Bargains with Fate

Psychological Crises and Conflicts in Shakespeare and His Plays

Bargains with Fate

Psychological Crises and Conflicts in Shakespeare and His Plays

Bernard J. Paris, Ph.D.
University of Florida
Gainesville, Florida

With a Foreword by
Theodore I. Rubin, M.D.

 INSIGHT BOOKS

Plenum Press • New York and London

Library of Congress Cataloging-in-Publication Data

Paris, Bernard J.
   Bargains with fate : psychological crises and conflicts in
Shakespeare and his plays / Bernard J. Paris ; with a foreword by
Theodore I. Rubin.
      p.   cm.
   Includes bibliographical references and index.
   ISBN 0-306-43760-0
   1. Shakespeare, William, 1564-1616--Knowledge--Psychology.
2. Shakespeare, William, 1564-1616--Biography--Psychology.
3. Dramatists, English--Early modern, 1500-1700--Psychology.
4. Fate and fatalism in literature. 5. Psychoanalysis and
literature. 6. Psychology in literature.   I. Title.
PR3065.P37   1991
822.3'3--dc20   90-28612
                                                              CIP

Grateful acknowledgment is made for permission to reprint excerpts from the following material:

Neurosis and Human Growth: The Struggle Toward Self-Realization by Karen Horney, M.D., by permission of W. W. Norton & Company, Inc. Copyright 1950 by W. W. Norton & Company, Inc. Copyright renewed 1978 by Renate Patterson, Brigitte Swarzenski, and Marianne von Eckardt.

Our Inner Conflicts: A Constructive Theory of Neurosis by Karen Horney, M.D., by permission of W. W. Norton & Company, Inc. Copyright 1945 by W. W. Norton & Company, Inc. Copyright renewed 1972 by Renate Mintz, Marianne von Eckardt, and Brigitte Horney Swarzenski.

ISBN 0-306-43760-0

© 1991 Plenum Press, New York
A Division of Plenum Publishing Corporation
233 Spring Street, New York, N.Y. 10013

An Insight Book

Printed in the United States of America

For Mark

Foreword

Karen Horney was a psychoanalytic pioneer who freed herself and many others from the confines of a rigid, biologically oriented orthodoxy. She understood the enormous influence of culture on human behavior and the fact that Homo sapiens is much more than an instinct-driven machine, however complex. She did not believe that anatomy is destiny but rather that one's biology can be used by a mind that far transcends instinct commands. She believed that people can change and grow whatever their age and condition and that they are capable of choice.

Although Horney is important for her resistance to Freud's phallocentric version of feminine psychology and for her emphasis on the importance of culture, she has not yet received the recognition that she deserves as perhaps our greatest anatomist of human character structure. In reading Horney, we learn of the influence of pride in our lives and of self-idealization, and we gain greater insight into our inner conflicts. As an anatomist of personality, Horney always had an intense interest in literature, and especially in the characters created by the great literary artists, many of whom are our most gifted natural psychologists. Seeing literature from the perspective of her theories greatly enriches our understanding not only of the text but also of ourselves and of others, and this enriched understanding fosters human compassion.

So far there has been a paucity of serious applications of Horneyan theory to literature, but in this work and others, Bernard Paris has done much to remedy the situation. Indeed, Paris is remarkably qualified for the task that he has undertaken. He is an accomplished literary critic with a distinguished record of publications and a superb Horneyan theorist. In fact, his skill in applying the theory easily rivals that of psychoanalysts with years of clinical practice.

In *Bargains with Fate,* Paris opens our eyes to Shakespeare's plays in a way that is possible only for those who are experts in human psychology as well as in literature. He not only illuminates the motivations of the leading characters in Shakespeare's great tragedies, but also makes connections between Shakespeare's inner life and his monumental achievement. He demonstrates convincingly that Shakespeare's work is an extension of his personality, and by so doing he brings that work closer to our own lives. By enabling us to identify with the author and his characters, he helps us to see the enduring humanity of people from a culture that, on the surface, seems quite remote, and this gives us a sense of connectedness not only to the past, but to the present and future as well. Reading this book is more than a literary eye-opener; it is also a therapeutic experience. Real art and the best literary criticism bring us into contact with the essence of humanity—our own and that of others in all times and places; and that is what Bernard Paris has done in this fascinating study.

If Horney were alive, I am sure that she would be grateful for the excellence of this book, which demonstrates superbly how well her theory works with literature, and especially with Shakespeare, the world's greatest and perhaps most elusive author. On behalf of Karen Horney, of myself, and of the many people who will profit from his work, I wish to thank Bernard Paris for this superb demonstration of the fruitful interaction between theory, literature, and self-understanding—an interaction that issues in a heightened capacity for empathy with everything human. This book should stimulate further interest in the Horneyan study of literature and in a more humanistic approach to the study of behavior. As I have said elsewhere, in charting the brain, we must not lose sight of the mind.

Theodore Isaac Rubin, M.D.

President Emeritus of the American
Institute for Psychoanalysis

Acknowledgments

This book has been a long time in the making, and I have incurred many debts of gratitude. My work on Shakespeare began with an essay on *Hamlet,* which was written in 1975 while I held a Guggenheim Fellowship that had been awarded for another project. I wish to thank the foundation again for this support. I commenced work on this project while I was at Michigan State University and completed it at the University of Florida. Both universities have been generous in providing me with research leaves, clerical help, and travel support, and I am grateful to the Division of Sponsored Research at the University of Florida for grants that have funded research assistance. Catherine R. Lewis assisted me splendidly for three years.

While I was at Michigan State University, Clint Goodson, Jay Ludwig, Philip McGuire, Douglas Peterson, Lawrence Porter, Randal Robinson, Robert Uphaus, and Evan Watkins gave me valuable critiques of my work in progress; and I received not only helpful feedback but also sustaining friendship and encouragement from Herbert Greenberg, Alan Hollingsworth, Diane Wakoski, and the late Glenn Wright. At the University of Florida, I am indebted to Ira Clark, Alistair Duckworth, Robert Thomson, Gregory Ulmer, Bertram Wyatt-Brown, and the late Judson Allen for their often challenging responses to the chapters I showed them. To my colleagues in the Institute for Psychological Study of the Arts—Robert de Beaugrande, Andrew Gordon, Norman Holland, and Ellie Ragland-Sullivan—I am grateful for their comradeship and intellectual stimulation. I owe special thanks to Norman Holland and Sidney Homan, who have read much of my work and with whom I cochaired the Florida Conference on

Shakespeare's Personality and coedited the book that resulted (Norman N. Holland, Sidney Homan, and Bernard J. Paris, eds., 1989 *Shakespeare's Personality*). Other colleagues here and abroad have been generous in taking the time to comment on portions of this work. These include A. A. Ansari, Maurice Charney, Jackson Cope, Herbert Coursen, Barbara Freedman, G. K. Hunter, H. S. Kakar, Harry Keyishian, A. D. Nuttall, Marvin Rosenberg, Ruth Rosenberg, Judith Rosenheim, Michael Warren, Herbert Weisinger, and Richard Wheeler. I am grateful to all, and to my graduate and undergraduate students at both universities who helped me to refine my ideas by allowing me to think aloud in their presence and letting me know when I didn't make sense.

As someone who came to Shakespeare studies in midcareer, I am grateful to my teachers—that is, to all those scholars and critics whose books and essays have formed the background of this study and have defined the issues with which I engage. Since I have decided to summarize critical debates rather than give extensive documentation, the list of works cited at the end of this book mentions only a fraction of those writings from which I have benefitted. I have also learned much while attending the meetings of the Shakespeare Association of America; their seminar format has given me many opportunities to engage co-workers in the field and to test my mettle as a Shakespearean.

I have been given similar opportunities in the field of psychoanalysis by the Association for the Advancement of Psychoanalysis, which has elected me to Honorary Membership and to the editorial board of its journal and has invited me to address its scientific meetings on several occasions. As someone whose formal training is in the humanities, I was particularly gratified to have my psychoanalytic interpretations well received by those who teach and apply the theory I am using. Alexandra Symonds, Mario Rendon, and Andrew Tershakovec stand out in my mind as Horneyan analysts who have been especially supportive over the years. My interpretation of Desdemona has been enriched by the contributions of the analysts who participated in a workshop I conducted for the association in 1979.

I have also had the benefit of trying out my ideas in a variety of other public forums. Earlier versions of portions of this book have been presented at (in chronological sequence) Michigan State University, Duke University, the State University of New York at Stony Brook, the South Atlantic Modern Language Association, the All-India English Conference (Madras), the Indian Institute of Technology (Delhi), Fairleigh Dickinson

University, the University of Florida Department of English, the Sixth American Imagery Conference, Simon Fraser University, the University of Washington, the University of Florida Department of Psychiatry, UCLA, the University of Southern California, the European-American Conference on the Psychology of Literature (Pécs, Hungary), the Group for the Application of Psychology (University of Florida), the Florida Conference on Shakespeare's Personality, the University of Illinois, the IPSA Conference on Literature and Psychology, and the Columbia Shakespeare Seminar. I have profited greatly from the feedback I received on these occasions.

Some of my ideas have appeared in articles also, and I have adapted these, as well as portions of *Shakespeare's Personality* and *Third Force Psychology and the Study of Literature,* for this volume (for a complete listing, see p. 288). I am grateful to the University of California Press, the Fairleigh Dickinson University Press, and the editors of *The Aligarh Journal of English Studies, The American Journal of Psychoanalysis, The Centennial Review,* and the *Revue Belge de Philologie et d'Histoire* for permission to use previously published material. I also wish to thank W. W. Norton & Company for permission to quote from the writings of Karen Horney.

In Part II of this book, I have drawn on interpretations that are fully developed in *Character as a Subversive Force in Shakespeare: The History and Roman Plays,* which will be published (1991) by Fairleigh Dickinson University Press. One reason why this book was so long in preparation is that I had to complete my analysis of all of Shakespeare's plays before I could conclude my discussion of his authorial personality, and this has led me to write two books concurrently. Readers may refer to *Character as a Subversive Force* not only for discussions of the history and Roman plays but also for an expanded treatment of critical issues.

I have large debts of a more personal nature that I wish to acknowledge here. My wife, Shirley, has been empathic, caring, and patient during the many years I have been working on this project. She has studied Shakespeare with me and has been, as always, my first reader and critic. She and my children, Susan and Mark, have helped me with their love through some very trying times. I have already dedicated a book to Susan; Mark, this one is for you. In 1985, I was operated on for a brain tumor that turned out to be benign. It was the size of a tennis ball and was situated on the language center of my brain. Without the skill and dedication of Dr. Albert Rhoton and his neurosurgical team, I would not have been able to finish this book. Dr. Rhoton, my next book is for you. I was helped through this time by many other caring people, to all of whom I am deeply grateful. I wish especially to mention my sister and brother-in-law, Hinda and Harvey Cohen, Catherine Lewis, and Emily Maren. I am thankful to be writing these acknowledgments.

Bernard J. Paris

Gainesville, Florida

Contents

II. SHAKESPEARE'S PERSONALITY

Introduction

The enduring appeal of Shakespeare's major tragedies derives in large part from the fact that they contain brilliantly drawn characters with whom people of widely differing backgrounds have been able to identify. Hamlet, Iago, Othello, Desdemona, Lear, Macbeth, and Lady Macbeth belong to worlds that are very different from ours and they often speak, think, and act in alien ways; but beneath all the differences they are so true to the essentials of human psychology that, as Elizabeth Montagu observed in 1769, we feel, "every moment, that they are of the same nature as ourselves" (quoted in Nuttall 1983, 67). Interpretations of these characters change with changing modes of understanding, and past ways of explaining their behavior, including Shakespeare's, no longer satisfy us; but Shakespeare was gifted with such remarkable powers of psychological intuition and mimetic characterization that his tragic heroes and heroines have a life of their own and have seemed like fellow human beings to people of subsequent ages and cultures. We can use twentieth-century psychoanalytic theories and our knowledge of ourselves as an aid to understanding them, and our understanding of them contributes, in turn, to our insight into ourselves and our conception of human behavior.

In this study of Shakespeare's four major tragedies and the personality that can be inferred from all his works, I shall employ a psychoanalytic approach inspired by the theories of Karen Horney, which I have found to be highly congruent with Shakespeare's portrayal of characters and relationships. In Part I, I examine the major tragedies as dramas about individuals with conflicts much like our own, who are in a state of psychological crisis as a result of the breakdown of their bargains with fate. In

Part II, I describe Shakespeare's authorial personality by reading the entire corpus as though it were the expression of a single, developing psyche with its own bargains, crises, and conflicts.

BARGAINS WITH FATE

I shall explain the psychodynamics of "bargains with fate" in a systematic way in Chapter 1, and there will be many illustrations throughout the book, but I want to make clear from the outset how I am using this term. What it immediately suggests to many people is the widespread practice of promising to reform when in trouble, or to perform acts of contrition, devotion, or restitution. Sickbed and battlefield conversions are common occurrences, with the bargain being that if our wishes are granted, we will behave as we think the force with which we are negotiating dictates that we should. This type of bargaining has rich psychological implications and deserves further study, but the bargains with fate that I am concerned with here are of a different kind. They are those in which we believe that we can control fate by living up to its presumed dictates not after it grants our wishes but before. If we think, feel, and behave as we are supposed to, we will receive our just deserts, whatever we may think they are. Fate is often conceived of as God, of course, and its dictates as His will; but our bargain can be with other people, with ourselves, with impersonal forces, with what we take to be the structure of the universe. As I shall argue in Chapter 1, the terms of the bargain are often not really determined by external forces but by the dictates of our predominant defensive strategy. Bargaining is a magical process in which conforming to the impossibly lofty demands of our neurotic solution (which Horney calls "a private religion") will enable us to attain our impossibly lofty goals.

This kind of bargain with fate is widespread and varied. Although it is often part of a private religion, it is also a prominent feature of many organized religions, and it figures in major works of Western literature from the Bible to the present day. The bargain will vary according to the defensive strategy from which it emanates. Horney has described five defensive strategies—self-effacement, narcissism, perfectionism, arrogant-vindictiveness, and resignation—each of which generates bargains that reflect its view of the world and its value system.

One kind of self-effacing bargain is epitomized by Moses Herzog's "childish credo" from Mother Goose:

I love little pussy, her coat is so warm
And if I don't hurt her, she'll do me no harm.
I'll sit by the fire and give her some food,
And pussy will love me because I am good.

Part of Moses's bargain is that if he does not hurt other people, they will not hurt him and that he will gain love by being good. He feels that he has been a wonderful husband to Madeleine and a devoted friend to Valentine Gersbach; but instead of loving him and doing him no harm, they cuckold him; and he feels unfairly treated by other "sharpies" as well. His benign view of human nature and of the world order is shattered, and he is thrown into a psychological crisis that resembles Hamlet's in many ways (see Paris 1986, 66–78).

An arrogant-vindictive character like Raskolnikov has a different kind of bargain from Herzog's. Raskolnikov wants power above all, and according to the dictates of his solution, to get it he must prove himself able to violate the traditional morality without feeling guilt, like his hero Napoleon. He tries to live up to his end of the bargain by killing the old moneylender, but he is so conscience-stricken afterward that he cannot use her money as he had intended and he gives himself away. Raskolnikov's psychological crisis is precipitated, like Macbeth's, not by the failure of life to honor his magic bargain, but by his own inability to live up to its terms (see Paris 1978b).

Literature does not always portray the failure of bargains; sometimes it shows them working, though often at a great cost. The narcissistic Lord Jim has a dream of glory in which he is as "unflinching as a hero in a book." Again and again Jim flinches, and he seems irretrievably lost after he jumps from the *Patna;* but his bargain, like Lear's, is that life is bound to fulfill his impossible dream as long as he holds onto his exaggerated claims for himself; and Conrad provides him with a "clean slate" in Patusan. Jim's weaknesses lead him to fail once again, but he refuses to believe that anything is lost, and he makes his dream come true by meeting his death with "a proud and unflinching glance" (see Paris 1974). Another character whose bargain succeeds through death is the perfectionist Antigone, who welcomes Creon's decree because it gives her the opportunity to gain eternal glory by proving her rectitude. By observing the rites of burial for her slain brother, she violates the law of the state and is condemned to death, but this is a price she gladly pays in order to demonstrate her devotion to family and her obedience to divine law. Her reward will come from the supernatural realm.

The kind of bargaining in which a resigned person might engage is well illustrated by Elizabeth-Jane in Thomas Hardy's *The Mayor of Casterbridge*. Whereas the ambitious Henchard seeks to master life through a sometimes ruthless aggressiveness, Elizabeth-Jane sees the world as an absurd place in which there is no relation between what people get and what they deserve, and in which passive acceptance is better than striving. Her bargain is that if she expects little of life, she will not be disappointed; and her resignation, like that of Horatio, makes her impervious to the "slings and arrows of outrageous fortune." When she marries the man of her dreams, at the end, she feels threatened by her happiness and must keep reminding herself of its meaninglessness and impermanence. She turns her "unbroken tranquility," which is one of the highest values of the resigned person, into further evidence of the capriciousness of fate, since it is quite out of keeping with what her unhappy youth had led her to expect. Uncomfortable at being "forced to class herself among the fortunate," she soothes herself by remembering that happiness is "but the occasional episode in a general drama of pain." This attitude enables her to remain steeled against misfortune instead of being deluded by her success. By refusing to feel very happy, moreover, she shows a proper fear of destiny and maintains an inconspicuousness that will not arouse the envy of either her fellow human beings or the fickle forces of fate.

I could provide many more examples and treat each one in far greater detail, but my purpose here is merely to suggest how widespread and various is the practice of bargaining with fate and to give a preliminary sense of how it works. I have found it not only in every period of Western literature, but also in myself and my contemporaries. I trust that my detailed analyses of the bargains of Shakespeare and his characters will sensitize the reader to the many manifestations of this phenomenon.

THE RECIPROCAL RELATION BETWEEN PSYCHOANALYTIC THEORY AND LITERATURE

This book is an interdisciplinary work that is intended as a contribution not only to the study of literature but also to the elucidation of certain aspects of experience that have been dealt with in different ways by both psychoanalysis and Shakespeare. It is addressed to students and lovers of Shakespeare, including actors who seek to comprehend the motivations of the characters they are playing and directors who want to stage Shakespeare's plays as dramas about human beings who are in conflict with each other and with themselves. It is addressed also to those who are interested in literature as a source of psychological insight.

I believe that psychoanalytic theory has much to contribute to our understanding of Shakespeare, that it permits a conceptual clarity that cannot be derived from literature alone. But Shakespeare has a contribution of at least equal importance to make to the theories that help us to understand him. There is a reciprocal relation, I propose, between psychoanalytic theory and the literary presentation of the phenomena it describes. Theory provides categories of understanding that help us to recover the intuitions of the great writers about the workings of the human psyche; and these intuitions, once recovered, become part of our conceptual understanding of life. Just as the good analyst learns something from every patient, so the student of literature finds himself gaining greater insight into human behavior because of the richness of artistic presentation. Even the most sophisticated theories are thin compared to the complex portrayals of characters and relationships that we find in an artist like Shakespeare. Taken together theory and literature offer a far more complex comprehension of human experience than either provides by itself.

Literature has more to offer the student of human nature than an enrichment of psychoanalytic theory. It is the product of a different mental process than that which produces analytic systems, and it makes available a different kind of knowledge. Theory gives us *formulations about* human behavior, whereas literature gives us *truth to* experiences of life. The analyst and the artist often deal with the same phenomena, but the artist's grasp of psychological process is of a more concrete and intuitive nature, deriving, as it often does, from a gift for mimesis. The artist's genius is in embodying and structuring observations, rather than in analyzing them. Literature is so enduring in part because it operates below the level of changing conceptualizations, including those of the artist.

Because of its concrete, dramatic quality, literature enables us not only to observe people other than ourselves, but also to enter into their experience of life; to discover what it feels like to *be* these people and to confront their situations. We can gain in this way a phenomenological grasp of experience that cannot be derived from theory alone, and not from case histories either, unless they are also works of art. Because literature provides this kind of knowledge, it has a potentially sensitizing effect, one that is of as much importance to the clinician as it is to the humanist. Literature offers us an opportunity to amplify our experience in a way that can enhance our empathic powers, and because of this it is a valuable aid to clinical training and to personal growth.

PSYCHOANALYSIS, SHAKESPEARE, AND ME

It is my experience, then, that psychoanalytic theory illuminates literature, that literature enriches theory, and that combining theory and literature enhances both our intellectual and our empathic understanding of human behavior. The process I am describing involves not just theory and literature but also our own personalities and our insight into ourselves. There is a triangular interaction between literature, theory, and the individual interpreter. Our literary and theoretical interests reflect our own character, the way in which we use theory depends upon whether we have simply studied it or have assimilated it into our experience, and what we are able to see in and to take away from literature depends upon our theoretical perspective and our access to our own inner life.

I used psychoanalytic theory for self-understanding before I employed it in the study of literature. In 1958, Ted Millon, then a colleague at Lehigh University, suggested that people in the humanities might find such theorists as Erich Fromm, Karen Horney, and Harry Stack Sullivan to be valuable. When I read these writers, along with Sigmund Freud, C. G. Jung, Theodore Reik, Erick Erikson, and others, I found Horney the most compelling, for she not only described my behavior in an immediately recognizable way, but she seemed to have invaded my privacy and to have understood my insecurities, my inner conflicts, and my unrealistic demands upon myself.

Soon after this I entered psychotherapy, and though I often used my readings in conjunction with my efforts at personal growth, I did not connect them with the study of literature until one memorable day in 1964 when I was teaching *Vanity Fair*. While arguing that the novel is full of contradictions and is thematically unintelligible, I suddenly remembered Karen Horney's statement that "inconsistencies are as definite an indication of the presence of conflicts as a rise in body temperature is of physical disturbance" (1945, p. 35), and in the next instant I realized that the novel's contradictions become intelligible if we see them as part of a system of inner conflicts. The novel was still confused thematically, but its inconsistencies could be explained in psychoanalytic terms (Paris, 1974). I have been unfolding the implications of that "aha" experience ever since.

As I began to read literature from a new perspective, I undertook to educate myself more thoroughly in psychoanalytic thought. I audited psychology courses, read systematically, and consulted experts to assure that my expositions of theory were correct. It was in therapy, of course, that I received my most valuable education. The knowledge that I gained there gave me both a deeper understanding of theory and the ability to recognize the portrayals of psychological phenomena in literature that most criticism ignores and to which I had been blind before. After wondering for a while if I was in the right profession, I developed an approach to literature that permitted me to combine my literary training with my psychological insight and to use the study of literature as a means to continued self-understanding and growth (Paris 1974, 1978a, 1986).

Despite the fact that I had by now read a great deal of theory and that my therapist was relatively orthodox, Karen Horney's ideas continued to impress me the most. Once I began to use them in the study of literature, I found that they were highly congruent not only with my own experience but also with works from a wide variety of cultures and periods (including those of Shakespeare) and this enhanced my sense of their explanatory power and range of applicability.

I wish to stress the fact, however, that although psychoanalytic theory has helped me to arrive at an understanding of literature, my understanding of psychoanalytic theories in turn has also been influenced by literature. I began my work on Shakespeare with an essay on Hamlet (Paris 1977), whom I saw as being in a state of psychological crisis because the desecration of his father's memory and the triumph of Claudius meant that the world did not reward the virtues of people like himself. His "bargain with fate" had failed. As I analyzed the other major tragedies, I realized that Iago, Othello, Desdemona, King Lear, Macbeth, and Lady Macbeth were also in states of crisis because their bargains were breaking down. Their bargains were different from each other and from Hamlet's, but the psychodynamic structure was the same. I thought that the concept of bargains was Horney's, but when I went back to see what she had said about it, I could not find the term in her works, though she does speak occasionally of "deals." My recognition of bargains in Shakespeare was facilitated by my knowledge of Horney, but my study of Shakespeare has led me to a much fuller understanding of the phenomenon than can be found in her works.

THE PSYCHOANALYTIC STUDY OF CHARACTER

Some readers may have questions about my analyzing Shakespeare's characters in motivational terms and using modern psychoanalytic concepts to do so. This is not the place for a full discussion of these issues, which I have treated elsewhere at length (Paris 1974, 1978a, 1991), but I should like to say a few words about them.

For more than a half-century, Shakespearean critics have attacked the approach of A. C. Bradley, who, in *Shakespearean Tragedy,* talked about the major characters as though they were real people and tried "to realise fully and exactly the inner movement which produced these words and no other, these deeds and no other, at each particular moment" (1963, 2). I do not agree with all of Bradley's interpretations, though they are usually quite astute, but I share his objectives. Shakespeare created some of the greatest psychological portraits in all of literature, and it is highly appropriate to discuss them in motivational terms.

It is essential to recognize that there are different kinds of characterization that require different strategies of interpretation. A useful taxonomy is that of Scholes and Kellogg (1966), which distinguishes between aesthetic, illustrative, and mimetic characterization. *Aesthetic characters* are stock types who may be understood primarily in terms of their technical functions and their formal and dramatic effects. *Illustrative characters* are "concepts in anthropoid shape or fragments of the human psyche parading as whole human beings." We try to understand "the principle they illustrate through their actions in a narrative framework" (p. 88). Behind realistic literature there is a strong "psychological impulse" that "tends toward the presentation of highly individualized figures who resist abstraction and generalization" (p. 101). When we encounter a fully drawn mimetic character, "we are justified in asking questions about his motivation based on our knowledge of the ways in which real people are motivated" (p. 87). A *mimetic character* usually has aesthetic and illustrative functions, but numerous details have been called forth by the author's desire to round out his psychological portrait, to make his character lifelike, complex, and inwardly intelligible, and these will go unnoticed if we try to understand the character only in functional terms.

A frequent complaint against Bradley is that he takes characters out of the work and tries to understand them in their own right. He did not do this to the extent that his critics contend; but given the nature of mimetic characterization, it is not an unreasonable procedure. Mimetic characters are part of the fictional world in which they exist, but they are also autonomous beings with an inner logic of their own. They are, in E. M. Forster's phrase, "creations inside a creation" (1949, 64) who tend to go their own way as the author becomes absorbed in imagining a human being, motivating his behavior, and supplying his reactions to the situations in which he has been placed.[1]

Some people object to the use of modern theories to explain Shakespeare's characters on the grounds that Shakespeare could not possibly have conceived of his characters in twentieth-century terms. Shakespeare had to make sense of human behavior for himself, as we all do, and he undoubtedly drew upon the conceptual systems of his day. To see his characters in the light of Renaissance psychology is to recover what may have been his conscious understanding of them, but it does not help us do justice to his mimetic achievement or make the characters intelligible to us.

We cannot identify Shakespeare's conceptions of his characters with the characters he has actually created, even if we could be certain of what his conceptions were. The great artist sees and portrays far more than he can comprehend. One of the features of mimetic characters is that they have a life independent of their author and that our understanding of them will change, along with our changing conceptions of human nature. Each age has to reinterpret these characters for itself. Any theory we use will be culture-bound and reductive; still, we must use some theory, consciously or not, to satisfy our need for conceptual understanding. In our age, there are many theories available, each of which may work with corresponding intuitions in Shakespeare.

A major weakness of psychoanalytic studies of literary characters has been their use of a diachronic mode of analysis that explains the present in terms of the past. Because of their reliance upon infantile experience to account for the behavior of the adult, they must often posit events in the character's early life that are not depicted in the text. This results in the generation of crucial explanatory material out of the premises of the theory, with no corroborating evidence except the supposed results of the invented experiences, which were inferred from these results to begin with. This procedure has resulted in a justifiable distrust of the psychoanalytic study of character. Because of its emphasis upon infantile origins, modern psychoanalytic theory has, ironically, made literary characters seem less accessible to motivational analysis than they did in the days of Bradley.

The approach I shall use is not subject to this objection, since Horney's theory focuses upon the character structure and defensive strategies of the adult. It permits us to establish a causal relationship between past and present if there is enough information, but it also enables us to understand the present structure of the psyche as an inwardly intelligible system and to explain behavior in terms of its function within that system. As a result, we can account for a character's thoughts, feelings, and actions on the basis of what has actually been given. If the childhood material is present, it can be used; but if it is absent, it need not be invented. Because Horney's theory describes the kinds of phenomena that are actually portrayed in literature and explains these phenomena in a synchronic way, it permits us to stick to the words on the page, to explicate the text.

SHAKESPEARE'S PERSONALITY

I shall be analyzing not only the dramatic characters in the tragedies, but also the character structure of the author as it can be inferred from all of his works. This procedure, too, requires a brief comment, since some critics celebrate what John Keats has called Shakespeare's "negative capability" and argue that his personality is difficult or impossible to detect in his works. "Shakespeare's poetry is characterless," proclaimed Samuel Taylor Coleridge; "it does not reflect the individual Shakespeare" (quoted in Schoenbaum 1970, 253). According to Virginia Woolf, the reason "why we know so little of Shakespeare is that his grudges and spites and antipathies are hidden from us. We are not held up by some 'revelation' which reminds us of the writer. All desire to protest, to preach, to proclaim an injury, to pay off a score, to make the world the witness of some hardship or grievance was fired out of him and consumed. Therefore his poetry flows from him free and unimpeded" (1957, 58–59). This is a widely held view of Shakespeare; one can find many similar statements.

An equal (or possibly a larger) number of critics defend the idea that Shakespeare revealed himself in his works. Writing in 1959, L. C. Knights observed that "our whole conception of Shakespeare's relation to his work, of what he was trying to do as an artist whilst at the same time satisfying the demands of the Elizabethan theatre, has undergone a very great change indeed." "The 'new' Shakespeare," he observes, "is much less impersonal than the old . . . . we feel the plays (in Eliot's words) 'to be united by one significant, consistent, and developing personality': we feel that the plays . . . 'are somehow dramatizing . . . [a] struggle for harmony in the soul of the poet.' We take it for granted that Shakespeare thought about the problems of life, and was . . . interested in working towards an imaginative solution . . ." (1965, 192). This "new" view is, of course, an old view as well. "Is it really conceivable," asked Bradley, that a man could portray such "an enormous amount and variety of human nature, without betraying anything whatever of his own disposition and preferences? I do not believe that he could . . . even if he deliberately set himself to the task" (1963, 214).[2] I am on the side of those who maintain that Shakespeare revealed himself in his works. I believe that his plays dramatize a "struggle for harmony," that he is working in them "towards an imaginative solution" of his problems, and that they betray, to some extent at least, his "disposition and preferences." In Part II, I shall attempt to make inferences about Shakespeare from his works. I do not claim to be describing the whole personality of the author, but only those aspects of it that lend themselves to my approach. As in my discussions of characters, I shall employ a synchronic mode of analysis; that is, I shall focus upon the structure of the psyche that is expressed by the plays rather than upon the origins of that psyche in Shakespeare's early experience.[3]

The personality I shall describe is not necessarily that of Shakespeare the man. When we use the name of the author, we may be referring to the implied author of one of his works, to the authorial personality that can be inferred from several or all of his works, or to the historical person who, among other things, wrote the books that bear his name. Clearly there is a relationship between the man and the works, but we must be very careful when we try to infer the historical person from his artistic creations. As W. H. Auden has observed, the relation between an author's "life and his works is at one and the same time too self-evident to require comment—every work of art is, in one sense, a self-disclosure—and too complicated ever to unravel" (1964, xviii). We must recognize that the historical person has a life independent of his works, that many of his attitudes and attributes may never appear in his fiction, and that those that do appear may have been disguised or transformed by the process of artistic creation. We must allow for artistic motivations, for generic requirements, and for the inner logic of individual works. The psychological traits of the authorial personality may or may not be traits of the historical person. To determine whether they are, we need a wealth of independent biographical data against which to test our inferences. In the case of Shakespeare, the biographical record is notoriously scanty. I cannot help feeling that I am learning something about Shakespeare the man when I examine the characters, the attitudes, and the strategies of defense that frequently recur in his works, but there is no way of confirming this.

My discussion of Shakespeare's personality will have two aspects. I shall try to describe the authorial personality that is implied by his corpus as a whole; and I shall *speculate* from time to time about *possible* relationships between the personality I infer from his works and the inner life and experience of Shakespeare the man. Many of us have a psychological need to imagine the author, and most people who have read or seen much of Shakespeare have developed, I suspect, their own version of his personality. Mine has been shaped by my particular way of looking at things, and it may offer readers ideas for *their* Shakespeare that they could not have found anywhere else.

PART I

The Major Tragedies

CHAPTER 1

Bargains, Defenses, and Cultural Codes

HISTORICAL VERSUS PSYCHOLOGICAL PERSPECTIVES

Shakespeare's tragic heroes and heroines are such compelling figures, I think, because they are confronting situations that throw them into a state of internal crisis. Bernard McElroy has observed this and has offered an historical explanation. According to McElroy, what happens in these plays is that "the world-picture" of the hero is "undermined"; and then "torn by several equally possible concepts of reality or else plunged into a chaotic abyss," he struggles "to reimpose upon the world" a "meaning which it must have if it is to be endurable" (1973, 28). Stressing the fact that "Shakespeare lived in an era of intellectual, religious, and social transition" (p. 9), McElroy sees the tensions in the tragic heroes as products of cultural and ideological conflicts. The heroes are susceptible to being undermined because of certain characteristics they all share, such as self-awareness, a tendency to universalize, and a craving for absolutes; but these are thematic necessities rather than traits of personality. A character's behavior is to be understood as predicated much more "upon his world-view" (p. 20) than upon psychological "motives."

I think McElroy is right in saying that the experience of the central characters is one in which their subjective world collapses and they must struggle to restore meaning to their lives. This is what has given the tragedies such immediacy to a wide variety of audiences. I see psychology rather than ideology, however, as the fundamental cause of their crises, and I feel that the characters' behavior is more predicated on motives than upon their worldviews. I trace their worldviews to their personality structures and their vulnerability to their unresolved conflicts and the unrealistic nature of their beliefs. These characters exist within pluralistic societies that offer a variety of worldviews, and they are receptive to the ones that are most congruent with their dispositions. Since they have inner conflicts, they may be receptive to several worldviews, and this will result in the kinds of dilemmas McElroy describes. Their intellectual confusion is not the cause, however, but the result of their psychological state; and the tensions within their culture affect them as they do because they correspond to, and in some cases exacerbate, their internal conflicts. An historical perspective has its value; but if the tragedies were primarily about conflicting worldviews in the Renaissance, they would not affect us so powerfully or have such a capacity to illuminate the experience of those for whom their ideological issues are no longer vital.

My thesis about the major tragedies is that they portray characters with inner conflicts that are very much like our own who are in a state of psychological crisis as a result of the breakdown of their bargains with fate. The concept of "bargains" was inspired by the theories of Karen Horney, who described the phenomenon, though she did not use the term. To facilitate my discussion of Shakespeare, I shall begin with an exposition of Horney (see also Rubins 1978; Westkott 1986; Paris 1986), whose theory will help us to recover his psychological intuitions and to describe the personality implied by his works. Readers familiar with Horney will note that my theoretical account of bargains is more complete and systematic than hers. Having gotten the idea from Horney, I learned much more about it from Shakespeare and have incorporated some of the insights derived from literature into the theory that facilitated but did not specifically contain those insights. After my exposition of Horney, I shall show how an historical approach like McElroy's can be combined with a psychological approach like mine if we correlate the defensive strategies described by Horney with the cultural codes that we find in Shakespeare's plays.

KAREN HORNEY: INTRODUCTION

Karen Horney (née Danielsen) was born in a suburb of Hamburg (Germany) on September 15, 1885. She attended medical school in Freiburg and completed her studies at the Universities of Göttingen and

Berlin. She married Oskar Horney in 1909, was in analysis with Karl Abraham in 1910–11, received her M.D. in 1915, and became a founding member of the Berlin Psychoanalytic Institute in 1920. She came to the United States in 1932, when Franz Alexander invited her to become the Associate Director of the Chicago Psychoanalytic Institute, moved to New York in 1934, broke with the New York Psychoanalytic Society in 1941, and founded the American Institute for Psychoanalysis in the same year. She died in 1952. (See Rubins 1978 and Quinn 1987 for biographies.)

Horney's early essays on feminine psychology took issue with the then orthodox views on penis envy and feminine masochism. Between 1937 and 1950, she published a series of books—*The Neurotic Personality of Our Time, New Ways in Psychoanalysis, Self-Analysis, Our Inner Conflicts,* and *Neurosis and Human Growth*—that developed a sophisticated theory of her own. Horney's thought went through three stages. In her early essays, mostly written in Germany, she tried to revise Sigmund Freud's phallocentric view of feminine psychology while remaining within the framework of classical theory (see Westkott 1986 and Quinn 1987). After she came to the United States, her quarrel with Freud became more pervasive and serious. In *The Neurotic Personality of Our Time* (1937) and in *New Ways in Psychoanalysis* (1939), she replaced biology with culture and disturbed human relationships when explaining neurotic development, and she shifted to a predominantly structural paradigm. In her last two books, she described in a systematic way the strategies of defense that individuals develop in order to cope with the frustration of their psychological needs.

It is Horney's structural paradigm, I think, that has made it almost impossible for classical theorists to assimilate her contribution. Although, like Freud, Horney sees our problems as originating in early childhood, she does not see the adult as simply repeating earlier patterns, and she does not explain adult behavior through analogies with childhood experience. Once children begin to adopt defensive strategies, their particular system develops under the influence of external factors, which encourage some strategies and discourage others, and of internal necessities, whereby each defensive move requires others to maintain its viability. The character structure of the adult had its origins in early childhood, but it is also the product of a complicated evolutionary history, and it can be understood in terms of the present constellation of defenses.

Although Horney's structural approach has generated resistance to her theory, it is the source of much of its strength. It makes it especially suitable, as I have said, for the analysis of literary characters. One of the chief objections to the psychoanalytic study of character has been its reliance upon early experiences not contained in the text to account for the behavior of the adult; but Horney's theory enables us to analyze characters in terms of their existing defenses, which are often quite fully portrayed. Horney's synchronic paradigm also makes her theory very useful for self-understanding, because the dynamics she describes are frequently available to introspection (as I have found in my own experience).

Horney is often thought of as belonging to the "cultural school" that flourished in the 1930s. After her first book, however, her emphasis was less on culture than on intrapsychic processes and interpersonal relations. I find it useful to place her mature theory in the context of what Abraham Maslow has called "Third Force" psychology (1968, vi). What distinguishes Third Force theorists from Freudians and behaviorists is their contention that man is not simply a tension-reducing or a conditioned animal, but that there is present in him a third force, an "evolutionary constructive" force, that urges "him to realize his given potentialities" (Horney 1950, 15).[1] Horney believes that each person has a biologically based inner nature, a "real self," that it is his object in life to actualize. She would have agreed with Maslow, I believe, in holding that part of the real self is a set of basic needs that must be met if the individual is to achieve full psychological growth. These are, in the order of their strength, physiological survival needs, needs for a safe and stable environment, needs for love and belonging, needs for self-esteem, and the need for a calling or vocation in which we can use our native capacities in an intrinsically satisfying way (Maslow 1970). Maslow also posits needs for beauty, knowledge, and understanding that he does not integrate into his hierarchy and a number of conditions, such as freedom and diversity of choice, that are essential to self-actualization.

Horney sees healthy human development as a process of self-realization and unhealthy development as a process of self-alienation. When his needs are relatively well met, the individual will develop "the clarity and depth of his own feelings, thoughts, wishes, interests . . . . ; the special capacities or gifts he may have; the faculty to express himself, and to relate himself to others with his spontaneous feelings. All this will in time enable him to find his set of values and his aims in life" (1950, 17). The psychologically deprived person develops in a quite different way. According to Horney, self-alienation begins as a defense against "basic anxiety," which is a "profound insecurity and vague apprehensiveness"

(1950, 18) generated by feelings of isolation, helplessness, fear, and hostility. As a result of this anxiety, the child "cannot simply like or dislike, trust or distrust, express his wishes or protest against those of another, but he has automatically to devise ways to cope with people and to manipulate them with minimum damage to himself" (1945, 219). He copes with others by developing the interpersonal strategies of defense that we shall examine next, and he seeks to compensate for his feelings of worthlessness and inadequacy by an intrapsychic process of self-glorification. These strategies constitute his effort to fulfill his frustrated, and therefore highly intensified, needs for safety, love and belonging, and self-esteem. They are also designed to reduce his anxiety and to provide a safe outlet for his hostility.

INTERPERSONAL STRATEGIES OF DEFENSE

There are three main ways in which children, and later adults, can move in their efforts to overcome feelings of weakness and to establish themselves safely in a threatening world. They can adopt a self-effacing or compliant solution and move toward people, or they can develop an aggressive or expansive solution and move against people, or they can become detached or resigned and move away from people.[2] Each of these defensive strategies involves a constellation of behavior patterns and personality traits, a conception of justice, and a set of beliefs about human nature, human values, and the human condition. Each involves also a bargain with fate in which obedience to the dictates of that solution is supposed to be rewarded.

In each of the defensive moves, one of the elements involved in basic anxiety is overemphasized: helplessness in the compliant solution, hostility in the aggressive solution, and isolation in the detached solution. Since under the conditions that produce basic anxiety all of these feelings are bound to arise, individuals will come to make all three of the defensive moves compulsively; and because these moves involve incompatible character structures and value systems, they will be torn by inner conflicts. To gain some sense of wholeness, they will emphasize one move more than the others and will become predominantly self-effacing, expansive, or detached. The other trends will continue to exist, but will be condemned and suppressed. When, for some reason, submerged trends are brought closer to the surface, the individuals will experience severe inner turmoil and may become paralyzed, unable to move in any direction at all. When their predominant solution fails, they may embrace one of the repressed strategies.

As we discuss the interpersonal strategies of defense and the types of personality to which they give rise, let us keep in mind the fact that we shall find neither characters in literature nor people in life who correspond exactly to Horney's descriptions. Her types are composites, drawn from her experience with people who share certain dominant trends but who differ from each other in many important ways. The Horneyan typology helps us to see how certain traits and behaviors are related to each other within a psychological system; but once we have identified a character's predominant solution, we must not assume that he has all the characteristics Horney ascribes to the self-effacing, expansive, or resigned constellations. He has, moreover, his own personal history, cultural background, and structure of inner conflicts, and he is confronted by a unique set of challenges. It is important to remember also, as Horney observed, that "although people tending toward the same main solution have characteristic similarities, they may differ widely with regard to the level of human qualities, gifts, or achievements involved" (1950, 191). One of the unavoidable dangers of psychological analysis is that it does not do justice to a whole range of human qualities that make people with similar defenses different from each other and quite variable in their attractiveness and humanity.

The person in whom compliant trends are dominant tries to overcome his basic anxiety by gaining affection and approval and by controlling others through his need of them. He seeks to attach others to him by being good, loving, self-effacing, and weak. Because of his need for surrender and for a safe expression of his aggressive tendencies, he is frequently attracted to his opposite, the masterful expansive person: "to love a proud person, to merge with him, to live vicariously through him would allow him to participate in the mastery of life without having to own it to himself" (Horney 1950, 244). This kind of relationship often develops into a "morbid dependency" in which a crisis can occur if the compliant partner comes to feel that his submission is not gaining the rewards for which he is sacrificing himself.

The values of the compliant person "lie in the direction of goodness, sympathy, love, generosity, unselfishness, humility; while egotism, ambition, callousness, unscrupulousness, wielding of power are abhorred" (Horney 1945, 54). Because "any wish, any striving, any reaching out for more feels to him like a dangerous or reckless challenging of fate," he is severely inhibited in his self-assertive and self-protective activities (Horney 1950, 218). He embraces Christian values, but in a compulsive way, because they are necessary to his defense system. He must believe in turning the other cheek and must see the world as displaying a providential order in which virtue is rewarded. His bargain is that if he is a peaceful, loving person who shuns pride and does not seek his own gain or glory, he will be well treated by fate and by other people. If his bargain is not honored, he may despair of divine justice, he may conclude that he is the guilty party, or he may have recourse to belief in a justice that transcends human understanding. He needs to believe not only in the fairness of the world order, but also in the goodness of human nature, and here, too, he is vulnerable to disappointment.

In the compliant person, according to Horney, there are "a variety of aggressive tendencies strongly repressed" (1945, 55). These tendencies are repressed because feeling them or acting them out would clash violently with his need to be good and would radically endanger his whole strategy for gaining love, justice, protection, and approval. His compliant strategies tend to increase his hostility, for "self-effacement and 'goodness' invite being stepped on" and "dependence upon others makes for exceptional vulnerability" (1945, 55–56). But his inner rage threatens his self-image, his philosophy of life, and his bargain; and he must repress, disguise, or justify his anger in order to avoid arousing self-hate and the hostility of others.

There are many predominantly compliant (or self-effacing) characters in Shakespeare, the most striking of whom are Henry VI, Helena in *A Midsummer-Night's Dream,* Antonio in *The Merchant of Venice* (Paris 1989b), Silvius in *As You Like It,* Viola (*Twelfth Night*), Hamlet, Desdemona, Duke Vincentio (*Measure for Measure*), Antony (Paris 1991), Timon of Athens, Prospero (*The Tempest*), and the poet of the Sonnets (Lewis 1985). There are other characters in whom self-effacing trends are subordinate, and in the characters I have mentioned there are usually inner conflicts.

The person in whom expansive tendencies are predominant has goals, traits, and values that are quite the opposite of those of the self-effacing person. What appeals to him most is not love, but mastery. He abhors helplessness, is ashamed of suffering, and needs "to achieve success, prestige, or recognition" (Horney 1945, 65). There are three expansive types: the narcissistic, the perfectionistic, and the arrogant-vindictive.

The narcissistic person seeks to master life "by self-admiration and the exercise of charm" (Horney 1950, 212). He has an "unquestioned belief in his greatness" and feels that "he *is* the anointed, the man of destiny, . . . the great giver, the benefactor of mankind" (1950, 194). Often a spoiled child, he grows up feeling the world to be a fostering mother and himself a favorite of fortune. His insecurity is manifested in the fact that he "may speak incessantly of his exploits or of his wonderful qualities and needs endless confirmation of his estimates of himself in the form of admiration and devotion" (1950, 194). His bargain is that if he holds onto his dreams and to his exaggerated claims for himself, life is bound to give him what he wants. If it does not, he may experience a psychological collapse, since he is ill-equipped to cope with reality. The most fully developed narcissists in Shakespeare are King Lear and Richard II (Paris 1991).

The person who is perfectionistic has extremely high standards, moral and intellectual, on the basis of which he looks down upon others. He takes great pride in his rectitude and aims for a "flawless excellence [in] the whole conduct of life" (Horney 1950, 196). Because of the difficulty of living up to his standards, he tends "to equate . . . *knowing* about moral values and *being* a good person" (1950, 196). While he deceives himself in this way, he may insist that others live up to "his standards of perfection and despise them for failing to do so. His own self-condemnation is thus externalized" (1950, 196). The imposition of his standards on others leads to admiration for a select few and a critical or condescending attitude toward the majority of mankind. The perfectionistic person has a legalistic bargain in which being fair, just, and dutiful entitles him "to fair treatment by others and by life in general. This conviction of an infallible justice operating in life gives him a feeling of mastery" (1950, 197). Through the height of his standards, he compels fate. Ill-fortune or errors of his own making threaten his bargain and may overwhelm him with feelings of helplessness or self-hate.

The predominantly perfectionistic characters in Shakespeare include Talbot in *1 Henry VI,* Humphrey, Duke of Gloucester in *2 Henry VI,* Titus Andronicus, Henry V (Paris 1991), Brutus (Paris 1991), Angelo in *Measure for Measure,* Othello, Cordelia, Kent, Macbeth (before the murder), and Coriolanus (Paris 1991). Again, despite their similar defenses these characters are quite different from each other in their human qualities and inner conflicts.

The arrogant-vindictive person is motivated chiefly by a need for vindictive triumphs. Whereas the narcissistic person received early admiration and the perfectionistic person "grew up under the pressure of rigid standards," the arrogant-vindictive person was "harshly treated" in childhood and has a need to retaliate for the injuries he has suffered (Horney 1950, 221). His philosophy tends to be that of an Iago or a Nietzsche. He feels "that the world is an arena where, in the Darwinian sense, only the fittest survive and the strong annihilate the weak" (Horney 1945, 64). The only moral law inherent in the order of things is that might makes right. In his relations with others he is competitive, ruthless, and cynical. He trusts no one, avoids emotional involvement, and seeks to exploit others in order to enhance his feelings of mastery. Self-effacing people are fools toward whom he is sometimes drawn, despite his contempt, because of their submissiveness and malleability.

Just as the compliant person must repress his hostile impulses in order to make his solution work, so for the arrogant-vindictive person "any feeling of sympathy, or obligation to be 'good,' or attitude of compliance would be incompatible with the whole structure of living he has built up and would shake its foundations" (1945, 70). He wants to be hard and tough and regards all manifestation of feeling as a sign of weakness. He despises the Christian ethic and is "likely to feel nauseated at the sight of affectionate behavior in others" (1945, 69). His reaction is so extreme because "it is prompted by his need to fight all softer feelings in himself. Nietzsche gives us a good illustration of these dynamics when he has his superman see any form of sympathy as a sort of fifth column, an enemy operating from within" (1945, 69–70). He fears the emergence of his own compliant trends because they would make him vulnerable in a hostile world, would confront him with self-hate, and would threaten his bargain, which is essentially with himself. He does not count on the world to give him anything but is convinced that he can reach his ambitious goal if he remains true to his vision of life as a battle and does not allow himself to be influenced by his softer feelings or the traditional morality. If his expansive solution collapses, self-effacing trends may emerge.

Many arrogant-vindictive characters can be found in Shakespeare. The most notable include Richard III (Paris 1991), Shylock (Paris 1989b), Cassius (Paris 1991), Iago, Edmund, Goneril, and Regan (*King Lear*), Lady Macbeth and Macbeth (after the murder).

The basically detached person pursues neither love nor mastery; rather, he worships freedom, peace, and self-sufficiency. He handles a threatening world by removing himself from its power and by shutting others out of his inner life. To avoid being dependent on the environment, he tries to subdue his inner cravings and to be content with little. He believes, "consciously or unconsciously, that it is *better* not to wish or expect anything. Sometimes this goes with a conscious pessimistic outlook on life, a sense of its being futile anyhow and of nothing being sufficiently desirable to make an effort for it" (1950, 263). He does not usually rail against life, however, but resigns himself to things as they are and accepts his fate with ironic humor or stoic dignity. He tries to escape suffering by being independent of external forces, by feeling that nothing matters, and by concerning himself only with those things that are within his power. His bargain is that if he asks nothing of others, they will not bother him; that if he tries for nothing, he will not fail; and that if he expects little of life, he will not be disappointed. The detached person withdraws from himself as well as from others. His suppression of feeling is part of an effort not only to avoid frustration, but also to escape from the conflict between his expansive and compliant trends.

There are only a few predominantly detached characters in Shake-speare (Jacques in *As You Like It*, Horatio and Thersites in *Troilus and Cressida*, and Apemantus in *Timon of Athens*), but detachment is often an important defense when other solutions collapse, as it is for Richard II (Paris 1991) and Antony and Cleopatra (Paris 1991).

INTRAPSYCHIC STRATEGIES OF DEFENSE

While interpersonal difficulties are creating the movements toward, against, and away from people, and the conflicts between these trends, concomitant intrapsychic problems are producing their own defensive strategies. To compensate for his feelings of self-hate and inadequacy, the individual creates, with the aid of his imagination, an "idealized image" of himself that he "endows . . . with unlimited powers and . . . exalted faculties" (Horney 1950, 22). The idealized image quickly leads, how-ever, to increased self-hate and additional inner conflict. Although the qualities with which the individual endows himself are dictated by his predominant interpersonal strategy, the repressed solutions are also repre-sented; and since each solution glorifies a different set of traits, the ide-alized image has contradictory aspects, all of which the individual must try to actualize. Since he can feel worthwhile only if he *is* his idealized image, everything that falls short is deemed worthless, and a "despised image" develops that becomes the focus of self-contempt. A great many people shuttle, says Horney, "between a feeling of arrogant omnipotence and of being the scum of the earth" (1950, 188). Whereas the idealized image is modeled on the predominant interpersonal strategy, the despised image reflects the strategy that is being most strenuously repressed. A predominantly compliant person like Hamlet, for example, would despise himself if he behaved like Claudius, whereas a predominantly arrogant-vindictive person like Iago would despise himself if he were "direct and honest" like Cassio, Othello, or Desdemona.

The idealized image evolves into an idealized self and the despised image into a despised self, as the individual becomes convinced he really is the grandiose or awful being he has imagined. Horney posits four kinds of selves: the real self; the idealized self; the despised self; and the actual self. The real (or possible) self is not an entity but a set of biological predispositions that require favorable conditions if they are to be actualized. The real self can be actualized only through interaction with the environment, and the degree and form of its actualization are heavily dependent upon external conditions, including culture. Under unfavorable conditions, the individual loses touch with his real self and his behavior is dictated by compulsive defensive strategies rather than by spontaneous feelings, interests, and wishes. Among these strategies is the creation of an idealized image, which in turn generates a despised image and intensifies self-hate. The idealized self is unrealistically grandiose, and the despised self is unrealistically worthless and weak. The actual self is what a person really is—a mixture of strengths and weaknesses, health and neurosis. The distance between the actual and real selves will depend upon the degree to which the person's development has been self-actualizing or self-alienated.

With the formation of the idealized image, the individual embarks upon a "search for glory," as "the energies driving toward self-realization are shifted to the aim of actualizing the idealized self" (1950, 24). The idealized image generates a whole structure of intrapsychic defenses that Horney calls "the pride system." These include "neurotic pride," "neurotic claims," and "tyrannical shoulds," all of which ultimately intensify self-hate.

Neurotic pride substitutes a pride in the attributes of the idealized self for realistic self-confidence and self-esteem. Threats to pride produce anxiety and hostility; its collapse results in self-contempt and despair. There are various devices for restoring pride, including retaliation, which reestablishes the superiority of the humiliated person, and loss of interest in that which is threatening. Also included are various forms of distortion, such as forgetting humiliating episodes, denying responsibility, blaming others, and embellishing. Sometimes "humor is used to take the sting out of an otherwise unbearable shame" (1950, 106).

On the basis of his pride the individual makes "neurotic claims" upon the world and his fellows. The specific content of his claims will vary with his predominant solution, but in every case he feels that his bargain with fate should be honored and the he should get what he needs in order to make his solution work. The claims are "pervaded by expectations of magic" (1950, 62). When they are frustrated by experience, the individual may react with despair, with outraged indignation, or with a denial of the realities that have broken in upon him. If things get bad enough, he may change his solution. Another possibility is that he may refuse to accept the implications of what has happened and may hold onto his claims as a "guaranty for future glory" (1950, 62). His claims intensify his vulnerability because their frustration threatens to confront him with the sense of worthlessness from which he is fleeing.

The individual's search for glory subjects him to what Horney calls "the tyranny of the should." The function of the shoulds is to compel a person to live up to his grandiose conception of himself. The shoulds are generated by the idealized image, and since the idealized image is, for the most part, a glorification of the self-effacing, expansive, and detached solutions, the individual's shoulds are determined largely by the character traits and values associated with his predominant defense. His subordinate trends are also represented in the idealized image, however, and, as a result, he is often caught in a "crossfire of conflicting shoulds." As he tries to obey contradictory inner dictates, he is bound to hate himself whatever he does, even if, paralyzed, he does nothing at all. The shoulds are impossible to live up to not only because they are contradictory, but also because they are unrealistic: we should love everyone; we should never make a mistake; we should always triumph; we should never need other people, and so forth. A good deal of externalization is connected with the shoulds. The individual feels his shoulds as the expectations of others, his self-hate as their rejection, and his self-criticism as their unfair judgment. He expects others to live up to his shoulds and displaces his rage at his own failure to do so onto them. The shoulds develop as a defense against self-loathing, but they aggravate the condition they are employed to cure. The "threat of a punitive self-hate" makes them "a regime of terror" (1950, 85).

The shoulds are the basis of the individual's bargain with fate. No matter what the solution, his bargain is that his claims will be honored if he lives up to his shoulds. He will control external reality by obeying his inner dictates. He does not see his claims as unreasonable, of course, but only as what he has a right to expect, given his grandiose conception of himself, and he will feel that life is unfair if his expectations are frustrated. His sense of justice is determined by his predominant solution and the bargain associated with it. Whereas Hamlet feels that the world is an unweeded garden because good people like his father are dishonored while the vicious Claudius triumphs, Iago is outraged because although he has lived up to his code of selfishness and deceit, the virtuous Cassio has won the lieutenancy. Each character feels that he has obeyed the shoulds of his solution and is in a state of psychological crisis because his claims have not been honored. The bargains of Hamlet and Iago are diametrically opposed and so, consequently, is their sense of what is just.

Self-hate is the end product of the intrapsychic strategies of defense, each of which tends to magnify the individual's feelings of inadequacy and failure. Essentially self-hate is the rage the idealized self feels toward the self we actually are for not being what it "should" be. In large part self-hate is an unconscious process, since it is usually too painful to be confronted directly. The chief defense against awareness is externalization, which takes two forms, active and passive. Active externalization "is an attempt to direct self-hate outward, against life, fate, institutions or people" (Horney 1950, 115). In passive externalization "the hate remains directed against the self but is perceived or experienced as coming from the outside." When self-hate is conscious, there is often a pride taken in it that serves to maintain self-glorification: "The very condemnation of imperfection confirms the godlike standards with which the person identifies himself" (1950, 114–15). Horney saw self-hate as "perhaps the greatest tragedy of the human mind. Man in reaching out for the Infinite and Absolute also starts destroying himself. When he makes a pact with the devil, who promises him glory, he has to go to hell—to the hell within himself" (1950, 154).

My view of the major tragedies is that the leading characters have embraced one or more of the defensive strategies Horney has described; that their values, their sense of identity, and their worldviews have been determined in large part by the strategy they have embraced; and that their bargains with fate are bound to fail because they are part of delusional systems that have little to do with either internal or external reality. In each play, there is something that challenges the protagonist's bargain and precipitates a psychological crisis. Either the character violates the dictates of his predominant solution, as is the case with Macbeth, or the world around him fails to honor his claims, as is the case with Hamlet, Iago, Othello, and Lear. When the character fails to live up to his shoulds, he is subject to intense self-hate and fear of retribution. When his claims are not honored, his idealized image is threatened, his belief in justice is shaken, and his version of reality is called into question. In either case, his predominant solution is undermined, his subordinate trends are activated, and he experiences intense inner conflict. In the process of trying to restore his pride and to repair his defenses, he behaves in ways that are terribly destructive to himself and to others.

CULTURAL CODES IN SHAKESPEARE

It is possible to combine an historical approach like Bernard McElroy's with a psychological approach like mine by correlating cultural codes in Shakespeare with the defensive strategies Horney described. I shall base my description of cultural codes mainly upon the first tetralogy (the three *Henry VI* plays and *Richard III*), but these codes are present throughout Shakespeare's works and play an important role in the tragedies.

There are four codes that must be discriminated in the first tetralogy: the code of martial and manly honor, the code of loyalty, duty, and service, the code of personal ambition, and the code of Christian values. Each of these codes has both cultural and psychological determinants, and there are conflicts between the codes both within the culture and within individuals.

In *Shakespeare and the Renaissance Concept of Honor*, Curtis Brown Watson points out that the Renaissance concept of honor is derived from pagan humanism and is frequently in conflict with the teachings of Christianity (1960, 3).[3] For example, the code of honor enjoins the taking of private revenge, whereas Christianity opposes it; and Christianity condemns pride, while the code of honor regards it as sublime.

I shall divide the Renaissance concept of honor into two separate codes: the code of martial and manly honor and the code of loyalty, duty, and service. Both codes have pagan sources, but the second code represents a more advanced stage of social evolution than the first. The code of martial and manly honor originated in the tribal state of social organization and was embraced by a wide variety of cultures, from the crudely barbaric to the highly civilized. It predated the Greek and Roman moralists upon whom the Renaissance drew; and it forms a part, but by no means the whole, of their value system. Its primary virtue is fortitude, which is only one of the four cardinal virtues of the ancients, the others being prudence, temperance, and justice. Within this code, honor means fame, glory, reputation, and power, which are to be acquired by displaying martial courage and prowess. The code of loyalty, duty, and service defines virtue primarily as moral rectitude, rather than as manly strength and valor. Within this code, honor means honesty, trustworthiness, and fidelity, and a concern for the public good—Brutus's rather than Cassius's conception of honor. Ideally, the two codes are part of a single system of values in which the individual displays loyalty to and martial valor in behalf of the community; and in some of Shakespeare's most highly approved characters, such as Talbot (*1 Henry VI*) and Henry V, this combination occurs. Often, however, the code of martial and manly honor is embraced in a way that is independent of, or even in conflict with, the code of loyalty, duty, and service. The two codes must therefore be examined independently, as well as in terms of their interrelationship.

The basic tenets of the code of martial and manly honor are set forth by Talbot in his description of what Knights of the Garter should be:

> Valiant and virtuous, full of haughty courage,
> Such as were grown to credit by the wars;
> Not fearing death, nor shrinking for distress,
> But always resolute in most extremes. (*1 Henry VI*, IV, i)[4]

Courage is the highest value in this code and cowardice is the greatest source of shame. Men hope to win honor through their bravery, and in order to do so, they must display it in battle. Warfare is welcomed, therefore, rather than avoided or abhorred, and peace is regarded as effeminate. A man's honor is not safe until he has proved his resoluteness in the face of extremity; hence, the manner of his death is of the utmost importance. The hero cannot always be triumphant, but he can always preserve his honor by remaining undaunted no matter what befalls him. Any threat to one's honor requires some sort of pride-restoring behavior, the most common form of which is revenge. The death of a friend, a comrade, and especially of a family member must be avenged by inflicting worse suffering upon the perpetrator.

The code of martial and manly honor is essentially secular in nature. It permits men to live in an absurd universe, full of violence and suffering, without losing faith in the meaning of life. Believers in this code do not indulge in self-blame or penitence, but rather attribute their defeats to blind forces beyond their control. Men cannot control their fates, but they can maintain their honor by demonstrating their ability to confront without flinching all that can be done to them. "Though Fortune's malice overthrow my state," proclaims the captured King Edward, "My mind exceeds the compass of her wheel" (*3 Henry VI,* IV, iii). In a sense men do control their fates by being resolute in extremes. There is a notion of justice in this code, but it does not depend upon any sort of Providence. Justice is getting the honor that is your due (in life and after death) and being avenged on those who have injured you. Men live and die for a kind of secular immortality, which lies in being remembered for their deeds and their fortitude.

Whereas the code of martial and manly honor is secular in nature, the code of loyalty, duty, and service has a religious dimension. It emphasizes the "natural" virtues of justice and prudence, but it also posits a supernatural order within which these virtues will be rewarded. When going into battle, the believers in this code rely upon the justice of their cause, as well as upon their martial prowess. Indeed, battles are often seen as a form of trial by combat in which victory goes to the righteous. A vivid example of the belief in the power of virtue is Gloucester's confidence that his enemies' plots against him cannot succeed:

> I must offend before I be attainted;
> And had I twenty times so many foes,
> And each of them had twenty times their power,
> All these could not procure me any scathe
> So long as I am loyal, true, and crimeless. (*2 Henry VI,* II, iv)

Richmond attributes his triumph at the battle of Bosworth not only to his arms but to God.

In the code of loyalty, duty, and service, the emphasis is less upon acquiring personal power and glory than upon fulfilling one's obligations to the community and to one's superiors. The world it posits is not the capricious one to which the code of martial and manly honor is adapted, but a highly evolved society that is part of a universal order and that is ruled by law. The hierarchical structure of society is seen as divinely ordained, and the purpose of life is not to rise above one's place, but to do the duties that belong to it. Personal ambition is an evil in this code, but ambition for one's country is admirable. As we can see in the case of Talbot, service to king and country often takes a military form. In Othello's phrase, the big wars make ambition virtue.

In *2 Henry VI,* Eleanor, Duchess of Gloucester, is married to a man who fails to live up to her idea of manhood, which is derived neither from the code of martial and manly honor nor from the code of loyalty, duty, and service, but rather from the code of personal ambition, the cultural source for which, in Shakespeare's time, was the Machiavellian philosophy as understood by the Elizabethans. Like Lady Macbeth, she dreams of gaining the crown and tries to infuse her husband with the same ambition: "Put forth thy hand, reach at the glorious gold./ What, is't too short? I'll lengthen it with mine!" (I, ii). When Gloucester indignantly rejects her treacherous suggestions, she scorns his "base and humble mind." In her value system, a man is someone who fights his way to the top without regard for duty, morality, or the lives of others.

The Shakespearean Machiavel does not (consciously) believe in any of the traditional values of his society. Indeed, it is his freedom from such values that establishes him in his own mind as a "realist" and permits him to act out his aggressive impulses. He pursues the power and glory that are celebrated by the code of martial and manly honor, but without following the rules of conduct set forth by that code. He has no concern with displaying an honorable courage or winning in a fair fight. He values revenge, as does the believer in manly honor, but tends to pursue it in a devious or treacherous way. For him, might makes right, and the end justifies the means. There is no moral order in the universe and no foundation for society's structure and values. The code of loyalty, duty, and service is simply a means by which those in power are able to exploit their fellows. Life is a battle of each against all in which the strongest rise to the top and then must protect their position by ruthlessly suppressing their competitors. The Machiavel has no compunction about the havoc he wreaks while pursuing his personal ambition. We either exploit others or are exploited by them. Those who believe in Christian values are, perhaps, the most readily manipulated. We must not allow ourselves to be weakened by "the milk of human kindness" or duped by such sentimental notions as love, charity, mercy, and fellow feeling.

The Machiavel is proud of his ability to see through the other codes, though for purposes of deception he often professes belief in them. Richard III, for example, frequently pretends to be meek, peaceloving, and devoid of ambition. The Machiavel becomes his own law-giver, the source and arbiter of values. He sees his transcendence of law as a kind of courage, which indeed it is, since it puts him at odds with his society and with his own cultural conditioning. He tries to tell himself that conscience "is but a word that cowards use,/ Devis'd at first to keep the strong in awe" (*Richard III*, V, iii), but he is not always successful.

In many ways, the Christian code is compatible with the code of loyalty, duty, and service, but it is in sharp contrast to the codes of martial and manly honor and of personal ambition. While the proud men around him are scrambling for power, Henry VI feels that he is God's "far unworthy deputy" (*2 Henry VI,* III, ii) and wishes that he were a subject rather than a king (IV, ix). He believes that "things ill-got [have] ever bad success" (*3 Henry VI,* II, ii) and attributes the troubles of his reign to the weakness of his claim to the throne. For Henry the world is a providential order in which evil is punished and virtue is rewarded. Vengeance belongs not to man but to the Lord. Instead of pursuing revenge, Henry refuses to judge, "for we are sinners all" (*2 Henry VI,* III, iii), and he forgives those who trespass against him. He asks God's pardon not only for Winchester, who is dying in torment because of his crimes, but even for Richard, his own murderer.

In *Richard III,* Christian values are articulated by King Edward, who seems to have undergone a deathbed conversion. This previously arrogant and self-indulgent man now does "deeds of charity" and seeks to make "peace of enmity, fair love of hate" (II, ii). When he hears of Clarence's death, he fears divine justice. Indeed, the dramatization in the play as a whole of the power of conscience and the inevitability of retribution exemplifies the Christian code.

CULTURAL CODES AND DEFENSIVE STRATEGIES

The four codes we have been examining have, as I have said, both cultural and psychological determinants. Each code is generated in part by the logic of social development and acts as a conditioning force upon individual members of the culture. Each code is also an expression of psychological needs and is embraced by its proponents not simply because it is there, but because it is congruent with their personalities. In analyzing influence, we must not underestimate the importance of receptivity. Unless individuals live in a truly monolithic culture, they are exposed to a great variety of influences, but are deeply affected only by those to which they are psychologically predisposed. Henry VI, Gloucester, and Richard III are all members of the same culture, but they embrace different codes because they have different character structures.

The four codes can be seen as embodiments of the kinds of defensive strategies that Horney has described. The movements against, away from, and toward other people are human elaborations of the basic defenses of the animal kingdom—fight, flight, and submission. All the strategies are encoded in almost every culture; but each culture has its characteristic attitudes toward the different strategies, its own formulations of and variations upon them, and its own structure of inner conflicts (see Paris 1986, 90–94). The code of Christian values is in many ways an embodiment of the self-effacing solution. In both there is an exaltation of humility, suffering, and sacrifice, reliance on a powerful protector, and a belief in the power of innocence. The code of loyalty, duty, and service parallels the perfectionistic solution in which living up to one's high moral standards gives one a feeling of superiority and an assurance of being fairly treated by fate and by other people. The code of personal ambition corresponds closely to the arrogant-vindictive solution; in both, the world is perceived as a jungle in which might makes right and the strong annihilate the weak. The only way to succeed is to repress one's softer feelings and to ignore the traditional morality. The code of martial and manly honor does not correlate as closely to Horney's descriptions of defensive strategies, but it clearly provides a socially sanctioned outlet for the pursuit of mastery and the release of aggression. Like Horney's solutions, each code involves a distinctive set of beliefs about human nature, human values, and the human condition, an idealized image, and a pride system. In each code there is also a bargain with fate in which obedience to the dictates of the code is supposed to ensure success.

Shakespeare depicts two other codes that also correspond closely to Horneyan defensive strategies—namely, the codes of aristocratic privilege and of stoic detachment. The code of aristocratic privilege derives from a social structure in which some are superior to others because of their birth. Those at or near the top feel like favorites of fortune who are above the laws and conditions that govern ordinary mortals. The code of aristocratic privilege contributes to the psychological pattern that Horney describes as narcissism, in which there are weak shoulds but enormous claims that have been fostered by overindulgence. The degree of narcissism tends to vary with rank. Kings like Richard II and Lear, for whom life has been easy and who have always been told that they are "everything," feel that they should get what they want simply because they are who they are. In the *Henry VI* plays, York is a narcissist (among other things) whose claims to the throne are not being honored and who is full of rage as a result. The code of aristocratic privilege is often combined with other codes in that loyalty, duty, and service are owed to those who are above one in the hierarchy and expected from those beneath, and any denial of one's prerogatives calls for a martial response. The predominantly Christian or self-effacing person, like Henry, does not feel entitled to his exalted position and does not know how to use the power attached to it.

The correlations between stoicism and the defensive strategy of detachment are evident. Both seek invulnerability to the slings and arrows of outrageous fortune by mastering the emotions. If one desires nothing, one cannot be frustrated; if one is indifferent to life, one cannot be defeated by death. In Shakespeare, stoical detachment sometimes takes the form of withdrawal into a quiet life, but more often it is presented as a "philosophical" way of dealing with pain, adversity, or evil, as in Gaunt's advice to Bolingbroke (*Richard II*, I, iii), Friar Laurence's to Romeo (III, iii), Antonio's to Leonato (*Much Ado*, V, i), or the Duke's to Brabantio (*Othello*, I, iii). The essence of this advice is that "What cannot be preserved when Fortune takes,/ Patience her injury a mockery makes" (*Othello*, I, iii). We triumph over fortune by not suffering. Hamlet admires Horatio because he "is not passion's slave" but has been "As one, in suffering all, that suffers nothing" (III, ii). Stoical detachment as a defense is most fully portrayed in Apemantus in *Timon of Athens*.

The connection between social codes and personality structures is present in Shakespeare from the very beginning. In the *Henry VI* plays, for example, where characters are relatively undeveloped, those who embrace Christian values display self-effacing traits, the exponents of loyalty, duty, and service are perfectionistic, and those who pursue personal ambition are arrogant-vindictive types. In his portrait of Richard III, his first great realistic character, Shakespeare explores the psychological sources of Machiavellian behavior and shows his understanding of inner conflict. Although Richard scornfully rejects the codes of Christian values and of loyalty, duty, and service, he has an unconscious allegiance to them, since he cannot violate their dictates without experiencing anxiety and self-hate. Fine as the portrayal of Richard is, he is, for the most part, a rather static figures who merely repeats his strategies. He does have a psychological crisis on the eve of the battle of Bosworth, but it comes late in the play and passes quickly as he represses his inner conflicts and reaffirms his dominant solution. Many splendid psychological portraits can be found in other plays of the 1590s; but it is in the major tragedies, of course, that Shakespeare has depicted most fully the interplay of culture and personality, the crises that arise when a character's bargain is threatened, and the dynamics of inner conflicts.

CHAPTER 2

Hamlet

HAMLET'S PROBLEMS

What are Hamlet's problems? Why does he delay? Is he uncertain about the right course of action, unsure of the ghost, afraid of damnation, traumatized by the disillusionment, excessively introspective, or paralyzed by inhibitions of which he himself is not wholly aware? Ernest Jones argued that Hamlet's difficulties center in reality "about a sexual problem," the manifestations of which "are transferred on to more tolerable and permissible topics, such as anxiety . . . about immortality and the salvation of the soul, philosophical considerations about the value of life, the future of the world, and so on" (1954, 67). Although I do not feel Hamlet's problems to be primarily sexual, I agree with Jones that his philosophical concerns are psychologically determined. I agree also, however, with Paul Gottschalk's objections to the generality of Jones's explanation and its failure to analyze the conscious material of the play:

> After all, the play takes place largely on the conscious level, and its philosophical, religious, and political content is considerable . . . we cannot fully appreciate the play, even from the psychoanalytic point of view, without understanding how Hamlet's inner problem . . . finds expression in these . . . ideas that body forth the deeper workings of the mind. To my knowledge, such an interpretation has not been done. (1972, 101)

It is such an interpretation that I propose to offer here.

Hamlet's problems begin before he encounters the ghost, learns of his father's murder, and accepts his mission of revenge. He is from the outset an angry brooding figure, full of conflicts, who is in an obvious state of psychological crisis.[1] He is disgusted with life, longs for death, and is seething with repressed hostility. He has been traumatized by a devastating experience. The precipitating event, as we learn in his first soliloquy, is his mother Gertrude's desecration of his father's memory by her hasty and incestuous marriage to a man whom Hamlet reviles. The central problem of the play for T. S. Eliot is why Hamlet reacts so intensely to his mother's behavior. Shakespeare cannot make Hamlet's emotion intelligible, says Eliot, "because it is in *excess* of the facts as they appear . . . his disgust is occasioned by his mother, but . . . his mother is not an adequate equivalent for it; his disgust envelops and exceeds her" (1950, 125). The facts as they appear would be disturbing to almost any man, but, as Eliot's remarks make clear, not everyone would react as Hamlet does. To understand Hamlet's feelings we must try to enter into his experience and comprehend his character. We can do this, I think, without reconstructing his childhood, but we shall have to infer from evidence in the text the attitudes, beliefs, and expectations from life that Hamlet has held as an adult and that have been undermined by the events following the death of his father.

Before his father's death, Hamlet is a man who strives hard to be good, who believes in the nobility of human nature, and who expects virtue to be rewarded, on earth and in the hereafter. He values love, dutifulness, and constancy, shuns pride, ambition, and revenge, and has a religious dread of sin. He admires aggressiveness in soldiers who fight to uphold their martial and manly honor, but he abhors violence, scheming, and duplicity within the state or in private life. He is morally fastidious and detests cynics, drunkards, lechers, and Machiavels. He tends to equate fair appearances with inner virtue, and he is proud of his mother's beauty, his father's distinction, and his own good looks. He strives to be a model prince, and he anticipates ascending the throne in due course and being a just and valiant king. He admires his father greatly and has modeled his idealized image upon his exalted conception of him.

In his personal relations, Hamlet is highly idealistic. He venerates his parents, is dutiful toward them, and wants their affection and approval. He sees them as a devoted couple and hopes to have for himself a love relationship similar to theirs. He glorifies women and is romantic and pure in his dealings with them. He is much maligned by Polonius and Laertes when they warn Ophelia against him. That is why when he curses her in act 3, scene 1, he says "be thou as chaste as ice, as pure as snow, thou shalt not escape calumny." In order to live up to his high moral standards, he has repressed his sexuality. He is fearful of lust in himself and is disgusted by it in others. He has warm relations with men and an exalted conception of friendship. We can see this in his dealings with Horatio and when he conjures Rosencrantz and Guildenstern "by the rights of our fellowship, by the consonancy of our youth, by the obligation of our ever-preserved love" to be direct with him (II, ii).

Before his father's death Hamlet has a secure place in his parents' affection, he is loved by the multitude, and he is "the expectancy and rose of the fair state" (III, i).[2] He has good friends, is happy at Wittenberg, and is romantically in love with Ophelia. He has great pride in his father, a strong sense of his own worth, and a firm confidence in the triumph of right. His kind of people are in power, his values are being honored, and the future looks bright.

The death of his father and the events that follow upset this situation and threaten Hamlet in a number of ways. His father's shocking, untimely death deprives Hamlet of a loved parent and sets him brooding on mortality and the "base uses" to which even the greatest of men may return (V, i). When Claudius becomes king, Hamlet is further alienated from the world in which he was formerly so much at home. His own noble qualities have been passed over, and the crown has been given to a man who is the opposite of both his father and himself. Claudius is untrustworthy, undeserving, a disgrace to the state. While this man has been elevated, Hamlet's own position has been diminished. He speaks of himself as a "poor . . . man" (I, v) and complains of being "most dreadfully attended" (II, ii). He does not dwell upon his political frustrations because he has taboos against ambition, but others assume he is brooding about them, and no doubt he is in a repressed way. His whole demeanor shows that he is feeling abused. At a more conscious level, his faith in the political order has been profoundly disturbed, and he cannot help feeling that life is unjust. His fair visions of the future have been mocked by events.

The most devastating blow to Hamlet is, of course, his mother's marriage to Claudius. Her disloyalty to his father's memory makes him question the constancy of woman's love, and her attraction to Claudius makes him feel that women are utterly capricious in their sexual choices (see III, iv, 63–81). Hamlet had not been disturbed by his mother's sexual attraction to his father, for it was sanctified by love and marriage, and he looked forward to receiving such affection from his own wife. But his mother's attraction to Claudius is unholy. He cannot believe that she loves this vile creature, with whom she has entered into an incestuous union.

}

Her guilty sexuality arouses so much disgust partly because it violates his moral standards, is a blow to his family pride, and partly because it threatens his own repression of lustful feelings: if lust "canst mutine in a matron's bones,/ To flaming youth let virtue be as wax" (III, iv). His mother's guilt undermines his lofty conception of women, shatters his confidence in fair appearances, and diminishes his hope of finding for himself a pure, faithful, loving wife. His distrust of her increases his sense of alienation and makes him feel all the more an outcast in the world. His hostility makes him afraid of his own violent impulses. He would hate himself if he acted out his rage and violated his taboos against filial impiety.

However important the preceding factors may be, the major reason why his mother's behavior fills Hamlet with such rage and despair is that, because of his powerful identification with his father, he feels the wrongs Gertrude has done to the dead king as though they had been done to himself. Hamlet is angry with his mother on his father's behalf.

> That it should come to this!
> But two months dead: nay, not so much, not two:
> So excellent a king; that was, to this,
> Hyperion to a satyr; so loving to my mother
> That he might not beteem the winds of heaven
> Visit her face too roughly. Heaven and earth!
> Must I remember? why, she would hang on him,
> As if increase of appetite had grown
> By what it fed on: and yet, within a month—
> Let me not think on't—Frailty, thy name is woman!—
> . . . .
> —why she, even she—
> O God! a beast, that wants discourse of reason,
> Would have mourn'd longer—married with my uncle,
> My father's brother, but no more like my father
> Than I to Hercules. (I, ii)

Hamlet's grievances against Gertrude in his first soliloquy are very similar to sentiments later expressed by the ghost:

> O Hamlet, what a falling-off was there!
> From me, whose love was of that dignity
> That it went hand in hand even with the vow
> I made to her in marriage, and to decline
> Upon a wretch whose natural gifts were poor
> To those of mine!
> But virtue, as it never will be moved,

> Though lewdness court it in a shape of heaven
> So lust, though to a radiant angel link'd,
> Will sate itself in a celestial bed,
> And prey on garbage. (I, v)

Both speeches stress the nobility of King Hamlet, the sexual depravity of Gertrude, and the inferiority of Claudius to his brother. There is in both a sense of outrage that this faithful, loving husband, this radiant angel, this Hyperion, has been betrayed by his wife and replaced in her affections by the bestial Claudius. Both speeches express profound disillusionment with Gertrude, this "seeming virtuous queen" (I, v), who posts "with such dexterity to incestuous sheets" (I, ii). The similarity of these speeches vividly reveals the extent to which Hamlet is reacting to his mother's behavior from his father's perspective.

Hamlet's identification with his father may be partly the effect of mourning, but the main reason for his identification is that he has modeled himself upon his father and glorified those qualities in himself that he shares with him. He and his father have similar character structures. Both strive to be noble, good, and loving, and both expect these qualities to be rewarded. They are conscientious, dutiful, religious men who exalt women, are faithful to their oaths, and place a high value upon sexual purity. They have lived up to their shoulds, but their claims have not been honored, and their bargain is in ruins. Instead of receiving fair treatment, the king is betrayed by his wife, murdered by his brother, and prematurely forgotten by everyone except Hamlet. Claudius has committed the most heinous of sins, but instead of being punished, he has gained through his villainy the throne and the queen. King Hamlet's spirit cannot rest in peace but is compelled to return from the grave, seeking vengeance.

Hamlet and the ghost of his father revile Claudius because he is the opposite psychological type. He is a wily, lecherous, underhanded schemer, a man whose very looks reveal his gross and cunning nature. He is such a good actor, however, that he deceives many members of the court (and a number of critics as well). He is not without ability, but his "gifts" are those of a Machiavel. For the Hamlet-type of man, it is unbearable for the Claudiuses of the world to gain the prizes that should be the reward of virtue. If the Claudiuses are triumphant and the Hamlets are ignominiously treated, then the world is "an unweeded garden,/ That grows to seed; things rank and gross in nature/ Possess it merely" (I, ii). It is striking that when Hamlet finally confronts his mother in the closet scene, what he dwells upon most passionately is the comparison between Claudius and his father. How *could* she have turned from her husband, upon whom "every god did seem to set his seal,/ To give the world assurance of a man"—to this "mildew'd ear," this "villain," this "king of shreds and patches"? (III, iv). Claudius is not merely subhuman, he is one of the more disgusting animals—"a paddock, . . . a bat, a gib." Because of his identification with his father, Hamlet feels Gertrude's preference for Claudius as a rejection of himself. He gains evident relief when he moves her to self-detestation and repentance and gains her promise of loyalty to him rather than to Claudius.

There is something more, I think, to the repugnance that Hamlet feels toward Claudius. Claudius represents the sexual and aggressive drives that Hamlet represses in himself. He is what Hamlet is afraid of becoming. Hamlet's father is an external embodiment of his idealized image; Claudius symbolizes his despised self. When Claudius's successes undermine his solution, Hamlet's repression is threatened and he becomes all the more afraid of his forbidden impulses. He cannot help doubting the efficacy of virtue (what has it done for his father?), and he is enraged with Gertrude, by whom he feels betrayed. His taboos are still in operation, however, and he is afraid of becoming a monster. His attacks on Claudius are partly an externalization of his loathing for those parts of himself against which he is struggling and partly a reaffirmation of his own nobility. They reinforce his pride in his virtue and assure him that he can never become like the bestial creature he condemns.

"THIS TOO TOO SOLID FLESH"

The disgust with life and longings for extinction that Hamlet expresses in his first soliloquy are the reactions of a man whose most cherished beliefs have been shattered and whose strategy for dealing with the world has proven to be ineffective. He is obsessed with the injustice of life and is full of rage, anxiety, and despair. His father was the kind of man that Hamlet has aspired to be, and his memory has been foully dishonored. What promise does life hold for Hamlet in a world such as this? His father's fate seems also to be his own. Claudius has already stepped between the election and his hopes. His mother's act "calls virtue hypocrite," "makes marriage vows as false as dicer's oaths," and renders "sweet religion" a mere "rhapsody of words" (III, iv). Will he, too, be mocked by the objects of his affection, betrayed by the people to whom he has been faithful, abandoned for base creatures by those from whom he deserves loyalty and appreciation? Even before he learns of the murder, the fate of his father shows that the world is not a moral order but an unweeded garden, a jungle in which good people are abused, the vicious triumph, and fair appearances are untrustworthy. This is not a world with which his kind of person can cope or in which he sees much hope of reward. He wants to escape by melting away into nothingness. Hamlet still believes in God, but he had expected justice on earth, and he has been cruelly disappointed.

Hamlet's oppression is the result not only of his disillusionment, but also of his repressed hostility. He is full of bitterness and rage, but he cannot express his feelings directly to Claudius and Gertrude. He mutters asides, quibbles with words, and accuses them with his display of mourning and melancholy. They have secured the blessings of the court, but he shows them through his behavior that he does not accept what they have done. His tactics make them deeply uncomfortable, and they respond by being defensive and placatory. They reaffirm their own sorrow, assure him that he is next in line to the throne, and try to argue him out of his "excessive" grief. Hamlet wants to get away from the poisonous atmosphere of Elsinore, but the king and queen feel too threatened to let him out of their sight, and Hamlet agrees to remain with every appearance of filial respect: "I shall in all my best obey you madam" (I, ii). As soon as he is alone, however, he pours out his accusations in his first soliloquy, which ends, "But break, my heart, for I must hold my tongue" (I, ii).

Hamlet's behavior reflects his fierce inner conflicts. He is furious with Gertrude and wants to express his outrage, to hurl accusations, to say the things he finally does say in the closet scene. He has strong taboos against such behavior, however, especially toward a mother, and all he can do is to accuse her with his misery and grief. His hostility is so great that he is afraid of losing control and of doing something for which he could never forgive himself. He is caught, in part, between conflicting demands of his compliant side. As a good son, he owes it to his father to honor his memory and to protest its desecration by others; but he has to be respectful and obedient toward his mother. Even to himself Hamlet does not complain of his own injuries, but only of those inflicted upon his father. Because of his self-effacing tendencies, Hamlet can feel anger on another's behalf much more readily than on his own. To fight for others is virtuous, but to resent the thwarting of his own desires would be a sign of selfishness. Hamlet makes occasional references to feeling slighted; but it is not until later, when he has become much more aggressive, that he expresses open resentment at what has been done to him.

The wish for death with which Hamlet's first soliloquy opens has several sources. It is in part a desire to escape from a world in which he despairs of receiving love and justice and in part, a desire to throw off the burden of his inner conflicts. It is also a product of turning against the self, a frequent defense in the self-effacing solution where there is a powerful taboo against violence, especially toward a parent. Hamlet's suicidal fantasies provide both an outlet for his destructive impulses and a defense against acting them out. He harbors murderous impulses toward his mother, but he cannot permit himself even to feel them. What he is aware of is that he wants to die. One object of suicide is to make others feel guilty, and this is surely a motive for Hamlet. But self-murder is also a sin. Hamlet can no longer believe that goodness will be rewarded in this world, but he still expects evil to be punished, both here and hereafter. The penalty for suicide is eternal damnation. If he could only melt away without any act of his own, he would at once escape his pain, retain his virtue, and show others how they have destroyed him.

HAMLET AND THE GHOST

As his death wishes indicate, Hamlet is already in an impossible position for his kind of person. His encounter with the ghost intensifies the pressure on him both to be aggressive and to be good. The wrongs done to his father are far greater than Hamlet had imagined. He had been betrayed by Claudius and Gertrude while he was alive and then murdered in his sleep by his own brother—"Of life, of crown, of queen, at once dispatch'd" (I, v). Because the manner of his death denied him the opportunity to purify his soul, he must suffer the purgatorial torments whose horror he suggests so vividly. The ghost feeds Hamlet's already seething indignation and puts him under heavy pressure to prove his love by avenging him.

Hamlet cannot help feeling ambivalent about being an avenger. He is prompted to his revenge by the codes of martial and manly honor and of loyalty, duty, and service; but there is both in Christianity and in Hamlet's self-effacing defense system a strong taboo against vindictive behavior. "I could accuse me of such things," he tells Ophelia, "that it were better my mother had not born me: I am very proud, revengeful, and ambitious" (III, i). He cannot pursue his revenge openly, moreover, like a soldier on the field of battle, but must plot like a Machiavel. It is a matter of love, duty, and manliness for Hamlet to carry out the ghost's commission, and he swears to do so; but he can neither obey nor disobey the ghost's commands without incurring self-hate.

The ghost himself is not a single-minded revenger. He is protective toward Gertrude and fearful of his son's damnation: "But, howsoever thou pursuest this act,/ Taint not thy mind, nor let thy soul contrive/ Against thy mother aught" (I, v). Hamlet is supposed to be aggressive, but also to be good; to avenge his father, but not to taint his mind; to stop the incest, but not to contrive anything against his mother. The ghost's conflicting messages correspond to Hamlet's own inner conflicts and contribute to his paralysis.

The ghost's sufferings, moreover, reinforce Hamlet's fear of sin and punishment in the afterlife. His father was a good man, but his spirit is doomed to undergo horrible torments until the "foul crimes done in [his] days of nature/ Are burnt and purged away" (I, iv). If these are his father's sufferings, what might Hamlet's be if he commits a sin greater than any of which his father has been guilty? He will not be a good son if he does not secure revenge, but to be an avenger is to descend into the arena with the Claudiuses of the world, to become like them, and to experience intense self-loathing and fear of divine retaliation.

When the ghost first announces that he has been murdered, Hamlet is most "apt" in the acceptance of his mission, and after the ghost departs, he is still breathing fire. He soon shows signs of inner stress, however. In the swearing scene he addresses the ghost with a strange levity that can only be understood as a release of tension. He quickly seizes upon the device of assuming an antic disposition. This has dubious value in his revenge scheme (Hamlet is almost totally inept as a plotter), but it permits him to manifest his inner turbulence and to release a good deal of aggression without being held responsible for his behavior. Hamlet needs at once to express and to disown his anger. As the first act ends, he is no longer "apt." Rather, he is oppressed that *he* is expected to take action: "The time is out of joint: O cursed spite,/ That ever I was born to set it right!" He is once again longing for escape. He wishes that he did not exist, that he had not been born. Hamlet wants to be loved, recognized, taken care of, rewarded for his goodness. He abhors the moral disorder of life and resents having to cope with the harsh realities of the historical process. He wants to *receive* justice, not to be burdened with the task of reestablishing it.

At the end of act 1, then, Hamlet is in deep psychological trouble, as his interpersonal and his intrapsychic strategies begin to break down. He despairs of having his claims honored and of living up to his shoulds. As a consequence, he is filled with the rage that is his dominant emotion in act 1 and the self-hate that becomes so prominent in act 2. He is losing faith in justice, in other people, and in himself.

It is important to recognize that Hamlet has an idealized image that he is trying to actualize. He wants to live without sin; that is, without the taint of pride, revengefulness, and ambition and of coarse or illicit sexuality. He wants to be an ideal son, lover, prince, and friend, and he believes that his virtues will be appropriately rewarded. His bargain is threatened by the fate of his father and by his disillusionment with other people. If they are all really Claudiuses or Gertrudes, then he has no chance of receiving the love and honor that are his due. He also needs to have faith in the goodness of others for the sake of his idealized image. If he is to believe in his own nobility, mankind in general must have the capacity to be high-minded and pure, at least to curb the devil, if not to throw him out. If all are depraved, then he must be also. His mother's guilt and his father's purgatorial sufferings threaten his belief in himself; it is difficult for him to maintain the possibility of his own innocence when he seems to be surrounded by human corruption.

The greatest threat to Hamlet's sense of innocence is his own rage, of course. He represses himself severely and turns his destructive impulses inward to prevent them from escaping. He would rather die than do anything that would destroy his idealized image. He dreads becoming like Claudius, and he projects upon his uncle the self-hate that is generated by his own forbidden feelings.

Hamlet's encounter with the ghost makes it impossible for him to maintain his self-approval. His rage is intensified; and although it is also to a certain extent sanctified, he can never enact the ghost's commands without severe anxiety and guilt. Once he incorporates the ghost's demand for revenge into his idealized image, he becomes caught in a cross fire of conflicting inner dictates, and he is bound to hate himself no matter what he does. No wonder he wishes that he had never been born.

HAMLET'S CONFLICTS IN ACT 2

Approximately two months pass between acts 1 and 2. When we meet Hamlet again, he is distraught, demoralized, in a state of psychological torment. Before he appears on stage, we receive a moving account of him from Ophelia, to whom he has appeared "with a look so piteous in purport/ As if he had been loosed out of hell/ To speak of horrors" (II, i).

In his disillusionment with Gertrude, Hamlet has turned to Ophelia for reassurance. He desperately needs to believe in her goodness, in the purity of his own feelings, and in the ideal nature of their love. He is cut off from Ophelia, however, by Polonius's insistence that she deny Hamlet her presence. Hamlet cannot be angry with Ophelia for her obedience to her father, but he must be terribly frustrated by the whole situation. He may be struggling with lustful impulses when he appears in Ophelia's private chamber, but it is more likely that he is lonely and tormented and hopes to move her through a display of his suffering. He needs sympathy. His piteous looks, his profound sighs, his remarkable dishevelment do arouse Ophelia's concern, but she is too submissive a daughter to respond openly and Hamlet cannot make a more direct appeal for fear of compromising her with her father. The deprivation of Ophelia is another injustice. It leaves Hamlet all the more alone at a time when he desperately needs love and comfort.

Hamlet is not yet bitter toward Ophelia, but he is toward Polonius who is, in act 2, the chief object of his antic disposition. The antic disposition is, as T. S. Eliot has observed, "less than madness and more than feigned." It is "a form of emotional relief," "the buffoonery of an emotion which can find no outlet in action" (1950, 126). Polonius is a prime target for several reasons. Hamlet is hostile toward him not only because he has denied him Ophelia, but also because he is a vulgar schemer whose cynical view of human nature leads him to see Hamlet as a seducer. This is an insult to Hamlet's pride and it threatens his idealized image, especially since he is afraid that he may, indeed, be sinful. Another reason for Hamlet's hostility is that Polonius serves as a surrogate onto whom he can displace his feelings toward Gertrude and Claudius. Polonius represents the kind of worldly corruption that Hamlet detests so much in Claudius, and he is an inferior to whom Hamlet owes no special duty or respect. It is much easier for Hamlet to behave aggressively toward this man than toward his mother or uncle, especially when his behavior must be excused as madness. The pattern is similar to that in act 1. Hamlet cannot contain his venom, but neither can he discharge it directly upon its proper objects. He is full of impotent rage, but he gains some sense of power by making a fool of the crafty old man.

Hamlet continues to be obsessed, as he was in act 1, with the fickleness of fate and the depravity of man. His bitter remarks on these subjects run like a refrain through the second act: "To be honest, as this world goes," he tells Polonius, "is to be one man picked out of ten thousand" (II, ii). If we "use every man after his desert, . . . who should 'scape whipping?" If "the world's grown honest," as Guildenstern says, "then is doomsday near." Hamlet wants to believe in human goodness. He greets Rosencrantz and Guildenstern with great warmth ("My excellent good friends! . . . Good lads, how do ye both?"), pleads with them almost pathetically to be "even and direct" with him, but sees their hesitation ("Nay, then, I have an eye of you") and is disappointed once more. His eloquent speech on "What a piece of work is a man" then follows, in which he contrasts his former idealistic view of human nature with his present disillusionment. This is not the main reason, of course, why he has "lost all [his] mirth"; but it is a very bitter experience for him to have to give up his faith in human goodness, on which he has depended for safety and recognition, and to accept the Claudius–Polonius-aggressive view of human relations as a battle of each against all.

Hamlet is disenchanted not only with human nature, but also with all things of this world. This "goodly frame, the earth," seems to him "a sterile promotory" (II, ii). This "majestical roof fretted with golden fire" appears to him "a foul and pestilent contagion of vapours" (II, ii). Beneath all fair appearances there is a sordid reality. Our earthly realm is not a just order but is ruled by fortune.

Hamlet's attack on the capriciousness of fate is most fully articulated in the speech he asks the player to recite describing the murder of Priam: "Out, out, thou strumpet, Fortune! All you gods,/ In general synod, take away her power" (II, ii). The important distinction made here between fortune and the gods is repeated in the description of the grief of Hecuba. Anyone who witnessed her clamor, " 'Gainst Fortune's state would treason have pronounced"; but "if the gods themselves did see her then," they "would have made milch the burning eyes of heaven." In effect, Hamlet is raging against the absurdity of historical reality; but he is not an atheist. He still believes in a higher justice, in a transcendent moral order, that will punish evil in its own way and to which he is responsible. This seems to be not only Hamlet's position, but also that of the play. Even Claudius knows that though "In the corrupted currents of this world/ Offence's gilded hand may shove by justice/ . . . 'tis not so above;/ . . . there the action lies/ In his true nature" (III, iii).

It may well be that Hamlet grows more religious (and hence has more conscientious scruples) as his belief in earthly justice crumbles. Aggressive people often become self-effacing when their ambitions are thwarted. This is what happens to Claudius, for a moment, when the play within the play threatens his security and he considers repentance. Self-effacing people, on the other hand, may become more self-effacing when their solution does not work. In the absence of earthly rewards, they may seek the greater security of a divine, but invisible, justice.

The chief source of Hamlet's inner torment is that he is driven by irreconcilable needs. He has sworn to avenge his father, but two months have passed, and as yet he has done nothing. His failure to act makes him feel disloyal, unloving, and cowardly. He is tortured by self-hate. To escape his self-accusations he tries to stir up his passions to such a pitch that he can override his scruples and take his revenge. Any approach to action, however, heightens his fears of incurring damnation; and he delays again, thinks up a new plan, or longs to withdraw into stoical patience or the oblivion of death. Each retreat from action generates new self-hate, which pushes him once more toward violence. He loathes himself for his undutifulness and ineffectuality, but he is afraid that he will hate himself even more, and incur divine wrath as well, if he becomes a murderer.

Hamlet is hopelessly trapped in this situation. He oscillates from one set of shoulds to another; but nothing will satisfy his contradictory needs and permit him to escape his self-hate. Each side of him accuses and inhibits the other. As he is torn by inner conflicts, he begins to doubt his own sanity. One function of his antic disposition may be to reassure himself that he is not mad but is only acting. We can see the dynamics I have just described very clearly at work in his encounter with the players and in his second and third soliloquies.

HAMLET AND THE PLAYERS

Hamlet asks the First Player to recite the description of Priam's murder and the grief of Hecuba in order to stir, to express, and to justify his own emotions. The monstrousness of Pyrrhus feeds his loathing of Claudius, the horror of Priam's death revivifies his own horror at the murder of his father, and the attack upon fortune expresses his outrage at the cruelty of fate. Hecuba's grief assures him that his own mourning is appropriate and reinforces his indignation at his mother's behavior. The pity of the gods at the sight of Hecuba's despair feeds his self-pity and assures him that Heaven understands his feelings and is on his side.

The contents of the recitation, combined with the player's passion in reciting it, have a profound effect upon Hamlet, as we see when he is left alone. His second soliloquy is a series of self-denunciations: he is a "rogue," a "peasant slave," a "dull and muddy-mettled rascal," a "coward," an "ass," a "whore," a "drab," a "scullion" (II, ii). There is a massive release of self-hate here. Hamlet's self-accusations are a form of self-punishment, an expression of his profound sense of his own ignobility, and a part of his effort to become the noble Hamlet once more by rousing himself to action.

It makes Hamlet feel "monstrous" that the player is so moved by the woes of Hecuba while he "can say nothing . . . for a king,/ Upon whose property and most dear life/ A damned defeat was made" (II, ii), and he attacks himself by imagining what the player would do if he had "the motive and the cue for passion" that he has: "He would drown the stage with tears/ And cleave the general air with horrid speech,/ Made mad the guilty and appal the free." This is what Hamlet has been wanting to do ever since his mother's remarriage, but something has forced him to hold his tongue. He accuses himself of being "A dull and muddy-mettled rascal," a "John-a-dreams, unpregnant of [his] cause"; but he has, of course, been obsessed with his cause and with his inability to act. His description of himself suggests, however, that he has tried to escape his inner torments by a process of withdrawal, by a blunting of consciousness that leaves him dull and stuporous.

Can it be, Hamlet wonders, that he is a coward? This is partly self-accusation and partly a search for an explanation of his delay. Hamlet experiences his conflicts, but he does not understand them, and he keeps trying to make sense of his behavior. The accusation of cowardice brings him to the pitch of passion at which he has been aiming. No one treats him like a coward, but if they did, he "should take it," for he must be "pigeon-liver'd" or he would have killed Claudius long before this. Hamlet's pride is now stirred up, and he attacks himself for being content with mere verbal violence, like the scum of the earth, instead of acting courageously, like the son of a king.

His bloodthirsty mood quickly gives way, however, to more cerebral activity as he reverts to the plan he had already set in motion to trap Claudius with the play. The play is another device for being aggressive in an indirect way, for torturing Claudius without making an overt assault, either verbal or physical, upon him. Hamlet excuses himself for this further delay by questioning the reliability of the ghost. As numerous critics have pointed out, his doubts are in keeping with contemporary doctrines concerning ghosts, but Hamlet recalls these doctrines at this time because something within him is reacting against his earlier clamoring for vengeance, and he is troubled once more by fear of damnation.

"TO BE OR NOT TO BE"

When we see Hamlet next, he is again subdued by his inner conflicts. The famous third soliloquy is a rather confused meditation in which three possible alternatives are being considered: compliance, aggression, or detachment. Hamlet begins by asking whether it is better to be or not to be, but he immediately shifts to the consideration of another question:

> Whether 'tis nobler in the mind to suffer
> The slings and arrows of outrageous fortune,
> Or to take arms against a sea of troubles,
> And by opposing end them? (III, i)

This is the question by which he has been most deeply tormented. He wishes above all to be noble, but does this mean submitting to fate or attacking the evils of life in an attempt to correct them? Hamlet longs to escape from the buffetings of fortune and the agony of his dilemma by withdrawing into the oblivion of death, but suicide would be a sin and he has a dread of the afterlife.

Hamlet cannot come to rest in any solution. Submission will not work because he has sworn to avenge his father's murder and to stop the incest. He is too full of outrage, moreover, to accept the injustices of life, and he has a need to live up to his culture's conception of manliness. Aggression will not work because it exposes him to fears of sinfulness and damnation: "Thus conscience does make cowards of us all;/ And thus the native hue of resolution/ Is sicklied o'er with the pale cast of thought" (III, i). Hamlet is very much drawn to detachment as a defense; he would dearly love to attain a stoical independence of fate. He envies Horatio, who is "A man that fortune's buffets and rewards/ Hast ta'en with equal thanks" (III, ii); but Hamlet is much too tormented by outrageous fortune and by his own inner turbulence to achieve such philosophic calm. He hates himself, no doubt, for being "passion's slave," "a pipe for fortune's finger/ To sound what stop she please" (III, ii).

Since he cannot become invulnerable by self-mastery, such as Horatio's, Hamlet's detachment takes the form of a longing for death. In death he could escape both his inner conflicts, with their accompanying self-hate, and the injustices of life:

> For who would bear the whips and scorns of time,
> The oppressor's wrong, the proud man's contumely,
> The pangs of despised love, the law's delay,
> The insolence of office and the spurns

> That patient merit of the unworthy takes,
> When he himself might his quietus make
> With a bare bodkin? (III, i)

These wrongs are very largely those that "good" people suffer at the hands of aggressive types. Hamlet is "patient merit"; Claudius is "the unworthy."

Hamlet's fantasy of dying is generated not only by his craving for escape but also by his self-effacing trends. When the solution of a self-effacing person fails, he may be attracted to self-destruction because it provides an outlet for his rage, shows others what they have done to him, and preserves his moral superiority. As Horney observed, "going to pieces under the assault of an unfeeling world appeals to him as the ultimate triumph . . . . What else can a sensitive person in an ignoble world do but go to pieces! Should he fight and assert himself and hence stoop down to the same level of crude vulgarity? (1950, 236).

Hamlet cannot commit suicide, however, because of his fear of the afterlife. If death were truly an escape, it would be "a consummation devoutly to be wish'd"; but it is no more an oblivion than sleep. Hamlet has bad dreams, and "what dreams may come/ When we have shuffled off this mortal coil must give us pause." Hamlet fears damnation should he either kill himself or die in the pursuit of vengeance. Conscience, which binds him to this weary life, also prevents him from carrying out his great enterprise; and he finds himself unable to act, to submit, or to escape.

"GET THEE TO A NUNNERY"

This is the last time we see Hamlet moody and inert. His encounter with Ophelia and the Mousetrap scene release his anger, and he becomes capable of both verbal and physical violence. His self-effacing trends remain in evidence, and he develops a more and more profound sense of resignation, but his aggression is henceforth liberated, and he becomes at times a stereotypic avenger.

Hamlet is not angry with Ophelia when he encounters her at the end of his third soliloquy. He has been preoccupied with thoughts of conscience and the afterlife, and he regards Ophelia as a pure, spiritual being whose prayers he has need of ("Nymph, in thy orisons/ Be all my sins remembered"). The situation changes, however, when Ophelia wants to return his gifts: "their perfume lost,/ Take these again; for to the noble mind/ Rich gifts wax poor when givers prove unkind" (III, i). Hamlet's response is, "Ha, ha! are you honest?" This is the turning point in Hamlet's attitude toward Ophelia. Her withdrawal has frustrated but not embittered him, for she has behaved as a dutiful daughter. But her present behavior is false. Hamlet has not been unkind. It is difficult to understand Ophelia's motivations, since the queen, earlier in the scene, had given her blessing to the relationship. Perhaps Ophelia is hoping that Hamlet will respond to her action by protesting his love; but, whatever her motives, from Hamlet's point of view, she is going beyond what is required by obedience to her father, and he is deeply upset.

Hamlet's immediate reaction is to feel that her fair appearance, too, hides a reality of evil. All of his negative attitudes toward women, to which she has been the sole antidote, are now projected onto Ophelia. His sense of his own goodness is profoundly threatened by his loss of faith in her. As long as he idealized her and their relationship, he maintained his belief in the possibility of a pure and noble love. Now that he sees her as a bawd, he becomes bawdy-minded himself and loses faith in his own purity. She should not have believed him when he told her that he loved her; "for virtue cannot so inoculate our old stock but we shall relish of it: I loved you not" (III, i). What he is saying is that being depraved, like all men, he did not love, but lusted after her. With the undermining of his idealized image, his despised self emerges, and he turns upon himself savagely:

> Get thee to a nunnery: why wouldst thou be a breeder of sinners? I am myself indifferent honest; but yet I could accuse me of such things that it were better my mother had not borne me: I am very proud, revengeful, ambitious, with more offenses at my beck than I have thoughts to put them in, imagination to give them shape, or time to act them in. What should such fellows as I do crawling between earth and heaven? We are arrant knaves all; believe none of us. Go thy ways to a nunnery. Where's your father? (III, i)

This attack is not simply upon himself, of course, but upon human nature in general. Hamlet feels that even its best specimens, such as Ophelia and himself, are irremediably depraved. Men are all arrant knaves, and the only way women can remain virtuous is to go to a nunnery.

It is a traditional piece of staging that after Hamlet says "Go thy ways to a nunnery," he catches a glimpse of the eavesdropping Polonius, which leads him to ask, "Where's your father?" My reading of the play supports this bit of business, which seems essential if we are to understand what follows. Ophelia replies with a lie—"At home, my lord"—and

Hamlet's next remark is clearly intended for Polonius: "Let the doors be shut upon him, that he may play the fool no where but in 's own house."
   Hamlet now feels that Ophelia is totally false, and he is so enraged that for the first time in the play he makes a direct assault upon the object of his wrath: "If thou dost marry, I'll give thee this plague for thy dowry: be thou as chaste as ice, as pure as snow, thou shalt not escape calumny. Get thee to a nunnery, go: farewell. Or, if thou wilt needs marry, marry a fool; for wise men know what monsters you make of them. To a nunnery, go, and quickly too. Farewell" (III, i). This is not an act put on for the benefit of the eavesdroppers; Hamlet is not feigning madness here. He is expressing at last grievances that have been rankling in his bosom for months. He has been chaste as ice, but he has not escaped calumny. Women are light, deceptive, wanton creatures who make fools of the men who love them. In the self-effacing person, observes Horney, there is a "pervasive suppression of resentment . . . . Only when he feels driven to despair will the locked gates break open and a flood of accusations rush out" (1950, 232). This is what is happening to Hamlet here. In his belief in Ophelia, in her purity and love, lay his last hope that he could maintain his own nobility and escape the fate of his father. When Hamlet says that "We will have no more marriages," he means that he will never marry. He will not let any woman do to him what Gertrude has done to his father. His tirade ends with a threat against the life of Claudius so alarming to the king that he determines immediately to send Hamlet to England.

"YET HAVE I IN ME SOMETHING DANGEROUS"

This explosion of hostility seems to relieve Hamlet's oppression, to lift his spirits, and to fill him with energy. He is no longer brooding, indecisive, or sullen; and, for a while at least, his death wishes disappear. In his dealings with others he becomes vigorous, articulate, and combative. His speech to the players is brisk and authoritative, he declares his admiration for Horatio in a very forthright manner, and he seems eager for the play. When the court enters, he puts on his antic disposition and takes great pleasure in jabbing at everyone. He does not obey his mother when she bids him sit by her, and he is very bawdy with Ophelia. Hamlet is tormenting everyone with great success; his jibes are brilliant. *He* has been suffering; now it is time for *them* to squirm. The play is another expression of his accusations, and he drives its points home with his sarcastic and bellicose remarks. It is this needling, as much as the play itself, that forces

Claudius to lose his composure. When the king rises, distraught, and flees the scene, Hamlet is gay. He has had a great vindictive triumph. He has been oppressed with impotent rage, but now he has broken through the defenses of this "smiling, damned villain," and it is Claudius who is stricken. The tables are turned. He disposes of the inquiries of Rosencrantz and Guildenstern with great wit and energy ("though you can fret me, yet you cannot play upon me"—III, ii); and he makes a fool of Polonius when the latter comes to summon him to the queen.

What we see here is the energy of liberated aggression. With the final collapse of his hopes of love and innocence, Hamlet's angry self has risen to the fore and has swept away the constraints that have been paralyzing him. His initial plan has worked: his doubts about the ghost have been resolved and he has discomfited his enemies. He is no longer helplessly trapped by fears and conflicts. He is no longer tortured by self-hate. He feels powerful, on top of things, capable of violence. He has no developed plan, but he longs to strike another blow: "now could I drink hot blood,/ And do such bitter business as the day/ Would quake to look on" (III, ii). It is in this frame of mind that he encounters Claudius praying.

I believe that Hamlet is now capable of killing Claudius and that he does not do so in the prayer scene for precisely the reasons he gives. He is in the grip of his vindictive shoulds which demand not only Claudius's death, but a revenge in keeping with the nature of the offense. He is being governed by the talion principle: an eye for an eye, a tooth for a tooth. Claudius took his father "grossly, full of bread," and now "Tis heavy with him" (III, ii). According to his present logic, it would hardly be revenge to take Claudius "in the purging of his soul,/ When he is fit and season'd for his passage." He wants to kill him, rather, when he is "about some act/ That has no relish of salvation in't" so that "his soul may be as damn'd and black/ As hell whereto it goes."

"These diabolical sentiments are not Hamlet's," Kittredge hastens to assure us; "the speech is merely a pretext for delay" (Kittredge and Ribner 1967, xviii).[3] The sentiments are diabolical and they are Hamlet's. This speech is not an isolated event. Hamlet was proclaiming his readiness moments before "to drink hot blood"; and when he speaks of his schoolfellows at the end of act 3, he sounds very much like Iago:

> they must sweep my way,
> And marshal me to knavery. Let it work;
> For 'tis sport to have the enginer
> Hoist with his own petar: and 't shall go hard
> But I will delve one yard below their mines;

> And blow them at the moon: O, 'tis most sweet,
> When in one line two crafts directly meet. (III, iv)

Hamlet sends them to their deaths, no "shriving-time allow'd," and then assures Horatio that they "are not near [his] conscience" (V, ii). He concludes his last soliloquy by exclaiming, "My thoughts be bloody, or be nothing worth!" (IV, iv).

It is difficult to integrate all this with the picture of Hamlet built up in the first half of the play, to believe that the tender-minded prince has turned into a fiendish avenger. His task no longer seems a heavy burden but a source of malicious delight. We must remember that Hamlet has been feeling an enormous sense of injury and a rage so intense that its repression has been severely disturbing. The Machiavellian monster that he has fought so hard to contain is now free. Hamlet still has inner conflicts, as we shall see; but the aggressive side of him now seems to operate independently at times, as though it were a separate personality. He warns Laertes as they are grappling in Ophelia's grave:

> I prithee, take thy fingers from my throat;
> For, though I am not splenitive and rash,
> Yet have I in me something dangerous,
> Which let thy wiseness fear. (V, i)

Under the stress of his situation, the pressure of his inner conflicts, and the collapse of his dominant solution, Hamlet has become schizoid. Different parts of his personality now dominate him by turns, the conflict between them having been reduced by a process of compartmentalization.

What we see in act 3 is Hamlet becoming aware of the dangerous part of himself. For the most part he exults in it, but he is afraid of it in relation to his mother. Before he goes to her closet, he struggles to bring his matricidal impulses under control: "O heart, lose not thy nature; let not ever/ The soul of Nero enter this firm bosom" (III, iii). When he enters his mother's chamber, he is so aggressive that the queen cries out for help, and Hamlet strikes at the hidden Polonius in a discharge of the murderous impulses that have been thwarted by Claudius's praying and his taboos against harming his mother. Whether it could have been the king or not (there is internal evidence to support both contentions), Hamlet clearly wishes that it had been.[4] He is in too fierce a state to feel concern at this time for what he has done. He must pour out all the bitterness that has been festering within him before he can register the implications of his rash and bloody deed.

THE CLOSET SCENE

The closet scene is a cathartic experience for Hamlet. He unleashes at last, in a torrent of words, the accusations upon which he has been brooding. Gertrude has much offended his father; he wishes that she were not his mother. Her act has destroyed his belief in virtue, in marriage, in human constancy. Neither love, nor judgment, nor even madness can account for her choice of Claudius. Rather, it must reflect some bestial lust, some hellish perversion. It symbolizes for Hamlet the depravity of all women and the fate of all good men, which is to be deserted in favor of sleazy seducers. His loathing for Claudius is such that his mother's relations with him seem like copulation with a beast. He hammers at Gertrude to give up her lasciviousness, to resist the advances of "the bloat king," and to stay out of Claudius's bed. In doing so he is carrying out the ghost's commands to stop the incest.

But this does not account for the intensity of his disgust. He is revolted by the sexual successes of Claudius and jealous at the same time. Where do they leave goodness and romance? He is horrified at the animality of the woman who had always represented purity and restraint. His disgust is also a defense against the forbidden feelings that his mother's behavior arouses in him. These may well be incestuous, but they are also more generally sexual. The sexuality of supposedly good women is both demoralizing and threatening to Hamlet. If they are bawds, what is the value of his own chastity? If they cannot curb the devil, then surely he cannot either. His disenchantment with Ophelia released, we remember, a good deal of sexual aggression. In the closet scene he is so much the spokesman for virtue because he is afraid of becoming a sexual monster, like Claudius or Gertrude. He must dwell upon the utter repulsiveness of their behavior to reinforce his own repressions; and he needs to win Gertrude over to sexual abstinence so as to reaffirm his own values.

Except for the murder of Polonius, the closet scene goes well for Hamlet. He not only releases his pent-up feelings, but his words achieve their desired effects. He wants to "be cruel," to "speak daggers to her" (III, ii), and he is successful: "O, speak to me no more;/ These words, like daggers, enter in mine ears;/ No more, sweet Hamlet!" (III, iv). He catches the conscience of the Queen and makes her share his revulsion at what she has done. After the ghost appears, he overcomes her scepticism about his sanity and delivers a lecture in which he exhorts her to stay out of Claudius's bed:

> Refrain to-night,
> And that shall lend a kind of easiness
> To the next abstinence: the next more easy;
> For use can almost change the stamp of nature,
> And either curb the devil, or throw him out
> With wondrous potency. (III, iv)

This speech suggests some of Hamlet's own struggles to curb the devil. What is remarkable about it is its tone, which is that of a priest exhorting a sinner or of a parent urging a child to give up masturbation. Sex is a bad habit that can be broken.

The closet scene releases Hamlet from his obsession with Gertrude; we do not see him brooding about her hereafter. He has asserted his moral superiority, and she has accepted his rebuke. This assuages his anger, feeds his pride in both his potency and his virtue, and gives him a sense of having completed an important part of his mission. Henceforth his rage is directed exclusively against Claudius. The greatest part of his triumph is winning Gertrude's loyalty to his cause: "Be thou assured, if words be made of breath,/ And breath of life, I have no life to breathe/ What thou hast said to me" (III, iv). His deepest grievance against her has been her abandonment of the good Hamlets for the bad Claudius, but now this has been reversed.

MORE OSCILLATIONS

From the end of act 3 to the conclusion of the play, the different sides of Hamlet's personality assert themselves by turns, as well as, at times, simultaneously. He still has inner conflicts and a need to reconcile his various shoulds, but his compliant, aggressive, and resigned trends seem at times to separate out and to manifest themselves in relatively pure forms.

Having settled his account with the Queen, Hamlet is able to react to his killing of Polonius. He repents and promises to "answer well the death I gave him" (III, iv). A few moments later, however, he is relishing the thought of hoisting his enemies with their "own petar," and he treats Polonius's corpse most unceremoniously: "I'll lug the guts into the neighbor room." In act 4 we hear that "he weeps for what is done" (IV, i), but he is fiercely aggressive in his few appearances on stage. He calls Rosencrantz a "sponge" (IV, ii), tells Claudius that if his messenger does not find Polonius in heaven, he should "seek him i' the other place" himself (IV, iii), and accuses himself, in his final soliloquy, of not having been bloody minded enough (IV, iv).

In this soliloquy Hamlet's aggressive side is dominant. He attacks his compliant tendencies and accuses himself, once more, of delay:

> Now, whether it be
> Bestial oblivion, or some craven scruple
> Of thinking too precisely on the event,
> A thought which, quartr'd, hath but one part wisdom
> And ever three parts coward, I do not know
> Why yet I live to say "This thing's to do;"
> Sith I have cause and will and strength and means
> To do 't. (IV, iv)

His self-accusations are, in part, irrational. His revenge is not dull, and it needs no spurring. Hamlet has delayed, it is true, and for very much the reasons he gives; but he is not delaying now, though, knowing his past record, he may be fearful of lapsing once more into paralysis. No longer has he the "means/ To do 't," at least not immediately. The Mousetrap has set in motion a plot against him, and the murder of Polonius has put him on the defensive. The king is on guard, and Hamlet's energies are taken up by his efforts to parry the moves against him.

Hamlet is a revenge play in which the obstacles are at first within the hero and then outside of him. Once Hamlet becomes capable of action, no suitable occasion arises, until the end. After the play and the murder of Polonius, Hamlet is swept along by events he has little power to control. What we see in his self-accusations is a new set of unrealistic shoulds. It is no longer perfect innocence, but aggressive potency that Hamlet demands of himself, whatever the obstacles.

Hamlet is not only attacking himself for his inaction, he is also justifying his intended violence by making it seem a matter of reason and honor. The celebration of man's "large discourse,/ Looking before and after" is both an assault upon his own mental paralysis (it "fusts" in him unused) and an elevation of his bloody thoughts into a manifestation of "god-like reason." It is not rationality that Hamlet is displaying here, of course, but his capacity for rationalization. The example before him is hardly one that Hamlet would find admirable in his Christian frame of mind. Twenty thousand men are prepared "to fight for a plot/ . . . Which is not tomb enough and continent/ To hide the slain" (IV, iv). In his present mood Hamlet sees this as glorious and Fortinbras as a great man. His "spirit with divine ambition puff'd," Fortinbras is ready "To find quarrel in a straw/ When honour's at the stake." This glorification of bellicosity and ambition and of a readiness to die is the expression of Hamlet's aggressive shoulds that are punishing him for his own lack of a fiery spirit. His dominant emotion is shame, which is what we feel when we have injured our pride. These people are ready to fight and die for "a straw," "an eggshell," whereas he, whose honor is so much more at stake, has "let all sleep." To restore his pride, he must think nothing but bloody thoughts from now on. His situation is not really comparable to that of Fortinbras, of course, since it requires a form of aggression that is much more spiritually risky and morally complex than the pursuit of martial glory. If all Hamlet had to do was to fight a battle, he would have acted long before this.

In act 5, Hamlet returns from England, after a considerable absence from the stage. In the first scene, he proclaims his love for Ophelia, which he can afford to feel now that she is dead, and in scene 2 he describes how he has sent Rosencrantz and Guildenstern to their deaths, "Not shrivingtime allow'd." He assures Horatio that they are not near his conscience, but his next speech suggests that he may be protesting too much:

> Does it not, thinks't thee, stand me now upon—
> He that hath kill'd my king and whored my mother,
> Popp'd in between the election and my hopes,
> Thrown out his angle for my proper life,
> And with such cozenage—is 't not perfect conscience,
> To quit him with this arm? and is 't not to be damn'd,
> To let this canker of our nature come
> In further evil? (V, ii)

It is evident that Hamlet still has a strong need to justify his behavior and to assure himself that he will not incur damnation by carrying out his revenge. He defends his past and intended violence by citing all the wrongs that have been done to him. The plot against him, which he has done so much to bring about, justifies his own plotting and assuages his guilt. He may have needed to create a situation in which he is forced to act in self-defense in order to feel that it is "perfect conscience" to kill the king. He is still worried about damnation, but now that Claudius is an active antagonist, he can assure himself that he will be damned if he does *not* act to stop the spread of evil. His inner conflicts are still operative, but he has found a way to reconcile his aggressive and his self-effacing values. The only way to be good is to be aggressive.

IN THE HANDS OF PROVIDENCE

What is most striking about Hamlet in act 5 is his sense of himself as being in the hands of Providence. The success of his rash invasion of Rosencrantz and Guildenstern's cabin shows that "There's a divinity that shapes our ends,/ Rough hew them how we will" (V, ii). The fact that he had his father's signet in his purse shows once again that heaven is "ordinant." He has profound misgivings about the fencing match with Laertes, but he ignores his premonitions and resigns himself to what will be: "We defy augury: there's a special providence in the fall of a sparrow. If it be now, 'tis not to come; if it be not to come, it will be now; if it be not now, yet it will come: the readiness is all: since no man has aught of what he leaves, what is 't to leave betimes? Let be" (V, ii). This speech also shows Hamlet's readiness to die. He expects heaven to direct him to his revenge (he still has no plan), but he also expects to die himself and does not wish it otherwise.

These attitudes are the expression of a defensive posture that begins to develop at the end of act 3, when Hamlet reacts to the death of Polonius:

> For this same lord,
> I do repent: but heaven hath pleased it so,
> To punish me with this and this with me,
> That I must be their scourge and minister.
> I will bestow him, and will answer well
> The death I gave him. So, again, good night.
> I must be cruel, only to be kind:
> Thus bad begins and worse remains behind. (III, iv)

By killing Polonius, Hamlet has irrevocably destroyed his claim to innocence. This liberates his aggressive impulses, which manifest themselves powerfully, as we have seen. But Hamlet also has a need to assuage his guilt and to reconcile the new state of affairs with his self-effacing side.

According to the logic of the self-effacing solution, worldly misfortune is a sign of guilt, a penalty of sin. Hamlet sees his killing of Polonius not only as a sin in itself, but also as a punishment for his basic guilt, a sense of which emerges whenever his pride in his goodness is undermined. It is an act by which he pays for past transgressions and for which he must be punished if divine justice is to be affirmed. Hamlet has a need to die in payment for the death he has given. He is self-protective in the interests of his mission, but he is content to die in the enactment of it, and he behaves in ways that court his own destruction.

With the collapse of his idealized image, Hamlet defends himself against self-hate and despair partly by switching to an aggressive value system that glorifies toughness and violence, and partly by seeing himself as an agent of the divine plan. These two defenses cannot be integrated philosophically or thematically, but they can coexist quite readily in a system of psychological conflicts. The question of whether it is nobler to suffer life's evils or to take arms against them is no longer an issue. Hamlet is eager now to feel himself in the hands of Providence and to interpret events as divinely ordained. This helps him at once to disown his actions and to assure himself of their righteousness; he must be cruel only to be kind. His pride in his goodness having been crushed, Hamlet clings to a posture of humble submission, of acquiescence to the demands of a higher justice. He no longer tries to control his fate or to transcend the limitations of human nature: he acknowledges his sinfulness, accepts the fact that he must dirty his hands, and trusts God to bring about a just resolution.

From the closet scene onward there is a strong element of resignation in Hamlet. He has reacted to the shattering of his dreams with terrible cries of pain, but after he assimilates the meaning of his rash and bloody deed, there is nothing left to hope for but the completion of his mission. His fate is settled; he must purge the world of evil and be punished himself for the crimes he commits in so doing. Bad has begun "and worse remains behind." Hamlet accepts the will of heaven and readies himself to die. The death of Ophelia produces a momentary outburst of passion, but it does not really seem to give him much pain. He has become immune to the slings and arrows of outrageous fortune by developing not only a wish for death, but an indifference to life— "what is't to leave betimes?"

A WISH-FULFILLMENT ENDING

Once Hamlet adopts an attitude of submission, his solution does work, for the ending is like a wish-fulfillment dream conceived from Hamlet's point of view. It satisfies his needs for punishment, revenge, vindication, and escape. The plotters against him are hoist with their own petard. Claudius inadvertently kills the queen and then is dispatched himself with the instruments he has aimed at Hamlet. Evil does not triumph after all. Laertes is "justly killed with [his] own treachery" (V, ii). The

Queen and Hamlet are also punished. Hamlet gets his wish for his own death and for that of his mother, but he is guilty neither of matricide nor of suicide. Providence has arranged all. Hamlet is forgiven by Laertes for causing his death and that of Polonius, and his own death at once justifies and pays for the murder of Claudius. He is still concerned with his nobility, his reputation, and his friend Horatio is there to save his "wounded name." He chooses the next king with his dying breath and then goes to "felicity," while Horatio lives on "in this harsh world . . ./ To tell [Hamlet's] story." He receives tributes from Horatio and from Fortinbras that testify to his spirituality and to his manliness:

> *Hor.* Now cracks a noble heart. Good night, sweet prince;
> And flights of angels sing thee to thy rest!
>
> . . . .
>
> *Fort.*   Let four captains
> Bear Hamlet, like a soldier, to the stage;
> For he was likely, had he been put on,
> To have proved most royal. (V, ii)

Although at the cost of his life, Hamlet's conflicts are almost miraculously resolved at the end. We mourn his death but rejoice in his triumph. We have been struggling with his conflicts through our identification with him, and when he gets what he wants, our needs are also satisfied.

Hamlet is the tragedy of a man who needs to be innocent but who is thrust into a situation in which both action and inaction lead to guilt. His existential problem is the necessity for taking harsh measures to deal with a harsh world; his personal problem is his inability to take those measures decisively enough because of his inner conflicts. Shakespeare wants to show us what happens to a man who, out of his desire to maintain his nobility, cannot cope with the evils of life, and he also wants to celebrate that nobility. The ending does both: it shows Hamlet being destroyed by the fruits of his inaction (along with others, in a seemingly casual slaughter), and it grants his wishes, leaving a final impression of him in the words of Horatio and Fortinbras.

CHAPTER 3

Othello

Othello is, like *Hamlet,* a story of revenge. There are two revenge plots in this play. Iago revenges himself upon Othello by inducing him to believe that his wife is unfaithful, and Othello revenges himself upon Desdemona by murdering her in their marriage bed. Instead of having a protagonist whose self-effacing tendencies paralyze him in a situation that calls for aggressive action, we have in this play two characters who behave more aggressively than is warranted by the offenses to which they are reacting. Here the tragedy arises from the hero's taking his revenge not too slowly, but too fast.

As in the case of *Hamlet,* much critical discussion has focused on the motivations of the characters, with some critics doubting that they are intelligible as human beings at all. The most difficult things to explain have been Iago's motives for initiating his diabolical plot, Othello's vulnerability to Iago's deception and the ferocity of his rage at Desdemona, and Desdemona's passivity under Othello's abuse after her boldness earlier in the play. Each of these characters has a bargain with fate that is threatened in the course of the play, and each responds with defensive behavior that precipitates his or her own destruction and the destruction of others. Bradley sees the tragedy as Iago's, and Leavis as Othello's character in action. Desdemona's character, too, contributes to her fate. The tragedy is the outcome of the psychological flaws of each of the characters *and* of their interaction. I shall consider the major characters in the order in which their bargains are threatened. The play opens with Iago's worldview breaking down, and part of his response is to undermine the solutions of Othello and Desdemona. As his poison works on Othello, Desdemona is driven to sacrifice her life in order to preserve her love.

IAGO'S CHARACTER

The precipitating events of the play are Othello's promotion of Cassio to the lieutenancy and his marriage to Desdemona. Iago is deeply disturbed by both of these events, and he reacts by plotting to displace Cassio and to destroy Othello's marriage. The questions we must answer if we are to understand Iago's behavior are: Why do these events affect him as profoundly as they do? Why does his revenge take the particular form that it does? Before I try to answer these questions, I shall attempt to describe Iago's character as it was before his crisis began; for it is only by understanding his anxieties, his defenses, and his objectives in life that we can appreciate the impact upon him of the precipitating events and the functions of his diabolical plot.

There are two scenes with Roderigo in act 1 that give us a great deal of insight into Iago's character. Near the beginning of scene 1, in the course of preparing Roderigo to understand his show of loyalty to Othello, Iago explains his philosophy of egoism:

> O sir, content you.
> I follow him to serve my turn upon him.
> We cannot all be masters, nor all masters
> Cannot be truly follow'd. You shall mark
> Many a duteous and knee-crooking knave
> That, doting on his own obsequious bondage,
> Wears out his time, much like his master's ass,
> For naught but provender, and when he's old, cashier'd:
> Whip me such honest knaves. Others there are
> Who, trimm'd in forms and visages of duty,
> Keep yet their heart attending on themselves,
> And, throwing but shows of service on their lords,
> Do well thrive by them, and when they have lin'd their coats,
> Do themselves homage: These fellows have some soul;
> And such a one do I profess myself. (I, i)

Iago has adopted an extreme form of the arrogant-vindictive solution; and this speech expresses the views of human nature, human values, and the human order that accompany that solution.[1] He sees the world as a jungle in which the strong exploit the weak and in which goodness does not pay.

There are two kinds of people in the world: the realists, who exploit others lest they be exploited themselves; and the fools, who trust other people's professions of loyalty and love and are abused as a result. Iago does not believe that everyone is like himself. He knows that there are "honest" folk about, but he scorns them as gulls and is convinced that they are destined to be victims. Indeed, he must victimize them himself in order to confirm his vision of the world.

Iago feels that there is a deception at the heart of master–servant relationships that are based on traditional notions of loyalty. The masters promise to look after their servants in return for faithful service, but in reality, they give them as little as possible and callously abandon them when they are no longer useful. For a man who understands this there is only one reasonable course of action: that is, to throw "shows of service" on his lord so that he may line his own coat and do "homage" to himself. Those who do this have "some soul," as opposed to the "knee-crooking knave[s]" who dote on their "own obsequious bondage." The deception involved here is perfectly justified as a response to the masters' deception of their servants.

Behind Iago's animus against masters lies, of course, an intense desire for power. His real grievance is not that masters do not reward their servants properly, but that he is not a master. An arrogant-vindictive person like Iago "cannot tolerate anybody who . . . achieves more than he does, wields more power, or in any way questions his superiority. Compulsively he has to drag his rival down or defeat him. Even if he subordinates himself for the sake of his career, he is scheming for ultimate triumph" (Horney 1950, 198). In such a person, aggressive attitudes are often "covered over with a veneer of suave politeness, fair-mindedness, and good fellowship" (Horney 1945, 63). This "front" represents "a Machiavellian concession to expediency" (Horney 1945, 63), and he is "extremely proud . . . of his faculty of fooling everybody" (Horney 1950, 193): "Heaven is my judge, not I for love and duty,/ But seeming so, for my peculiar end" (I, i). Iago feels a deep resentment of a system in which he has inherited a subordinate position, and he revenges himself upon it by subverting the values on which it is based. Through his deceit he controls his relationships with his superiors and overcomes his feelings of weakness and insignificance. By his reputation for honesty, we can see how successful he has been in duping his betters. They may order him about, but he consoles himself with the knowledge that, in a very real sense, he has them in his power.

A surprising number of critics have, like Bradley, seen Iago as a

"blunt, bluff soldier, who spoke his mind freely and plainly . . . and
. . . was given to making remarks somewhat disparaging to human nature"
(Bradley 1964, 214). The reason for this mistake is the assumption that Iago
speaks to everyone as he does to Roderigo, whom he treats as a fellow
conspirator and whom he despises for his stupidity. His reputation for
honesty has been gained not by bluntness, but by a strict course of hypocrisy
in which he has played the role of the absolutely devoted servant who can be
counted on for loyalty and integrity. He projects an image of himself not as a
cynic, but as an idealist.

The bargain of the compliant types whom Iago scorns is with their
masters. Iago's bargain is with himself. He trusts no one and has no belief
in a moral order either in human affairs or in the universe. Just as he is
concerned only for himself, so he assumes that those above him are
equally selfish and that no one will be looking out for him: "Were I the
Moor, I would not be Iago" (I, i). The speech to Roderigo makes very
clear the nature of Iago's pact with himself. If he is to succeed in this
crooked world, he must not be taken in by the traditional code of values,
which is simply an instrument by which the strong exploit the weak. He
must never be guilty of loyalty or of unselfish behavior; he must attend
constantly to his own interests; and, above all, he must always conceal his
true purposes and feelings:

> Heaven is my judge, not I for love and duty,
> But seeming so, for my peculiar end;
> For when my outward action doth demonstrate
> The native act and figure of my heart
> In compliment extern, 'tis not long after
> But I will wear my heart upon my sleeve
> For daws to peck at. I am not what I am. (I, i)

Iago's scorn of compliant types is, like his justification of duplicity, a
constant preoccupation. He is as obsessed with his loathing for honest
people as Hamlet is with his repugnance toward aggressive types. The
intensity of his contempt indicates that he feels threatened by virtuous
people and that he has inner conflicts. In his value system they are fools,
but in theirs he is a rogue. He feels vastly superior to them, but he is also
vaguely uncomfortable about violating traditional values, and his scorn of
those who adhere to them is part of his defense against self-hate. He is
genuinely proud of his devilishness, but he also protests too much.

In his first scene with Roderigo, Iago demythifies and inverts the
traditional code of loyalty. In his second scene, which occurs after Othello

and Desdemona justify their marriage to the Venetian senate, Iago mocks traditional notions of love and proclaims his belief in the supremacy of the will. Roderigo feels hopeless about ever possessing Desdemona and says that he will "incontinently drown" himself:

> *Iago.* O villainous! I have look'd upon the world for four times seven years; and since I could distinguish betwixt a benefit and an injury, I never found man that knew how to love himself. Ere I would say I would drown myself for the love of a guinea-hen, I would change my humanity with a baboon.
>
> *Rod.* What should I do? I confess it is my shame to be so fond; but it is not in my virtue to amend it.
>
> *Iago.* Virtue? a fig! 'tis in ourselves that we are thus or thus. Our bodies are our gardens, to the which our wills are gardeners; so that if we will plant nettles or sow lettuce, set hyssop and weed up thyme, supply it with one gender of herbs, or distract it with many, either to have it sterile with idleness or manured with industry—why, the power and corrigible authority of this lies in our wills. If the balance of our lives had not one scale of reason to poise another of sensuality, the blood and baseness of our natures would conduct us to most preposterous conclusions. But we have reason to cool our raging motions, our carnal stings, our unbitted lusts, whereof I take this that you call love to be sect or scion.
>
> *Rod.* It cannot be.
>
> *Iago.* It is merely a lust of the blood and a permission of the will. Come, be a man! (I, iii)

Iago's speech has a manipulative function in his relationship with Roderigo; but it also expresses his long-harbored and deeply felt sentiments on the subjects of love and will.

What men call "love" Iago sees as merely "a lust of the blood" (I, iii). Lacking the capacity to care for anyone but himself, he believes that the relations between men and women can only be based upon physical appetite. This is why he can convince himself, at times at least, as well as Roderigo, that Othello and Desdemona will soon tire of each other and that Desdemona is attracted to Cassio: "The food that to him now is as luscious as locusts, shall be to him shortly as bitter as coloquintida. She must change for youth; when she is sated with his body, she will find the error of her choice" (I, iii). Iago is right, of course, as far as his understanding goes. Sex without love becomes a burden, and variety is required in order to maintain the appetite. This has apparently been his experience with Emilia, who speaks bitterly of his loss of interest:

> 'Tis not a year or two shows us a man.
> They are all but stomachs and we all but food;
> They eat us hungerly, and when they are full,
> They belch us. (III, iv)

According to Iago, the only true and constant love a man has is for himself. To destroy himself because he longs for another, as Roderigo proposes to do, is "villainous!"

Roderigo says that it is his "shame to be so fond," and Iago agrees completely. He urges Roderigo to "be a man," that is, not to be a victim of his feelings. Iago scorns not only those who are loyal to their masters, but also those who are not masters of themselves. The arrogant-vindictive person despises in others "their compliance, their self-degrading, their helpless hankering for love. In short, he despises in them the very self-effacing trends he hates and despises in himself" (Horney 1950, 207). Iago is afraid of any emotion that would undermine his self-sufficiency, expose him to inner conflicts, or interfere with his calculated pursuit of his own interests. Love for him means weakness and vulnerability. He dreads the idea of being reduced to the pathetic state of a Roderigo, though he enjoys inducing such states in others, since this feeds his sense of superiority.

An essential feature of Iago's defense system is his belief in the supremacy of the mind: " 'Tis in ourselves that we are thus or thus." He relies upon his intellectual powers for the mastery of life, and he dreads anything that will disturb their functioning. When we are in the grip of passion, we are led "to most preposterous conclusions"—as he will later demonstrate in the case of Othello. "The mind," for a person of his type, "is the magic *ruler* for which, as for God, everything is possible" (Horney 1950, 183). Thus "another dualism is created. It is no longer mind *and* feelings but mind *versus* feelings; no longer mind *and* body but mind *versus* body" (Horney 1950, 183): "Our bodies are our gardens, to the which our wills are gardeners." The belief in the supremacy of the mind is, of course, unrealistic. It is part of Iago's idealized image, one of the tyrannical shoulds that keeps him in a state of anxiety. His hostility toward women may be the result, in part at least, of fear, since they pose a threat to his self-control.

Iago has not only a fear of loving, but also a hopelessness of being loved. He has abandoned love as a value, defended himself against his frustration by scorning what he cannot have, and tried to overcome his sense of worthlessness through the pursuit of mastery and triumph. His love need has persisted, however, and has given rise to feelings of loneliness, exclusion, and envy. Iago's need for love is difficult to see in the text because it has been turned by his defenses into a variety of aggressive behaviors. It is detectable, I think, in his role-playing, in his relationship with Emilia, and in his reaction to the marriage of Othello and Desdemona. Horney observed that the friendly "front" of an arrogant-vindictive person is frequently "a composite of pretence, genuine feelings, and neurotic needs . . . for affection and approval, put to the service of aggressive goals" (1945, 63). Iago needs to be liked, trusted, and approved; but he cannot admit these desires to himself because they conflict with his idealized image and would expose him to rejection. By playing the role of "honest Iago," he gains the confidence of Othello, Cassio, and Desdemona, which gratifies his need for intimacy and approval; but he defends himself against self-contempt and frustration by assuring himself that he is only fooling them to further his ambitions.

Iago treats Emilia harshly but he wants her to be devoted to him, and he is afraid of her infidelity. His scorn and abuse are partly a defense against the hurt that he fears she will inflict upon him. If he rejects her first, he will be less vulnerable to her expected rejection of him. In effect, his callous behavior and his philandering provide an excuse, as well as a retaliation in advance, for her betrayal of him. They are a protection against the self-hate that is aroused in him by every slight.

This defense does not work, however, for Iago is consumed by sexual jealousy. He suspects that Othello and Cassio have "leaped into [his] seat," the "thought whereof/ Doth like a poisonous mineral gnaw [his] inwards" (II, iii). Both Iago and Emilia are experts on jealousy. Emilia's description of husbands who "break out in peevish jealousies" (IV, iii) gives us a good insight into her life with Iago. She speaks with authority when she explains to Desdemona that "jealous souls . . . are not ever jealous for the cause,/ But jealous for they are jealous. 'Tis a monster/ Begot upon itself, born on itself" (III, iv). This passage leads me to believe that Iago is not simply manipulating Othello when he confesses that "it is my nature's plague/ To spy into abuses, and oft my jealousy/ Shapes faults that are not" (III, iii). It is to himself that Iago observes that "Trifles light as air/ Are to the jealous confirmations strong/ As proofs of holy writ"; and that "Dangerous conceits are in their natures poisons" which, when they "act upon the blood/ Burn like the mines of sulfur" (III, iii).

Iago's jealousy has, of course, many sources. It is based partly upon the feeling that no one can love him and partly upon a reasonable fear of Emilia's retaliation. It is very important for Iago to possess his wife completely, to feel that she is his chattel. The thought that she might escape his control or that others might triumph over him through her is tormenting. In addition, he needs her to be faithful as an indication that he is worthy of love. He cannot try to win love by being lovable—that is much too risky. He wants to be abusive and unfaithful to Emilia, but he wants her to be faithful to him, and part of this anguish at the thought of her infidelity comes from a feeling of personal rejection. Iago's jealousy is quite out of keeping with his idealized image of himself as a man of will and reason. It conducts him "to most preposterous conclusions" and fills him with shame and self-contempt.

IAGO'S CRISIS

It is not too difficult to understand, at this point, why the precipitating events in the play affect Iago as profoundly as they do. The lieutenancy was the immediate prize for which he had been scheming. Gaining it would have verified his estimate of his own abilities, assured him of Othello's love and admiration, and validated his bargain by proving that selfishness and deceit are the proper paths to success in this crooked world. It would have been a triumph not only over Othello, who would have been duped, but over the entire system by which Iago has felt himself to be unfairly treated. The promotion of Cassio denies Iago all of these satisfactions and deals him a staggering blow.

The play opens with Iago explaining to Roderigo why he hates Othello. He is outraged because Othello has failed to give him the recognition he deserves: "I know my price, I am worth no worse a place." His indignation is increased by the fact that the man who has been promoted to lieutenant over him is Michael Cassio, a "bookish" theorist who lacks Iago's experience in the field. He feels that Othello's choice is profoundly unfair, that "Preferment goes by letter and affection,/ And not by old gradation, where each second/ Stood heir to th' first" (I, i). Cassio has been promoted because he had greater influence and because Othello loves him more than Iago. Iago's feelings of being unloved and abused are profoundly stirred by this event; and his rage, which is always simmering below the surface, begins to boil. The fact that there is "no remedy" within the system gives him an intolerable feeling of helplessness.

The promotion of Cassio is a bitter defeat that threatens Iago's self-esteem, his value system, and, indeed, his whole strategy for dealing with life. He has played the role of faithful servant to advance his own interests and has had an immense pride in the success of his duplicity. But his scheming has, in fact, failed. Othello has benefitted from his service but has given the reward that he was expecting to someone else. Iago, the exploiter, has been exploited. The blow to his pride is all the worse because Cassio is precisely the kind of person Iago scorns. He really is loyal, he really is dutiful, and he really does love his master. In Iago's version of reality, Cassio is the kind of person who is exploited, whereas tough-minded fellows like himself beat the system. Iago's reaction to Cassio's success is similar in a way to Hamlet's response to the triumph of Claudius. If those kinds of people succeed, then the world is out of joint.

Anything that threatens Iago's version of the world also threatens his sense of righteousness. Iago's self-effacing trends are deeply repressed; but, as his obsession with compliant types indicates, they are there; and he is not without conscientious qualms. He justifies his behavior by seeing it as the only course of action that is adapted to a clear-sighted perception of reality. It is essential for him to feel that his mode of operating is the only way not simply to succeed, but even to survive. If honesty pays, as it does for Cassio, then his rationalization is seriously jeopardized, and he is in danger of having to confront his own villainy.

Iago hates Othello not only because he has promoted Cassio, but also because he is bitterly envious of the success the Moor has achieved through his marriage to Desdemona. Iago suffers from a pervasive envy of everyone who seems to possess something that he lacks, whether it be wealth and prestige, physical attractiveness, or the love of a devoted woman. This aspect of Iago's character is described in Horney's analysis of the sadistic person. Because of his intense, though unadmitted, frustrations, the sadistic person "hate[s] life and all that is positive in it":

> But he hates it with the burning envy of one who is withheld from something he ardently desires. It is the bitter, begrudging envy of a person who feels that life is passing him by. "Lebensneid," Nietzsche called it . . . others . . . sit at the table while he goes hungry; "they" love, create, enjoy, feel healthy and at ease, belong somewhere. The happiness of others . . . irritate[s] him. If he cannot be happy and free, why should they be so? (1945, 201–202)

Othello's marriage greatly exacerbates Iago's feelings of exclusion and failure. At the very same time that he has frustrated Iago's expectations, Othello has made a brilliant match that will ensure his own position: "he tonight hath boarded a land carrack./ If it prove lawful prize, he's made for ever" (I, i). Even more disturbing to Iago is Othello's fulfillment in love. His jealousy is aroused by the thought of a black man possessing a white woman (one who is inaccessible to him, moreover); and he is envious of the affection, loyalty, and admiration that the Moor will receive from the virtuous Desdemona. The promotion of Cassio has reminded Iago of Othello's power and of his inferior position. Othello's marriage adds to his prestige and makes Iago feel his own loveless state all the more poignantly.

As the play opens, then, Iago is undergoing a psychological crisis. He has lived up to his shoulds, but his claims have not been honored, and the validity of his bargain has been called in question. His pride has been hurt, his idealized image has been undermined, and he is threatened with unbearable feelings of envy and self-hate. His predominant responses are anxiety and rage; and these responses further threaten his pride system, since they make him feel vulnerable and are in conflict with his needs for mastery and self-control.

THE PSYCHOLOGICAL FUNCTIONS OF IAGO'S PLOT

Iago responds to his crisis by plotting revenge. He has certain practical objectives, such as gaining the lieutenancy, but the primary values of his plot are psychological. Through it he seeks to express his rage, to restore his pride, and to assuage his inner torments. Since almost everything goes his way until the very end, his plot has a fantastic quality that has led some critics to liken it to a work of art. As we shall see, it is highly self-expressive and is exquisitely adapted to his psychological needs.

The impulse to take revenge is such a common reaction to feeling injured that it may not seem to require a psychological explanation. What is clearly pathological about Iago's revenge is its disproportionate nature. Initially, he does not seek the deaths of his victims, but he does want to ruin their lives. Iago's revenge is so monstrous partly because the injuries he has received are so vastly magnified in his own mind. As we have seen, the promotion of Cassio is not simply a big disappointment; it is a terrible blow that threatens his whole system of defense. For an arrogant-vindictive person like Iago, moreover, it is very important to hurt his adversaries even more than they have hurt him. Such a person feels that an offender, "by his very power to hurt our pride, has put himself above us and has defeated us. By our taking revenge and hurting him more than he did us, the situation will be reversed" (Horney 1950, 103–104).

Iago's revenge must not only be disproportionate to what he feels to be an outrageous offense; it must also be a masterpiece of ingenuity and deception. Iago has an idealized image of himself as a consummate hypocrite and fiendishly clever schemer. He *should* be able to manipulate those who are less intelligent, less "realistic," and less self-controlled than he. The failure of his plan to exploit Othello by playing the role of devoted servant undermines this idealized image and threatens him with self-contempt. If he is to restore his confidence that he *is* his idealized self, he must be able, through his cleverness, to turn humiliation and defeat into a triumph of grandiose proportions. He will not simply revenge himself upon Othello; he will make the Moor thank him, love him, and reward him "For making him egregiously an ass/ And practising upon his peace and quiet/ Even to madness" (I, ii). It gives him an exquisite pleasure to ensure Cassio's destruction by acting as a friend and giving him good advice: "Divinity of hell!/ When devils will the blackest sins put on,/ They do suggest at first with heavenly shows,/ As I do now" (II, iii).

A person's idealized image is often modeled upon a hero who embodies in a glamorous or heightened form the characteristics that are prescribed by his solution. Julien Sorel and Raskolnikov, for example, seek to imitate Napoleon. Iago's model is the devil himself, and he takes an enormous pride in the thought that he is as good a deceiver as his own divinity. The joy Iago experiences as his plot unfolds so beautifully derives from his triumphant feeling that he is becoming his idealized self.

Iago needs to validate not only his idealized image, but also his bargain, which has been threatened by his own disappointment and by the success of others. As we have seen, Iago's preoccupation with self-effacing types indicates the presence within him of inner conflicts. So also does his remark in act 5 that Cassio has "a daily beauty in his life/ That makes me ugly" (V, i) and his justification of his revenge on the grounds that Othello and Cassio have slept with Emilia. At the same time that he exults in his knavery, he has a need to make his revenge seem normal by attributing it to the time-honored motive of having been cuckolded. It is because he has strong compliant trends that he needs to keep repressed that the good fortune of virtuous people is so threatening to him. According to his vision of life, we live in a "monstrous world" in which "To be direct and honest is not safe" (III, iii). Since fate is not destroying the honest people, he must do so himself to prove that his behavior is required by reality. If their bargain works, and his does not, he will be exposed to severe inner conflicts and unbearable self-hate. He must be a villain to avoid feeling like a monster.

To satisfy his needs, Iago must prove not simply that virtue does not pay, but that the so-called good qualities of his victims make them extremely vulnerable. Cassio is an "honest fool" whom Iago can easily exploit for his own purposes. He plays upon Cassio's compliancy to make him drunk, and upon his anxiety to be taken back to get him to plead incessantly for Desdemona's intervention. He knows that the "inclining Desdemona" holds it "a vice in her goodness not to do more than she is requested" (II, iii); and he is ecstatic at the thought that by getting Othello to misinterpret her pleading for Cassio he will "turn her virtue into pitch/ And out of her own goodness make the net/ That shall enmesh them all" (II, iii). What makes the whole plot work, of course, is the fact that "The Moor is of a free and open nature/ That thinks men honest that but seem to be so" (I, iii). By using their generosity, their credulity, and their need for love to destroy his victims, Iago confirms his view of the world and proves to himself that the only way to survive is to be ruthless, deceitful, and self-sufficient.

Finally, Iago's plot serves to assuage his envy. He envies Cassio's attractiveness to women, Othello's happiness in love, and the Moor's confidence and self-possession. All these things intensify his feelings of inferiority and his sense of the emptiness of his own life. He responds by trying to prove that what he envies is really dangerous or not worth having and by trying to make those he envies even more miserable than he is. Cassio's attractiveness becomes "a person and a smooth dispose/ To be suspected, framed to make women false" (I, iii); and thus it contributes to his undoing. Love is not worth having because it turns us into sick fools, like Roderigo, exposes us to the torments of jealousy, and conducts us to the most preposterous conclusions, as it does with Othello and Desdemona. One of Iago's chief objects, from the outset, is to do away with his envy of Othello by destroying Othello's marriage, his self-confidence, and his peace of mind.

Iago's primary effort in act 1 is to "poison [Othello's] delight" (I, i) in his marriage. He knows that Brabantio's opposition will not undo the marriage, but he hopes, at least, to interrupt its consummation and to throw "changes of vexation" upon Othello's "joy." The timing of the brawl that he precipitates between Roderigo and Cassio in act 2 may have a similar function, for Othello and Desdemona have not yet slept together and have just retired to enjoy the fruits of their marriage. Iago's envy at the sight of the lovers' ecstatic reunion in Cypress is evident: "O, you are well tun'd now!/ But I'll set down the pegs that make this music,/ As honest as I am" (II, i).

Horney's description of the sadist illuminates Iago's reactions: "The happiness of others and their 'naive' expectations of pleasure . . . irritate him. . . . He must trample on the joy of others. If he cannot be happy and free why should they be so? . . . if others are as defeated and degraded as he, his own misery is tempered in that he no longer feels himself the only one afflicted" (1945, 201–202). This passage helps to explain also Iago's need to undermine Othello's confidence and self-possession and to inflict upon him the torments of jealousy. Despite his pride in his self-mastery, there are many feelings over which Iago has no control. His entire plot, which he sees as a testimony to his all-conquering reason, is motivated by compulsive feelings of anxiety, envy, and rage. He is tormented most of all, perhaps, by his sexual jealousy, for this feeling conflicts with his pride in his will, violates his taboo against emotional involvement, and testifies to his profound feeling of insecurity. His self-hate is intensified by the sight of Othello's self-assurance and composure, which he displays not only in military matters, but also in his behavior toward Brabantio, Desdemona, and the senate.

It gives Iago an enormous satisfaction to make Othello uncertain of his worth, to undermine his sense of reality, and to drive him mad with jealousy. These are Iago's very own torments, which he inflicts upon Othello to a higher degree. Perhaps his greatest triumph comes when Othello is so overcome by emotion that he falls into a trance. His scorn of Othello is now so great that he begins to express it openly: "Marry, patience!/ Or I shall say you are all in all in spleen,/ And nothing of a man" (IV, i). Othello's loss of self-control is equally evident a few moments later when he strikes Desdemona in the presence of Lodovico.

> Is this the noble Moor [asks Lodovico] whom our full Senate
> Call all in all sufficient? Is this the nature
> Whom passion could not shake? whose solid virtue
> The shot of accident nor dart of chance
> Could neither graze nor pierce? (IV, i)

This description of Othello—who has just exited screaming "Goats and monkeys!"—must be exquisitely gratifying to Iago, for it provides a measure of his achievement.

Authors often have to manipulate their plots in order to show that virtue pays, that the self-effacing solution will be rewarded. There is much less need to do so in order to show that expansive solutions are bound, sooner or later, to fail. Pride does go before a fall, if only because it puts us out of touch with reality. A person like Iago has enormous pride in his intellectual powers. One of his needs is to produce a virtuoso performance in which he deceives Roderigo, Cassio, Othello, and Desdemona simultaneously, in a brilliantly integrated scheme, that must be improvised, moreover, as he goes along. For four acts everything works perfectly, but Iago has overreached himself, and in act 5 his plot suddenly unravels. When Emilia betrays him, he is so enraged by the blow to his feeling of mastery and the denial of his claim for loyalty that he kills her on the spot. Even if she had remained quiet, he would have been undone by Roderigo's accusations and the survival of Cassio. Iago now holds onto his pride in the only way left open to him. He will prove his self-control and thwart his tormentors by never speaking a word. The rest, we can be assured, is silence.

OTHELLO TRIUMPHANT

The great puzzle about Othello is the speed of his transformation from the commanding figure of act 1 into a murderously jealous husband. As soon as Iago begins to question Cassio's honesty in act 3, Othello becomes panicky, and within a very short time he is screaming for Desdemona's blood. His change is so quick and so radical that some critics have denied that it makes sense at all in motivational terms (e.g., Stoll 1933, 1940). Among those who have tried to understand Othello as a person, there have been two main ways of accounting for his transformation. Some critics have seen Othello as essentially a noble victim who is destroyed by his grand simplicity of nature, by his innocence of Venetian society, and, above all, by the diabolical cleverness of Iago. He does a terrible thing, but he reacts as most men would in a similar situation, and he is more sinned against than sinning.[2] Others have held that "Othello is not the noble Moor at all but has serious defects of character which cause his downfall" (Heilman 1956, 137). This "modern Othello" is "rootless, histrionic, . . . self-deceiving, . . . irritable, hasty, dependent, insecure—a pathetic image who lives in a fantasy of himself and others, who shrinks from reality into a world of 'pipe dreams' " (Rosenberg 1961, 186–187).[3]

My analysis will tend to confirm the "modern" view of Othello. I shall be less concerned with castigating our hero, however, than with understanding him. As the play opens, Iago's solution is being threatened, but Othello's is working to perfection. Act 1 shows Othello achieving a series of triumphs that vindicate his bargain and are like a dream come true. At the beginning of act 2, when he is reunited with Desdemona, Othello reaches the height of his bliss. After this, he begins his descent, not simply because of Iago's machinations, which are a necessary but not a sufficient cause of his downfall, but also because of the instability of his mental state and the fragility of his entire solution. His behavior in act 2 will be intelligible, I think, if we first examine his state of mind in act 1, the significance of his triumphs, and the earlier signs of his vulnerability. We shall then be in a position to understand not only the speed with which his confidence collapses and the source of his murderous rage, but also his insistence that he is an agent of justice and his behavior after he discovers his mistake.

Othello is, above all, ambitious. He aspires to fame and glory. He wants to be a great man, a conquering hero, a legendary figure. He mythologizes himself and his exploits, and he needs to have his grandiose conception of himself confirmed by the fidelity of his subordinates and the recognition of his superiors. He strives very hard to live up to his idealized image, and he bases his claims on the flawless performance of his duties. His bargain is, in part at least, that of the perfectionistic person: "Because he is fair, just, dutiful, he is entitled to fair treatment by others and by life in general. This conviction of an infallible justice operating in life gives him a feeling of mastery" (Horney 1950, 197).

What strikes us most forcefully about Othello in act 1 is precisely his feeling of mastery, his confidence that he is in control of his fate. In marrying Desdemona, he has violated the mores of Venetian society and has outraged her father, who is a very powerful man. When Iago warns him of Brabantio's opposition, Othello replies with magnificent assurance:

> *Oth.*   Let him do his spite.
> My services which I have done the signiory
> Shall outtongue his complaints. 'Tis yet to know,—
> Which, when I know that boasting is an honour,
> I shall promulgate—I fetch my life and being
> From men of royal siege; and my demerits
> May speak unbonneted to as proud a fortune
> As this that I have reach'd. For know, Iago,
> But that I love the gentle Desdemona,
> I would not my unhoused free condition
> Put into circumscription and confine
> For the sea's worth.
> *Enter CASSIO and OFFICERS with torches.*
> *Iago.* Those are the raised father and his friends:
> You were best go in.
> *Oth.* Not I. I must be found.
> My parts, my title, and my perfect soul
> Shall manifest me rightly. (I, ii)

Othello is not afraid of Brabantio because he feels that he deserves the proud fortune he has reached. He deserves it, moreover, not because of his royal birth, which he never reveals publicly, but because of his abilities, his accomplishments, and his moral perfection. He does not boast about his birth—though he is very conscious of it and is out to prove himself the equal of his royal forebears—because his claims for recognition are based on his personal merit. He does boast, of course, about his services, his adventures, and his soldierly qualities. The speech we are examining is, in fact, a boast—of his fearlessness, his merit, and his confidence that the signiory will endorse his marriage to Desdemona. Indeed, he presents himself not as a fortunate suitor who has won a socially superior woman, but as a man who out of love for her has given up his "free condition." Othello's reactions here are those of a man who feels that he *is* his idealized self and who is certain that his bargain will be honored.

Othello's self-assurance is even more striking when he is confronted with the direct hostility of Brabantio. He controls the potential combatants masterfully and listens calmly to Brabantio's foul accusations:

> Damn'd as thou art, thou hast enchanted her!
> For I'll refer me to all things of sense,
> If she in chains of magic were not bound,
> Whether a maid so tender, fair, and happy,
> So opposite to marriage that she shunn'd
> The wealthy curled darlings of our nation,
> Would ever have (t' incur a general mock)
> Run from her guardage to the sooty bosom
> Of such a thing as thou. (I, ii)

What is so impressive about Othello here is that he does not seem to be hurt or threatened by Brabantio's insults. He shows no anger or irritation, and he responds in an amazingly composed manner. The reasons, I think, are his confidence in his own worth, in Desdemona's love, and in the support of the council, which has just sent for him to deal with an emergency. Moreover, he takes a certain pleasure in Brabantio's accusations. The reasons Brabantio gives, both here and before the council, for believing that Othello must have used witchcraft upon Desdemona all contribute to Othello's glory. They verify his triumph over Desdemona's wealthy suitors and the power of his personal appeal, which has overcome all of the external obstacles to Desdemona's love. It is with a great pride that Othello delivers his "round unvarnish'd tale" of his "whole course of love—what drugs, what charms,/ What conjuration, and what mighty magic/ . . . I won his daughter" (I, iii). The mighty magic is his own history, his own merit, his own grandeur. Brabantio's words arouse no insecurity in Othello as long as he is identified with his idealized image— indeed, they feed his pride; but they remain in his mind and return to haunt him in act 3, when his self-confidence begins to falter.

Othello is in such an exalted state in act 1 because all his dreams are coming true. His search for glory has taken the form of military adventure. War appeals to him not only because of its "pride, pomp, and circumstance" (III, iii) and the opportunities it affords to gain recognition for his courage, toughness, and leadership, but also because it permits him to pursue his aggressive goals in a way that harmonizes with his need for moral perfection. By making "ambition virtue," "the big wars" enable Othello to combine martial and manly honor with loyalty, duty, and service (III, iii). By the time the play begins, he has reached the pinnacle of his military career. He has the reputation, the honors, and the position of trust and importance to which he has aspired. He is an indispensable man on whom the state depends completely in its times of trouble.

His marriage to Desdemona marks a new and very precious kind of triumph. It symbolizes his entry into the highest level of Venetian society. As Desdemona's husband, he will no longer be a hired soldier, "an extravagant and wheeling stranger/ Of here and everywhere" (I, i); he will be one of them. He will be the social as well as the military equal of the greatest men. In his mind, Desdemona is an exalted being whose acceptance confers upon him the status he feels is appropriate to his deserts: "She might lie by an emperor's side and command him tasks" (IV, i). It is a testimony also to his virtue ("I saw Othello's visage in his mind") and to his personal magnetism. When the Duke accepts the marriage, telling Brabantio that "If virtue no delighted beauty lack,/ Your son-in-law is far more fair than black" (I, iii), Othello's triumph is complete.

Desdemona's response is deeply gratifying to Othello in a variety of ways. She is an avid listener who is awe-struck by his tales of adventure and who confirms his sense of himself as a romantic figure. This is not a new experience for Othello; Brabantio, and presumably others like him, had shown a similar fascination with the story of his life. What Othello discovers in his conversations with Desdemona is that his exploits can win not simply admiration and popularity as a source of entertainment, but the love of a highborn, beautiful woman. They give him an appeal so powerful that it can overcome all the differences of age, race, and position. Winning Desdemona's love is a great social and sexual triumph; it is the ultimate reward for all his sacrifices. The fact that she deceives her father and defies the conventions of her society in order to marry Othello is proof of her adoration and of his greatness. He welcomes the opportunity to respond to Brabantio's accusations because it provides an occasion for the tale of his courtship, for the justification of his worthiness, and for Desdemona's public display of love, loyalty, and admiration.

Othello loves Desdemona, then, because she feeds his pride, confirms his idealized image, and validates his bargain with fate. She gives him something else very precious, moreover, that he probably has not received since he was a small boy. Othello's tales of adventure are also tales of suffering. Desdemona finds them not only glamorous, which is the usual response, but also "wondrous pitiful" (I, iii). Othello has received from other men recognition for his toughness, courage, and resourcefulness; he would not expect, or even want, them to pity his suffering. Desdemona gives him empathy, concern, and tenderness; she rouses and gratifies a softer side of his nature that is not in keeping with the code of manly behavior and that he has repressed, no doubt, since he left his mother's knee.

Othello's highest moment occurs in act 2, when he is reunited with Desdemona at Cyprus:

> If it were now to die,
> 'Twere now to be most happy; for I fear
> My soul hath her content so absolute
> That not another comfort like to this
> Succeeds is unknown fate. (II, i)

Othello must feel, indeed, like a favorite of fortune, for the storm has destroyed his enemies without harming either Desdemona or himself. His very joy makes him vulnerable, of course, as he is aware. Since he has realized his dream of glory, his "content" is "absolute." If he were to die now, he would be united forever with his idealized self. Nothing better can succeed "in unknown fate."

OTHELLO'S VULNERABILITY

Othello is feeling vulnerable here because he is experiencing the superstitious dread that accompanies supreme good fortune and because he is afraid that the rest of his life will seem anticlimactic. The deepest source of his vulnerability, however, lies beyond his perception, within his own character. He responds to life with rigid defenses, and he is dependent for his self-esteem upon an unrealistically grandiose conception of himself, one that denies many of his feelings and that can easily be threatened by reality. The self-assurance that he feels in act 1 is an intoxicating but unstable condition. It is based upon the confirmation, through his marriage to Desdemona and his importance to the state, of his idealized image of himself. Self-idealization is almost always an indication of insecurity; it is a compensatory process. It is impossible to recover the beginnings of Othello's need for self-idealization, since we know little of his early childhood; but the evidence we do have permits us to reconstruct some of its sources.

As we have seen, Othello has made a perfectionistic bargain with fate; he gains a sense of superiority and control by measuring up to his high moral standards, "by fulfilling duties and obligations" (Horney 1950, 196). Othello also displays many of the characteristics of the narcissistic person. The narcissist "is his idealized image and seems to adore it. This basic attitude . . . gives him a seeming abundance of self-confidence which appears enviable to all those [like Iago] chafing under self-doubts" (Horney 1950, 194). He tends to romanticize himself and others, endowing "his family and his friends, as well as his work and plans, with glowing attributes." His underlying insecurity is revealed by the fact that he speaks "incessantly of his exploits or of his wonderful qualities and needs endless confirmation of himself in the form of admiration and devotion." Othello's idealized image is a composite of the perfectionistic and the narcissistic solutions; and he has made, as we shall see, a double bargain with fate.

The narcissistic person "often is gifted beyond average, early and easily won distinctions, and sometimes was the favored and admired child" (Horney 1950, 194). Although we do not know how Othello was treated within his family, we do know that he is descended "from men of royal siege" (I, ii). He occupied a privileged position in his society and had reason to regard himself as a special person with a special destiny. He seems to have been a gifted warrior from an early age who was following in the footsteps of his illustrious forebears. His royal descent, his gifts, and his daring exploits may all have combined to give him a sense of himself as an exceptional being. This would function not only as a source of self-adoration, but also as a pressure to maintain his grandeur, and hence as a source of insecurity. He seems to have a need to reinforce the narcissistic component of his idealized image by driving himself to greater and greater accomplishments and by gaining the admiration of others, which he pursues, in part, by celebrations of himself. The narcissistic person feels himself to be the favorite of fortune (as he had been of his family or his society), and he often exposes himself to danger to demonstrate his invulnerability. Othello's many "hairbreadth scapes" are a testimony to his good luck. His calm in the midst of battle shows not only his fortitude, but also his confidence in destiny.

Although he has no doubt inherited a strict code of conduct on the observance of which his honor depends, Othello's strong perfectionistic trends may also be the product of his separation from his own society. Othello's project seems to be to achieve the status that was promised by his abilities and his birth, despite the fact that he is living in an alien world. Military prowess alone will not accomplish his purpose, for he is not content to be seen merely as a gifted barbarian. He has not only a narcissistic need for admiration and devotion, but also a perfectionistic need for approval and respect. It is to attain the latter things that he strives for a "flawless excellence in the whole conduct of life" (Horney 1950, 196).

When he enters a predominantly white society, Othello exchanges his privileged position for a disadvantageous one. The speeches of Iago, Roderigo, and Brabantio reveal with what prejudice he is viewed by the members of Venetian society. Iago characterizes him as an "old black ram," "the devil," and "a Barbary horse," while Roderigo calls him a "lascivious Moor" and "an extravagant and wheeling stranger/ Of here and everywhere." The speeches in which Othello is thus described are addressed to his "friend," Brabantio, who is sure that the other Venetian noblemen must "feel this wrong as 'twere their own;/ For if such actions may have passage free,/ Bondslaves and pagans shall our statesman be" (I, ii).

No one had spoken in this way to Othello before his marriage, of course, but he must have realized the difficulty of gaining genuine acceptance into Venetian society. He must have felt threatened in his self-esteem by these negative attitudes and have needed social acceptance all the more as a form of reassurance. He tries to maintain his self-esteem and to win the respect of others by being morally perfect. He must show the world and himself that he is not a bondslave and pagan, but a man who is thoroughly civilized and nobly Christian. He is not a lascivious Moor, but a sexually restrained man who confesses "to heaven/ . . . the vices of [his] blood" (I, iii). He has married Desdemona for love, and not simply "to please the palate of [his] appetite" (I, iii). He is not an "extravagant and wheeling stranger/ Of here and everywhere," but a man who identifies completely with the Venetian cause and who is utterly loyal and trustworthy.

This reconstruction of Othello's defenses will give us a better understanding of the significance of his triumphs and the sources of his vulnerability. Act 1 begins with attacks on Othello, behind his back, by Iago and Roderigo, and to his face, by Brabantio, as his marriage brings out the latent hostility of the Venetians toward him as a stranger, a barbarian, and a black man. The act concludes, so far as it concerns Othello, with his total vindication and his public acceptance by everyone except Brabantio. His words, his demeanor, the testimony of Desdemona, and the approval of the Duke all refute the prejudiced view of Othello and confirm both the narcissistic and the perfectionistic components of his idealized image. His double bargain is working. He has held onto his claims, and his dreams have come true. He is the favorite of fortune and of the state. By marrying a woman fit "to lie by an emperor's side" (IV, i), he has become the equal, if not the superior, of his royal forebears. He has accomplished this, in the face of racial prejudice, by virtue of his "parts, [his] title, and [his] perfect soul" (I, ii). Desdemona's "heart's subdued/ Even to the very quality of [her] lord"; she sees "Othello's visage in his mind" (I, iii). The Duke proclaims that his virtue makes him "far more fair than black" (I, iii). These triumphs produce in Othello a sense of having become his idealized self, a feeling that is heightened, at the beginning of act 2, by his supreme good fortune. He has had another of his "hairbreadth scapes."

Although the defensive strategies are designed to compensate for anxieties about our worth or adequacy, they all make us vulnerable to an intensified self-hate. A major source of Othello's anxiety is the combination of his need to live up to the exalted conception of himself he has derived from his royal lineage with his uneasy feeling that his blackness and his "primitive" origins may actually make him an inferior being. The words of Desdemona and the Duke quoted above indicate that Othello is worthy and attractive despite his blackness, and Othello seems to acquiesce in the terms of this praise. His compensatory self-idealization generates an additional source of anxiety, since it leads him to expect too much from life, from others, and from himself.

Othello's vulnerability begins to appear in act 1, when the feelings that have been aroused in him by Desdemona make him anxious about damaging his manly image. He has a strong need to show himself and others that being in love does not mean that he is getting soft. Thus, when the Duke is somewhat apologetic about "slubber[ing] the gloss of [his] new fortunes" by sending him off to Cyprus on his wedding night, Othello replies by boasting of his toughness and embracing the assignment (I, iii). He has a "natural and prompt alacrity" for hardship; the "flinty and steel couch of war" is his "thrice-driven bed of down." He will not allow himself to show any disappointment at these developments or any eagerness for the consummation of his marriage. Instead, he turns the occasion into another display of his readiness to serve and seeks admiration for his warlike qualities.

A few moments later, in supporting Desdemona's suit to accompany him, Othello is most emphatic in assuring the council that he does not want Desdemona with him "to comply with heat . . ./ But to be free and bounteous to her mind" (I, iii). He will never be distracted from his serious business by the allurements of love:

> And heaven defend your good souls that you think
> I will your serious and great business scant
> For she is with me. No, when light-wing'd toys
> Of feather'd Cupid steel with wanton dullness
> My speculative and offic'd instruments,
> That my disports corrupt and taint my business,
> Let housewives make a skillet of my helm,
> And all indign and base adversities
> Make head against my estimation! (I, iii)

Othello presents himself here as his idealized image. He is dutiful, self-possessed, and free both of sensuality and of selfishness. He asks that Desdemona be allowed to accompany him for her sake rather than for his own, suggesting that her need for him is greater than his for her. Othello is struggling with the emergence of his self-effacing trends. All of his codes generate strong taboos against his softer feelings, which threaten his idealized image in a variety of ways. He senses how important Desdemona is to him and is afraid of becoming a slave to love. As an antidote, he deprecates the power of Cupid's toys, mocks the idea that such a thing could happen to him, and reminds himself of the self-contempt he would feel if he should violate his standards and of the punishment that would surely follow. His protestation that Desdemona's presence could never distract him from his duties is highly ironic in the light of what happens later on.

The first obvious manifestation of Othello's vulnerability occurs in his handling of the fight between Cassio and Montano, when he loses his composure for the first time in the play. He experiences this situation as a challenge to his authority, which must be absolute; and he has a low tolerance for uncertainty, which threatens his sense of control. It is for this reason, among others, that he relies so heavily on Iago's account and does not investigate further; he is impatient to feel that he has found out the truth. Iago is very skillful, of course, in investing his testimony against Cassio with great credibility; he speaks with reluctance and appears to be engaged in Cassio's defense. Since Othello tends to idealize those around him, making them, in this way, fit complements to his own greatness, he has no disposition to suspect Iago's honesty.

Othello is deeply disturbed by Cassio's breach of conduct. The scene had opened with Othello's assigning Cassio the task of supervising the guard during the period of celebration: "Let's teach ourselves that honourable stop./ Not to outsport discretion" (II, iii). The perfectionistic person externalizes his shoulds and insists that others live up to them. Othello demands of Cassio the same discretion, the same sense of responsibility, that he demands of himself. Cassio's conduct is a gross violation of his standards, and he must condemn that conduct in order to reaffirm those standards. The eruption of domestic violence while he is in authority is particularly threatening to Othello because it arouses his anxiety about being considered uncivilized: "Are we turn'd Turks and to ourselves do that/ Which heaven hath forbid the Ottomites?/ For Christian shame put by this barbarous brawl!" The severity with which he first stops the fight and then punishes the offender shows how much he disdains this behavior. Such things must not happen under his command!

Desdemona's pleading for Cassio in act 3, scene 3 throws Othello into the kind of inner conflict he had feared in act 1. He has insisted that the offender, "though he had twinned with me, both at a birth,/ Shall lose me" (II, iii); and he has told Cassio that, though he loves him, he shall never again be his officer. He has made it very clear that personal affection shall not affect his decision in so serious a matter. When Desdemona begins to plead for Cassio, Othello is, therefore, understandably resistant. After a badgering speech in which Desdemona wonders what Othello could ask of her that she "should deny/ Or stand so mamm'ring on," Othello capitulates: "Prithee no more. Let him come when he will!/ I will deny thee nothing" (III, iii).

Given Othello's prior elevation of duty over the claims of love, he is bound to feel uncomfortable with his present behavior. Desdemona has induced him to act according to the terms of her own self-effacing bargain: I will do anything you want out of love for you, and you should do the same for me. Such compliant behavior is quite in keeping with Desdemona's value system and is a source of pride for her, but it is humiliating to Othello. He fears that people will say precisely the sort of thing that Iago has been saying behind his back:

> His soul is so enfetter'd to her love
> That she may make, unmake, do what she list,
> Even as her appetite shall play the god
> With his weak function. (II, iii)

"Our General's wife," Iago proclaims, "is now the General" (II, iii). Othello's inner tension is indicated by his request that Desdemona now leave him alone: "I will deny thee nothing./ Whereon I do beseech thee grant me this,/ To leave me but a little to myself" (III, iii). Othello is trying to control the resentment he feels toward Desdemona for having led him to act in a way that threatens his pride and makes him feel ashamed of himself. He does not want to show his resentment after having just made a sacrifice to prove his love, and so he asks her to go away so that he can regain his composure. There is a certain bitterness, however, in his invocation of their bargain. This scene leaves Othello in an agitated state of mind: he is uncomfortable with himself, resentful toward Desdemona, and less enchanted than he had been with his marriage.

OTHELLO'S TRANSFORMATION

We are ready now to consider Othello's transformation. It will not seem quite so rapid if we recognize that in a significant way it has already begun. Othello is no longer in the supremely confident state of mind that he enjoyed in act 1. He has begun to have sinking feelings, as his fantasies about himself and others have been shaken. Cassio has not proved to be the ideal lieutenant nor Desdemona the submissive wife that Othello had expected them to be, and he has not lived up to the image of himself that he had presented to the senate. Even before Iago begins to work on him, he is feeling anxious. This is one reason why Iago's hesitations frighten him so much; he has already had premonitions that he has only been dreaming.

Another reason for Othello's fright is, of course, his faith in Iago. He knows that such "stops" in "a false disloyal knave/ Are tricks of custom," but he has mythologized Iago, and he persists in seeing him as he needs him to be, as his honest friend and servant. His insensitivity to Iago as a person is indicated not only by his failure even to suspect his hypocrisy, but also by his unawareness of the injury he has done Iago by not promot-

ing him to the lieutenancy. Iago understands how Othello wants to perceive him, and he plays his role to perfection. He is a consummate actor
who deceives not only Othello, but everyone else as well. At the moment
when Iago begins to undermine Othello's faith in Desdemona, Othello
may be depending on him all the more because of his growing disenchantment with others.

The initial doubt that Iago raises is not primarily about Desdemona,
but about Cassio. Othello is especially vulnerable to this line of attack
because Cassio has disappointed him, and he becomes agitated as soon as
Iago begins to express his suspicions. Iago's hesitancy and conscientious
scruples at once increase his own credibility and intensify Othello's anxiety. They frustrate Othello's need for certainty and control and set his
imagination running wild by suggesting that Iago's suspicions are horrible
indeed. There is no way Othello can defend himself in this situation; and,
with growing desperation, he finally explodes: "By heaven, I'll know thy
thoughts!" (III, iii).

Only now does Iago implicate Desdemona by warning Othello to
beware of jealousy. Othello is relieved to know Iago's suspicions, and he
begins at once to rebuild his defenses:

> Why, why is this?
> Think'st thou I'd make a life of jealousy,
> To follow still the changes of the moon
> With fresh suspicions? No! To be once in doubt
> Is once to be resolv'd. Exchange me for a goat
> When I shall turn the business of my soul
> To such exsufflicate and blown surmises,
> Matching thy inference. 'Tis not to make me jealous
> To say my wife is fair, feeds well, loves company,
> Is free of speech, sings, plays, and dances well.
> Where virtue is, these are more virtuous.
> Nor from mine own weak merits will I draw
> The smallest fear or doubt of her revolt,
> For she had eyes, and chose me. No, Iago;
> I'll see before I doubt; when I doubt, prove;
> And on the proof, there is no more but this—
> Away at once with love or jealousy! (III, iii)

Othello is describing here, of course, not the way he really is, but the way
he needs to be. Jealousy would threaten him with the things he can least
tolerate: doubt, helplessness, indecision, uncertainty about his worth, and
enslavement by his need for love. He denies, therefore, that he could be

such a victim of "the green-eyed monster" as Iago has described and tries to allay his anxiety by reaffirming his idealized image of himself and Desdemona. This is his last boast, and its hollowness is evident. He is terrified of jealousy and incapable of objectivity. His perceptions have been conditioned throughout by his needs and fears.

Iago uses Othello's boast as an excuse to speak more frankly, and Othello's confidence in Desdemona quickly collapses under a direct assault:

> *Iago.* I know our country disposition well:
> In Venice they do let heaven see the pranks
> They dare not show their husbands; their best conscience
> Is not to leave't undone, but keep't unknown.
> *Oth.* Dost thou say so?
> *Iago.* She did deceive her father, marrying you,
> And where she seem'd to shake and fear your looks,
> She lov'd them most.
> *Oth.*   And so she did.
> *Iago.* Why, go to then!
> She that, so young, could give out such a seeming
> To seel her father's eyes up close as Oak—
> He thought 'twas witchcraft—. (III, iii)

Iago's techniques are so effective here that they would shake the faith of a man far less vulnerable than Othello. Iago knows the local mores much better than does Othello, and Othello can have no basis other than a complete trust in Desdemona for defending himself against the doubt raised by Iago's description of Venetian women. How can he have such a trust, however, when Desdemona did, in fact, deceive her father and conceal, for a time at least, her true feeling toward himself? Othello surely remembers, at this point, Brabantio's horrible warning: "Look to her, Moor, if thou hast eyes to see./ She has deceiv'd her father, and may thee" (I, ii). Desdemona's behavior toward her father had been a source of pride for Othello earlier, when he interpreted it as a testimony of her great love for him. Now it undermines his belief in her virtue and is the solid foundation upon which Iago builds his structure of deceit.

Othello's doubts about Desdemona weaken his confidence in himself as well—in his ability to distinguish between appearance and reality, and in his worthiness of Desdemona's love. Othello's attitudes toward himself and Desdemona are interdependent. He can believe in her love in act 1 because he feels deserving of it, and her love is the supreme confirmation of his idealized image. Anything that threatens his belief in himself threatens his belief in her, and anything that threatens his belief in her threatens his belief in himself. He is caught now in a vicious circle. He is susceptible to doubt about Desdemona's love because of the insecurities which that love was to put to rest. Once he begins to doubt, his insecurities are reactivated, and suspicion becomes easier than belief.

After Iago reminds him of Desdemona's deception of her father, Othello tries, feebly, to reaffirm his faith:

> Oth.   I do not think but Desdemona's honest.
> Iago. Long live she so! and long live you to think so!
> Oth.   And yet how nature erring from itself—
> Iago. Ay, there's the point! as (to be bold with you)
>   Not to affect many proposed matches
>   Of her own clime, complexion, and degree,
>   Whereto we see in all things nature tends—
>   Foh! one may smell in such a will most rank,
>   Foul disproportion, thoughts unnatural— (III, iii)

In act 1, Brabantio had argued that "For nature so prepost'rously to err,/ Being not deficient, blind, or lame of sense,/ Sans witchcraft could not" (I, iii). At that point Othello was so sure of his worth that he seemed completely unaffected by these charges. Now, with his faith in Desdemona shaken and his self-confidence sinking, it seems unnatural to Othello, too, that she should love him. Iago's chief ally here is Othello's self-hate. Even when he was his idealized self, Othello felt worthy *despite* his blackness: his virtue made him inwardly white. With his despised self rising to the fore, he feels the contempt for his blackness to which Brabantio had given voice. Now Desdemona's attraction to him is not a sign of his surpassing worth, but of her degradation. Iago understands this very well, and he seizes the opportunity to remind Othello of Brabantio's words and to reinforce his image of Desdemona. She is deceitful if she does not love him and unnatural if she does.

Othello's soliloquy, which occurs only 150 lines after Iago seriously begins his assault, indicates clearly that a decisive change in his images of Desdemona and himself has already taken place:

> Haply, for I am black
> And have not those soft parts of conversation
> That chamberers have, or for I am declin'd
> Into the vale of years (yet that's not much)
> She's gone. I am abus'd, and my relief

> Must be to loathe her. O curse of marriage,
> That we can call these delicate creatures ours,
> And not their appetites! . . .
>   Yet 'tis the plague of great ones;
> Prerogativ'd are they less than the base.
> 'Tis destiny unshunnable, like death.
> Even then this forked plague is fated to us
> When we do quicken. (III, iii)

Iago's tale of Cassio's dream and of the handkerchief are "confirmations strong/ As proofs of holy writ" (III, iii) because Othello is predisposed to believe in everything that points to Desdemona's guilt and to discount all evidence of her innocence.

Othello's soliloquy is remarkable not only for its revelation of his insecurities, but also for its portrayal of his strategies of defense. As long as Desdemona fed his pride, Othello needed to exalt her. Now that she is undermining him, he has a vested interest in tearing her down. In addition to protecting his pride by shifting the blame from himself to Desdemona, he is defending himself against self-hate by a process of externalization. Instead of despising himself, he will loathe her. Othello protects himself also by generalizing, depersonalizing, and reversing the significance of his situation. He is suffering from the "curse of marriage," from a "destiny unshunnable, like death." His is the common lot of married men— indeed, of mankind. It is a "plague," moreover, that especially affects "great ones," who are more vulnerable in this matter than "the base." A soliloquy that began with Othello's feeling his plight to be the result of his inferiority concludes with the reflection that it is man's inescapable fate and a sign of his own greatness.

Such measures, however, bring little relief. From this point on, Othello experiences great mental anguish. His belief in Desdemona has been dealt a mortal blow, but it is not yet dead, and the next several scenes are largely occupied with his agonies of doubt and demands for proof. As in the incident with Cassio, his impatience to be "satisfied" makes him all the more vulnerable to Iago's lies. The idea of Desdemona's guilt is so devastating to him, however, that even after he is convinced he needs repeated confirmations. It is a dreadful thing for him to have to give up his dream of glory, especially after he thought it had come true, and he is overwhelmed by the pity of it.

We can understand the intensity of Othello's reaction, I think, if we remember what Desdemona means to him. Before his marriage, he had invested his pride in his military exploits and in his moral perfection; after his marriage, he invests it in her. Her betrayal means that his bargain has not been honored and that he is his despised rather than his idealized self. His despair comes from his hopelessness about ever succeeding in his search for glory. The "pride, pomp, and circumstance of glorious war" (III, iii) mean nothing to him now because they no longer contribute to his personal grandeur. He must either live in Desdemona's love "or bear no life" (IV, ii).

It is only when we understand how badly Othello has been hurt that we can comprehend his murderous rage. Like Hamlet and Iago when their claims are not honored, he feels terribly abused and is consumed with indignation. He has a desperate need to restore his pride, to assuage his self-hate, and to overcome his feeling of helplessness by striking back, by hurting Cassio and Desdemona even more that they have hurt him. Since Desdemona has destroyed his life, simple murder seems an inadequate punishment: "O, that the slave had forty thousand lives!/ One is too poor, too weak for my revenge" (III, iii).

Othello reacts against his softness and indecision, against the self-effacing trends that have exposed him to such agony, and invests his pride now in the headlong violence of his behavior.

> *Iago.* Patience, I say. Your mind perhaps may change.
> *Oth.* Never, Iago. Like to the Pontic sea,
>   Whose icy current and compulsive course
>   Ne'er feels retiring ebb, but keeps due on
>   To the Propontic and the Hellespont;
>   Even so my bloody thoughts, with violent pace,
>   Shall ne'er look back, ne'er ebb to humble love,
>   Till that a capable and wide revenge
>   Swallow them up. (III, iii)

He repudiates the idea that his mind may change because that would mean giving in to "humble love" and accepting humiliation. Compulsively driven by his vindictive needs, he exalts hatred, bloodthirstiness, and revenge, which he swears with "the due reverence of a sacred vow." He not only appoints Iago his lieutenant, but he adopts, at this moment, Iago's inverted system of values.

AN HONORABLE MURDERER?

Othello is here at the peak of his fury. In act 4, his inner conflicts return. We see him trying to forget about the handkerchief, being overwhelmed by his grief, and looking, presumably, for more evidence as he witnesses Iago's interrogation of Cassio. His rage alternates with his anguish at having to relinquish his dream, and Iago must prod him into pursuing his revenge:

> *Oth.* Ay, let her rot, and perish, and be damn'd tonight; for she shall not live. No, my heart is turn'd to stone; I strike it, and it hurts my hand. O, the world hath not a sweeter creature! She might lie by an emperor's side and command him tasks.
>
> *Iago.* Nay, that's not your way.
>
> *Oth.* Hang her! I do but say what she is. So delicate with her needle! an admirable musician! O, she will sing the savageness out of a bear! Of so high and plenteous wit and invention!
>
> *Iago.* She's the worse for all this.
>
> *Oth.* O, a thousand times! And then, of so gentle a condition!
>
> *Iago.* Ay, too gentle.
>
> *Oth.* Nay, that's certain. But yet the pity of it, Iago! O Iago, the pity of it, Iago!
>
> *Iago.* If you are so fond of her iniquity, give her patent to offend; for if it touch not you, it comes near nobody.
>
> *Oth.* I will chop her into messes! Cuckold me! (IV, i)

Othello is also ambivalent at the time of the murder. When he hears Cassio calling for a surgeon, he is challenged to emulate Iago's behavior:

> Thou teachest me. Minion, your dear lies dead,
> And your unblest fate hies. Strumpet, I come.
> Forth of my heart those charms, thine eyes, are blotted.
> Thy bed, lust-stain'd, shall with lust's blood be spotted. (V, i)

He is determined not to let his softer feelings for Desdemona interfere with his resolution, and so he keeps up his rage by reminding himself of his wrongs and her corruption. When he enters their bedchamber, however, he is in a different state of mind. He sees himself as killing Desdemona in the name of a higher justice ("It is the cause, it is the cause, my soul"), and not out of a lust for personal revenge. His bloodthirstiness is gone, and he is full of tenderness and deep regret:

> One more, one more! [*kiss*]
> Be thus when thou art dead, and I will kill thee,
> And love thee after. One more, and this the last!
> So sweet was ne'er so fatal. I must weep,
> But they are cruel tears. This sorrow's heavenly;
> It strikes where it doth love. (V, ii)

We have here another transformation that needs to be explained.

When Othello is in the grip of his rage, he craves a bloody revenge, but he is not basically an arrogant-vindictive person, and he cannot be comfortable with himself when he acts in accordance with this solution. He will despise himself, however, if he allows himself to be abused. What we see in the murder scene is Othello's effort to reconcile his need for retaliation with his perfectionistic values. He is going to sacrifice the woman he loves in the name of justice, so that she won't "betray more men." He is not engaged in a personal vendetta, but is affirming the code of loyalty, duty, and service. Hence, his claim, even after he discovers his error, that he is "an honourable murderer . . ./ For naught I did in hate, but all in honour" (V, ii). Killing Desdemona in the name of justice permits him to feel his tenderness, longing, and regret; for he no longer has to feed his fury in order to get himself to carry out his revenge. The fact that he feels love for her, rather than hate, reinforces his pride in himself as a noble person. Moreover, he is prepared to give her time to pray so that she may reconcile her soul to heaven: "I would not kill thy unprepared spirit./ No, heaven forfend! I would not kill thy soul" (V, ii). He is not a barbarian, but a civilized Christian.

Desdemona's resistance upsets Othello's solution. His rage is just below the surface, and it emerges immediately when she begins to plead for her life: his eyes roll, he gnaws his "nether lip," and "Some bloody passion shakes [his] very frame." Desdemona's protestations of innocence change his mood entirely: "O perjur'd woman! thou dost stone my heart,/ And mak'st me call what I intend to do/ A murder, which I thought a sacrifice" (V, ii). When Desdemona begs that Cassio be sent for, Othello becomes once again the bloodthirsty revenger and does not even allow her time to pray. His later protestations to the contrary notwithstanding, he kills her in hate, partly because she has forced him to relinquish his nobility.

When Othello learns the truth, his pride is crushed, and he is overwhelmed by self-hate. He had told Emilia that he was "damn'd beneath all depth in hell/ But that [he] did proceed upon just grounds/ To this extremity" (V, ii). Now he feels that when they meet at the last judgment, Desdemona's look "will hurl [his] soul from heaven/ And fiends will snatch at it" (V, ii). The sight of Desdemona's corpse fills him with such rage at himself that he begs for punishment. The intensity of Othello's self-hate is a function of the hideousness of his deed, which has turned him into his despised self, and of his unbearable feeling that Desdemona *was* the woman of his dreams and that he has destroyed his own happiness:

> O Desdemona, Desdemona! dead!
> O! O! O! (V, ii)

Othello's lament is less for what he had done to Desdemona than for what
he has done to himself.

Through his last speech and his suicide, Othello makes a final effort
to salvage at least some of his pride. He is, as T. S. Eliot said, trying to
cheer himself up (1950, 110–111). His audience is at once himself, his
auditors, and posterity. He hopes to influence the image of himself that
will be carried back to Venice and passed on to future generations. He
acknowledges some errors; but by softening his faults and calling attention
to his virtues, he makes a case for himself as a man who deserves sympathy and admiration. He did not love Desdemona "wisely," but "too well."
This is accurate in a sense, but it puts too favorable an interpretation upon
his desperate need for her love as an affirmation of his worth. He was "not
easily jealous" (which is false), but he *was* "perplex'd in the extreme"
after he had been wrought upon by Iago. He ignores the fact that he has
murdered an innocent woman, and presents himself, rather, as a man who
"threw a pearl away"—that is, as a man who has done a terrible thing to
himself. He weeps at what he has done, and invites us to pity him. There
is a moral blindness in all this, a self-preoccupation, that is quite understandable in the circumstances, but that also justifies Eliot's strictures. The
speech is brilliant in its self-protective rhetoric.

Othello begins his speech by reminding his auditors of what he has
done for the state and he concludes by rendering his final service.

> Set you down this;
> And say besides that in Aleppo once,
> Where a malignant and a turban'd Turk
> Beat a Venetian and traduc'd the state,
> I took by th' throat the circumcised dog
> And smote him—thus!   *[He stabs himself.]* (V, ii)

Othello kills himself partly out of self-hate and a need for punishment; he
identifies himself with the malignant Turk who was an enemy of the state.
By killing himself in this way, however, he not only reminds his audience
of his earlier service, but he becomes again the state's defender, this time
against himself. He is an agent of justice and a loyal servant of the
Venetian cause. By being his own judge and executioner, he escapes his
humiliating position and gains some sense of mastery over his fate. Given
the utter hopelessness of his position, Othello manages to salvage a con-

siderable amount of pride and dignity. He dies poetically, kissing Desdemona; and he receives an immediate tribute from Cassio: "This did I fear . . ./For he was great of heart." The play ends with Othello once again seeming great and Iago being blamed completely for the tragedy.

> *Lod.* [To Iago] O Spartan dog,
> More fell than anguish, hunger, or the sea!
> Look on this tragic loading in this bed.
> This is thy work. (V, ii)

BEWITCHED DESDEMONA

Like Othello, Desdemona is a controversial character whose behavior has been difficult to understand. Is she little less than a saint, or a rebellious daughter who is rightly punished for her deception of her father? A Christ-like martyr, or a guilt-ridden woman who participates in her own victimization? Many critics have been struck by the disparity between her assertive behavior early in the play and her inability to defend herself later. This is the central puzzle of Desdemona's character, but it is by no means the only one. With the possible exception of Cleopatra, Desdemona is Shakespeare's most complex psychological portrait of a woman.[4] The glorifying rhetoric of the play tends to discourage an examination of her motives; but when we look at her closely, we find that her actions are as extreme as those of Iago and Othello and that her character, as well as theirs, contributes to the tragedy.

As the play opens, Desdemona has just behaved in a way that is quite outrageous from the point of view of her culture. She has fallen in love with a man of a different race, country, and color; and she is so determined to marry him despite what she knows would be her father's opposition that she conceals her intentions and weds without her father's consent. By doing this, she loses her father's affection and deals him such a blow that he soon dies of grief. Brabantio repeatedly characterizes her behavior as unnatural, but the rhetoric of the play works in Desdemona's behalf and lessens the impact of what she has done. The Duke says that Othello's tale would have won his daughter, too, and he tells Brabantio that his son-in-law's virtue makes him "far more fair than black" (I, iii). This makes the marriage seem natural and desirable. Desdemona's undutifulness is obscured when Brabantio, instead of arraigning her for her "treason of the blood" (I, i), asks her where she most owes obedience. This permits her to answer from the position of a married woman, whose first duty is to her husband. Her response is entirely proper, but it ignores the fact that she betrayed her father by her secret courtship and marriage. Despite the fact that Brabantio's reactions are not endorsed by the rhetoric of the play, they represent the conventional views of his society (which even Othello will soon embrace); and it is from them, I think, rather than from the response of the Duke, that we get the clearest sense of the extreme nature of Desdemona's behavior. Brabantio reacts to the news of the marriage with outrage and despair. These feelings give way, however, to utter amazement at Desdemona's behavior and to a conviction that she must have been bewitched. Her actions are so out of keeping with his sense of her character that Brabantio cannot believe them to have been voluntary:

> For I'll refer me to all things of sense,
> If she in chains of magic were not bound,
> Whether a maid so tender, fair, and happy,
> So opposite to marriage that she shunn'd
> The wealthy curled darlings of our nation,
> Would ever have (t' incur a general mock)
> Run from her guardage to the sooty bosom
> Of such a thing as thou—to fear, not to delight. (I, ii)

Brabantio's conviction is, in part, defensive: if Desdemona is bound in chains of magic, then she has not really rejected him. But it is mostly the product of his genuine bewilderment at behavior that is so incongruous with both the social norms and Desdemona's usual self.

> A maiden never bold;
> Of spirit so still and quiet that her motion
> Blush'd at herself; and she—in spite of nature,
> Of years, of country, credit, everything—
> To fall in love with what she fear'd to look on!
> It is a judgment maim'd and most imperfect
> That will confess perfection so could err
> Against all rules of nature, and must be driven
> To find out practices of cunning hell
> Why this should be. (I, iii)

Given Brabantio's view of his daughter—on which we must rely, I think, for our picture of the earlier Desdemona—it is no wonder that he must resort to witchcraft for an explanation of her behavior.

In his account of the courtship, Othello offers another explanation of

Desdemona's attraction to him. Desdemona was captivated by his tales of adventure and suffering, so much so that she dispatched "the house affairs" with haste in order to "come again, and with a greedy ear/ Devour up [his] discourse" (I, iii). Seeing this, he found means to draw a prayer from her that he would "all his pilgrimage dilate," which she had heard only in part:

> My story being done,
> She gave me for my pains a world of sighs.
> She swore, in faith, 'twas strange, 'twas passing strange;
> 'Twas pitiful, 'twas wondrous pitiful.
> She wish'd she had not heard it; yet she wish'd
> That heaven had made her such a man. She thank'd me,
> And bade me, if I had a friend that lov'd her,
> I should but teach him how to tell my story,
> And that would woo her. (I, iii)

If we combine the information contained in this passage, spoken by Othello, with Brabantio's descriptions of his daughter, we can gain considerable insight into Desdemona's character and begin to understand what it is that makes Othello so irresistible to her.

Before Othello's arrival, Desdemona is tender, modest, and compliant. Brabantio describes her as "perfection"; and she is, outwardly at least, an embodiment of the feminine ideal of her society. Inwardly, however, she is discontent; she has vague longings for a kind of life that is denied to her as a woman. The only future to which she can look forward is marriage to one of the "wealthy curled darlings" of her nation, but this is unappealing. With her mother dead, she has been mistress of her father's house. Should she marry one of these young men, she would merely be exchanging one set of domestic duties for another. She could not live vicariously through him, moreover, for his life would be hardly more exciting than hers. She feels stifled by her lot, but she sees no way of escaping it; and so she conforms, with a certain amount of resignation, to the norms of feminine behavior. Her inner uneasiness manifests itself only in her aversion to marriage.

The arrival of Othello has a profound effect upon Desdemona. At first, she is frightened and perhaps a bit repelled. She shakes and fears his looks and speaks dispraisingly of him to Cassio. But she is attracted by the very things she fears, his strangeness, his warrior's mien, his difference in color. He excites her, whereas the young men of her own class and country leave her unmoved. He is an exotic figure who embodies the romantic

possibilities of life from which she has felt excluded. As he tells his tales,
she enters into his experiences, feels for and with him, and participates
imaginatively in his life of adventure. Here, at last, is a man who can
rescue her from the constrictions of her social and sexual identity.
When Othello displays his interest, Desdemona encourages him to
propose, even though this means violating the feminine taboo against
being half the wooer. Her deepest wish is "that heaven had made her such
a man"; but since it has not, the best thing she can do is to marry Othello.
By merging her identity with his, she will gain possession of his exotic
past and will be able to share in his glorious future. Marriage to Othello
offers her a chance to escape the routine existence that had seemed to be
her lot and to enter the world of her dreams. She *must* seize this opportunity, even if it means incurring a general mock and rebelling against her
father.

We can understand now why Desdemona speaks so boldly to the
senate. If she is forced to remain at home while Othello goes off to war,
then the romantic life for which she has sacrificed so much will be denied
her:

> That I did love the Moor to live with him,
> My downright violence, and storm of fortunes,
> May trumpet to the world. My heart's subdu'd
> Even to the very quality of my lord.
> I saw Othello's visage in his mind,
> And to his honours and his valiant parts
> Did I my soul and fortunes consecrate.
> So that, dear lords, if I be left behind,
> A moth of peace, and he go to the war,
> The rites for which I love him are bereft me,
> And I a heavy interim shall support
> By his dear absence. (I, iii)

This speech makes very explicit the role that Othello's vocation has played
in arousing Desdemona's love. A number of commentators have glossed
"quality" as "profession," so that Desdemona is proclaiming, according
to Kittredge's note, that she has "fallen in love with [Othello's] profession
as well as himself." The "rites" for which she loves him are not the
"amorous rites" of which Juliet speaks, but the rites of war, of which she
will be deprived if she is left behind.[5] She is saying that she loves Othello
because he is a valiant warrior, full of honors, who offers her the opportunity to share his adventures.

It is not only Othello's background and profession, of course, but also her personality that accounts for the irresistibility of his appeal to Desdemona. Othello is a powerful, expansive male; and Desdemona, despite the boldness of the behavior that we have so far examined, is basically a self-effacing person. She could hardly be otherwise, given the expectations her society has of women. Brabantio feels that Desdemona has been "enchanted," "bewitched." From a psychological point of view, there is some truth to his theory; for there is a compulsive quality in Desdemona's relationship with Othello that is largely responsible for her rebellious behavior. "The self-effacing person does not choose," says Horney, "but instead is 'spellbound' by certain types," especially by members of the opposite sex who impress him "as stronger and superior" (1950, 243).

The relationship between a self-effacing and an expansive person is often initiated by a blow to the pride of the self-effacing person that makes him psychologically dependent upon the other. This blow often takes the form of an insult, the effects of which can be removed only by gaining the other's approval. In Desdemona's case, the initiating event is the fright she feels in Othello's presence. The effete young gentlemen of her own social set arouse in her no feelings of incompleteness, dependence, or sexual attraction. Her fear of Othello, however, makes her feel weak, and she needs to possess him in order to gain a sense of safety and reassurance. She wishes at once to submerge herself in him and to have him in her power.

It is the combination of Othello's aggressiveness not only with Desdemona's self-effacing tendencies, but also with her frustrated expansive side that accounts for the "magic" of his attraction for her. "Chafing under his enforced humility," says Horney, the self-effacing person "adores in others aggressive qualities which he lacks or which are unavailable to him" (1950, 220). "What accounts specifically for [the self-effacing person's] being fascinated or spellbound—i.e. for the compulsive element in such an infatuation—is the suppression of his expansive drives. . . . To love a proud person, to merge with him, to live vicariously through him would allow him to participate in the mastery of life without having to own it to himself. (Horney 1950, 244). Merging with Othello permits Desdemona to fulfill her expansive fantasies, but in a self-effacing manner, through her devotion to another. She endears herself to Othello through a display of womanly qualities, such as tenderness, admiration, and pity, at the same time that she identifies with his masculinity. As their relationship develops, Othello becomes transformed in her mind into a magnificent being. Since he is attracted to her, her aggrandizement of him becomes a form of self-idealization. It fills her with pride that such a wonderful hero can love her. She consecrates herself to "his honours and his valiant parts." Through him she can realize her craving for glory. Othello is the only man Desdemona has ever met who can fulfill both her self-effacing and her expansive needs. Marriage to him might have provided a workable solution to her inner conflict if he had been a socially acceptable suitor. Because he is not, she is forced to behave in uncharacteristically aggressive ways, pursuing Othello, deceiving her father, defying the mores of her society, and violating her filial duty. She sees herself, no doubt, as doing all this for love. Her need is so great that she can let nothing stand in the way of her relationship with Othello. While she is fighting for her marriage, she suppresses her feelings of guilt; but they contribute later, I think, to her inability to defend herself against her husband's unjust accusations.

"THE INCLINING DESDEMONA"

Desdemona's aggressiveness with Othello on Cassio's behalf must be distinguished from the rebellious behavior that is motivated by her own desires for herself. When she pursues Cassio's interest so vigorously, she is not being self-assertive but is engaged in the typical self-effacing project of fighting for somebody else. "While curtailed in any pursuit on his own behalf," the self-effacing person "is not only free to do things for others but, according to his inner dictates, should be the ultimate of helpfulness, generosity, considerateness, understanding, sympathy, love, and sacrifice" (Horney 1950, 220). This is precisely Iago's understanding of the "inclining Desdemona" who "is of so free, so kind, so apt, so blessed a disposition she holds it a vice in her goodness not to do more than she is requested" (II, iii). Such compliant behavior is glorified by the culture, but Iago understands perfectly well that it is compulsive, and he knows that once Cassio enlists her in his cause, she will behave with an excess of ardor. Desdemona does not disappoint him. She promises Cassio that Othello "shall never rest" until he has granted his suit and that she "shall rather die/ Than give [his] cause away" (III, iii). Her badgering of Othello makes him more vulnerable to Iago's manipulation, as we have seen; and her persistence in the face of his growing irrationality is foolish, to say the least. Even after the tense scene in which Othello demands to be shown the handkerchief, she repeats her promise to Cassio: "What I can do I will; and more I will/ Than for myself I dare" (III, iv).

Desdemona is driven into self-destructive behavior, then, by her need to be "the ultimate of helpfulness, generosity, . . . and sacrifice." "If I do vow a friendship," she assures Cassio, "I'll perform it/ To the last article" (III, iii). She is so moved by Cassio's plea partly because she identifies with him. "Thrice-gentle Cassio" (III, iv) is, like Desdemona, a self-effacing person who wishes to merge with the powerful Othello. Iago plays not only upon Desdemona's need to fulfill the wishes of others, but also upon Cassio's desperate need of Othello's approval. Cassio is so afraid his "General will forget [his] love and service" (III, iii) that he cannot allow his offense to cool before he begins his campaign for re-instatement. He is as importunate with Desdemona as she is with Othello:

> I do beseech you
> That by your virtuous means I may again
> Exist, and be a member of his love
> Whom I with all the office of my heart
> Entirely honour. I would not be delay'd. (III, iv)

We have here what Horney calls a relationship of "morbid dependency" in which the self-effacing person feels that he cannot exist without the expansive person's love. Since Desdemona has such a relationship with Othello herself, Cassio's plight moves her deeply. What has happened to Cassio is precisely what she could not bear to have happen to herself. It is to relieve her own anxieties, therefore, as well as Cassio's, that she so passionately pleads his cause. By doing so, however, she helps to bring about the very things she dreads.

Desdemona's advocacy of Cassio's cause is, finally, a test of her power, of her bargain with Othello. She expects their relationship to be one of mutual compliance in which she will submit to him completely and he will do what she wants in return. In her initial interview with Cassio, she is supremely confident of her ability to influence her husband: "Before Emilia here/ I give thee warrant of thy place" (III, iii). When Othello is hesitant, she invokes her bargain in quite explicit terms: "I wonder in my soul/ What you could ask me that I should deny/ Or stand so mamm'ring on" (III, iii). Othello capitulates, but, as we have seen, he is irritated with Desdemona and uncomfortable with himself. Desdemona is so preoccupied with her own needs that she is blind to what is going on inside her husband.

Now that we have understood the psychological sources of Desdemona's aggressiveness early in the play, we shall not be puzzled by her passivity later. She is aggressive largely in pursuit of goals that are dictated by her self-effacing solution. Her passivity is part of a defensive response when that solution is threatened. The self-effacing person is terrified of hostility, both in himself and in others, and "prefers to give in, to 'understand' and forgive" (Horney 1950, 219). He has a tendency "automatically to shoulder blame . . . he will accuse himself rather than others and tend to scrutinize himself or be apologetic in the face of obviously unwarranted criticism" (Horney 1945, 52). We can see these defenses at work in Desdemona when, after encountering Othello's hostility in the handkerchief scene, she begins to blame herself and to excuse her husband:

> Something sure of state . . .
> Hath puddled his clear spirit; and in such cases
> Men's natures wrangle with inferior things,
> Though great ones are their object.
> . . . .
> Nay, we must think men are not gods,
> Nor of them look for such observancy
> As fits the bridal. Beshrew me much, Emilia,
> I was (unhandsome warrior as I am!)
> Arraigning his unkindness with my soul;
> But now I find I had suborn'd the witness,
> And he's indicted falsely. (III, iv)

The tissue of rationalizations Desdemona develops here serves a number of functions. She wards off her fear of losing Othello's love by constructing a version of reality in which he is really angry with others and is merely displacing his irritation onto her. She defends Othello's character by seeing this kind of behavior as unusual for him, but typical of great men, who take out their frustration on inferior things, such as women. It is not he who is at fault for being cross, but she for having had unreasonable expectations. She handles her anger by accusing herself of having indicted Othello falsely.

"HIS SCORN I APPROVE"

When Othello begins to make his outrageous accusations, Desdemona consistently protests her innocence, but she never accuses him of irrationality or shows more than a fleeting resentment of his unfairness and cruelty. She certainly does not defend herself as vigorously as she had fought for Cassio. Instead, as Bradley observes, she often "acts precisely as if she were guilty" (1964, 206). Despite her protestations of innocence, she seems to feel that she is in some way responsible for Othello's anger. "Alas," she replies, when Othello tells her that he wishes she had never been born, "what ignorant sin have I committed?" (IV, ii). She does not know what she has done to deserve such harsh treatment, but she feels that she must somehow have brought it on herself. When Othello leaves, Desdemona tells Emilia to put out her wedding sheets, presumably as a proof of virginity; and then, when she is alone, she again expresses her sense of culpability: "Tis meet I should be used so, very meet. / How have I been behav'd, that he might stick/ The small'st opinion on my least misuse?" (IV, ii). I do not believe that Desdemona is being ironic here, or expressing indignation. Othello's abuse somehow feels right to her, but she does not know why, and she is genuinely puzzled as to the nature of her offense. Later, when she is singing "Willow," she brings in out of place the line, "Let nobody blame him, his scorn I approve"— (IV, iii). Here again she seems to be feeling that his behavior is justified and that she is to blame.

Given her innocence, Desdemona's reactions are inappropriate, to say the least. How are we to account for them? There is a good clue in Horney's observation that "a person in the clutches of self-contempt often takes *too much abuse* from others. . . . Even if indignant friends call it to his attention [as Emilia does with Desdemona] he tends to minimize or justify the offender's behavior" (1950, 136). There is in such cases a "defenselessness produced by the person's conviction that he does not deserve any better treatment." Desdemona may be so passive under Othello's abuse because she is suffering from self-contempt, the sources of which are largely unconscious. This is why she feels deserving of scorn but bewildered as to the nature of her offense. Her self-hate derives, I believe, from her earlier treatment of her father and from her failure to please her husband.

Desdemona has not deceived Othello in the way in which he imagines, but she has deceived her father. In the first act, she seems to be rigidly defending herself against any feelings of remorse or compassion; she makes no apology and shows Brabantio no tenderness whatsoever. Her feelings of guilt still seem to be repressed in act 4, but they manifest themselves indirectly, in relation to Othello. She has not done anything to Othello to deserve his scorn, but she feels that she deserves it because of what she has done to her father. She reacts to Othello's abuse in a masochistic way; her punishment pays for her guilt and makes her feel better.

It is Desdemona's unconscious guilt toward her father that accounts also for her slavish obedience to her husband. She is compensating for having been a disobedient daughter by being a perfectly dutiful wife. She is so obedient, in fact, that with a clear premonition of Othello's intentions, she prepares herself meekly for bed, sending Emilia away, according to her husband's orders, and leaving instructions that she should be shrouded in one of her wedding sheets. There are a number of other courses she could have followed had she been intent upon saving her life. One of the reasons why she embraces her death, I believe, is an unconscious wish to expiate her guilt toward her father. It is no accident that we learn of his death soon after the death of his daughter. Dramatically, this has the effect of making her death seem not quite so absurd.

Another reason why Desdemona feels self-contempt is that Othello is treating her with scorn. In the face of his abuse, her sense of her own worth sinks rapidly. If he treats her in this way, there must be something terribly wrong with her. Once they transfer their pride to each other, Othello and Desdemona are completely dependent upon each other's love and approval. Just as Desdemona's love confirms Othello's idealized image of himself, making him feel like an emperor, so Othello's love confirms Desdemona's sense of herself as an extraordinary woman, fit to lie by an emperor's side. The sense of grandeur that she derives from being his consort is strong enough to override her feelings of guilt toward her father. The prize has been worth the price. When Othello feels that he has lost Desdemona's love, that she has betrayed him, his idealized image collapses and his self-hate begins to emerge. He must not have been good enough for her after all; perhaps he was too old, too unpolished, or of the wrong color. The same things happens to Desdemona. If Othello is angry with her, then she must have some fault or defect that has cost her his love. She feels an unconscious guilt for not having lived up to her shoulds; she ought to have been able to please him perfectly, and thus to have retained his devotion. The collapse of her dream of glory makes her more vulnerable to feelings of guilt about her earlier transgressions.

When Othello's pride is hurt by Desdemona's supposed infidelity, he says that his "relief/ Must be to loathe her" (III, iii). Given her character structure and situation, Desdemona cannot respond in this way to Othello's mistreatment of her. She has, as Emilia says, forsaken "her father and her country, all her friends" (IV, ii) in order to marry Othello. Without him, she has nothing. She has transferred her pride to Othello, moreover, and must maintain her idealized picture of him to protect her investment. When Othello turns hostile, her solution begins to collapse, but she cannot allow this to happen. She must maintain the value of her bargain at all costs. His harshness becomes in her mind, therefore, a desirable characteristic. When Emilia says "I would you had never seen him," Desdemona replies: "So would not I. My love doth so approve him/ That even his stubbornness, his checks, his frowns—/ . . . have grace and favour in them" (IV, iii). Whatever he does, she will continue to approve him. Even after he has strangled her, she asks Emilia, with her last breath, to "commend" her to her "kind lord" (V, ii). Part of Desdemona's feeling of guilt derives from her need to defend Othello: she blames herself in order to excuse him.

"WHO HATH DONE THIS DEED?"

Desdemona needs to protect not only her pride in Othello, but also her pride in herself. She takes the blame to excuse him and protests her innocence to protect herself. Her emotions at this point are quite confused. She feels at once guilty and innocent, morally perfect and worthy of scorn. She maintains her self-idealization by being the chaste, obedient, and, above all, perfectly loving and self-sacrificial wife. Even if Othello shakes her off "to beggarly divorcement," she will always "love him dearly": "Unkindness may do much;/ And his unkindness may defeat my life,/ But never taint my love" (IV, ii). If she rebelled against him, she could no doubt save her life, but she would then have to admit that Othello was behaving like a maniac and to give up her project of being the perfect wife. As long as she submits, there are two things that will not be changed: her image of Othello and her image of herself. Once Othello turns against her, Desdemona adopts an extreme form of the self-effacing solution, which she maintains to the end. It contributes to her destruction, but it also preserves what is more important to her than life itself, her sense of union with her glorious hero. Her death enacts the scenario she had sketched out earlier in which she would remain perfectly loving even if Othello killed her.

Her death has other functions as well. It satisfies the need for punishment that arises from her feelings of guilt; and it is also a form of retaliation, the only kind that Desdemona can permit herself. She accuses Othello through her innocent suffering—"he'll be sorry when he realizes what he has done." Desdemona does not speak these words, but the plot enacts this fantasy. When Othello learns the truth, he is overwhelmed by his sense of loss and guilt, and all of his love for her returns. Allowing him to kill her is the most awful revenge Desdemona could have on Othello.

When Emilia asks, "who hath done this deed?" Desdemona at first replies, "nobody," and then she says, "I myself" (V, ii). The second answer has an element of truth, for not only does Desdemona cooperate in Othello's plans for her murder, but her submissiveness contributes to Iago's plot and prevents her from attacking her husband's delusion. The best answer, of course, would have been "everybody," including not only the principals but also Cassio and Emilia.

As has often been noted, *Othello* is, more than any other of Shakespeare's plays, a tragedy of character. It presents with remarkable intuitive insight the fatal interaction of three highly complex and disturbed individuals. Each has his bargain threatened in the course of the play, and each reacts in a way that has tragic consequences for himself and others. Iago and Othello react to feeling wronged by seeking revenge, and this is shown to be terribly destructive. When Emilia proposes that wives should retaliate when they have been mistreated, Desdemona is appalled: "Heaven me such uses send/ Not to pick bad from bad, but by bad mend!" (IV, iii). Desdemona has seemed to many critics to represent the Christian ideal of grace, since she loves and forgives the undeserving Othello; and she may have been so intended by Shakespeare, for the rhetoric is much in her favor. What the play actually shows, however, is that her self-effacing goodness is as fatal a flaw as the aggressiveness of Iago and Othello.

CHAPTER 4

King Lear

King Lear, writes Maynard Mack, is "the most remarkable compound of realism and artifice that Shakespearean dramaturgy ever achieved" (1972, 48). "At any given instant," he tells us, "characters may shift along a spectrum between compelling realism and an almost pure representativeness" (1972, 67). Although Mack makes some admirable attempts to describe the compound of realism and artifice in a way that does justice to both of its components, the main thrust of his argument is that, for the most part, the characters have "a mode of being determined by what they . . . represent in the total scheme of the play rather than by any form of psychic 'life' fluctuating among 'motives' " (1972, 66). "More of the play becomes intelligible," he contends, "if a view of it is taken that relates its conventions to literary modes to which it is genuinely akin, such as Romance, Morality play, and Vision, rater than to psychological or realistic drama, with which it has very little in common" (1972, 83). "In *Lear,*" he proclaims, "even more than in *Macbeth,* significance holds plot and character in an iron grasp" (1972, 74).

Mack is correct in stressing *King Lear's* combination of artifice and realism, but wrong, I believe, in denying its affinity with psychological drama. He acknowledges its realistic components, but then loses sight of them in the course of analyzing the play as parable, emblem, and allegory. While there is much in the play that should be understood in this way, there is also a great deal of psychological detail that simply will be lost unless we analyze *King Lear* as, in part at least, a highly realistic drama. Lear is an imagined human being who experiences a series of very complicated emotions. He speaks a large number of lines, many of which are of primary interest for their detailed expression of his internal states. To see Lear's speeches as always "more fully in the service of the vision of the play as a whole than true to a consistent interior reality" (1972, 68), as Mack insists we should, is to miss a large part of Shakespeare's achievement.

From a thematic point of view, *King Lear* seems to be a story of moral growth through suffering. The play has a tragic education plot in which the protagonist errs, suffers as a result of his errors, and develops insight, compassion, and a better set of values as a result of his suffering. His errors set in motion a chain of events, however, that results in his destruction. By the end of the play, he is purged of his faults and awakened to reality, but the change comes too late to save him from the consequences of his mistakes. Not all critics see Lear's development in this way, of course, but the majority do, and they tend to focus upon those of his speeches that fit the education pattern. The pattern is reinforced by the subplot, in which Gloucester undergoes a similar development, and by the commentary of Edgar, whose description of himself as a poor man "who, by the art of known and feeling sorrows,/ Am pregnant to good pity" (IV, vi) articulates the process of moral growth through suffering.

So much emphasis has been placed upon the positive side of Lear's development that critics have tended to lose sight of the fact that this is a play about a man who is driven out of his mind by a series of blows to his psyche. Criticism that focuses upon what Lear's suffering does *for* him needs to be supplemented by an analysis of its destructive effect. Like Hamlet, Iago, and Othello, Lear has a bargain with fate that is the product of his predominant strategy of defense. When his claims are not honored, his pride system is threatened, and he becomes overwhelmed by rage and anxiety. He makes desperate efforts to rebuild his defenses, but nothing avails, and he finally goes mad as a result of his inability to cope with the realities that have broken in upon him. Cordelia's forgiveness gives new meaning to his life, and, for a time, it looks as though his crisis has passed; but her death destroys his new solution and drives him into the hallucinatory state in which he expires. When we look at Lear's development from a psychological point of view, we shall see that though he does gain in awareness and has his sympathies enlarged, his growth is more intermittent and less complete than most critics would have us believe.

King Lear is not only a great character study but is also the most thematically complex of Shakespeare's tragedies. There has been a great deal of debate about what kind of universe the play is affirming. I shall try to clarify this issue by observing what happens to the strategies of defense that are embraced by the various characters. Another controversial aspect of the play is the gloomy ending produced by the death of Cordelia. I shall show how this ending fits into one of the dominant fantasies of the play, the punishment of the unjust parent, in a way that permits the wronged child to remain virtuous.

THE LOVE TEST

Most critics maintain that it is inappropriate to try to explain the motivation behind Lear's behavior in the opening scene. It is difficult, I grant, to understand Lear's motives as the scene unfolds, nor need we do so to find it dramatically effective. His behavior is intelligible in retrospect, however, after we have seen enough of him to form an idea of his character. This is the way in which we understand people in life and imagined human beings in literature: their actions come to make sense as we learn more about them. Not only is it possible, but it is quite important to our experience of the play as a whole to comprehend Lear's state of mind at the beginning; for if we do not, we cannot appreciate the causes of his psychological deterioration and the significance of his changes in attitude.

The precipitating event in this play is not the death of a father and a mother's remarriage, or failure to gain promotion, or loss of faith in a wife, but the failure of a daughter to produce the expected flattery. The disparity between Cordelia's provocation and Lear's response is a measure of Lear's irrationality. To understand why Lear reacts to Cordelia as he does, we must first understand what her behavior means to him; and, in order to do this, we must reconstruct the habits of mind, the emotional needs, and the fantasies that lay behind his division of the kingdom among his daughters and his proposal of the love test.

Lear is, like Richard II, a predominantly narcissistic person whose psychology has been profoundly affected by the experience of being a king.[1] His royal power has given him delusions of omnipotence. Indeed, an important part of his education lies in his becoming aware of these delusions and realizing his human limitations:

> They flatter'd me like a dog, and told me I had the white hairs in my beard
> ere the black ones were there. To say "ay" and "no" to everything I said!
> "Ay" and "no" too was no good divinity. When the rain came to wet me
> once, and the wind to make me chatter; when the thunder would not peace at
> my bidding; there I found 'em, there I smelt 'em out. Go to, they are not men

o' their words! They told me I was everything. 'Tis a lie—I am not ague-
proof. (IV, vi)

Lear has, it seems, been so shielded from the harsh realities of life that he
feels immune to the violence of the elements and the frailties of the flesh.
He does not know what the world is really like or what it is to be a man. At
court, his will has been law, and he has come to expect even the phenomena of nature to do his bidding. In the course of the play, he gains
insight not only into his human limitations, but also into some of the
sources of his mistakes about himself. Much like Richard, he attributes his
delusions to the effects of flattery. He is defending himself here by blaming others, but there is, nonetheless, much truth in his analysis. Surrounded as he has been for so many years by constant praise, deference,
and hypocrisy, it is no wonder that he is a poor judge of others and that he
"hath ever but slenderly known himself" (I, i).

The narcissistic person, observed Horney, was often "the favored and
admired child" (1950, 194). Lear has been treated like a spoiled child all
his life, and, as a result, he has become permanently infantile. The function of others is to satisfy his desires; if they do not do this, they have no
reason for existence. "Better thou/ Hadst not been born," he tells Cordelia, "than not t' have pleased me better" (I, i). Constant indulgence by
others has led him to expect immediate gratification, and he becomes
petulant at the slightest frustration. In the first two acts, we often see him
impatiently demanding food, service or attention. He is very jealous of his
prerogatives and becomes petulant at any real or imagined opposition. As
is typical in the narcissistic person, his idealized image is not compensatory in nature, but is derived from the special treatment he has received from
others.

Since he has always felt like his glorified self, Lear's project is not to
actualize his idealized image, but to maintain it. His bargain with fate is
that if he insists upon being treated in accordance with his exalted status,
his claims will have to be honored. Lear's claims are enormous, but since
he does not have to drive himself to become his idealized image, his
shoulds are unusually weak. His most powerful inner dictate is that he
should hold onto his claims. He does not recognize a larger system of
duties to which he is subject. He regards crown and country as personal
possessions and does not seem to comprehend that people have duties
other than to please him. This is why he cannot recognize the justice of
Kent's and Cordelia's behavior in the opening scene. The play begins with
Lear violating his duties both as king and as father, and it shows the price

he must pay in consequence. His folly has usually been discussed in ethical terms, but it also has a psychological dimension.

Lear seems to have a number of motives for giving up his throne and dividing his kingdom among his daughters. The major reason he gives is that he wants to "shake all cares and business from [his] age" and "Unburden'd crawl toward death" (I, i). Despite his advanced years, Lear shows no signs of inability to carry out his functions; he seems to be using his age as an excuse for greater self-indulgence. He has a dream of an idyllic state in which he will have all the perquisites of the crown while being spared its responsibilities. Instead of having to care for the kingdom, he will be cared for by his worshipful daughters, especially Cordelia, and he will be free to devote himself to riding, hunting, and other royal amusements. He does not realize that he is actually giving up his power; in his fantasy he will still be a commanding figure whose word will be law and who will be surrounded by obsequious followers. Indeed, for Lear the division of the kingdom is not a relinquishment, but is rather an exercise of power. Faced with the fact that he cannot have many more years to live, he does not wait to be stripped of his authority by death but rather seeks to preside over the distribution of his own estate and to reap the rewards of his magnanimity. His abdication is not a submission to fate, but an attempt to master it.

It is an attempt also, as many have observed, to buy the love of his daughters. In Lear's mind what he is doing is not only wise, since it will prevent future strife, but it is also incredibly generous, and he expects his daughters' undying gratitude. He is trying to put them so deeply in his debt that they will have to devote their lives to repaying him. By giving them all, he expects to get all from them in return. His generosity will justify his most extravagant claims.

There is, then, a self-effacing component to Lear's behavior as well as a narcissistic one. It seems evident that he has a great need of his daughters' devotion and that he is insecure about getting it. Perhaps with his advancing age he feels an increased dependency upon his children and wishes to guarantee their affection. He may be aware at some level of his deficiencies as a father, especially to Goneril and Regan, whose resentment he may sense. He seems to want to show that he *is* a kind, generous, loving father. Perhaps he hopes to placate them and to assure himself of their devotion by giving each of them a third of the kingdom. If so, it is quite blind of him to show favoritism once again to Cordelia. This will hardly endear him to his older daughters or prevent future strife. It is on Cordelia, of course, that he is really depending for tender loving care. He may feel threatened by her impending marriage and have a need to secure her through his generosity. Indeed, the whole plan may have been designed to provide his youngest daughter with a patrimony and himself with a secure haven. Shakespeare does not give us enough information to verify any of these explanations, though all of them are plausible and consistent with the evidence we have. What he does make plain is that Lear has deep needs for love, for care, and for adulation from his daughters and that he hopes to have these needs fulfilled through his division of the kingdom.

Lear proposes the love test as a means of getting an immediate return on his investment, a first installment, as it were, of the adulation with which he expects to be regaled for the rest of his life. What he is looking for is clear from the speeches of Goneril and Regan, who have excellent insight into his character and who give him exactly what he wants. The climax is to come in the speech of Cordelia, who loves him most, whom he loves most, and who is to receive the most opulent portion. The object of the love test is not to determine who shall get the largest share, but to give his daughters an opportunity to begin to repay him for what he has already decided to give; and since he is going to give Cordelia the most, he expects the most from her in return. Cordelia's response is so disappointing not only because she will not try to outdo her sisters in professions of devotion, but also because when she does speak, she says precisely what Lear does not want to hear. He wants to be assured that he alone counts, that nothing else matters, that her affection will not diminish when she takes a husband; but she tells him that she loves him "according to [her] bond; no more nor less" and that when she marries, her husband will take half of her love with him.

CORDELIA'S COMPULSIVENESS

Lear's reaction to Cordelia is so extreme as to seem unintelligible to many critics. It makes sense, I believe, in the light of his needs and his expectations. But before we analyze Lear's response, we must first have a look at Cordelia's behavior, for it is this that precipitates his outrage. Lear is not the only irrational party in this scene; the catastrophe with which the play begins is the product of a network of interactions between all the members of the family. Lear misconstrues Cordelia, to be sure; but he is correct about her pride and her lack of tenderness. There is something going on in Cordelia that compels her to be cold and ungiving and that prevents her from doing anything to reassure her father, once he is upset, or to assuage his anger. Cordelia's response to her father is as much in need of explanation as is his response to her. Cordelia is not a very fully developed character, but like many of the minor characters in this play, she is a distinct psychological type whose behavior is intelligible in the light of her defense system.

When Cordelia declares that she can say nothing in order to draw a third more opulent than her sister, she is not so much withholding from Lear the professions of love he desires as refusing to behave in a way that would make her the same as her sisters. Some critics feel that she is deeply angry with her father because of his irrational demands, and this may be so; but I believe that she is above all threatened by the pressure she is under to abandon her own values and to become like the creatures she despises. Her asides after the speeches of Goneril and Regan indicate her growing anxiety. Their extravagant expressions of devotion will render an honest statement of her own feelings feeble by comparison. She knows that her sisters are being hypocritical, and she cannot bear to behave like them, but she feels that this is what she would have to do in order to satisfy her father. She responds in a way that calls attention to the impropriety of her sister's replies and unmistakably distinguishes her from them:

> Why have my sisters husbands, if they say
> They love you all? Haply, when I shall wed.
> That lord whose hand must take my plight shall carry
> Half my love with him, half my care and duty.
> Sure I shall never marry like my sisters,
> To love my father all. (I, i)

These words have a terrible impact on Lear, but they are addressed less to him than to Goneril and Regan.

Cordelia's compulsive need to dissociate herself from her sisters makes her unable to respond to the other elements in the situation and has tragic consequences for both herself and her father. Cordelia is a person who cares above all about rectitude and self-respect, and her response to Lear is in keeping with her perfectionistic attitudes: "I love your Majesty/ According to my bond; no more nor less" (I, i). This reply is unimpeachably correct, as that other perfectionist, Kent, testifies; but it is cold, and it is ill-adapted to the situation. For Cordelia, Goneril and Regan embody all of the qualities that her solution condemns. She would become her despised self if she ever behaved like them.

It is her fear of incurring self-hate that prevents Cordelia from reassuring her father after he has been hurt and from attempting to assuage his anger. It is evident that she has been tender toward Lear in the past, and we see her behave in a most loving way upon her return to England; but the situation in the opening scene freezes her emotions. She seems afraid of giving any sign of warmth or concern. When she speaks again in this scene, it is to defend herself against her father's deprecations and to make sure France knows she has done nothing wrong:

> I yet beseech your Majesty,
> If for I want that glib and oily art
> To speak and purpose not, since what I well intend,
> I'll do't before I speak—that you make known
> It is no vicious blot, murder, or foulness,
> Nor unchaste action or dishonoured step,
> That hath depriv'd me of your grace and favour;
> But even for want of that for which I am richer—
> A still-soliciting eye, and such a tongue
> As I am glad I have not, though not to have it
> Hath lost me in your liking. (I, i)

Cordelia is here expressing pride in herself for not being like her sisters and is telling her father, in effect, that she would rather lose his favor than become like them. Again, it is important to observe that she makes no effort to correct his misunderstanding, to soothe his ruffled feelings, or to remind him of past evidences of her devotion, even though she knows that he has done a very destructive thing, not only to her, but to himself and the kingdom. She is afraid to be winning, to profess affection. The only thing she can profess is her own rectitude.

It may seem strange that even before France rescues her from the consequences of Lear's fury by choosing her to be his queen, Cordelia does not seem to be particularly upset about what has happened. This, too, can be explained in terms of her perfectionism. If she were predominantly self-effacing, as her later lack of resentment, forgiveness of injuries, and self-sacrificial behavior might lead us to suspect, she would be filled with anxiety by Lear's rejection and would have an overwhelming need to win him back. Her sense of worth does not depend, however, upon the love and approval of others, but upon her self-approbation; and this she has not lost. She has been treated very unfairly, but she never protests, for the loss of her father's favor and of her third of the kingdom is the price she has had to pay to maintain her self-image, and she has no regrets. She cannot be made really miserable as long as her pride in herself is intact.

THE COLLAPSE OF LEAR'S FANTASY

Lear's fantasy has been unfolding as he had dreamed it would until he encounters Cordelia's "Nothing." His initial response is not anger but incredulity—"Nothing?" He cannot believe, in view of the performance of his other daughters and his own kind intentions, that Cordelia will not give him what he wants; and so he asks her twice to mend her speech. Cordelia's statement that she loves him according to her bond is a denial of the bargain he is making with his daughters and a frustration of his irrational claims. Because he is giving his daughters more than they have a right to expect, he feels justified in demanding from them more than a mere fulfillment of their duty. Lear is most hurt by Cordelia's insistence that she "shall never marry like [her] sisters,/ To love [her] father all." He has loved her more than anyone else, and he needs a special sign of love from her, an assurance that he can count on her to care for him in his declining years.

It is not difficult to understand why Lear is deeply hurt by what he takes to be Cordelia's unloving behavior, nor why he responds with anger. His rage, however, is greatly in excess of the occasion, as is the magnitude of his retaliation. Lear's retaliation is so extreme because of his need to restore his pride. Cordelia's violation of his claims raises the possibility that they have no solid foundation and that others will also violate them. His rage is a way of affirming his claims, and his punishment of Cordelia serves as a warning to others that they had better not repeat the offense. Lear is deeply humiliated at being rejected (as he feels) in such a public way by the person upon whom he had meant to bestow the greatest sign of his favor. He is trying to humiliate her in return and to make himself invulnerable to further hurts by denying his need for her love and rejecting her completely. He wards off the self-doubts that have been aroused by Cordelia's frustration of his wishes by attributing his disappointment to her distorted nature. Above all, Lear is attempting to demonstrate his power. Since he cannot get Cordelia to do what he wants by means of his generosity, he tries to deprive her of everything, including a husband, and to restore in this way his sense of potency. Lear emerges from this scene as the greatest victim of his spite. Cordelia is claimed by France; and Lear is left, deprived of her support, to the "professed bosoms" of his "pelican daughters."

"TO PLAINNESS HONOUR'S BOUND"

Lear behaves in a self-defeating way again with Kent when that loyal counselor defends Cordelia, accuses him of folly, and urges him to revoke his gift to Goneril and Regan. Here, too, a threat to his pride produces blinding rage and excessive retaliation. Once again, however, the irrationality is not all on Lear's side; there is something compulsive in Kent's reaction as well. In the interaction between these two, Lear behaves much as he had with Cordelia, and Kent behaves much as Cordelia had with her father. Kent's counsel is good, just as Cordelia's response is proper; but his behavior, like hers, is provocative, and for similar reasons.

Kent, too, is a perfectionist, which is why he and Cordelia have such a strong admiration for each other. Just as Cordelia has a need to preserve her rectitude in the face of her father's demands and her sisters' example, so Kent has a need to resist the pressure upon him to hold his tongue. Kent speaks not so much out of a concern for Lear, which would have been better served by a greater degree of tact, as out of a need to obey his own inner dictates: "Think'st thou that duty shall have dread to speak/ When power to flattery bows? To plainness honour's bound/ When majesty falls to folly." Lear's anger and his threats only make Kent all the more determined to speak his mind, and in the bluntest of terms. Otherwise, he would feel like the sycophants by whom Lear is surrounded; and his self-hate would be unbearable. His martyrdom, like Cordelia's, is the mark of his virtue.

Kent's motives in this scene become clearer when we see his interaction with Oswald later. "No contraries hold more antipathy," he proclaims "Than I and such a knave" (II, ii). Kent is a man who stands up for what is right, whatever the consequences, even to the King. Oswald is a mere instrument of his mistress's will—in Cornwall's term, a "silly-ducking observant" (II, ii). Kent is threatened by "Such smiling rogues as these" who "smooth every passion/ That in the natures of their lords rebel" and know "naught (like dogs) but following" (II, ii). Oswald is to Kent what Goneril and Regan are to Cordelia, an embodiment of his despised self, of what he would most hate to become. In the opening scene, Kent feels under pressure to behave in the contemptible way he has just described. Like Cordelia, he responds in terms of his need to protect his pride, independently of what the situation calls for or of how Lear will react. He will do his duty and preserve his honor whatever the cost.

RHETORIC VERSUS MIMESIS

Despite its elements of ritual and romance, the opening scene of *King Lear* is a taut psychological drama in which the characters' reactions to each other are dictated by their emotional needs and their strategies of defense. Lear, Cordelia, and Kent, and even Goneril and Regan, are to be understood not only in terms of theme and archetype, but also as imagined human beings whose behavior is inwardly motivated. Lear is the dominant figure, but his personality forms only one component in a set of complex interactions. Goneril and Regan respond to his demand for love in a way that is typical of arrogant-vindictive people: in order to gain the prize being dangled before them, they do not hesitate to profess sentiments they despise and that are the opposite of what they really feel. As we have seen, it is the combination of her father's demands, her sisters' response, and her own psychological needs that makes Cordelia so punctilious and ungiving. If she were not so afraid of seeming to be like her sisters, she would have been able to show Lear some warmth, and he might not have reacted in such an explosive manner. Similarly, if Kent had not had to prove that he is not one of the smiling rogues he so despises, he would have been able to give Lear his good advice in a less offensive manner; and, at the least, he would not have been banished. It is difficult to say how much difference it would have made if Kent and Cordelia had been less rigid, given the degree of Lear's irrationality, but it is clear that their defensive behavior makes things worse and contributes to the tragedy.

I am not suggesting, of course, that my view of Cordelia and Kent is the one Shakespeare means us to have. The rhetoric of the opening scene works strongly in favor of these characters, who are presented as the innocent victims of Lear's irrationality. In the thematic structure of the play, they function as truth-tellers, moral norms, Lear's good angels. The play begins with them being unfairly condemned, and it moves toward their vindication as Lear comes to see how loving and loyal they are and how monstrous are Goneril and Regan. My view of Cordelia and Kent is at odds with Shakespeare's because there is a conflict between Shakespeare's psychological portrait of these characters and the rhetoric with which he surrounds them. This often occurs when characters combine aesthetic, illustrative, and mimetic functions. The tension between Kent's illustrative and mimetic aspects has aroused little comment that I know of; but there has been considerable controversy about Cordelia. Some critics agree with Kent that she "justly think'st and has most rightly said" (I, i), while others have been disturbed, as was Coleridge, by "some little faulty admixture of pride and sullenness" in her response to her father (quoted in Harrison and McDonnel 1962, 94). Both groups of critics are partially correct. One group is responding to Cordelia's illustrative function, while the other is reacting to the mimetic portrait. It is simply not true, as Maynard Mack contended, that in this play "significance holds . . . character in an iron grasp" (1972, 74). It is because character is often in conflict with significance that the play produces so many confusing effects.

There is no confusion of effect concerning Lear in the opening scene. The play begins as a tragedy of character in which the protagonist's flaws are chiefly responsible for the catastrophe. Goneril and Regan are necessary but not sufficient causes, for it is Lear who gives them the power to hurt him. The comments of Kent, of France, of Goneril and Regan in the first scene and of Gloucester in the second make clear the baselessness and folly of Lear's behavior. They are quite in keeping with a psychological analysis of his character. Theme and mimesis are in complete harmony here.

Shakespeare's treatment of Lear begins to change toward the end of the first act. As Lear is treated more and more harshly by his daughters, our sympathies shift to him. Cordelia's marriage to France and the loyalty of Kent defuse the anger toward Lear that had been generated by the opening scene. Since one of his victims has prospered and the other has returned to serve him, his injustice to them does not continue to feed our indignation. The Fool evokes compassion for Lear by emphasizing what an awful thing he has done to himself and by giving us a glimpse of the self-hate he must be feeling. Lear would not tolerate his bitter jibes if they did not satisfy a need for self-condemnation. He has brought his suffering upon himself, but it seems terribly unfair that he should be receiving it at the hands of these daughters, whom he has not wronged as he has Cordelia. Despite his mistakes, moreover, he is still a father and a king, and it is painful to see him treated with such disrespect. The villain of the opening scene has become the wronged and suffering victim.

This shift in Shakespeare's treatment of Lear tends to obscure certain aspects of his psychological portrait. Though it is possible to reconstruct Lear's motivations in the opening scene, he becomes much more of a mimetic character as the play proceeds and we are given a detailed picture of his actions and feelings. If we respond to the rhetoric of the play, however, we shall see him less and less as the irascible, vindictive, overly impetuous man of the opening scene and more and more as a man who is reacting in the only way possible to a truly horrifying situation. As the mistreatment of Lear becomes increasingly outrageous, his responses come to seem normal. His stupendous rages, and even his madness, are presented as natural reactions to the extremity of his situation.

BLOWS AND DEFENSES

I do not wish to deny the awfulness of what is done to Lear by his daughters, but I do wish to emphasize the fact that he reacts in terms of his individual psychology. It is easy to recognize the irrationality of his rage in the opening scene since it is so out of proportion to its external causes. The provocations of Goneril and Regan are so great that we may lose sight of the fact that Lear is still overreacting. Everyone would find it difficult to cope with the situation by which he is confronted, but not everyone would react to it with the same self-destructive fury. Lear is overwhelmed by the actions of his daughters not only because they are so monstrous, but also because they constitute a series of unbearable blows to his pride. Given the intensity of his reactions to the relatively minor frustrations of the opening scene, it is not surprising that he is driven mad by the total rejection of his claims that he encounters later.

The affronts to Lear begin with Oswald's impertinence, to which he responds with characteristic choler. The first truly severe blow to his pride comes when Goneril complains of his "insolent retinue" and warns him that if he should sanction their behavior, "the fault / Would not scape censure" (I, iv). Lear is stunned, incredulous, unable to assimilate the fact that he is being spoken to in this way by his daughter. His sense of identity is profoundly threatened by such disrespect. It is no wonder, then, that he explodes with rage when Goneril asks him to reduce his train and threatens to "take the thing she begs" if he does not accede to her desire. He has given her half of the kingdom, and he has anticipated in return a constant display of gratitude and affection. Goneril, however, will not even honor the public and minimal terms of his bargain, his reservation of a hundred knights to be supported by his daughters. Her behavior is a shattering blow to his dream of an honored old age and to his sense of potency and grandeur.

Lear's habitual response to anything that he perceives as a threat is to restore his pride through immediate retaliation. Now that he has given up his power, however, he cannot punish the offender. All he can do is to call Goneril names and bestow a series of curses upon her. The violence of his language is a substitute for the actual violence that he would like to visit upon his daughter. *King Lear* is a play of magnificently articulated anger. Hamlet's rage is that of a son toward a mother, and he represses it until the closet scene. Lear's is the rage of a father toward his children, and he expresses it from the beginning without inhibition. His rage grows greater and greater not only because he is subject to increasingly severe indignities, but also because of his inability to retaliate. His verbal fireworks are an effort to reduce the pressure of his frustrated vindictiveness and to give himself a feeling of power. He counts upon his position as father and king to have a magical influence with the gods. His curses are a way of affirming his claims and maintaining his sense of importance.

In this scene (I, iv), we see Lear being treated with more disrespect than he has ever encountered in his life, at the very time when he feels most deserving of affection. He has received so far only a small taste of the mistreatment he is in for, but he fears already that he is going mad (I, v). Many things are driving Lear mad, but the chief of them is his sense of the unfairness of Goneril's behavior, of her monstrous ingratitude. Lear has both a narcissistic bargain with fate in which he feels entitled to be indulged because of his status as a special person and a self-effacing bargain with his daughters in which he is entitled to overwhelming love and gratitude for having been "so kind a father!" (I, v). Goneril's behavior violates both of these bargains, and it is therefore unbearable. In evaluating Lear's response, we must remember that he has not heard Goneril's conversations with Regan and with Oswald, as we have, and that she has not begun to display the full measure of her viciousness. Even before he discovers the loss of fifty followers, he calls her a "marble-hearted fiend," a "detested kite," and a "degenerate bastard" (I, iv). Lear's abusiveness is appropriate to the true nature of his daughter, but here it is in excess of the occasion, as is the vehemence of his curses. Bad as Goneril is in act 1, scene 4, nothing has happened as yet to justify the ferocity of Lear's rage or to threaten with madness a man who was not extremely vulnerable.

Lear's experience with Regan is a repetition of his experiences with Goneril, only now the situation is much more serious, since she is his last resource. Given his performance with Cordelia and Goneril, Lear is remarkably self-controlled with Regan and Cornwall. When Regan tells him that he should return to her sister and ask forgiveness, Lear explodes with rage, but he directs it toward Goneril, though Regan gets the message that similar curses are in store for her if she should cross him. Angry as he is with Regan, Lear simply cannot afford to be rejected by her, and so he lets his rage out in safe ways and refuses to register the full meaning of her behavior. This is in contrast to his almost immediate denunciations of Cordelia and Goneril and is a sign of his desperation.

Lear is brought to a crisis when he is forced to realize that Regan, too, is against him. She asks why he needs even fifty followers and tells him to bring no more than twenty-five when he comes to her. Lear capitulates for the first time; despite his earlier protestation that he would "rather . . . abjure all roofs" than return to Goneril, he now says that he will go with her. Goneril and Regan close in: what needs he twenty-five, ten, five, or even one? At first Lear delivers an eloquent response to their arguments ("O, reason not the need!"). Man needs more than the bare necessities; he requires symbols to attest to his status. He soon begins to lose control, however, and in the remainder of the speech he gives passionate expression to the chaotic emotions that are warring within him:

> But, for true need—
> You heavens, give me that patience, patience I need!
> You see me here, you gods, a poor old man,
> As full of grief as age; wretched in both.
> If it be you that stirs these daughters' hearts
> Against their father, fool me not so much
> To bear it tamely; touch me with noble anger,
> And let not women's weapons, water drops,
> Stain my man's cheeks! No, you unnatural hags!
> I will have such revenges on you both
> That all the world shall—I will do such things—
> What they are yet, I know not; but they shall be
> The terrors of the earth! You think I'll weep.
> No, I'll not weep.
> I have full cause of weeping, but this heart
> Shall break into a hundred thousand flaws
> Or ere I'll weep. O fool, I shall go mad! (II, iv)

Lear begins by asking the heavens to give him patience, but within a few lines, he is asking the gods to touch him "with noble anger." This is the first of several efforts by Lear to be patient, none of which is successful. A kind of stoical acceptance of the slings and arrows of outrageous fortune is one means by which he could attempt to cope with his situation, but, like Hamlet, he is too full of rage for this, and it is alien to his character structure. To resign himself to what is happening would mean giving up his bargain with fate, and, along with it, his claims and his idealized image. Rage, however, constitutes an affirmation of his claims, an insistence that he will never tolerate being treated badly. Lear's rage signifies his nonacceptance of what has happened. To bear it tamely is to be a weakling and fool.

Lear welcomes his anger not only as a means of affirming his claims, but also as a way of protecting himself against the self-effacing trends that are threatening to emerge. At first he turns to the heavens as his ally, but he soon begins to suspect them of turning his daughters' hearts against him. He is overcome by the pathos of his situation: he is "a poor old man,/ As full of grief as age," who has been betrayed by both his daughters and the heavens, and he feels himself to be on the verge of tears. He had felt shame when Goneril made him weep (I, iv) and the same feeling is operative here. In addition, he is fighting an impulse to move his daughters to compassion by displaying himself as pathetic. To do this would be to try to control the world in a feminine way, through tears and suffering. The use of such "women's weapons" would fill him with self-hate, and it is partly to defend himself against this that he calls for a "noble anger."

Anger is the response that is most in keeping with Lear's sense of his dignity and power. His impulse, as always, is to restore his pride through retaliation. The trouble with anger as a coping strategy here, however, is that there is no way he can act it out. He wants to visit revenges upon his daughters that will be "the terrors of the earth," but he has no concrete ideas as to what he might do. Even as he delivers them he recognizes that his threats are empty, and he is overcome once again with an impulse to weep. He would rather see his heart break into a hundred thousand pieces, however, than give them that satisfaction.

The speech ends with Lear telling the Fool that he is going to go mad. He feels this way because he can find no means of coping with his situation. Goneril and Regan seem all-powerful and he seems totally helpless. Cordelia is coming to the rescue, but Lear knows nothing of this. He moves in this speech from one defensive strategy to another, but nothing will work. He is stymied, much as Hamlet was at the end of the "To be or not to be" soliloquy. He cannot endure, he cannot submit, and he cannot retaliate. It is no wonder that he feels overwhelmed.

"IN SUCH A NIGHT AS THIS!"

Being shut out in the storm is the ultimate outrage, the one that causes Lear finally to lose his mind. There is a good deal of rhetoric in the play that emphasizes the monstrousness of Goneril's and Regan's behavior; their treatment of Lear is a violation of what is owed not only to his age, rank, and paternity, but to his bare humanity. Even animals deserve shelter in such a tempest: "Mine enemy's dog," says Cordelia, "Though he had bit me," should "have stood that night/ Against my fire" (IV, vii). The ferocity of the storm is also emphasized to increase our sense of outrage and to explain its effects upon Lear. Kent has never seen "such sheets of fire, such bursts of horrid thunder" (III, ii).

Confronted with such an extreme situation, Lear has a series of extreme reactions, but it is important to recognize once again that his reactions are also the product of his character. "In high rage" (II, iv), he goes out into the storm of his own volition, and he seems to relish its violence. Critics have treated the storm scenes in largely thematic terms, but whatever their illustrative significance, Lear's mental states are portrayed in great detail and with marvelous psychological insight. His relationship to the storm is very complicated and goes through a number of stages.

At first the storm seems to relieve the pressure on Lear by providing an outlet for his violent emotions and restoring his sense of potency:

> Blow, winds, and crack your cheeks! rage! blow!
> You cataracts and hurricanoes, spout
> Till you have drench'd our steeples, drown'd the cocks!
> You sulph'rous and thought-executing fires,
> Vaunt-couriers to oak-cleaving thunderbolts,
> Singe my white head! And thou, all-shaking thunder,
> Strike flat the thick rotundity o' th' world,
> Crack Nature's moulds, all germains spill at once,
> That make ingrateful man! (III, ii)

Lear here identifies with the storm and sees it as an expression of his rage, an externalization of his fury. He invokes the storm's destructiveness as a way of gaining a sense of power; the storm is to be the instrument of his revenge. He had said that he would do things that would be "the terrors of the earth" (II, iv), and now he asks the storm to punish ungrateful man by bringing the race to an end. This gives us a good idea of the magnitude of his sense of injury and the intensity of his vindictive impulses. The only thing that will assuage his rage at the injustice of his fate is the destruction of the species.

In one part of the above speech Lear invites the thunderbolts to singe his white head. This points to another aspect of his relation to the storm; and it leads, I think, to the next speech in which he sees himself no longer as the director of the storm's violence but as its victim. Lear invites the

pelting of the storm in this and other speeches because he wants to dramatize the awful state to which he has been reduced by the injustice of his
daughters and to feed in this way both his rage and self-pity. His first
speech is dominated by rage and the next by self-pity:

> Rumble thy bellyful! Spit, fire! spout, rain!
> Nor rain, wind, thunder, fire are my daughters.
> I tax not you, you elements, with unkindness.
> I never gave you kingdom, call'd you children,
> You owe me no subscription. Then let fall
> Your horrible pleasure. Here I stand your slave,
> A poor, infirm, weak, and despis'd old man.
> But yet I call you servile ministers,
> That will with two pernicious daughters join
> Your high-engender'd battles 'gainst a head
> So old and white as this! O! O! 'tis foul! (III, ii)

In these two speeches taken together, Lear moves from seeing the storm as
his agent, to seeing the storm as neutral, to seeing the storm as the
minister of his daughters; and his sense of his own potency diminishes
dramatically.

Lear cannot see the storm as his agent and himself as its object
simultaneously. He moves, therefore, from identifying with it to seeing it
as neutral. It is not the instrument of his rage, but neither is he angry with
it, since he has no claims upon it, as he has upon his daughters, and it is
not directed against him personally. Since he never gave it kingdom, he
cannot tax it with unkindness. As his self-pity grows, however, he comes
to feel the storm to be the agent of his daughters, and he is overcome by
the pathos and injustice of his situation. There is a similar situation at the
end of act 2 in which Lear sees the gods first as his allies and then as the
forces behind the malevolence of his daughters. There Lear began with an
appeal for patience; here he turns to patience after his sense of power
dissipates and his rage gives way to undignified self-pity: "No, I will be
the pattern of all patience; I will say nothing."

Lear's next effort at obtaining relief takes the form of seeing the
storm as an agent of the gods, who will punish sinners—most of all,
presumably, those who have sinned against him. This is triggered by
Kent's remark that "Man's nature cannot carry/ Th' affliction nor the
fear," which arouses Lear's hope that the storm will strike terror into those
who have so far escaped punishment:

> Let the great gods,
> That keep this dreadful pudder o'er our heads,

Find out their enemies now. Tremble, thou wretch,
That hast within thee undivulged crimes
Unwhipp'd of justice. Hide thee, thou bloody hand;
Thou perjur'd, and thou simular of virtue
That art incestuous. Caitiff, in pieces shake
That under covert and convenient seeming
Hast practis'd on man's life. Close pent-up guilts,
Rive your concealing continents, and cry
These dreadful summoners grace. I am a man
More sinn'd against than sinning. (III, ii)

As we have seen, what is most unbearable to Lear is his sense of the injustice with which he has been treated by his daughters. Since they are now in authority, there is nowhere he can go to obtain redress of his grievances, and he is powerless to avenge himself. To satisfy his needs, he turns the storm here into a minister of justice that will find out those who have hitherto sinned with impunity. The sins he mentions are not specifically those of his daughters, though there seems little doubt that at the bottom of this speech is a hope that the fury of the storm will break down the icy composure of even a Goneril and a Regan and will perhaps induce them to repent. The failure of his personal bargain leads Lear, like Hamlet, to a vision of widespread corruption.

The concluding sentence of the speech—"I am a man/ More sinn'd against than sinning"—does not follow logically from what has gone before, but its psychological connection is not difficult to infer. Although Lear's dominant emotion in the first three acts is the rage that arises from his sense of injustice, he also has feelings of guilt because of his own injustice to Cordelia. As he calls upon the gods to strike terror into sinners, he begins to fear that he is directing their wrath at himself. His assertion that he is a man more sinned against than sinning is at once an acknowledgment of guilt and a defense against punishment. It is an effort to direct the attention of the gods to their greater enemies; namely, those who have sinned against him. The two efforts that Lear makes to take comfort from the storm both end in failure, the first with his feeling the elements to be instruments of his daughters and the second with the emergence of his feelings of guilt. He has reached another impasse, and he announces again that madness is imminent.

At this point an important development occurs, as he becomes sensitive for the first time to the plight of another. He seems interested in the hovel that Kent has mentioned as much for the Fool's sake as for his own. By the time they reach the hovel, however, Lear's mood has changed, and he refuses to enter. His profession of indifference to the storm is a way of dramatizing the "tempest in [his] mind," of showing what his daughters have done to him. He wants to remain out of doors in order to feed his rage and intensify their guilt:

> But I will punish home!
> No, I will weep no more. In such a night
> To shut me out! Pour on; I will endure.
> In such a night as this! O Regan, Goneril!
> Your old kind father, whose frank heart gave all!
> O, that way madness lies; let me shun that! (III, iv)

The very awfulness of the night is a kind of satisfaction to him because it heightens the pathos of his plight. He is acting out a scenario he had envisioned earlier when he said that rather than return to Goneril, he would

> abjure all roofs, and choose
> To wage against the enmity o' th' air,
> To be a comrade with the wolf and owl—
> Necessity's sharp pinch! (II, iv)

His suffering is a way of accusing his daughters; to alleviate it by going inside is to diminish their criminality.

We see in this scene some familiar psychological patterns. The thought of his daughters' ingratitude arouses Lear's rage and his desire for retaliation. Buoyed by the feeling of strength generated by his anger, he determines not to weep and vows to endure. As he dwells upon the awfulness of the night, however, his rage gives way to self-pity: how could they have done this to their old kind father? This threatens his sense of control and arouses fears of going mad. It is not only self-pity, but also his sense of injustice by which Lear is afraid of being overwhelmed. He cultivates this sense of injustice in order to feed his rage; but when his feeling of potency passes, he is left with no way to cope with the unfairness of his fate. To retain his sanity, he tries then to shun the very emotions he has just been attempting to cultivate.

Note that Lear still perceives himself as the magnanimous father. He has gained no insight into his behavior in dividing the kingdom, which was neither kind nor frank, but was, as we have seen, a crass attempt to manipulate his daughters. They have treated him terribly, to be sure; but the disparity between his behavior toward them and theirs toward him is not as great as he imagines. If he could see this, he would not be so maddened by his sense of injustice. Lear never understands his limitations as a father—except, of course, in his rejection of Cordelia; and the rhetoric of the play calls no attention to them after the opening scene.

Lear declines once again to enter the hovel, but this time he wants to stay out in the storm so as to take refuge from his mental pain: "This tempest will not give me leave to ponder/ On things would hurt me more" (III, iv). He says that he will go in, however, after he has prayed, and he urges the Fool to enter. In this speech Lear shows a remarkable growth in compassion:

> Poor naked wretches, whereso'er you are,
> That bide the pelting of this pitiless storm,
> How shall your houseless heads and unfed sides,
> Your loop'd and window'd raggedness, defend you
> From seasons such as these? O, I have ta'en
> Too little care of this! Take physic, pomp;
> Expose thyself to feel what wretches feel,
> That thou mayst shake the superflux to them
> And show the heavens more just. (III, iv)

This speech has been discussed primarily in thematic terms, and quite understandably so, since it exemplifies the education pattern of the play. Lear's suffering seems to have humanized him, to have made him aware of the feelings of others and of his own earlier insensitivity. This pattern is repeated with Gloucester, who makes a similar speech to Poor Tom after he has been blinded (IV, i). Prosperity leads to pride and moral blindness. Suffering chastens pride, generates sympathetic insight, and produces a desire to relieve the sufferings of others. If men in power undergo such suffering, they will create a more just distribution of wealth.

In "Poor naked wretches" have we encountered at last one of those speeches that are "more fully in the service of the vision of the play as a whole than true to a consistent interior reality" (Mack, 1972, 68)? The speech is assuredly in the service of the vision of the play, but this does not preclude the possibility of its also being consistent with Lear's internal development. Having been thwarted in every attempt to find a bearable relationship to the storm, Lear here adopts a more self-effacing attitude. This often happens in an expansive person when his pride has been crushed. Lear's turning to prayer suggests a submissive relationship to the gods, whom he has hitherto tended either to curse or to command. Seeing himself as having been unjust gives him some relief from his outrage at the injustice with which he has been treated—we feel less indignant with others when we are aware of our own sins; and seeing his suffering as medicinal enables him to find meaning and value in his ordeal. He avoids arraigning the heavens by blaming men for the apparent unfairness of fate. There may even be an effort to make a bargain here in which Lear is promising to be a better king if he is returned to power.

I do not mean to suggest that Lear does not experience some genuine growth as a result of his suffering. It enlarges his imagination, enabling him to feel with those in like circumstances. His self-pity is turned here into pity for others, whose loves he had not had a sense of before. But there has been a tendency, I suggest, to overestimate how much Lear has learned and its importance in his overall development. Lear's experiences of sympathy and insight come and go, leaving little residual effect. They are transitory phases rather than stages in a steady moral growth. It is understandable that he should have a dawning awareness of what life is like for the poor naked wretches of the world and a realization of his earlier blindness. It is also understandable that this should be a rather fleeting experience. Suffering does makes us conscious of what others have been through, and we think that henceforth we shall be more understanding and compassionate. Our blindness returns, however, when the pain passes or when we become preoccupied with our own problems again. Suffering can have an enlarging effect, but it tends more often to narrow us. Shakespeare shows us both of these phenomena in his portrayal of Lear. Immediately after the speech in which he seems more in touch with reality than he has ever been before, Lear begins to interpret everything in the light of his own predicament. He is obsessed not with the injustice of life to a number of people, but with his daughters' treatment of him.

"UNACCOMMODATED MAN": LEAR AND "POOR TOM"

During his experiences with Goneril and Regan and in the storm, Lear has frequently felt himself to be on the verge of insanity. He becomes progressively more disturbed, but he does not step over the edge until his encounter with Gloucester's son Edgar, disguised as "Poor Tom." There is a powerful psychological interaction between these two that deserves examination. Edgar is acting out impulses that Lear has been struggling to control, and this spectacle liberates Lear's irrationality and invites his emulation. Until his encounter with Poor Tom, Lear has been trying to cope with his situation and to keep hold of his sanity. He sees, through Edgar's example, that going mad is the ultimate way of dramatizing what has been done to him, and he comes to regard Poor Tom as his mentor.

By exposing himself to the pelting of the storm, Lear was showing how badly he had been victimized, but in Poor Tom he sees a man whose state is worse than his own. He immediately interprets Tom's case in the light of his own experience: "Didst thou give all to thy daughters, and art come to this?" (III, iv). By doing this he is also viewing his own case in the light of Tom's and is claiming for himself an equivalent suffering. Poor Tom expands his imagination by showing him how low a man can descend, and Lear has an irresistible desire to join him in the depths. This is one reason why he tears at his clothes. As he had observed in his "Reason not the need" speech (II, iv), clothing symbolizes status; it distinguishes men from each other and man from the beasts. Poor Tom shows Lear how little there is separating man from the lower animals: "Thou art the thing itself; unaccommodated man is no more but such a poor, bare, forked animal as thou art" (III, iv). Since Lear has been stripped of his status and has been denied even shelter in the storm, he too, is an unaccommodated man, and his fine clothes are a mockery. By tearing them off, he seeks to define his true status and to show how low he has been brought. The lower he gets, the greater the epic quality of his suffering. At the same time, he is acting out his feeling that, with the collapse of his pride, he is now his despised self.

Lear has such a powerful reaction to Edgar in the role of "Poor Tom" because the two men are responding to similar plights with similar psychological mechanisms. Both have been victimized, Lear by his daughters and Edgar by his father, and both respond to the injustice by degrading and mortifying themselves. In order to escape from those who are searching for him, Edgar decides "To take the basest and most poorest shape/ That ever penury in contempt of man, / Brought near to beast" (II, iii). This can be explained as an effective disguise, but there are also psychological reasons why Edgar assumes this particular role. He is adopting the defense of warding off danger through self-punishment and lowliness. In addition, as Janet Adelman has observed, he creates in Poor Tom "a creature through whom he can safely express his sense of helpless victimization, of utter vulnerability and confusion" (1978, 14). Lear sees in Poor Tom a creature who embodies in a most vivid way these aspects of his own condition. Poor Tom is a role for Edgar, of course; and as a result, "emotions that might otherwise threaten to overwhelm him can . . . be disowned and controlled even as they are allowed expression" (Adelman 1978, 15). Lear's madness is real; he is unnerved by the spectacle of Tom acting out his own threatening emotions.

The role of Poor Tom allows Edgar to express not only his self-pity and sense of victimization, but also his feeling of rage; and here, too, there are similarities with Lear. Since Edgar's is the rage of a good son toward a parent, it is, like Hamlet's, turned against himself. As Janet Adelman has observed: "In his own person, Edgar never expressed direct anger against his father . . . ; just when we might expect to see him expressing anger and the desire for revenge or self-justification, we see him stripping and inflicting pain on himself in the person of Poor Tom. . . . The . . . masochism of Poor Tom serves Edgar well: for by turning the punishment against the self, he can avoid turning it against the world" (1978, 17). By turning the punishment against himself, however, he is, in an indirect way, also turning it against the world. By assuming such a base shape, he is accusing his father, much as Lear is accusing his daughters by exposing himself to the storm.

It is not typical for Lear, of course, to express his rage by turning it against himself; he would much prefer to turn it against others and to express it through violent retaliation. He is reduced by his impotence to employing a self-effacing device, and Edgar shows him a way of carrying his self-mortification much further than he had done so far. Lear recognizes Edgar's infliction of pain upon himself as a response to rejection:

> Is it the fashion that discarded fathers
> Should have thus little mercy on their flesh?
> Judicious punishment! 'Twas this flesh begot
> Those pelican daughters. (III, iv)

These lines suggest that Lear's masochistic behavior is an expression not only of frustrated rage, but also of self-hate. With the collapse of his pride, his despised self emerges, and he feels somehow to blame for what has happened to him. He may need to punish himself not only for begetting those pelican daughters, but also for his stupidity in putting himself in their power.

His strongest impulse, however, is still to punish *them:* "To have a thousand with red burning spits/ Come hizzing in upon 'em—" (III, vi). The only way he can have what he wants is by hallucinating it, and this is what we see him doing in the farmhouse scene, in which he arraigns his daughters, using Poor Tom and the Fool as judges. In this scene again, however, though he begins as the punisher, he ends as the victim. After arraigning his daughters, he imagines Regan escaping: "Stop her there!/ Arms, arms, swords, fire! Corruption in the place!/ False justicer, why hast thou let her 'scape?" (III, vi). He cannot get away from his feeling that the world is corrupt and that justice does not exist. He is consumed by self-pity and sees even the little dogs barking at him.

"LET COPULATION THRIVE"

In the fourth act, Lear is in the grip of his madness, which reaches its climax in scene 6. The sense of universal corruption and injustice that we saw developing earlier is fully expressed during his encounter with Gloucester. In response to Gloucester's "Is't not the King?" Lear delivers a discourse excusing adultery:

> Ay, every inch a king!
> ....
> I pardon that man's life. What was thy cause?
> Adultery?
> Thou shalt not die. Die for adultery? No.
> The wren goes to't, and the small gilded fly
> Does lecher in my sight.
> Let copulation thrive; for Gloucester's bastard son
> Was kinder to his father than my daughters
> Got 'tween the lawful sheets. (IV, vi)

His thoughts of adultery are triggered by Gloucester, whom, in some fashion, he recognizes and who is the man, perhaps, to whom he is offering a pardon. He is overcome by a sense of injustice at the thought that Edmund has been kinder to Gloucester than Goneril and Regan have been to him, which is excruciatingly ironic under the circumstances. Lear's sense of the unfairness of his own fate has undermined his belief in a moral order. There is no virtue, only the pretence; and why should anyone be virtuous anyway, since bastards treat their fathers better than do lawful children? If sin is rewarded and virtue is punished, why obey the law? Chastity is merely a plague of custom that is contrary to the course of nature. Lear comes close here to sharing Edmund's vision of life as a jungle, a vision that is sponsored in Edmund, too, by a sense of injustice that leads him to reject the social order.

Lear's next two speeches are attacks on authority. They continue the theme that there is no justice, since those who do the punishing are as corrupt as those they correct. Now that Lear is so vulnerable himself, he identifies with the perspective of the downtrodden, who must pay for their sins while the rich and powerful can get away with anything. The corrupt justices, the dogs who are obeyed in office, the high and mighty whose "furr'd gowns hide all" refer, no doubt, to his persecutors. It should be noted, however, that Lear is not protesting the innocence of the victims, only the equal guilt of those in authority: everyone is corrupt. He seems to be in the grip here of his own guilt and self-hate, triggered, perhaps, by the proximity of Cordelia, against which he defends himself by saying that "None does offend." The more guilty Lear feels, the less able he is to pass judgment on others. How can he say that anyone else has offended when his offenses have been so great? Indeed, his attack upon authority is directed at least in part against himself. He understands the unfairness in the administration of justice because of his own sins in office. His vision of the universality of corruption is at once a generalization from what has been done to him and what he has done to others and a way of warding off his own feelings of self-hate. If everybody does it, then he is not so bad. He is engaged simultaneously in attack and defense.

Other conflicting emotions come to the surface in the remainder of the scene. He tells Gloucester that he must be patient, but then his rage surfaces again, and he has a fantasy of revenge:

> It were a delicate stratagem, to shoe
> A troop of horse with felt. I'll put't in proof,
> And when I have stol'n upon these son-in-laws,
> Then kill, kill, kill, kill, kill, kill! (IV, vi)

Also at variance with his counsel of patience is his characterization of the world as a "great stage of fools." Lear has always felt like the favorite of fortune, but now he feels mocked by fate. When he is taken by Cordelia's men, he calls himself "the natural fool of fortune," indicating the total collapse of his pride.

PARADISE REGAINED

Lear is saved by his reconciliation with Cordelia, which provides him with an escape from his maddening plight and gives him something to live for. In speech after speech and scene after scene, he has oscillated from one emotional stance to another, unable to find an adequate way of responding to his situation. In the presence of Cordelia, he relieves his guilt by admitting his folly and asking for forgiveness; and he is absolved by Cordelia, who treats him with great tenderness. He now has a solution that can work, and he embraces his hitherto repressed self-effacing trends. His rage is dead, his sense of injustice is gone, and he is no longer concerned with revenge. He wishes to live now only for love.

This change is evident after Cordelia's forces are defeated and she and Lear are being led off to prison. Cordelia must find a defense against "false Fortune's frown," and she is still obsessed with Goneril and Regan;

but Lear is indifferent both to the loss of the battle and to the behavior of his elder daughters, upon whom he no longer needs to vent his indignation. Although Cordelia is "cast down" at her father's fate, Lear seems oblivious to the consequences of the defeat for her. He welcomes a situation in which he will have her entirely to himself, and he envisions a continual repetition of their reconciliation scene, which was his moment of salvation: "We two alone will sing like birds i' the cage:/ When thou dost ask me blessing, I'll kneel down,/ And ask of thee forgiveness" (V, iii).

Now that his self-effacing side is uppermost, Lear turns against his proud, ambitious, worldly self and feels remote from all of the things by which he was once obsessed:

> So we'll live,
> And pray, and sing, and tell old tales, and laugh
> At gilded butterflies, and hear poor rogues
> Talk of court news; and we'll talk with them too—
> Who loses and who wins; who's in, who's out—
> And take upon's the mystery of things,
> As if we were God's spies; and we'll wear out,
> In a wall'd prison, packs and sects of great ones,
> That ebb and flow by th' moon. (V, iii)

He is aware of the fleeting nature of pomp and power, and he envisions himself and Cordelia observing the rise and fall of others with an amused curiosity, a cosmic detachment. Embedded in prison and in his love relationship with Cordelia, he feels immune to the vicissitudes of fortune. From their position of safe lowliness, they will outlast the "packs and sects of great ones" who are pursuing worldly success.

The one thing that Lear is anxious about is being separated from Cordelia. He believes in the magical potency of her sacrifice, however; and he is convinced that now he has found her again, they can never be parted. But the gods do not throw incense upon Cordelia's sacrifice, and Lear's new solution is shattered by her death. This is more than Lear can bear, and he once again becomes mentally distracted. Three times he imagines that Cordelia is alive, first when he thinks that the feather stirs, next when he thinks that she has spoken, and finally when he hallucinates the movement of her lips. His death seems clearly meant to be a parallel to Gloucester's, whose heart burst smilingly " 'Twixt two extremes of passion, joy and grief" (V, iii). Just before he thinks he sees the movement of Cordelia's lips, Lear is once again overwhelmed by the injustice of life, in which lower creatures have breath but Cordelia has none. To escape from his unbearable emotions, he imagines the movement of her lips, and this brings him to the extreme of joy. When he thought the feather stirred, he said, "If it be so,/ It is a chance which does redeem all sorrows/ That ever I have felt." This is his state of mind, presumably, at the end. Lear dies, like Gloucester, from the shock of such joy in the midst of his despair. Under the circumstances, it is an extremely fortunate death.

SPIRITUAL REBIRTH?

In the preceding analysis, my primary object has been to do justice to Shakespeare's mimetic genius and psychological insight by discussing Lear as an imagined human being. Whatever else Shakespeare was doing in this play, he was certainly creating a remarkably subtle portrait of a particular man confronting a particular crisis in his life, and many of the details of the play are there primarily for the sake of this portrait. Maynard Mack felt that in this play "significance holds . . . character in an iron grasp" (1972, 74). It is my impression that Shakespeare's mimetic portrait of Lear is never sacrificed to thematic or formal necessities.

There are frequently tensions, however, between form, theme, and mimesis. One of the reasons for this is that Lear is a realistic character who tends to escape his intended thematic significance. He is one of those "creations inside a creation," of which E. M. Forster spoke, who are "often engaged in treason against the main scheme of the book" (1949, 64). As we have seen, the play seems to have a tragic education plot in which "the declining action which is the dogging of the hero to death, is complemented by a rising action, which is the hero's regeneration" (Fraser, 1963, xxvi). Many critics speak of Lear's spiritual rebirth, his growth in feeling and insight, and there is much in the play that suggests this design. When we look at the play from a psychoanalytic perspective, however, it becomes difficult to regard it as a "transcendent dream of human redemption" (McElroy 1973, 161).

Lear's realizations are often quite transitory and his sympathetic impulses come and go. His suffering makes him morally sensitive at times, but its predominant effect is to increase his rage and to reinforce his obsessions. Although he learns a great deal about his human limitations and the true nature of others, he remains blind to many things, including his own behavior as a father. When Cordelia comes to his rescue, his rage gives way to guilt; and when she forgives him, he begins to live for love.

The play is about the crushing of Lear's pride, which leads him to become self-effacing. From some perspectives this may look like spiritual growth, but from my perspective it is not. Lear's "let's away to prison" speech shows little sensitivity to Cordelia, a new kind of magic bargain, and a strong tendency toward embeddedness. When his new solution is destroyed by Cordelia's death, he is once again maddened with rage and grief. Lear dies not reconciled to reality, but escaping from it.

"ALL'S CHEERLESS, DARK, AND DEADLY"

Some critical disagreements about *King Lear* arise from the fact that one critic is interpreting the play in terms of its thematic clues, while another is responding to the mimesis. In other cases, however, disagreements arise from the fact that the thematic clues themselves are confusing. No play of Shakespeare's seems more to invite thematic analysis, but it is very difficult to determine what the play is about. Is it about a proud, willful, foolish king who brings destruction on himself and others, as the opening scene suggests; or is it about an "old kind king" (Kent's words in act 3, scene 1) whose daughters are marble-hearted fiends and who is subjected to indignities that are almost beyond belief? The most problematic issue in the play is whether it is affirming a just or an irrational order. Is this a Christian play or a foreshadowing of our own absurdist drama? The play seems to be moving toward the triumph of right, but poetic justice is suddenly violated by the death of Cordelia. I shall approach these problems by examining the various solutions that are dramatized in the play and observing their fates. I shall look at the ending in terms of the function it serves in the play's underlying fantasy, which is that of a wronged child whose offending parent is punished in a way that permits her to retain her innocence.

One of the reasons why *King Lear* seems so allegorical is that, as Bradley observed, "with the possible exception of Lear, no one of the characters strikes us as psychologically a wonderful creation" (1964, 263). In *Othello,* the tragedy arises from the interaction of four characters with well-developed personalities. In *Lear,* we seem to be witnessing "a conflict not so much of particular persons as of the powers of good and evil in the world" (Bradley 1964, 262–63). With few exceptions, the characters surrounding Lear are divided into two strongly contrasted groups: "Here we have unselfish and devoted love, there hard self-seeking" (Bradley 1964, 263). While it is true that only Lear is highly individualized, many of the other characters are distinct psychological types. The evil characters—Goneril, Regan, Edmund, and Cornwall—are all arrogant-vindictive people who have much in common with Claudius and Iago; and the good characters are either self-effacing or perfectionistic.

Shakespeare's treatment of the arrogant-vindictive characters is perfectly clear. Much of the rhetoric of the play is designed to arouse our horror and indignation at their behavior. They are hypocritical, disloyal, ungrateful, and ruthless in the pursuit of their goals. They seem to be governed by no moral restraints; to further their lust and ambition they are ready to kill brother, sister, husband, father, king—anyone who gets in their way. The shocking nature of the play derives in part from their violation of some of the strongest taboos and deepest pieties of human civilization. The possibility of their success constitutes a profound threat to the continuance of the moral order. After Cornwall blinds Gloucester, with Regan's approval, we have the following exchange between two servants:

> *Sec. Serv.* I'll never care what wickedness I do,
>   If this man come to good.
> *Third Serv.* If she live long,
>   And in the end meet the old course of death,
>   Women will all turn monsters. (III, vii)

Albany expresses similar sentiments when he finally turns on Goneril:

> Tigers, not daughters, what have you performed?
> . . . .
> If that the heavens do not their visible spirits
> Send quickly down to tame these vile offences,
> It will come,
> Humanity must perforce prey on itself,
> Like monsters of the deep. (IV, ii)

Moral anarchy is averted, of course, by the punishment of all the villains. Everything in the play contributes to the idea that evil cannot prosper long.

Albany and Edgar affirm the moral order to be supernatural in origin. When Albany hears of Cornwall's death, he says this shows that there are "justicers" above (IV, ii); and he speaks of the deaths of Goneril and Regan as the "judgment of the heavens" (V, iii). Edgar says that "the gods are just"; the "dark and vicious place" where Gloucester begot Edmund "cost him his eyes" (V, iii). Edmund, who has rejected traditional values, agrees now with his brother: "Thou hast spoken right, 'tis true;/ The wheel is come full circle; I am here" (V, iii). The collapse of his solution convinces him of the incorrectness of his world view. A hitherto repressed side of his personality emerges, and he even attempts to do some good by trying to save Lear and Cordelia.

Everything in the play supports the idea that the arrogant-vindictive solution is bound to fail; but it should be noted that only the speeches I have cited attribute this to a supernatural agency. The gods do not intervene in the action, as they do in some of the Romances. The villains perish through a natural course of events. Cornwall is killed by a servant who cannot tolerate his outrage upon Gloucester. There are people in the world who believe in the traditional values and who will defend them at the risk of their lives. Goneril and Regan perish in the jungle of their own making; when appetite reigns, no one is safe. Edmund dies, however, in a trial by combat. The theory behind such a trial is that right makes might, that heaven will side with the good. This point is not emphasized in the play, however, and the defeat of Cordelia in battle seems to indicate the silence of the gods. Even if Edgar had not challenged him, Edmund would have been undone by the disclosure of Goneril's letter. Lear and Gloucester are also punished for their sins in a natural way.

Shakespeare repudiates the arrogant-vindictive characters not only by showing their defeat in the action, but also by creating a number of foils to them, whom he presents in a favorable light. These include not only Kent, Cordelia, Albany, and Edgar, but also the Fool, who remains loyal despite his clear vision of Lear's impending downfall; Gloucester, who determines to succor Lear even if he must die for it; the servant who stands up to Cornwall; the servants and the old man who aid Gloucester; and Lear in his humbled condition. *King Lear* cannot be said to present a dark view of human nature, for though there are four truly vicious characters, virtue is well represented. There is no confusion about the traits and values that Shakespeare affirms, though there may be some question, as I have suggested, about the motives of those who display them.

The problem in the play does not arise, then, from the triumph of evil, for the vicious characters all receive their just deserts, and in ways that are highly appropriate. It is the fate of the good characters, and especially of Cordelia, that has aroused so much controversy. There are two groups of characters whose suffering seems undeserved: Lear and Gloucester, who are more sinned against than sinning, and Edgar, Cordelia, and Kent, who are presented as being virtuous. Although nothing in the play contradicts the idea that the gods are just in their punishment of evil, nothing supports the idea that they reward the good and protect the innocent. As numerous critics have observed, the pious hopes of Edgar and Albany are usually disappointed. When Edgar leaves Gloucester before the battle, he urges him to "Pray that the right may thrive" and assures him that "If ever I return to you again,/ I'll bring you comfort" (V, ii). He returns, however, to announce the defeat of Cordelia. When Albany learns that Edmund has ordered the death of Cordelia, he exclaims, "The gods defend her!" (V, iii). Lear then enters with Cordelia dead in his arms. These juxtapositions seem highly significant. Edmund is proven wrong in his assumption that traditional values can be violated with impunity, but Albany and Edgar are not vindicated in their belief in the triumph of right.

The play's treatment of the problem of evil consists not only of its portrayal of unjust suffering, but also its dramatization of the efforts of various characters to come to terms with this aspect of the human condition. Lear, as we have seen, never finds a way of coping with the unfairness of his fate. He is most at peace during the brief interlude after his reunion with Cordelia, but he is overwhelmed once again by her death. Some critics feel that Lear's spiritual rebirth redeems his suffering, but Lear never feels that way, and the degree of his regeneration is problematic. The major consequence of his suffering is not growth, but psychological deterioration. He says at the end that if Cordelia lives, it "redeem[s] all sorrows/ That ever I have felt" (V, iii); but the fact is that she is dead.

It is Gloucester, of course, who most directly arraigns the gods, and it is in his story that we have the most extended portrayal of a man who is trying to come to terms with his suffering. Despite his irreverent remark about the gods, Gloucester is not a cynic or a rebel, but a pious man who cherishes the traditional values. When he learns of his mistake, he immediately asks for forgiveness: "O my follies! Then Edgar was abus'd./ Kind gods forgive me that, and prosper him!" (III, vii). When he compares the gods to "wanton boys" who "kill us for their sport" (IV, i), he is not thinking of the injustice of his lot but is trying to ward off his self-hate. The comment occurs in a speech that is triggered by the appearance of Poor Tom:

> I' th' last night's storm I such a fellow saw,
> Which made me think a man a worm. My son
> Came then into my mind, and yet my mind
> Was then scarce friends with him. I have heard more since.
> As flies to wanton boys are we to th' gods.
> They kill us for their sport. (IV, i)

When we look at Gloucester's remark in its context, we see that it is an effort to reduce his sense of guilt at his own injustice to Edgar by attributing such things to the capriciousness of fate. It is a most uncharacteristic sentiment that Gloucester never repeats.

Through Gloucester, Shakespeare explores a self-effacing response to suffering. He does not rage against Edmund as Lear does against Goneril and Regan, and he is disposed to regard his suffering as a punishment for his sins. He moralizes on the fact that his wretchedness will make Poor Tom happier:

> Heavens, deal so still!
> Let the superfluous and lust-dieted man,
> That slaves your ordinance, that will not see
> Because he does not feel, feel your pow'r quickly;
> So distribution should undo excess,
> And each man have enough. (IV, i)

The problem is that these pious sentiments do not enable Gloucester to accept his fate, any more than Lear's similar insights in the "poor naked wretches" speech prevented him from going mad shortly thereafter. Gloucester gives his purse to Poor Tom in order to be led to Dover, where he can kill himself.

Gloucester wishes to die not only to escape his pain, but also to avoid the sin of rebellion. Before his attempted suicide at Dover, he tells the gods that he would live out his life if he "could bear it longer and not fall/ To quarrel with your great opposeless wills" (IV, vi). Edgar, his therapist and spiritual counselor, works hard at getting him to accept his affliction, but to little avail. Gloucester says that he will do so when Edgar convinces him that he has been preserved by the gods; but after his encounter with Lear, he asks the gods to kill him now so that he will be able to accept their will. He welcomes the prospect of dying by Oswald's sword, and he is "in ill thoughts again" the last time we see him on the stage. The battle has been lost, and Edgar wants to help him escape, but he refuses to move: "No further, sir. A man may rot even here" (V, ii). Edgar admonishes him again: "Men must endure/ Their going hence, even as their coming hither;/ Ripeness is all." Gloucester assents—"And that's true too"—but he has assented before without its having had any permanent effect. Gloucester wants to have a properly submissive attitude toward his fate, but his anguish is so great that he cannot maintain it. He is a pious man who is trying to live by religious ideas, but he is unable to do so with any consistency.

Neither Lear nor Gloucester seems to offer a workable response to the harshness of the human condition. One is driven to madness and the other to suicidal despair. Gloucester cannot practice what Edgar preaches, but what about Edgar himself? Edgar is one of the victims whose fate is completely unfair, but he neither rages nor suffers despair, though he does experience some dark moments. He is not always able himself to bear free and patient thoughts. When he sees his blinded father being led by an old man, he exclaims, "World, world, O world!/ But that thy strange mutations make us hate thee, / Life would not yield to age" (IV, i). Even if the last lines of the play are not his, he seems to share in the overwhelming gloom of the final scene. If they are his, they have a devastating impact upon his earlier pieties: "The weight of this sad time we must obey;/ Speak what we feel, not what we ought to say" (V, iii). These lines have a similar effect whether they are Edgar's or Albany's, for both of these characters have been spokesmen for orthodox attitudes that seem impossible to maintain in the face of Lear's and Cordelia's fates.

As I tried to show earlier, Edgar's response to being wronged is not as patient and rational as his counsels to Gloucester might lead one to expect. He is full of rage that he turns against himself and expresses through self-mortifying behavior. He debases himself as a form of protest and accusation. He seems charitable and forgiving toward his father, but his behavior is subtly vindictive. This becomes clear when he does not reveal himself to Gloucester after he learns that he has been vindicated:

> Ah dear son Edgar,
> The food of thy abused father's wrath!
> Might I but live to see thee in my touch,
> I'd say I had eyes again! (IV, i)

This is a perfect moment for Edgar to be reconciled with his father. He works hard at curing Gloucester's despair, but he contributes to it through his concealment of his identity.

In addition to Edgar, the other innocent victims are Kent and Cordelia. They respond in a perfectionistic way to the injustice of their fate, whereas Edgar's response, like Gloucester's, is self-effacing. Like Edgar, Kent continues to do his duty to the man by whom he has been wronged. He displays no anger at what has been done to him, partly because it has not damaged but fed his pride. By serving where he stands condemned, he attains the epitome of moral perfection. He seems to feel that nothing can touch him as long as he remains true to the code of loyalty, duty, and service. When he is placed in the stocks, he objects to the insult to Lear;

but he seems undisturbed on his own account: "A good man's fortune may grow out at heels" (II, ii). He does not require just treatment (in the short run, at least) because virtue is its own reward.

Kent is broken at the end of the play not by his own suffering but by that of others—or so it seems. Edgar tells of his meeting with Kent just after the death of Gloucester:

> While I was big in clamour, came there a man,
> Who having seen me in my worst estate,
> Shunn'd my abhorr'd society; but then, finding
> Who 'twas that so endur'd, with his strong arms
> He fastened on my neck, and bellowed out
> As he'd burst heaven; threw him on my father;
> Told the most piteous tale of Lear and him
> That ever ear receiv'd; which in recounting
> His grief grew puissant, and the strings of life
> Began to crack. Twice then the trumpets sounded,
> And there I left him tranc'd. (V, iii)

It seems to be the sufferings of Edgar, Lear, and Gloucester that produce such overpowering grief in Kent. It is when he finds out "who 'twas that so endur'd" that he begins to lose his composure. Kent does not demand justice for himself, but he does seem to claim it for others, and the failure of heaven to honor such claims is a terrible blow to his solution. The topsy-turvy world of the play eventually undermines his sense of order.

Kent is so moved by Edgar's situation because it is close to his own: both are under a sentence of death, imposed by a man whom they have loved and to whom they have been totally loyal. Both have been forced to assume degrading disguises in order to escape detection, and both have continued to serve where they stand condemned. Kent is experiencing his feelings about his own unjust fate by grieving over the sufferings of others, especially of Edgar. He bellows out at the heavens not only on their behalf, but on his own as well. His solution does not collapse completely, for he remains dutiful; but he is given hereafter to dark statements, and he loses his desire to live. He seeks out Lear in order to bid him "good night" forever. When Lear enters carrying the dead Cordelia, Kent asks, "Is this the promis'd end?"; and after he reveals his identity to Lear, he proclaims that "All's cheerless, dark, and deadly." When Lear dies, he discourages Edgar's efforts to revive him: "O, let him pass! He hates him much/ That would upon the rack of this tough world/ Stretch him out longer" (V, iii). The world is a torture chamber from which death is a welcome escape. Kent's last words announce his own imminent demise. The traumatic events of the play have crushed this physically strong and morally vigorous man of forty-eight. The breakdown of Kent contributes greatly to our sense of the darkness of the ending.

Cordelia is in many respects similar to Kent; he may have been her mentor. Despite the fact that her father disowns her, she continues to do her duty. She returns to rescue the man who has said that he would deny her all succor. Since she has strong taboos against the kind of aggressiveness that characterizes her sisters, she must make it clear that it is not "blown ambition" that brings her to England, "But love, dear love, and our ag'd father's right" (IV, iv). Her mission fails with her defeat in battle, but since she has behaved nobly, she is not unhappy for herself— only for Lear. Cordelia's solution does not break down as dramatically as Kent's, but the last time we see her alive she is weeping, and not, I think, for her father, since he is looking forward to their future in prison together. Cordelia believes in a moral order in which the wicked are punished: "Time shall unfold what plighted cunning hides./ Who covers faults, at last shame them derides" (I, i). This belief is vindicated by the fate of her sisters, but her own fate makes it impossible to believe that innocence is protected.

I have tried to suggest that it is not only the existence of so much undeserved suffering that makes *King Lear* such a dark play, but also the fact that none of the characters offers a workable response to this aspect of the human condition. Terrible things happen in all of Shakespeare's tragedies, but at the end we are usually left with the sense that order is being restored. Albany makes a gesture in this direction when he says that "All friends shall taste/ The wages of their virtue, and all foes/ The cup of their deservings" (V, iii), but this is followed immediately by the death of Lear and Kent's prediction that he will soon follow his master. Albany is in charge at the end, and, especially if the last lines are his, his comments are as gloomy as Kent's.

Albany is a very weak figure, moreover, to bear such responsibility. Goneril despises him because of his self-effacing traits. She complains of his "milky gentleness" and "harmful mildness" (I, iv), and she attacks him later as a "Milk-liver'd man" (IV, ii). There are a couple of scenes in which the worm turns, but for the most part Albany is confused and indecisive. His main effort in the final scene is to get rid of the responsibility that has fallen upon him since he is not a man who is comfortable with power. After observing that Lear "knows not what he says," Albany announces that he will resign his absolute power to him for as long as he lives. When Lear dies, he tries to bestow the leadership of the country upon Edgar and Kent, but Kent declines by announcing that he will soon die, and Edgar makes no gesture of acceptance. The gored state desperately needs someone to sustain it, but Albany does not seem to be the man.[2]

There is no ray of light in the final scene, nothing to dispel our sense that all is "cheerless, dark, and deadly." A delusional joy leading to death seems to be the best that life has to offer. Authority is in the hands of a good man who is unfit to be a leader. The emphasis is not upon the purgation of evil and the emergence of a new order, but upon the great burden of woe everyone is carrying and the magnitude of the suffering that has taken place. The last lines of the play reject the traditional sources of comfort. When the characters speak what they feel at the end of *King Lear,* they find nothing reassuring to say.

THE DEATH OF CORDELIA

The death of Cordelia is one of the most disturbing things in Shakespeare, so much so that for over one hundred years Nahum Tate's happily ending version of the play held the stage. One reason for this is that the play seems to be moving in the direction of poetic justice when Lear suddenly enters carrying Cordelia's body. Up to this point, the evil ones have been punished and the virtuous have been vindicated. In a sense, the whole play is a love test that reveals the hypocrisy of Goneril, Regan, and Edmund and the devotion of Edgar, Cordelia, and Kent. Lear and Gloucester have seen the error of their ways, and even Edmund has undergone a conversion. His effort to save Cordelia comes too late, however. Her death is so shocking partly because it seems so accidental; it does not strike us as an inevitable consequence of the plot. Nor was it thrust upon Shakespeare by his sources, since in them this part of the story ends happily and Cordelia's death does not occur until later. We cannot help wondering, therefore, why Shakespeare chose to end the play in this fashion.

The death of Cordelia is required, of course, by the tragic education plot in which the hero grows as a result of his errors but also sets in motion a chain of causes that leads to his destruction. In such a story the lessons are always learned too late. Although Cordelia's death has an accidental quality, it is the direct result of Lear's folly at the beginning of the play. It is the severest consequence of his mistakes. We may also explain it thematically as part of the dark view of life that Shakespeare seems to be setting forth in this play. It is his final and most compelling instance of unjust suffering, one with which none of the characters can cope. Another way of approaching the problem is to ask how Cordelia's death fits into the dominant fantasy of the play. This is a difficult question to answer because the play seems to be governed at different times by different fantasies. It begins as the story of a foolish father who is very unfair to his child, but it quickly becomes the story of a wronged father who is badly mistreated by his children. Gloucester's story follows a similar pattern. Is the main subject of the play paternal unfairness or filial ingratitude? Is Shakespeare writing from the perspective of a wronged child or of a wronged father, or from some combination of both?

The beginning and end of the play are governed by the perspective of the child. Cordelia and Edgar are wronged at the outset and vindicated at the end. Initially we have strong sympathy with them and antipathy toward their irrational parents. Most of the play is governed, however, by the perspective of the father. What is done to Gloucester and Lear is outrageous. There is an aura of sanctity about fathers and kings that makes the actions of the evil children seem utterly monstrous and heightens our sympathy for their victims. The wronged children themselves sympathize with their fathers; their behavior, along with that of Kent, shows what is owed to such authority figures. A great deal of the energy of the play is expressed in Lear's rage, which comes to seem like a justified response to the indignities to which he is subjected. From the perspective of the father, the death of Cordelia is an excessively cruel blow to a man who has already suffered too much. He has learned love and humility, and he is now being deprived of his only consolation. His death in response to hers is a proof of his love for his child.

The death of Cordelia has more inevitability, I believe, if we view the play as a fantasy written from the child's point of view. In the child's fantasy, to die as a result of the parent's injustice is the ultimate form of revenge. *King Lear,* too, is a play about revenge. Goneril and Regan take revenge on Lear for his domineering ways, his favoritism to Cordelia, and his persistence in remaining alive. Edmund revenges himself on Gloucester for the humiliation he has suffered as a bastard and upon Edgar for the privileges he enjoys as a legitimate child. Cornwall takes revenge on Gloucester for siding with Lear, and Albany says that he will revenge Gloucester's eyes. Gloucester, Albany, and Edgar believe that "winged vengeance" (III, vii) will overtake the evildoers. Lear's is a story of frustrated revenge. What drives him mad is not only the wrongs he has suffered, but also his inability to retaliate.

What is striking in this play is that those who have been most wronged —Edgar, Cordelia, and Kent—are presented as being completely devoid of vindictiveness. I assume that, in writing the play, Shakespeare was drawing upon his feelings both as a wronged father and as a wronged child. Most men who live to a certain age have been both. The feelings of the wronged father are expressed with great force and directness; and although Lear is impotent in his desires for revenge, a moral order is affirmed that demands respect for authority and that punishes the evil children. The feelings of the wronged child, however, are disguised and repressed. There is a great deal of outrage in the play at the mistreatment of fathers by children, but very little at the mistreatment of children by fathers, and that is quickly dispelled by our sympathy for the fathers' suffering. What seems to be missing in the play is the rage of Edgar and Cordelia.

Also missing is the ambivalence that a child would feel toward a father like Lear. Shakespeare gives the love to Cordelia and the hatred to Goneril and Regan, and he then shows what hideous monsters are children who take revenge on a parent. He does not present in a realistic way the complexities of the situation, the mixed feelings that must be felt toward an irrational authority figure. He could have done so, of course, by embodying the conflicting responses in one character instead of splitting them as he does. It is this splitting that makes the play seem so allegorical. The play generates mixed feelings in the audience toward Gloucester and Lear, but it does not portray them in the characters.

This statement is not entirely true, of course, for Edgar's rage is not missing, but is only disguised. When he says that Lear is childed as he is fathered (III, vi), he is making a very bitter remark about Gloucester; a remark that points to the double focus of the play. Edgar conceals his vindictiveness from himself and from us by having great pity for Gloucester and by trying to cure him of his despair; but his delay in revealing himself is a major cause of Gloucester's death, as he himself seems to realize: "Never (O fault!) reveal'd myself unto him/ Until some half hour past" (V, iii). It should be noted that he kills Oswald and Edmund, but in ways that conceal his aggressiveness. He wishes that Oswald had had another "deathsman" (IV, vi), and he is quick to exchange charity with Edmund (V, iii). Edgar appears to be charitable to his father and brother, but he has had his revenge.

What about Cordelia? What has happened to her anger with Lear for his unjust treatment of her? She must feel resentment at her father's rejection, but the only vindictiveness she displays is toward her sisters.

She tries to make them look bad in the love test, she denounces them before she leaves for France, and she returns to do battle with them on her father's behalf. After her defeat she seems eager to see them, presumably to express her scorn and indignation. Toward the father who has disowned her, however, she is all tenderness, pity, and concern. She is not simply charitable; she denies that there is anything to forgive. Her desire for revenge on her father is far more deeply repressed than is Edgar's. It does not show up in her behavior, except in a few very oblique ways; but it seems to be enacted by the plot, in which Lear is severely punished for what he does to her.

The main action of the play may be seen as a fantasy conceived from the child's point of view, a fantasy of vindication and revenge. Marvin Rosenberg has called this "the *Lear* myth" and has cited its folk tale analogues and its psychological sources: "First, a father—often seeking the affection of his daughters—rejects the true love of a good child, and mistakenly favors bad ones; the good child at first suffers in silence, while the father is severely punished for his error, and learns to be sorry he was so wrong. Second, the good child saves him from his pain and sorrow; he begs forgiveness, and the good child grants it" (1972, 327). This pattern is often part of a childhood fantasy in which "the parent suffers—dies— because he wrongs the dreamer, who himself may die, or at least endure noble martyrdom: for the suffering and death of the child dreamer is . . . the worst possible punishment for the father" (1972, 327).[3]

From the child's point of view, Lear is an irrational father who favors the bad children and wrongs the good one. He is punished for this, but not by the good child; for if the good child were to punish the father, or even to be hostile toward him, she would not be the good child any more. The father is punished in a poetically just fashion by the bad children into whose hands he has foolishly put himself. It should be noted that Cordelia makes no effort to save Lear from his folly. At the end of the first scene, she seems to be anticipating that Goneril and Regan will be her avengers:

> The jewels of our father, with wash'd eyes
> Cordelia leaves you. I know you what you are;
> And like a sister, am most loath to call
> Your faults as they are nam'd. Love well our father.
> To your professed bosoms I commit him;
> But yet, alas, stood I within his grace,
> I would prefer him to a better place! (I, i)

There is bitterness here toward Lear, who has chosen Goneril and Regan as his "jewels," as well as toward her sisters. She knows what they are and what they will do to her father. Committing him to their bosoms is like passing sentence upon him. What is going to happen is not her fault, however; she would have cared for him if only he had let her.

Subsequent developments must be extremely gratifying to Cordelia. Her sisters are shown for what they are, she is vindicated, and her father is repentant. By coming to his rescue, despite his rejection, she proves her own nobility. She dwells upon the horror of her sisters' treatment of Lear with pity and indignation, but also I think, with a kind of satisfaction that their true colors have been revealed so dramatically (IV, vii). It is not difficult for Cordelia to forgive her father, for not only does this accord with her sense of duty, but the hostility that she has repressed has been acted out by her sisters.

Lear's punishment, like Gloucester's, consists not only of his own suffering, but also of the suffering of his innocent child. The discovery of the degradation to which he has reduced Edgar is part of the shock that kills Gloucester, and it is Cordelia's death that deals the final blow to Lear. It is the ultimate vindication of her goodness, since she loses her life in coming to his rescue; and it is the ultimate proof of his folly, since this is what it has led to. It is also the ultimate way of making him sorry and of receiving the testimony of his love. His grief is so intense that it cannot be borne; and, when he thinks that she is alive, his joy is so great that it kills him. The gloom of the ending is, among other things, a tribute to Cordelia.

I am not suggesting that Cordelia dies on purpose in order to produce these effects. The play is not her fantasy, but Shakespeare's, and it is he who obtains the satisfactions to be derived from the death of the innocent child. As we shall see when we analyze Shakespeare's personality, the Cordelia fantasy satisfies his need for innocent revenge, of the sort that Hamlet was unable to encompass. The solution that Shakespeare imagines for Cordelia is not realistic, of course; for it depends upon his manipulation of the action in such a way that her father is punished while she incurs no guilt. In this respect, *King Lear* is akin to the Romances. There the villains are punished either by the gods or by other people, which permits their innocent victims to be avenged without losing their virtue.[4]

CONCLUSION

Maynard Mack contended that *King Lear* has much more in common with "Romance, Morality play, and Vision" than it does with "psychological or realistic drama" (1972, 83). I hope that my analysis of Lear has shown that the play contains at least one great psychological portrait. Mack ridiculed the idea of assuming "that the relation of Lear to his speeches is the same as that of (say) Hedda Gabler to hers" (1972, 29), but that is precisely the way in which Lear's speeches should be understood. The play is realistic not only in its characterization of Lear, but also in its portrayal of the human condition. It shows the inadequacy or self-destructiveness of all the defensive strategies; none of the characters are able to master fate or to cope with the unfairness of life. In this play, Shakespeare shows us things not as they should be, but as they are.

Mack is correct, however, in pointing to the affinities of *King Lear* with Morality play and Romance. The moral dimension of the play resides in its critique of Lear's narcissism and of the Machiavellian behavior of Goneril, Regan, and Edmund, and in its affirmation of perfectionistic and self-effacing values. None of the solutions work, but from an ethical point of view, some are vastly better than others. There is good and evil in human beings, whatever the nature of the cosmic order; and it is preferable to be good, even if virtue is not always rewarded. Although no one makes out well in this play, Albany and Edgar fare the best, while the virtuous characters who are destroyed win our love and admiration. As we have seen, the allegorical aura of the play derives, in part, from its portrayal of extreme forms of the various solutions. The Machiavellian characters show no trace of conscience or inner conflict, except for Edmund at the end; and the vindictive trends of the good characters are either disguised or displaced into the plot. This makes these characters seem like fragments of the human psyche rather than whole human beings—though, as I have tried to show, they are recognizable psychological types.

King Lear is akin to romance in its indulgence of some of our wishes. Despite the apparent triumph of grim reality, there is a powerful element of wish fulfillment in this play, from both the father's and the child's point of view. This accounts for many of our positive emotional responses, and it mitigates the effects of the realism. Things sometimes work out as they should. Although Lear's curses seem impotent at first, his ungrateful daughters are soon destroyed. There is the fantasy not only of the wronged but also of the forgiven father. Cordelia loves her father despite his injustice, and she gives him a proof of devotion that far exceeds his own unreasonable expectations. Their idyllic reunion does not last long, but Lear dies happy in the belief that she is alive. Cordelia is granted the punishment of the erring father and the evil sisters and the restoration of her father's affection. What is most important of all to such a perfectionistic person is that her virtue be recognized and admired. She does not succeed in mastering fate through the height of her standards, but part of her bargain works. In a sense, the gods do throw incense upon her sacrifice, or at least the playwright does. In the last two acts, there is a series of tributes to her virtue, which is established for all time by her death. From the child's point of view, there is a sense of triumph at the end because although Cordelia dies, her search for glory succeeds.

CHAPTER 5

Macbeth

Less discussion has been devoted to character and motive in twentieth-century criticism of *Macbeth* than in criticism of any of the other major tragedies. L. C. Knights' "How Many Children Had Lady Macbeth?" seems effectually to have inhibited subsequent critics from building upon the insights of Bradley. As G. K. Hunter has observed, it has "become something of a cliche of modern criticism to say that the essential structure of *Macbeth* is 'to be sought in the poetry' (L. C. Knights), that the characters 'are not shaped primarily to conform to a psychological ver-isimilitude, but to make explicit the intellectual statements with which the play is concerned' (Irving Ribner), that Lady Macbeth, Macbeth, and Banquo 'are parts of a pattern, a design; are images or symbols' (A. P. Rossiter)" (1977, 6). In his 1973 survey of Shakespearean criticism, Ronald Berman reported that "there has been no better study of the character of the principals" than Bradley's (125), and the situation has not changed greatly since then. Even psychoanalytic critics have eschewed the analysis of motives. They have been "content," as Norman Holland said, "to consider the characters as projections of psychological impulses rather than [as] portraits of those impulses in 'real' people. The witches, ghosts, and prophecies of *Macbeth* would seem almost to force this kind of reading, and it is no bad thing" (1966, 230). The fullest discussion of character occurs in Marvin Rosenberg's *The Masks of Macbeth* (1978), and one of the most striking things about his account is how much more actors, actresses, and directors have contributed to our understanding of the principals than have literary critics.[1]

Nevertheless, as Hunter observed, "the reaction (even of critics) to stage-figures as if to real people is not finally repressible, and few treatments succeed in ignoring the hero altogether" (1977, 9). Among critics who have discussed character and motive in this play, the chief problems have been in accounting for Macbeth's commission of the murder in spite of his powerful feelings against it, and the transformation of the principals, in which the tender-minded Macbeth becomes a callous murderer while the "fiendlike" Lady Macbeth is destroyed by conscience. Simon Lesser echoed many earlier critics when he observed that "a priori, nothing seems more improbable than the idea that a man with such an unrelenting conscience as Macbeth's would embark on a career of crime" (1977, 233). Freud felt the transformation of Macbeth and Lady Macbeth to be inexplicable: "What . . . [the] motives can have been which in so short a space of time could turn the hesitating, ambitious man into an unbridled tyrant, and his steely-hearted instigator into a sick woman gnawed by remorse, it is, in my view, impossible to divine" (1958, 97).

Freud could make no sense of these characters because "the childlessness of Macbeth and the barrenness of his Lady" were the only causes he could adduce for their transformation, but the time scheme of the play does not allow these causes to become operative. He therefore abandoned the attempt to understand them as realistically portrayed individuals and followed Ludwig Jekel's suggestion that Shakespeare has split up one character "into two personages, each of whom then appears not altogether comprehensible until once more conjoined with the other" (1958, 98). Thus,

> the stirrings of fear which arise in Macbeth on the night of the murder, do not develop further in him, but in the Lady. It is he who has the hallucination of the dagger before the deed, but it is she who later succumbs to mental disorder. . . . Thus is fulfilled in her what his pangs of conscience had apprehended; she is incarnate remorse after the deed, he incarnate defiance—together they exhaust the possibilities of reaction to the crime, like two disunited parts of the mind of a single individuality, and perhaps they are the divided images of a single prototype. (1958, 98–99)

What Freud failed to perceive was Lady Macbeth's inner conflicts before and Macbeth's after the murder. Macbeth and Lady Macbeth are separate, brilliantly portrayed personalities whose behavior makes sense when we have understood their motivational systems.

When we look at these characters as imagined human beings, we see that once again Shakespeare has portrayed people who are undergoing a psychological crisis as a result of the breakdown of their bargains with fate. In the plays we have examined so far, the characters have had their bargains violated by other people, by external events. The case of Macbeth is somewhat different. At the beginning of the play, Macbeth is a perfectionistic person whose solution has been highly successful. He has lived up to his shoulds, and his claims have been honored. He precipitates his psychological crisis himself by violating the code of loyalty, duty, and service to which he subscribes in order to act out the Machiavellian tendencies that are reinforced by his wife. Once he violates his own bargain, he is overwhelmed by fear and self-hate. He tries to cope with his crisis by wholeheartedly embracing the arrogant-vindictive solution, but he cannot really do so, and he sinks into despair.

Lady Macbeth also discovers the futility of this solution. Like Claudius, Iago, Edmund, Goneril, and Regan, she is ready to violate the most sacred values of her society in the pursuit of her ambitions. Her solution breaks down when she finds that success does not bring the joy she had anticipated and that conscience cannot be repressed. Macbeth would not have murdered Duncan without the prodding of his wife; and Lady's Macbeth's deterioration is related, I believe, to the growing brutality of her husband, which deprives her of her mission and leaves her prey to her guilt. Shakespeare has given us in this play not only two marvelous mimetic characters, but also a brilliant picture of their relationship.

MACBETH'S INNER CONFLICTS—BEFORE THE MURDER

A number of critics have pointed to the fact that our first image of Macbeth is that of a bloody man, and they see this as a foreshadowing of his later violence. What impresses me most about the Macbeth of the early scenes is his horror at the thought of shedding Duncan's blood, despite his fearlessness in confronting the terrors of battle. We are meant to have a positive reaction to Macbeth's feats of slaughter. He is a warrior-hero like Talbot, Bedford, Henry V, and Coriolanus whose aggressiveness is glorified because it expresses itself in fighting for his country. Bloodthirsty behavior is honored in Shakespeare as long as it conforms to the rules of war and is directed against enemies of the state. It is condemned when it is an agent of merely personal ambition and when it involves treachery and revolt. If we are to understand Macbeth's inner conflicts at the beginning of the play, we must recognize that in his moral code, as in that of his culture, there is an immense difference between killing in battle and murder, especially the murder of a king. The one is sanctioned by the codes of loyalty, duty, and service and martial and manly honor; the other is a "horrid deed" that is bound to bring retribution.

In her soliloquy upon the receipt of Macbeth's letter, Lady Macbeth provides some excellent insights into her husband's conflicts:

> Yet I do fear thy nature.
> It is too full o' th' milk of human kindness
> To catch the nearest way. Thou wouldst be great;
> Art not without ambition, but without
> The illness should attend it. What thou wouldst highly,
> That wouldst thou holily; wouldst not play false,
> And yet wouldst wrongly win. (I, v)

Macbeth is an ambitious man who wants more than he can legitimately have but who is prevented from going after it by powerful compliant and perfectionistic tendencies. His compliance is indicated by the milk imagery that is consistently employed by aggressive characters in Western literature to describe self-effacing behavior (cf. Goneril on Albany), and his perfectionism is indicated by his need for righteousness. Macbeth is a man who is deeply committed to the values of his society and who has invested his pride in living up to them. His reply to Duncan's expression of gratitude sets forth his genuine beliefs:

> The service and the loyalty I owe,
> In doing pays itself. Your Highness' part
> Is to receive our duties; and our duties
> Are to your throne and state children and servants,
> Which do but what they should by doing everything
> Safe toward your love and honour. (I, iv)

Under the circumstances, this speech seems hypocritical, but it is an expression of the code upon which Macbeth has so far molded his life.

Macbeth has a powerful need to be great but an even more powerful need to be good. His solution to his inner conflict has been to search for glory in acceptable ways, through loyal service to the state. He is a man of honor who exults, like Othello, in "the big wars that make ambition virtue." As the play opens, he is receiving all of the recognition he can reasonably expect. In act 1, scene 1, alone he is described as "brave Macbeth," "valour's minion," "valiant cousin," "justice . . . with valour armed," "Bellona's bridegroom," and "noble Macbeth." These are the "golden opinions" that mean so much to him. He is named Thane of Cawdor and is promised an even "greater honour" (I, iii). The problem is that, whetted by his success and by his encounter with the witches, Macbeth's ambition and his sense of his deserts cannot be satisfied by anything Duncan can do for him. Indeed, Duncan may feed Macbeth's discontent by acknowledging his inability to reward him properly: "More is thy due than more than all can pay" (I, iv). Macbeth's need for greatness threatens to get out of control and to violate his need to be good.

Macbeth's inner conflict is evident in his reaction to the witches' prophecy. He starts and is "rapt" because the witches have brought to the surface a fantasy he has been trying to repress. He wants to believe that the supernatural soliciting is good, but he is afraid it is not: "If good, why do I yield to that suggestion/ Whose horrid image doth unfix my hair/ And make my seated heart knock at my ribs/ Against the use of nature?" (I, iii). Since he can imagine no honorable way to the throne, the thought of becoming king arouses images of himself murdering Duncan; but this is a violation of everything he believes in, and he reacts with a feeling of horror. At the beginning of this speech Macbeth is entranced by the prospect of his imperial destiny, but within a few moments he finds himself in the throes of an anxiety attack. He feels weak, he trembles, and he has palpitations of the heart. The brave warrior who has always been undaunted in the face of "present danger" is unmanned by his "horrible imaginings." His thoughts of murder activate all his taboos against it, and he is overwhelmed by his dread of the self-hate and retribution to which he would be exposed should he violate his own most sacred values. He defends himself against his terror by renouncing his criminal intentions: "If chance will have me King, why, chance may crown me,/ Without my stir." Having chance crown him is the perfect solution, for it permits Macbeth to realize his dream of glory without having to sacrifice his rectitude. The thought of this solution so reduces his anxiety that he regains the use of his faculties and is able to attend to the people around him.

Macbeth's inner conflict has only momentarily subsided, of course. The reduction of his anxiety permits the reemergence of his aggressive impulses. When he invites Banquo to a further discussion of what has occurred, he seems to be keeping his options open for conspiratorial action. He writes his letter to Lady Macbeth between this scene and the next. As Lesser has observed, "One does not have to examine Macbeth's letter searchingly to see that one of its aims is to induce his wife to persuade him to murder Duncan" (1977, 222). His use of his wife to goad him is one of his devices for "outwitting conscience" (1977, 220). He responds to Duncan's gratitude with an at least partially sincere statement of his code of loyalty, duty, and service (I, iv); but when Duncan names Malcolm his successor, he feels that chance is not going to crown him, and his regicidal impulses rise to the surface once more: "Stars hide your fires!/ Let not light see my black and deep desires./ The eye wink at the hand; yet let that be,/ Which the eye fears, when it is done, to see" (I, v). There is a great deal of conflict here. Macbeth is profoundly uncomfortable with his dark desires; he fears divine judgment and wants them hidden from the forces of good in the universe. After his earlier anxiety attack, he is doubtful of his ability to carry out the murder, so he hopes somehow to be able to do it without being aware of it himself. He foresees the difficulty he will have in getting around the internal obstacles to such a deed and the horror he will feel afterward if he is somehow able to do it. This speech expresses the wish that the murder will take place despite his fears and scruples.

When Macbeth arrives at Inverness, he seems fully intent upon the murder.

Lady M.	Great Glamis! worthy Cawdor!
	Greater than both, by the all-hail hereafter!
	Thy letters have transported me beyond
	This ignorant present, and I feel now
	The future in the instant.
Macb.	My dearest love,
	Duncan comes here to-night.
Lady M.	And when goes hence?
Macb.	To-morrow, as he purposes.
Lady M.	O, never
	Shall sun that morrow see! (I, v)

Macbeth is not simply informing his wife of Duncan's arrival but is responding to her excitement over his great expectations by offering her Duncan's arrival as the means by which these expectations are to be realized. When she asks when Duncan goes hence, his reply— "To-morrow, as *he* purposes"—indicates that he has no intention of allowing him to depart. Macbeth and Lady Macbeth are more in tune in this scene than they will ever be again. They pick up each other's cues in a way that makes us feel they are reading each others' minds. The only thing about which Lady Macbeth is concerned is the obviousness of her husband's evil intentions: "Your face, my Thane, is as a book where men/ May read strange matters . . . / . . . look like the innocent flower,/ But be the serpent under 't" (I, v). He is serpent enough here to meet even her standards; he needs to work, however, on his hypocrisy.

When we next see Macbeth he is once again in conflict. He has left the chamber while Duncan is still dining because he has become so agitated that he must reconsider his course. As Lady Macbeth observes, the "fitness" of circumstances "unmake[s]" him (I, vii). As the moment approaches when he must carry out his murderous intentions, he becomes prey once more to his anxieties. He seems to have gotten over one of the major obstacles to the crime, for he is ready to "jump the life to come" (I, vii) in exchange for absolute power on earth. What torments him in this soliloquy is the fear that after having made such a terrible sacrifice, he will still have to face earthly retribution:

> But in these cases
> We still have judgment here, that we but teach
> Bloody instructions, which, being taught, return
> To plague th' inventor. This even-handed justice
> Commends th' ingredient of our poison'd chalice
> To our own lips. (I, vii)

Underlying this speech is Macbeth's deep belief that reality conforms to the traditional code of morality. Characters like Iago and Edmund see such values as duty, loyalty, and the acceptance of one's place in society as part of a myth that has been promulgated by those in power to maintain their dominance. They have neither divine sanction nor social necessity, and they can be ignored with impunity. Macbeth does not see these values as arbitrary, however, and he is convinced that by violating them he will set in motion a train of events by which he himself will be punished.

Macbeth's fears are, in part, reality based, but his sense of the inevitability of retribution is greatly intensified by his perfectionistic bargain. Part of every bargain is a belief not only in the rewards of living up to one's shoulds but also in the penalties for violating them. Receiving "justice" means both having our claims honored when we have fulfilled the terms of our bargain and being punished when we have failed to do so. Macbeth's conviction of an infallible justice operating in life gives him a feeling of mastery when he is virtuous, but it fills him with dread when he thinks of committing a crime. It derives less from reality than from his own sense of what is fair. It is difficult to see this because his belief is borne out by the action of the play. It corresponds to the reality of the *Macbeth* world, the laws of which seem to be those of the perfectionistic solution.

Macbeth's sense of justice expresses itself not only in his fear of retribution but also in his rehearsal of the moral objections to the murder.

Activated by the imminence of their violation, both his perfectionistic and his self-effacing shoulds fill him with a sense of horror. He is Duncan's kinsman, his subject, and his host, "who should against his murder shut the door,/ Not bear the knife myself." He would be violating three sacred bonds by doing the deed. How could he live with himself after?

> Besides, this Duncan
> Hath born his faculties so meek, hath been
> So clear in his great office, that his virtues
> Will plead like angels, trumpet-tongu'd, against
> The deep damnation of his taking-off;
> And pity, like a naked new-born babe,
> Striding the blast, or heaven's cherubin, hors'd
> Upon the sightless couriers of the air,
> Shall blow the horrid deed in every eye,
> That tears shall drown the wind. (I, vii)

We have here our first direct evidence of that softer side of Macbeth about which his wife was concerned when she received his letter. Duncan is a meek, mild, over-trusting, over-generous person who is so excessively grateful that Macbeth must remind him that the service he has received was his due. A Machiavel scorns men like Duncan and has no qualms about moving against them. Macbeth, however, honors Duncan for his Christian virtues and feels that they add to the heinousness of the murder. The killing of so virtuous a man is an outrage against justice and will assure the murderer's damnation. Pity for Duncan will spread so rapidly that everyone will know of his "horrid deed," and it will be so intense that this seemingly ineffectual sentiment will become a powerful force. Macbeth envisions universal mourning for Duncan and universal detestation of himself. He is, in part, externalizing his own emotions, of course (see Rosenberg 1978, 261).

The soliloquy concludes with Macbeth recoiling against his ambition:

> I have no spur
> To prick the sides of my intent, but only
> Vaulting ambition, which o'erleaps itself
> And falls on th' other side. (I, vii)

His reflections have shown him that he has no justification for the murder and that all considerations, practical and moral, militate against it. Even if he were willing to sacrifice his immortal soul, he would still be faced with retribution, self-hate, and the judgment of his fellows. The only thing driving him is his ambition, which he now sees as an unholy overreaching that is bound to lead to a fall. Macbeth defends himself against his anxieties as he had done earlier, by abandoning his criminal intentions.

Macbeth announces his decision in the ensuing conversation with his wife, telling her that he has "bought/ Golden opinions from all sorts of people" that should not be "cast aside so soon" (I, vii). Macbeth is a man who has lived for recognition, and, as the play opens, he is receiving it in a greater degree than he has ever done before. He has come to feel that if he commits the murder he will be severely judged for violating his sacred trust and for killing so virtuous a man. Now he is a national hero whose exploits are being widely acclaimed. If he kills Duncan, he will lose forever the "golden opinions" he has hardly begun to enjoy.

MACBETH AND LADY MACBETH

It is not surprising that people have had difficulty understanding how a man with so many powerful motives against it could actually have committed the crime. One reason for this difficulty, I believe, is that Shakespeare has given us a far more effective representation of Macbeth's anxieties about the murder than he has of the "vaulting ambition" that is driving him to it. Macbeth has many fantasies about the horrors of regicide but few about the glories of kingship. The forces holding him back are dramatized so vividly that it is hard to see how they could be overcome. The strength of his ambition must be inferred from his reactions to the witches' prophecies and from his willingness to sacrifice his soul, but we *see* the strength of his fears and scruples.

We can understand Shakespeare's method through a modification of the Jekels-Freud hypothesis. Shakespeare has not split up one character "into two personages," but it is true that neither of them is "altogether comprehensible" unless "conjoined with the other" (Freud 1958, 98). Macbeth and Lady Macbeth are doubles in the sense that each has as a dominant trend the subordinate side of the other. Macbeth's ruthless, aggressive side is displayed most fully not in him but in his wife, while her fears and scruples are expressed most directly by her husband. Each gives us insight into the less exposed parts of the other. There has been considerable debate about the degree of responsibility that should be assigned to Macbeth and to Lady Macbeth. The outcome is the product of the *interaction* between these two people. He stirs her up so that she will reinforce his aggressive impulses, but she has powerful reasons of her own for wishing to do so. After he tells her that he "will proceed no further," she literally badgers him into doing what she wants; but she could not have affected him so powerfully if she had not struck a responsive chord in his nature. To understand this crucial scene, we must analyze it from the perspective of both participants. We must know what is driving Lady Macbeth and why her husband is so susceptible to her manipulation.

It is impossible to know why Lady Macbeth is as she is, but the structure of her personality is clear. She is a woman who has modeled herself not upon any of the feminine ideals of her culture but upon the Machiavellian model of manhood. She wants to achieve absolute mastery and is prepared to use any means necessary to attain it. She has an idealized image of herself as totally cruel, unscrupulous, and devoid of sentiment. She despises the self-effacing traits and values that are normally associated with womanhood and seeks to eliminate all traces of them in herself. She has a sense of rivalry with men and a need to prove that she is as good as they are. She has lived, so far, a life of frustration. Because of the constrictions of her feminine lot, she has had no outlet for her aggressiveness. Like most ambitious women in Western literature, she is dependent upon a man for the realization of her dreams. She has invested her hopes in Macbeth, who shares her craving for mastery; but she is afraid that he is too tender-minded to cut his way to the top.

Her husband's letter throws Lady Macbeth into a state of intense excitement. The opportunity for which she has been waiting has finally arrived. The witches' prophecies confirm her own vision of greatness, and they have roused up Macbeth's ambition, perhaps to the requisite pitch. She is worried about the soft and scrupulous side of his nature, but she is determined not to lose this chance, and she is confident of her ability to "chastise with the valour of [her] tongue/ All that impedes" him from gaining "the golden round" (I, v). She has mixed feelings about Macbeth's inner impediments. They make her anxious, but they also give her an opportunity to feel that his acquisition of the crown will be *her* doing. When she sees that Macbeth is clearly intent upon the murder, she tries in another way to feel in control of the situation. She lectures him on the art of hypocrisy and tells him that he should put "This night's great business into my dispatch." He must "Only look up clear"; she'll do "all the rest." She wishes to be the power behind the most powerful man in the state.

Lady Macbeth is not free of inner conflict. Her second soliloquy is triggered by anxieties about herself that are aroused by the news of Duncan's imminent arrival:

> Come, you spirits
> That tend on mortal thoughts, unsex me here,
> And fill me, from the crown to the toe, top-full
> Of direst cruelty! Make thick my blood;
> Stop up th' access and passage to remorse,
> That no compunctious visitings of nature
> Shake my fell purpose nor keep peace between
> Th' effect and it! Come to my woman's breasts
> And take my milk for gall, you murd'ring ministers,
> Wherever in your sightless substances
> You wait on nature's mischief! Come, thick night,
> And pall thee in the dunnest smoke of hell,
> That my keen knife see not the wound it makes,
> Nor heaven peep through the blanket of the dark
> To cry "Hold, hold!" (I, v)

Having the opportunity to act out her aggressive impulses stirs up her opposing tendencies and threatens Lady Macbeth with feelings of guilt. When this sort of thing happens to Macbeth, he defends himself by relinquishing his criminal intentions. Lady Macbeth, however, is more afraid of her arrogant-vindictive shoulds than she is of anything else. She has the opportunity to actualize her idealized image of herself as a ruthlessly aggressive person, and she could never forgive herself if she were prevented from doing so by her softer feelings. Thus, she calls upon the powers of evil to reinforce her "fell purpose" and to aid in the repression of her self-effacing side. That she has softer feelings is evident in her concern to stop up "remorse" and the "compunctious visitings of nature." She is no more able than Macbeth to confront the actual murder, and, like him, she invokes total darkness so that she will not see Duncan's blood. She is afraid that the sight of heaven's light will rouse up her conscience and prevent her from doing the deed.

These are not the thoughts of a totally cold, calculating, "fiendlike" woman, but of a woman who wants to be that way and is afraid that she cannot. If we have understood this soliloquy, we should not be surprised by Lady Macbeth's psychological deterioration. Driven by her need to become her glorified self and her fear of self-hate if she does not, she convinces herself that she can repress her conscientious feelings completely. Macbeth has a great deal more self-knowledge than his wife, since he knows the torments that await him if he murders the king and decides to desist. Lady Macbeth's blindness extends, of course, to her husband, whom she understands very well, but only up to a point. She is aware of his inner conflicts, but she does not appreciate their strength. She sees them, moreover, from her own perspective, as obstacles to her search for glory, rather than from his, as signs that he should not commit the crime. She has a compulsive need to turn him, as well as herself, into her idealized image of a man, and she cannot afford to see that neither of her projects is realistic.

Lady Macbeth's hopes receive a blow when her husband begins to back out, and she responds with a furious attack, using every device at her command to bend him to her will (I, vii). We must recognize that her situation is different from that of Macbeth. He has been heaped with honors, and for him to go ahead with the murder is to sacrifice the rewards his heroism has bought. Lady Macbeth feels that she has arrived at the turning point of her life. This is her golden opportunity to exercise real power, to escape her woman's lot. Either she will become her glorified self or live out the rest of her days in despair, full of hatred of herself and bitter contempt for her husband. She would regard it as a shameful failure if she allowed Macbeth's scruples to triumph. She had expected his resistance and had anticipated this scene in which she "chastise[s] with the valour of [her] tongue/ All that impedes [him] from the golden round" (I,v).

The energy of her attack derives not only from the need to convert Macbeth, but also from a need to reassure herself. His scruples arouse her inner conflicts and force her to reaffirm her Machiavellian values. She is afraid of what she accuses her husband of fearing. She, too, shrinks from being the same in act as she is in desire. She, too, would be "a coward" in her "own esteem" if she let " 'I dare not' wait upon 'I would.' " In part at least, she is displacing onto Macbeth the scorn she feels for the side of herself to which he is appealing. When Macbeth says that he dares "do all that may become a man," she must reject his ideal of manhood and reaffirm her own. She implies that even though she is a woman, she is a better man than he is, for she would dash out the brains of her nursing babe rather than go back on her word, as Macbeth is doing. She unsexes herself again by reaffirming the dominance of the aggressive side of herself over her womanly feelings. Her triumph in this scene is complete. She not only masters her husband, but she also gains his admiration. He tells her to "bring forth men-children only," for her "undaunted mettle should compose/ Nothing but males" (I, vii). This confirms, in effect, her idealized image of herself.

We can understand now, I think, why Lady Macbeth is so impassioned, but we have yet to explain why her harangue has such a potent effect upon her husband. Like Iago, Lady Macbeth is a great psychologist who understands other people's vulnerabilities and is a genius at exploiting them. She attacks her husband initially by trying to make him feel that he will be despicable if he allows his scruples to stand in his way. She subjects him to a shrinking process from which he emerges "green and pale," "afeared," a "coward," and as pathetic as "the poor cat i' th' adage." The opposite terms in the speech are "hope," "valour," "desire," and "ornament of life"—all of which Macbeth is giving up because of his moral nausea. She portrays the situation as a test not only of his manliness, but also of his love, and she implies the withdrawal of her own affection. Given Macbeth's dependency upon her, this is a powerful form of emotional blackmail. If he is to have her love, he must prove his love for her; and he can do this only by killing Duncan. She is playing upon his softer side in order to get him to commit the murder.

She is also playing upon his aggressive side. She is the voice of his arrogant-vindictive dictates, which were drowned out in his soliloquy by his opposing trends. He is now caught in a cross fire of conflicting shoulds. He knows that he will hate himself if he violates his code of honor, but Lady Macbeth makes him see that he will also hate himself if he does not commit the murder: "Wouldst thou have that/ Which thou esteem'st the ornament of life,/ And live a coward in thine own esteem,/ Letting 'I dare not' wait upon 'I would' "? (I, viii) His wife's contempt would not affect him as strongly as it does if he did not feel that he would, in fact, despise himself as a coward—not because he is a warrior, as many critics have said, but because part of him shares her Machiavellian value system. He is profoundly uncomfortable about committing the murder, but he is also uneasy about being afraid to do it. His fear comes out in his soliloquies, but he does not allow others to see it. The reasons he gives Lady Macbeth for not wanting to proceed are genuine, but they conceal his moral anxieties. His wife ignores his stated reasons and goes straight to his fear: "Was the hope drunk/ Wherein you dress'd yourself? Hath it slept since?/ And wakes it now to look so green and pale/ At what it did so freely?" (I, viii) She senses his ambivalent feelings about being afraid to proceed and tries to reinforce the shame that derives from the aggressive side of his personality.

Macbeth defends himself against his wife's attack and his own threatening self-hate by reaffirming his perfectionistic code: "I dare do all that may become a man./ Who dares do more is none." Lady Macbeth counters with her arrogant-vindictive notion of manhood: "When you durst do it, then you were a man;/ And to be more than what you were, you would/ Be so much more the man." (I, iii) Macbeth is at a great disadvantage in this confrontation, for his wife's arguments reverberate strongly within him, whereas she is scornful of his. The fact that his inner conflicts are much closer to the surface than hers makes him extremely vulnerable. She can influence him, but he cannot win her to his position. If he refuses to go along, he will lose her approval; but if he kills Duncan, he will be "so much more the man."

The conclusion of Lady Macbeth's speech is brilliant, both rhetorically and psychologically:

> I have given suck, and know
> How tender 'tis to love the babe that milks me.
> I would, while it was smiling in my face,
> Have pluck'd my nipple from his boneless gums
> And dash'd the brains out, had I so sworn as you
> Have done to this. (I, vii)

She had reminded him earlier that it was he who had initiated the scheme, and she now reproaches him for being ready to break his oath. There has been considerable speculation as to what Lady Macbeth is referring to here, since we do not see Macbeth either break the enterprise to her or swear to do the murder in any of the preceding scenes. My own feeling is that he has done neither, though in act 1, scene 5, there is a tacit understanding between them. The important point is that Lady Macbeth succeeds in making Macbeth feel that it was his idea in the first place, that he has committed himself to it, and that he would be contemptible if he backed out now. She compares herself to him in a way that is extremely threatening to his pride. She presents herself as a woman engaged in the most womanly of all acts who has more guts and determination than he. The effect of her speech is to establish an order of loyalties. If she had made such a commitment to him, she would place it above her bond to her child. The implication is that his pledge to her ought to come before his loyalty to Duncan. Macbeth does not want to kill Duncan because of his innocence. Lady Macbeth parallels Duncan's innocence with that of the nursing babe, which she would kill while it was smiling in her face. She is asking him to do nothing more cruel than she is prepared to do herself. The image of milk reminds us of Lady Macbeth's fear that her husband is "too full o' th' milk of human kindness/ To catch the nearest way." She is trying here to exorcise the softer feelings that are holding him back by pointing out that she has such feelings also but that she would not let them stand in her way. The milk of human kindness is epitomized by a nursing mother. What more tender feelings, what more sacred bond could Macbeth cite as a reason for not proceeding?

Macbeth's resistance is swept away by the onslaught of his wife. The forces propelling him toward the murder are stronger now than those holding him back. Although gaining the throne is what initially prompted him to think of killing the king, it is no longer his major motivation. As Bradley has observed, "the deed is done in horror and without the faintest desire or sense of glory, . . . as if it were an appalling duty" (1964, 358). Macbeth is driven less by his search for glory than by fear of his wife's rejection and of his own self-contempt. He is compelled to live up to the idealized image of a man that is dictated by Lady Macbeth and by the corresponding side of his own idealized image.

Macbeth still hesitates, asking what would happen if they should fail; but his question indicates that he has capitulated, since he is concerned now not with the moral but with the practical aspects of the murder. He is looking for reassurance, which his wife is quick to provide. Especially comforting to him is her plan to place the guilt on Duncan's "spongy officers." If everyone thinks that the chamberlains have done it, he may escape the retribution he has feared, and the loss of golden opinions. Lady Macbeth's confidence, resourcefulness, and "undaunted mettle" reduce his anxieties and help to persuade him that he can get away with the crime.

MACBETH'S INNER CONFLICTS—AFTER THE MURDER

Macbeth is still not single-minded, of course, any more than he was when he decided against the murder. His inner conflicts are evident even in the moment of his resolution. He speaks of the murder as a "terrible feat" and tells his wife that "false face must hide what the false heart doth know" (I, vii). His language reveals that he is still feeling considerable moral discomfort. His hallucination of the dagger in the next scene is a sign of intense psychological stress. At first the hallucination seems to be generated by his aggressive side. The handle of the dagger is toward him, inviting his grasp, and the dagger seems to marshal him "the way that [he] was going" (II, i). Before his eyes, however, the dagger becomes covered with blood, as though his compunctious side were reminding him once more of the horror of what he is about to do. Macbeth reacts to this by dismissing the dagger as an illusion and invoking the forces of evil to put him in harmony with the act he is going to perform. He engages in a desperate effort to persuade himself that evil is now his good. He sustains the illusion long enough to permit him to murder Duncan, but it collapses as soon as he has done the deed.

Caught as he is in a cross fire of conflicting shoulds, Macbeth is bound to suffer no matter what he does. He is damned if he does not kill Duncan and damned if he does. He returns from the murder in a panic-stricken state. He could not say "Amen" when he "had most need of blessing," and he has heard a voice cry "Sleep no more./ Macbeth does murder sleep" (II, ii). He has violated his need to be holy, and hence he cannot say Amen. He had feared damnation before the murder, and now he is sure that he is lost. He had thought he was ready to pay this price, but he finds that he is not. His auditory hallucination derives, in part, from his belief in an "even-handed justice." According to the *lex talionis,* if you murder a man in his sleep then you may be murdered in yours. When we sleep, we are most vulnerable, least in control of our fate. We are dependent upon other men, upon the protection of a stable order. It is not only Duncan, it is also this order Macbeth has murdered. He fears that he will no longer feel safe enough to sleep, that he has deprived himself of the "chief nourisher in life's feast." His sleep does, in fact, become disturbed, as does that of Lady Macbeth.

It is noteworthy that Macbeth speaks of "the innocent sleep." Sleep is innocent in the sense that it is a state in which we do no harm and also in the sense that it comes more readily to those who are pure of heart. As with the chamberlains, saying one's prayers is a prelude to sleep. Duncan, presumably, is sleeping the sleep of the innocent. Having killed Duncan in his sleep intensifies Macbeth's sense of guilt. He has killed an innocent man in his most defenseless and innocent state. It is not only his fear but also his guilt that accounts for his later insomnia. Inability to sleep is a fitting punishment for having murdered his own innocence.

Macbeth is so overwhelmed by fear and guilt that he fails to carry out an essential part of the plan. Instead of planting the bloody daggers on the sleeping grooms, he carries them away, thus incriminating himself. As a number of critics have observed, Macbeth seems unconsciously to be seeking punishment. He is so appalled by what he has done that he vehemently rejects Lady Macbeth's instructions to return the daggers and to smear the grooms with blood. "To know my deed," he tells her later in the scene, " 't were best not know myself." His habitual values are dominant once again, and he regards the self implied by his deed with horror and loathing. This comes out most vividly, perhaps, in his obsession with his bloody hands. He speaks of them as a "sorry sight" and wonders if they can ever be purified:

> What hands are here? Ha! they pluck out mine eyes!
> Will all great Neptune's ocean wash this blood
> Clean from my hand? No. This my hand will rather
> The multitudinous seas incarnadine,
> Making the green one red. (II, ii)

There is no power on earth great enough to cleanse him; rather, everything will be contaminated by his touch. It is not simply his hand, of course, but his whole moral being that is irrevocably stained with guilt. His impulse to pluck out his eyes derives in part from a desire to assuage his guilt through self-punishment and, in part, from a wish to blind himself to what he has done. He wanted before the murder to trick his conscience by having "the eye wink at the hand" (I, v). He has now done that which "the eye fears . . . to see"; and he has an impulse to try to escape the reproaches of conscience by putting out his eyes. Macbeth is in such agony at having committed the murder that he wishes his deed could be undone: "Wake Duncan with thy knocking! I would thou couldst!"

THE MURDER OF BANQUO

Macbeth's transformation from a reluctant, conscience-ridden conspirator into a cunning and brutal murderer begins in the very next scene. Despite his panic immediately after the murder, he is remarkably self-possessed when Duncan's death is discovered. He eloquently expresses his sorrow, boldly kills the chamberlains, and effectively defends this precipitous action. The murder of the grooms was not part of the original plan. It is Macbeth's idea, and it is a very good one, for it makes it much easier to pin the guilt for Duncan's death on them. When next we see Macbeth, he is planning the murders of Banquo and Fleance; and after his encounter with Banquo's ghost, he immediately begins to plot against Macduff. By the end of the play he is a "butcher" (V, viii) who has turned Scotland into a country where "Each new morn/New widows howl, new orphans cry, new sorrows/Strike heaven on the face" (IV, iii). Given Macbeth's inner conflicts before the murder and his fear and revulsion after, how can we account for his growing brutality through the rest of the play? This may be the central puzzle of Macbeth's character.

Macbeth has a number of motives for wanting to kill Banquo, the chief of which are fear, feelings of inferiority, and anguish at the thought of Banquo's line succeeding to the throne. Macbeth's fear arises less from any specific threat posed by Banquo than from feelings of anxiety with which Banquo has little to do. Ironically, the measures he has taken to gain "sovereign sway and masterdom" (I, v) have made him feel far more vulnerable than he has ever felt before. By his murder of Duncan, he has turned the world into a jungle in which no one can be trusted and no one is safe. In this struggle of each against all, he must get others before they get him. Since he expects retribution for having violated the code of loyalty, duty, and service, no amount of power can make him feel safe. His mental agony is so great that he envies the man he has murdered:

> Duncan is in his grave;
> After life's fitful fever he sleeps well.
> Treason has done his worst. Nor steel, nor poison,
> Malice domestic, foreign levy, nothing,
> Can touch him further. (III, ii)

Macbeth's fears are widespread and overwhelming. He fears poison in his food and either lies awake in "restless ecstasy" (III, ii) or is visited by terrifying dreams. He is afraid of domestic malice and of foreign invasion. Why, then, does he say that "there is none but [Banquo]/ Whose being I do fear"? There are several reasons: Macbeth's fears are generated less by external threats (at this point) than by the violation of his own value system. He is full of self-hate and expectations of punishment. To recognize the intrapsychic sources of his anxiety would leave Macbeth in despair. What steps could he take to find peace? He needs to believe that his fears have a tangible, specific, external source in order to feel that there is something he can do about them. He defends himself against his fears by attributing them to one person and then imagining that he can rid himself of them by disposing of their source. Banquo is a logical focus for his fears because he is a formidable person who has good reason to suspect Macbeth's wrongdoing. Macbeth sees Banquo as a better man than himself. Banquo's "temper" is as "dauntless" as his; but Banquo has "a wisdom that doth guide his valour/ To act in safety" (III, i), while his own daring has led him to sacrifice his peace and security.

Macbeth is psychologically oppressed by the existence of Banquo, who makes him feel foolish, inadequate, and morally inferior. Banquo possesses a "royalty of nature" (III, i) that Macbeth feels to be lacking in himself. He represents the code of loyalty, duty, and service that Macbeth has violated; he had similar temptations but did not give way. Because he has dreamt of the Weird Sisters, he struggles against going to sleep: "Merciful powers,/ Restrain in me the cursed thoughts that nature/ Gives way to in repose!" (II, i). Before the murder, Macbeth tried to tempt him by saying that it would "make honour" for him if he "cleave[d] to [his] consent"; but Banquo was firm in his reply: "So I lose none/ In seeking to augment it, but still keep/ My bosom franchised and allegiance clear,/ I shall be counsell'd" (II, i). These words must continue to rankle Macbeth, for he has done that which Banquo refused to do: he has sacrificed integrity in the pursuit of worldly fortune. Banquo represents to Macbeth his perfectionistic shoulds, his earlier self. He is what Macbeth wishes he still were instead of what he has become. Comparing himself to Banquo fills Macbeth with self-hate. He externalizes this self-hate actively by hating Banquo and passively by imagining himself to be the object of Banquo's aggression. One of his reasons for killing Banquo is to alleviate his self-contempt and sense of inferiority by removing the person who triggers these feelings. It is part of his effort to escape the perfectionistic side of his nature, which is largely responsible for his mental torment.

One of Macbeth's strongest reasons for wanting to kill Banquo (and Fleance) is his anguish at the thought of Banquo's line succeeding to the throne. Macbeth did not kill Duncan to establish a dynasty, but to gain the throne for himself. His obsession with the matter of his successor is a reflection of his disillusionment with the kingship. He feels, like Lady Macbeth, that "Naught's had, all's spent,/ Where our desire is got without content" (II, ii). His scepter has brought him no satisfaction, but in order to get it, he has defiled his mind, put rancours in the vessel of his peace, and sold his soul to the devil.[2] He now needs to found a dynasty in order to compensate for the emptiness of his triumph and the apparent meaninglessness of his sacrifice. Since he has given his "eternal jewel" to "the common enemy of man" (III, i), his heaven must now be on earth, his immortality in his descendants. Only if they succeed to the throne will there be a sufficient measure of glory to justify his sacrifice. The Weird Sisters have prophesied, however, that not he but Banquo will be "father to a line of kings" (III, i). It maddens Macbeth to feel that Banquo is going to get through his heirs the glory that he has pursued, but without compromising his honor, betraying his royalty of nature, or losing his soul. Macbeth will have paid the price and Banquo will reap the reward. His enemy is not simply Banquo; it is fate, which has ordained that Banquo's line shall be kings. For him to have sacrificed everything in order to make "the seeds of Banquo kings" is too unfair to be borne: "Rather than so, come, Fate, into the list,/ And champion me to th' utterance!" (III, i).

By killing Banquo and Fleance, then, Macbeth is not only trying to assure his safety and to cut off a rival line, but is also trying to master fate, to force it to honor his bargain. The futility of this enterprise is made evident by the escape of Fleance, which brings on his "fit again" (III, iv). Macbeth would feel "Whole as the marble, founded as the rock" if both Banquo and Fleance had been killed because this would have established his independence of external ordinances. He is aspiring to the position of lawgiver, not merely in the state, but in the universe. If he can prove that he is above fate, then he may not be subject to the retribution he fears. The escape of Fleance shows that he is not a free agent but is "bound in" by an external order whose laws he has violated. As a result, his anxieties are intensified. His attempt to master fate leaves him more rather than less exposed to "saucy doubts and fears" (III, iv).

It is striking that after vacillating so much before the murder of Duncan, Macbeth moves against Banquo with an apparent absence of inner conflict. His conscientious side is still present, with its fear of retribution, but it has been repressed. Consciously, he has adopted the Machiavellian code and is attempting to live up to the idealized image it prescribes. We can see this most clearly in the scene with the murderers in which his conception of manhood parallels Lady Macbeth's. He mocks the gospel notion of forgiveness and encourages the murderers' vindictive impulses. The more villainous they are, the higher they rank in the order of manhood. When they agree to commit the murders, he commends them in language that reminds us of Iago: "Your spirits shine through you" (III, i). At this point for Macbeth "fair is foul, and foul is fair"; he has inverted his former values.

Macbeth's inner conflicts are brought to the surface by the appearance of Banquo's ghost. It is impossible to say whether Shakespeare meant for the ghost to be real or an hallucination. If it is supposed to be the latter, then it is Macbeth's conscientious side emerging and haunting him with what he has done. This is, of course, Lady Macbeth's interpretation. She calls it "the very painting of [his] fear" and reminds him of "the air-drawn dagger" (III, iv). Given Macbeth's earlier hallucinations, it seems likely that Shakespeare meant for the ghost to be one also. If the ghost is real—and Macbeth at first thinks it is—then its effect is to reaffirm the moral order and to exacerbate his fear of retribution:

> It will have blood, they say; blood will have blood.
> Stones have been known to move and trees to speak;
> Augures and understood relations have
> By maggot-pies and choughs and rooks brought forth
> The secret'st man of blood. (III, iv)

Macbeth is in the grip here of a mystic belief that murder will out, that a supernatural order will see to his punishment. He is as panic-stricken as he was after the murder of Duncan. His arrogant-vindictive defense system has broken down, his suppressed trends have emerged, and he is almost overwhelmed by anxiety.

MACBETH'S TRANSFORMATION

At this moment, a major turning point in Macbeth's development occurs. He expresses resentment toward Macduff, who did not attend the feast, and determines to embark upon a course of reckless cruelty. One would think that the appearance of Banquo's ghost might deter him from future crimes, or at least make him more fearful of the consequences; but it seems to have the opposite effect. Instead of shrinking from further violence, he embraces it wholeheartedly. Up to this point, he has not been a bloody tyrant, but he becomes one now. Henceforth we see neither hesitation before nor moral discomfort after his crimes. His inner conflicts seem to disappear. How are we to account for this change?

The change in Macbeth is a direct reaction to the anxiety he has just experienced. He defends himself against his fear of being punished by determining ruthlessly to eliminate anyone who threatens him: "For mine own good/ All causes shall give way" (III, iv). If he is not to succumb to his dread of the moral order, he must defy it. His idealized image of himself as a "man" has been undermined by his response to the ghost and by Lady Macbeth's mockery. He turns his anger at his own weakness onto Macduff and resolves to show both his wife and himself what kind of man he is by pursuing a course of unrestrained violence. Macbeth is defending himself most of all against the threat of psychological collapse that is posed by the emergence of his guilt. He senses that to think of "these deeds . . . after these ways" (II, ii) will make him mad. The emergence of his conscientious side can only fill Macbeth with self-hate and anxiety, for there is no longer any way he can put himself in harmony with it. Because Macbeth is more perfectionistic than self-effacing, repentance is not an option that he considers. Salvation for him comes from obeying the law; once he has broken it, he feels himself to be doomed. He has stepped in blood so far that there is nothing to be gained by going back and nothing to be lost by going forward. His only hope of avoiding a total breakdown is to rebuild his arrogant-vindictive defense system and to identify himself with it completely. If he is not to be destroyed by his conscientious side, he must destroy it first.

There are two major ways in which Macbeth hopes to accomplish this—by inuring himself to violence and by acting on impulse. He now sees the ghost as an hallucination that was caused by his inexperience, and he determines to harden himself by a steady course of violence: "My strange and self-abuse/ Is the initiate fear that wants hard use./ We are yet but young in deed" (III, iv). This is a way of dismissing what has just happened, as well as of assuring himself that he will be able to avoid such visitations in the future. Thinking about his murderous intentions has tended to fill him with horror. He will put an end to this by purposely acting on impulse: "Strange things I have in head, that will to hand;/ Which must be acted ere they may be scann'd" (III, iv). He wants to anesthetize himself so that he will be free of moral anxiety both before his crimes and after.

The first victims of Macbeth's impulsive violence are Macduff's wife and children. He moves against them for several reasons. One of the strange things he had in mind was the murder of Macduff, but he put it off until he had visited the three witches. When Macduff escapes, Macbeth is angry with himself for having delayed and resolves never to do so again: "From this moment/ The very firstlings of my heart shall be/ The first-lings of my hand" (IV, ii). He had gone to the witches in order to learn "by the worst means the worst" (III, iv), but he still had hoped for a reversal of their earlier prophecy and he is furious at hearing once again that Banquo's issue will be kings. He is full of rage at himself, at Macduff, and at destiny; and he takes out this rage on Macduff's wife and children. By murdering them, he will punish Macduff for his defection and will restore his sense of power. He needs to prove to himself that he can actually carry out the murderous impulses that flit through his mind: "No boasting like a fool!/ This deed I'll do before this purpose cool" (IV, ii). The murder of Lady Macduff and her children has little practical purpose, but it serves a multitude of psychological needs. It is the means by which Macbeth acts out his rage, relieves his feelings of impotence, and actu-alizes his idealized image of himself as a man who can commit the most heinous crimes without flinching. It is the first step in his effort to kill his conscience by accustoming himself to murder. Macbeth's further crimes are not presented in any detail but are conveyed to us in a general way through a series of laments for Scotland and denunciations of Macbeth and by Macbeth's own feeling that he has "supp'd full with horrors" (V, v).

THE VILLAIN AS HERO

Although the concluding acts of *Macbeth* are rather flat compared with the opening three, they contain, nonetheless, some impressive achievements. *Macbeth* lacks the sustained richness of *Hamlet, Othello,* and *Lear,* but it has fewer confusing effects, and its conclusion is more satisfactory. In no other tragedy does the death of the main character satisfy so many demands while causing so few frustrations, and in no other tragedy does the gesture toward optimism at the end seem so well justified. Shakespeare has achieved a very complex effect, moreover, by making us regard Macbeth as both a monstrous and a sympathetic figure. He achieves this, in part, by keeping Macbeth's victims and adversaries one-dimensional, while Macbeth remains a mimetic character. We are moved by the suffering of Macduff and his family, but Macbeth's suffering moves us more. We admire Malcolm's virtue and sagacity (at least some of us do), but he seems a pale figure beside the more vividly drawn Macbeth. As the appeal of Satan in *Paradise Lost* indicates, a mimetically portrayed villain has much more human interest than any aesthetic or illustrative character—even God himself. We want the forces of good to win and to put an end to Macbeth's reign of terror, but we continue to care more about Macbeth than about any other character because we know him so much better.

Macbeth retains our sympathy also because his effort to kill his conscience fails and he remains a tortured human being. Heilman complained that Macbeth is spared "the ultimate rigour of self-confrontation, the act of knowing directly what he has been and done" (1977, 36). This is true, of course, at least at the conscious level; and it is a sign of Shakespeare's psychological realism; for after the appearance of Banquo's ghost, Macbeth tries to defend himself, as we have seen, by denying his feelings of guilt. If Shakespeare had made Macbeth "face the moral record" as Heilman wished (1977, 37), he would have falsified his character, as Garrick did by having him repent. Macbeth's feelings of guilt are still present, however, and are the source of much of his distress. They are too deeply repressed to be directly available to our observation, but Shakespeare makes us aware of them by having Angus and Menteith comment on Macbeth's psychological state:

> Ang.   Now does he feel
> His secret murders sticking on his hands.
> Now minutely revolts upbraid his faith-breach.
> Those he commands move only in command,
> Nothing in love. Now does he feel his title
> Hang loose about him, like a giant's robe
> Upon a dwarfish thief.
> Ment.   Who then shall blame
> His pester'd senses to recoil and start,
> When all that is within him does condemn
> Itself for being there? (V, ii)

These speeches are given great weight by the following scene, in which Macbeth is trying to control the panic caused by the desertions of which Angus speaks. We do not see Macbeth condemning himself in the way Menteith describes, but he displays the effects that Menteith attributes to his sense of guilt.

Macbeth's "pester'd senses . . . recoil and start" from the moment of his first encounter with the witches. As the moment for the murder approaches, he has the vision of the dagger, and afterwards he hears voices proclaiming that he has murdered sleep. His early starts and hallucinations and his later nightmares are produced by a fear of retribution that derives from his self-condemnation. Surely, it is this fear and not mere physical cowardice with which Macbeth is struggling in the scene that follows the comments of Angus and Menteith. The fate he has dreaded since before the murder of Duncan seems now to be imminent. His thanes are flying from him, and his enemies are closing in. He clings to the words of the apparitions in order to convince himself that he is not shaking with fear or sagging with doubt, but he is protesting too much. His fear is evident in his reaction to the servant who enters:

> Macb.   The devil damn thee black, thou cream-fac'd loon!
>   Where got'st thou that goose look?
> Serv.   There is ten thousand—
> Macb.   Geese, villain?
> Serv.   Soldiers, sir.
> Macb.   Go prick thy face and over-red thy fear,
>   Thou lily-liver'd boy. What soldiers, patch?
>   Death of thy soul! Those linen cheeks of thine
>   Are counsellors to fear. What soldiers, wheyface?
> Serv.   The English force, so please you.
> Macb.   Take thy face hence. (V, iii)

The vehemence of Macbeth's attack on the servant has two sources. The fear of others is very threatening to him since it reinforces his own fear, which is barely under control. He is eager to get the boy out of his sight, and later in the scene he tells Seyton to "Hang those that talk of fear." His severity is also the product of his self-hate. He is externalizing the rage and contempt he feels toward himself for being afraid and thus failing to live up to his idealized image. He does not need Lady Macbeth to shame him now; he is trying through his attack on the boy to shame himself.

Macbeth is struggling in this scene not only with fear of retribution but also with despair. At this point, there is no way in which he can succeed. Even if he were to repel the invaders, he would not really be cheered; for he has lost the things he had always cherished most highly and that are still of great importance to him— "honour, love, obedience, troops of friends" (V, iii). Instead of having "golden opinions from all sorts of people" (I, vii), he now has merely "mouth-honour" from people who are compelled to give him homage while hating them in their hearts. Since life has nothing to offer, Macbeth feels that he has "liv'd long enough." His conversation with the doctor is a further expression of his despair. Although they are ostensibly discussing his wife, Macbeth is clearly speaking of himself. His mind, too, is diseased; the same "perilous stuff" (V, iii) that weighs upon her heart weighs upon his. Perhaps life would be bearable if there were some potion that could erase the memories that haunt him and cleanse his "stuff'd bosom" of its guilt, but he can no more restore his peace of mind than he can recover the golden opinions he has lost.

Macbeth's darkest expression of despair occurs in the speech that follows upon the death of his wife. Many critics feel that Macbeth reacts to the news with callousness or indifference, but the grimness of his reflections indicates that he finds it deeply disturbing:

> To-morrow, and to-morrow, and to-morrow
> Creeps in this petty pace from day to day
> To the last syllable of recorded time;
> And all our yesterdays have lighted fools
> The way to dusty death. Out, out, brief candle!
> Life's but a walking shadow, a poor player,
> That struts and frets his hour upon the stage
> And then is heard no more. It is a tale
> Told by an idiot, full of sound and fury,
> Signifying nothing. (V, v)

The death of his wife fills Macbeth with a sense of the futility of all their striving. Now he feels quite sincerely what he said upon the death of

Duncan: "from this instant/ There's nothing serious in mortality;/ All is but toys" (II, iii). Life is so transitory and insubstantial that it is foolish to take anything seriously. We aspire to fame and glory, but after our brief hour upon the stage, we disappear and are forgotten. Viewed from the perspective of death, our hates and loves, agonies and triumphs, have no ultimate meaning. they are but "sound and fury,/ Signifying nothing." These are not Shakespeare's sentiments, of course, but Macbeth's, who is generalizing from the emptiness of his own existence to the absurdity of the human condition.

This speech is not only an expression of despair but also a defense against it. Lady Macbeth's death threatens Macbeth by making him feel the futility of his life and by intensifying his own fear of dying. He defends himself by withdrawing to a detached perspective from which nothing matters. Life is meaningless because of death, and death has no significance because life is such a burden. Macbeth is looking at time from both a subjective and a cosmic perspective. From the subjective perspective, it moves with agonizing slowness through a series of empty tomorrows. From the cosmic perspective, life is so ridiculously short—a brief candle, an hour upon the stage—that it seems like "a walking shadow." Both perspectives make death more acceptable: the subjective because it makes death a release from the wearisome round of tomorrows; the cosmic because it makes our lives seem unreal and their duration of little significance. If life is so empty, burdensome, and brief, what difference does it make whether we die now or a little later? Macbeth's sense of absurdity is a defense not only against his fear of death, but also against his frustration and self-hate. Despair about life in general is much easier for him to handle than is a sense of personal defeat. If all lives are futile, if all men are mocked by fate, then his own life has not been such a tragic disaster. He can blame his suffering on the idiotic nature of existence rather than upon himself.

As the play draws to a close, Macbeth oscillates between courage and fear, hope and despair. His hope is based upon the words of the apparitions, which give him a feeling of invulnerability until they prove to be equivocal. He is confident his "castle's strength/ Will laugh a siege to scorn" (V, v) until he hears that Birnam Wood has begun to move. With this blow to his hope of an escape from retribution, his death wish grows stronger. One of the reasons we admire Macbeth is that although he has received two terrible blows in this scene—his wife's death and the moving of Birnam Wood—he does not, in fact, "pull in resolution" but determines to fight on in spite of everything: "Blow wind, come wrack,/ At least we'll die with harness on our back" (V, v). This pattern is repeated in his encounter with Macduff. Macbeth exults in his sense of invulnerability when he fights the young Siward—"swords I smile at, weapons laugh to scorn,/ Brandish'd by man that's of a woman born" (V, vii); but his "better part of man" is "cow'd" when he learns that Macduff was ripped untimely from his mother's womb. He knows now that he is lost, but once again he rallies his spirit: "Yet I will try the last. Before my body/ I throw my warlike shield. Lay on, Macduff,/ And damn'd be him that first cries, 'hold, enough!' " (V, viii). Macbeth still seems heroic because despite the hopelessness of his situation his energy does not fail. He wavers again and again, but in the end he stands up to psychological pressures under which most men would collapse. Although his courage is not morally redemptive, it establishes his martial and manly honor and earns our respect.

THE DEATH OF MACBETH

Macbeth's death is extraordinarily satisfying, because it is in harmony with our sympathy and admiration for him and also with our abhorrence and need to see him punished. It completes the pattern of his psychological development and also the pattern of the larger aesthetic and thematic structure of which he is a part. Even though he fights to the end, it is clear that Macbeth wants to die. He has been afraid all along of a retributive justice operating in the universe, and only death can rid him of this fear. It pays for his guilt, satisfies his need for punishment, and gives him the quiet sleep for which he had so envied Duncan. Now "nothing/ Can touch him further" (III, ii). It is an escape, moreover, from a life of which he has grown weary, a life in which there is no hope of joy, of success, of freedom from inner torment. Despite his death wish, Macbeth does not succumb to the temptation to "play the Roman fool and die/ On [his] own sword" (V, viii). He resists also the temptations to flee and to yield. He maintains his pride and dies in a way that fulfills his image of himself as a fearless warrior. The manner of his death not only earns our respect, it enables him to retain his own.

Macbeth's death completes the moral pattern of the play, which is that of the perfectionistic solution. Macbeth is rewarded as long as he is faithful to the code of loyalty, duty, and service but is punished in the ways he anticipates when he violates it. As in all of Shakespeare's tragedies, there are a number of innocent victims; but with respect to the villains, at least, there is an even-handed justice. The play opens on this note as "the merciless Macdonwald" is unseamed by Macbeth and his head is fixed upon the battlements (I, ii). The merciless Macbeth meets a similar fate at the end. It is extremely satisfying that Macbeth is killed by Macduff, the victim of his most outrageous atrocity. It is also satisfying that Macbeth is defeated by the forces of Malcolm, the young prince whose father he killed and whose place he has usurped. The perfectionistic Banquo does not get his just deserts, but the perfectionistic Malcolm does.

The death of Macbeth is in harmony not only with the aesthetic and thematic patterns of the play but also with its realistic dimension, for it is the product of a natural sequence of events that flows from his character. Macbeth brings it on himself as a result of his inability to cope with the violation of his perfectionistic values. Although it has numerous affinities with the morality play, *Macbeth* also has much in common with a realistic novel like *Crime and Punishment*. Like Raskolnikov, Macbeth has inner conflicts before and after his crime, and it is his guilt and fear more than anything else that are responsible for his downfall. The compelling power of both works derives in large part from their brilliant portrayal of the effects of crime upon the psychology of the criminal.[3] A. P. Rossiter contended that "*Macbeth,* like *Richard III,* is best interpreted through its themes and imagery, not through character" (1961, 209). I feel that *Macbeth* and *Richard III* are very much alike in the importance that character has in the development of theme (see Paris 1991). Both plays dramatize through their concrete psychological portraits the inescapability of conscientious feelings, not only in a perfectionist like Macbeth, but also in arrogant-vindictive people like Lady Macbeth and Richard. It is less the external consequences of their crime than their internal deterioration that brings about the downfall of Macbeth and his wife. If he had not been so afraid, Macbeth might have gotten away with his crime; and his fear, as we have seen, is largely psychological in origin. To cope with it, he embarks upon a series of actions that turns everyone against him and brings about the very thing he dreads. *Macbeth* is the tragedy of a man who violates his own bargain with fate and then, as a result of the psychological consequences, compulsively destroys himself.

The death of Macbeth is satisfying, finally, because it signals the lifting of a nightmarish oppression and the restoration of order. A vision of that restoration is held out in act 3, scene 6. The forces are gathering against Macbeth so that

> we may again
> Give to our tables meat, sleep to our nights,
> Free from our feasts and banquets bloody knives,

Do faithful homage and receive free honours—
All which we pine for now.

Our feeling about the prospects for the future will depend upon our estimate of Malcolm, who is in charge at the end of the play. He has often been maligned, but we have more reason to believe that the state will prosper under him than under a Fortinbras, an Albany, or an Edgar. What makes Malcolm such a positive figure is that he combines virtue with realism, more successfully, perhaps, than any other of Shakespeare's characters. He is a good man who is able to cope with the evil in the world. When his father is murdered, Malcolm immediately senses his danger and flees. Banquo, another good man, stays around too long. Duncan was too trusting; his greatest weakness was his inability to detect a traitor. The long scene between Malcolm and Macduff shows Malcolm's ability to deal with the appearance-reality problem that had baffled his father and that undoes so many of Shakespeare's characters. Malcolm is neither too trusting nor too cynical. He knows that some men are evil, but he does not assume, therefore, that all men are. A virtuous appearance is not necessarily a sign of virtue, but it may be:

That which you are, my thoughts cannot transpose.
Angels are bright still, though the brightest fell.
Though all things foul would wear the brows of grace,
Yet grace must still look so. (IV, iii)

Malcolm understands that evil people try to appear virtuous in order to take in good men like himself, and he therefore tries to get Macduff to prove his virtue. He does not see people in terms of a predetermined view of human nature, but recognizes the necessity of testing reality. We have good reason to believe that Malcolm will be a more effective king than was his father and that the ending promises not simply a return to things as they were but the institution of a better order.

PART II

Shakespeare's Personality

CHAPTER 6

Shakespeare's Conflicts

"A DEEPLY DIVIDED MAN"

As J. B. Priestley has observed, "until his final years," Shakespeare "was a deeply divided man, like nearly all great writers. There were profound opposites in his nature, and it is the relation between these opposites . . . that gives energy and life to his work" (1964, 82). Critics have tended to define these opposites in terms of masculine and feminine traits. In *The Personality of Shakespeare,* Harold Grier McCurdy concluded that Shakespeare "was predominantly masculine, aggressive," but that his "masculine aims have a way of running counter to the feminine components in him, which incline toward idealistic love and domestic virtues" (1953, 159). In *Psychoanalysis and Shakespeare,* Norman Holland presented a similar picture of Shakespeare. According to these critics, the division in Shakespeare's personality is between an aggressive, vindictive, power-hungry side, that generates "images of . . . violent action" (Holland 1966, 142), and a gentle, submissive, idealistic side, that dislikes cruelty and is given to loving-kindness and Christian charity. Shakespeare is afraid of his feminine side and employs "aggressive masculinity . . . as a defense against it" (Holland 1966, 141–142); he can express tenderness and charity only when his aggressive needs have been fulfilled.

This view is in conflict with the traditional picture of a "gentle Shakespeare" (Ben Jonson) who is "civil," "upright," and "honest" (Henry Chettle) and "of an open and free nature" (Jonson). In the heyday of what Samuel Schoenbaum calls "subjective biography," most critics held the softer side of Shakespeare's personality to be dominant (see Dowden 1910). Brandes felt that Shakespeare's strong reaction to evil was partly the result of his idealism: "the natural tendency of his youth had been to see good everywhere" (1899, 420). He wanted to be generous, but ingratitude made "it hard for him to be helpful again" (1899, 451). Bradley also saw Shakespeare as being of a gentle and idealistic rather than of a proud, ambitious, or aggressive nature: "Now such a free and open nature . . . is specially exposed to the risks of deception, perfidy, and ingratitude. . . . such experiences will tempt it to melancholy, embitterment, anger, possibly even misanthropy. . . . These affections, passions, and sufferings of free and open natures are Shakespeare's favourite tragic subject" (1963, 325). "It is perhaps most especially in his rendering of the shock and the effects of *disillusionment* in open natures," Bradley concluded, "that we seem to feel Shakespeare's personality."

In what is perhaps the most sophisticated attempt to relate Shakespeare's works to "the evolving temperament of [the] author," Richard Wheeler finds "a division in Shakespeare's imagination" between masculine and feminine modes of forming an identity and of relating to the world (1981, 32). The masculine mode involves "the assertion of self-willed . . . autonomy over destructive female power or over compliant feminine goodness," while the feminine mode seeks a "trusting investment of self in an other" and "turns on the mutual dependence of male and female" (1981, 221). Wheeler's understanding of the opposites in Shakespeare derives from the theories of Margaret Mahler, which posit an initial state of oneness or symbiosis with the mother, followed by a process of separation and individuation that is essential to the establishment of an autonomous identity. This process is subject to a variety of disturbances that produce powerful needs for a renewal of merger or for the assertion of independence. Both the movement toward merger and the movement toward autonomy have destructive potentialities: "the longing for merger threatens to destroy precariously achieved autonomy; the longing for complete autonomy threatens to isolate the self from its base of trust in actual and internalized relations to others" (1981, 206). Wheeler does not find one side of Shakespeare's personality to be dominant. Rather, he sees a continual "interaction of conflicting needs for trust and autonomy" (1981, 207), both within individual plays and in the corpus as a whole.

Like many other critics, I, too, see Shakespeare as "a deeply divided man" whose works reflect his inner conflicts. I shall describe these conflicts in Horneyan terms, not because they are the best possible terms for everyone to use, but because they fit certain aspects of Shakespeare very well and have the greatest heuristic value for me. Those who are not as comfortable with them as I am can translate the insights they yield into their own mode of discourse, as I do with the insights of others. It seems to me, in fact, that the critics I have been citing describe Shakespeare in terms that are quite compatible with mine. The vengeful, aggressive, power-hungry side of Shakespeare corresponds to what I call his arrogant-vindictive trends, whereas the forgiving, submissive, idealistic side corresponds to his compliant tendencies. McCurdy and Holland depict a Shakespeare who is predominantly aggressive but who has powerful, though submerged, self-effacing trends. Brandes and Bradley describe a man who believes in the world-picture of the self-effacing solution and whose aggressive tendencies emerge as a result of his disenchantment. What Wheeler describes as the trust/merger pattern in many ways parallels Horney's account of the self-effacing solution in which the individual counts on other people for love and protection and tends to merge with them in relationships of morbid dependency. The autonomy/isolation pattern seems to involve both the movement away from and the movement against other people. Since Horney's theory is predominantly synchronic, not much work has been done tracing the early origins of the defensive moves she describes (but see Feiring 1983). It is possible that Horney and Mahler can be integrated by seeing the Horneyan strategies as originating in the vicissitudes of the separation/individuation process. Fear of separation generates the movement toward other people, whereas fear of reengulfment (or perhaps lack of adequate initial symbiosis) generates longings for power and independence.

From a Horneyan point of view there is more than one conflict in Shakespeare. There are conflicts between perfectionistic and compliant and perfectionistic and arrogant-vindictive trends, as well as impulses toward detachment. Shakespeare's major conflict, however, is between his arrogant-vindictive and his self-effacing tendencies. Horney does not identify these tendencies as masculine or feminine, since she does not believe that they are biologically linked to either sex; but she notes that Western culture has tended to reinforce aggressive behavior in males and compliant behavior in females and to frown on compliant men and aggressive women. Because such linkages occur both culturally and in Shakespeare's works, it makes a certain amount of sense to speak of Shakespeare's conflict as occurring between the masculine and feminine components of his nature. I prefer the Horneyan terminology, however, which does not presuppose distinctively masculine and feminine psychologies.

In the remaining chapters of this book, I shall describe Shakespeare's personality by examining the ways in which his plays manifest his conflicts, his fantasies, and his "struggles for harmony" (Knights 1965, 192). In this chapter, I shall examine his attitude toward the various defensive strategies and their relation to each other within his character structure, and I shall show how he tried to resolve one of his major inner conflicts through an analysis of *Measure for Measure*. Although I shall draw upon the corpus as a whole, I shall focus mainly on the realistic plays, beginning with the first tetralogy. I shall indicate the place of all the strategies in Shakespeare's personality, but his attitude toward self-effacement is so complex that it requires separate treatment. In Chapter 7, I shall examine his ambivalence toward this solution in the sonnets, the comedies, *Troilus and Cressida,* and *Antony and Cleopatra;* and in Chapter 8, I shall argue that *Timon of Athens* marks a turning point in Shakespeare's development because the breakdown of Timon's self-effacing bargain leads to the leap of faith that is affirmed in the Romances. In the concluding chapter, I shall analyze *The Tempest,* which is Shakespeare's most brilliant effort to find "an imaginative solution" of his problems.

SHAKESPEARE'S TREATMENT OF CULTURAL CODES AS EXPRESSIONS OF HIS PERSONALITY

Looking at the first tetralogy, we can readily understand why some critics see Shakespeare's personality as predominantly aggressive. The plays are full of extremely competitive characters, both male and female; and, though some of them are treated as villains, others are glorified for their courage, ferocity, and military success. To understand Shakespeare's presentation of aggression and what it tells us about his personality, we must recognize that there are at least three kinds of aggression in his plays each of which is sanctioned by a different code and each of which receives a different rhetorical treatment.

Just as the codes that the characters embrace tell us something about their personalities, so Shakespeare's treatment of these codes and their proponents tells us something about his. In *The Moon and Sixpence,* Maugham has one of his characters observe that in the creation of rogues "the writer gratifies instincts deep-rooted in him, which the manners and customs of the civilized world have forced back into the mysterious recesses of the unconscious. In giving to the character of his invention flesh and bones he is giving life to that part of himself which finds no other means of expression" (1919, 203). Shakespeare's preoccupation with Machiavels may indicate that portraying their ruthless behavior gratifies a repressed part of his personality, but his conscious attitude is clearly one of horror and condemnation. The rhetoric of his plays consistently portrays them as monsters who threaten to destroy the social order. To see Shakespeare as having a predominantly aggressive personality because he portrays such characters frequently is to ignore his treatment of them, which is invariably negative. If they express a side of his personality, it is a side by which he feels threatened and that he needs to repudiate.

There is a violent side of Shakespeare's personality to which he gives direct expression, however, through his treatment of martial and manly behavior; and it is his glorification of such behavior, I suspect, that has led some critics to see him as predominantly aggressive. There is much relishing of bloodthirstiness, conquest, and revenge in the first tetralogy. Indeed, the first scene of what may have been Shakespeare's first play opens with a celebration of the martial prowess of Henry V. Although the English nobles squabble amongst themselves, they all admire the "valiant Talbot" (*1 Henry VI*, I, i) who displays the ruthlessness, vindictiveness, and violence that McCurdy attributed to Shakespeare (1953, 159–161). When Salisbury is killed by the French, Talbot vows to avenge his death in the most bloodthirsty manner: "Your hearts I'll stamp out with my horse's heels, / And make a quagmire of your mingled brains" (I, iv). He threatens Bordeaux with "the fury of [his] three attendants,/ Lean famine, quartering steel, and climbing fire" (IV, ii) if it does not surrender on his terms. As these lines indicate, this play frequently anticipates *Henry V*. In both plays, there is a glorification of British ferocity and valor, a delight in the humiliation of the French, and an enjoyment of the violent behavior that is unleashed by war.

In both of these plays, aggressiveness is combined with loyalty, duty, and service, and this combination permits the aggressiveness to be expressed without conflict or guilt. Almost any form of violence is acceptable when it is directed against the French. The pursuit of national glory justifies all. In the first tetralogy, the code of martial and manly honor is presented positively, however, not only in perfectionists like Talbot, Bedford, and Warwick (in Part II), but also in Machiavels. Characters like Suffolk, Margaret, York, and Richard attain a surprising stature when they behave according to this code, so that Shakespeare seems to admire the code for its own sake and not only when it is linked to a national cause. Suffolk does not fear death but is resolute in extremes, and Margaret is equally resolute in confronting the loss of her lover: "Oft have I heard that grief softens the mind/ And makes it fearful and degenerate./ Think therefore on revenge and cease to weep" (*2 Henry VI*, IV, iv). York also faces death resolutely, and Richard reacts to the loss of his father according to the code: "Tears, then, for babes; blows and revenge for me!/ Richard, I bear thy name; I'll venge thy death/ Or die renowned by attempting it" (*3 Henry VI*, II, i). When we first encounter Richard in Part II, he seems less a Machiavel than a fierce fighter; and whenever he displays his martial side, Shakespeare treats him in a positive manner. When villains like Richard and Macbeth die fighting bravely, this creates a confusion of effect. They have preserved their "honor" in terms of the martial code, but they are unredeemed in other respects.

The only form of combat that Shakespeare seems to condemn is that which takes place in civil wars, which, by their very nature, involve a violation of the code of loyalty, duty, and service. The most horrible consequences of internal strife are portrayed in the famous scene in which Henry witnesses the grief of a father who has killed his son and of a son who has killed his father. Each is overwhelmed by guilt because he has "murdered where [he] should not kill" (*3 Henry VI*, II, v). Despite this scene, however, Part III frequently glorifies martial behavior, even in civil war. Part II ends with Warwick proclaiming that "'twas a glorious day./ Saint Alban's battle, won by famous York,/ Shall be eterniz'd in all age to come" (V, iii). There is nothing to suggest that the victory was not, indeed, glorious; and Shakespeare, through his drama, is eternizing it. There *is* an aggressive side to Shakespeare's personality that keeps looking for acceptable outlets. The code of martial and manly honor provides such an outlet.

The most acceptable outlet, as we have seen, is martial behavior that is sanctioned by the code of loyalty, duty, and service. This is exemplified by Talbot in Part I, who is glorified more than any other character in the tetralogy. The next most highly glorified character is Humphrey, Duke of Gloucester, that model of "honour, truth, and loyalty" (*2 Henry VI*, III, i), who is the chief protagonist of Part II. He believes that his enemies cannot "procure [him] any scathe/ So long as [he is] loyal, true, and crimeless" (*2 Henry VI*, II, iv). He is the first of Shakespeare's characters who has a distinct bargain with fate that is shattered by the course of events. Lord Say has a similar bargain that also fails to protect him. Indeed, both of these characters refuse to take adequate precautions for their safety because of their perfectionistic beliefs. Shakespeare favors the code of loyalty, duty, and service, which he sees as the foundation of all social order; but he seems to be sceptical, in the *Henry VI* plays at least, about the belief in a just universe upon which it is based.

The code of Christian values is exemplified in the first tetralogy primarily by Henry VI. Henry displays humility, patience, and pity, eschews revenge, and submits himself to the will of God. He is the opposite of the Machiavels who dominate these plays and is a constant target of their criticism. Shakespeare's attitude toward Henry seems to be ambivalent. He both admires and scorns his self-effacing attributes and he discharges his scorn through his arrogant-vindictive characters, in a way that permits him to disown it. Henry's critics lack the Christian virtues, but Henry lacks the martial and manly qualities that are necessary for the kingship. This is articulated by Clifford as he is dying:

> And, Henry, hadst thou sway'd as kings should do,
>
> . . . .
>
> I and ten thousand in this luckless realm
> Had left no mourning widows for our death,
> And thou this day hadst kept thy chair in peace.
> (*3 Henry VI*, II, vi)

Henry shows himself again and again to be pathetically weak, nowhere more vividly, perhaps, than in his inability to save Gloucester, whom he knows to be innocent. He compares himself to a helpless cow that can only run "lowing up and down" when the butchers take her calf "to the bloody slaughter house" (*2 Henry VI*, III, i). He wishes that he were a private citizen; and when he is restored to the throne by Warwick, he gives up his power, hoping, in typical self-effacing fashion, to "conquer fortune's spite/ By living low, where fortune cannot hurt" him (*3 Henry VI*, IV, vi).

Like Gloucester, Henry has bargains that do not work. He, too, believes in the power of innocence: "Thrice is he arm'd that hath his quarrel just,/ And he but naked, though lock'd up in steel,/ Whose conscience with injustice is corrupted" (*2 Henry VI*, III, ii). The amazing thing is that he persists in this belief *after* the murder of Gloucester, which seems not to have disillusioned him. His naiveté, like Gloucester's, makes him more vulnerable to those who are plotting against him. Another of his bargains is that if you are good to people, they will love you in return. He feels that his generosity, mildness, and mercy should have won the people's hearts, but "they love Edward more" (*3 Henry VI*, IV, viii), and he is grievously disappointed. He believes that "God . . . will succour" him (2 *Henry VI*, IV, iv) because of his piety and innocence, but God's care for him is not much in evidence. The self-effacing solution does not fare very well in the *Henry VI* plays.

Indeed, none of the solutions fares very well. In the *Henry VI* plays, Shakespeare seems to have been particularly interested in the conflict between the Machiavellian code and the others. In each part he shows those who are unscrupulously pursuing their personal ambition undermining the values of the other codes and destroying those who live by them. In Part I, the martial Talbot is destroyed because of the intrigues of the power-hungry nobles. In Part II, the loyal Gloucester is pulled down by a pack of conspirators who unite only for the purpose of destroying him. In Part III, it is the "gentle," mild, and virtuous" Henry who falls prey to the Machiavels. In all three parts, the arrogant-vindictive characters destroy not only those who differ from them, but each other as well. In *Richard III*, they are defeated at last by the forces of good.

According to Jan Kott, there are two kinds of historical drama. The first "is based on the conviction that history has a meaning . . . and leads in a definite direction" (1974, 36). The second originates "in the conviction that history has no meaning and stands still, or constantly repeats its cruel cycle" (1974, 37). Kott felt that "the latter concept of historical tragedy was nearer to Shakespeare" (1974, 37), and the *Henry VI* plays seem to support his position. In *Richard III*, however, historical reality is not absurd but has a meaning and leads in a definite direction. In the three parts of *Henry VI*, Shakespeare is showing what happens when the Machiavellian pursuit of personal ambition undermines the codes that hold together the social and political orders. The world becomes a jungle in which power governs all and nothing is sacred. *Richard III* is a reaffirmation of the codes of loyalty, duty, and service and of Christian values that had hitherto seemed so impotent. Clarence warns his murderers that God "holds vengeance in his hand/ To hurl upon their heads that break his law" (I, iv), and the play seems to bear him out. It is full of curses that invoke punishment for wrongs, many of which were committed in the preceding plays, and all of the curses are efficacious. In the *Henry VI* plays, the ambitious characters tend to destroy each other in their scramble for power. In *Richard III*, this is presented as part of a process by which God uses their ruthlessness toward each other as part of a system of retributive justice. Richard is defeated, however, not by other Machiavels, but by forces of good both within and outside of himself.

In *Richard III*, Shakespeare is out to show, through action and through characterization, that crime does not pay and that conscience is inescapable. Like *Macbeth,* this play asks whether a human being can, indeed, sin with impunity, and the answer is a resounding NO. The Machiavellian world view is false. Crime or the intention to commit crime activates the conscience, even in hardened men. The murderers of Clarence are troubled by conscience before the deed, and one of them repents afterward. The dialogue between them (II, iv) is similar to conversations between Macbeth and his wife. Despite the fact that they are "flesh'd villains," the murderers of the princes are stricken "with conscience and remorse" (IV, iii); and Tyrrel, who commissioned them, is deeply shaken. Sometimes it is misfortune or the threat of retribution that activates the conscience. Clarence's accusing dream occurs while he is in prison and fills him with remorse. Buckingham, who was as proud of his villainy as Richard, recognizes the justice of his fate as he is about to be beheaded: "Wrong hath but wrong, and blame the due of blame" (V, i). Both Richard and Buckingham swear great but insincere oaths in order to get people to believe them. They do this with ease because they do not believe in the religious doctrines that make an oath a sacred thing. In the case of Buckingham, the very fate that he had called upon his head if he should be lying comes to pass, and he undergoes a religious conversion.

Richard does not undergo a conversion, but he has "timorous dreams" (IV, i) and an attack of conscience on the eve of the battle of Bosworth. The play explicitly rejects his naturalistic explanation that "conscience is but a word that cowards use,/ Devis'd at first to keep the strong in awe" (V, iii). Richard believes that might makes right: "Our strong arms be our conscience, swords our law!" The battle of Bosworth shows, however, that right makes might. It is a trial by combat in which Humphrey's and Henry's belief in the power of righteousness is finally vindicated. The inexperienced Richmond is outnumbered by Richard, but the justness of his cause makes up for his military inferiority: "Every man's conscience is a thousand men,/ To fight against this guilty homicide" (V, ii). Richmond is God's "captain," his minister of "chastisement" (V, iii). He does not seek the crown of England out of a lust for power, as the Yorks had done, but out of loyalty, duty, and service to God.

DEFENSES AND INNER CONFLICTS

What authorial personality can we infer, then, from the first tetralogy? Shakespeare seems to have a powerful aggressive side that delights in ruthlessness, vindictiveness, and violence when they are sanctioned by the code of martial and manly honor. He glorifies belligerence especially when it is combined with loyalty, duty, and service, as in the case of Talbot; but in *2 Henry VI a*and *3 Henry VI,* he gives epic stature to the warriors who are pursuing personal ambition and precipitating civil strife. He honors the bargain of the martial code by keeping alive the memory of those who have lived and died by its dictates. The aggressive side of his personality is also expressed in his portrayal of Machiavels, through whom he vicariously experiences and then punishes his own lawless impulses. He seems to need to show himself (and his audiences) again and again what would happen if we allowed the Machiavellian value system and worldview to dominate, and his very obsession with doing this suggests that he is threatened by and needs to suppress such trends in himself.

Shakespeare has also a strong perfectionistic side. He opposes perfectionistic to Machiavellian values and prefers to subordinate the code of martial and manly honor to that of loyalty, duty, and service. He glorifies perfectionistic characters, like Duke Humphrey, and wants to believe in the perfectionistic version of reality and in its bargain with fate. In the *Henry VI* plays, however, he presents the world as the Machiavels see it, as an amoral process in which the strong devour the weak. The perfectionistic solution is vindicated in *Richard III.* In this play, there is a God in the heavens who sanctions the code of loyalty, duty, and service and the hierarchical order upon which it is based. He punishes the wicked, avenges the innocent, and honors Richmond's bargain with fate. The tetralogy as a whole suggests that Shakespeare is torn between a naturalistic and a perfectionistic view of reality and that he is so threatened by the former that he is driven in *Richard III* to abandon the more realistic mode of the earlier plays and to introduce a supernatural dimension. *Richard III* has a wish-fulfillment quality: it is full of magical curses, gestures, and rituals; and there is a deus ex machina that is not really necessary, since Richard's downfall is the natural product of his faults. Shakespeare seems to be forcing his perfectionistic version of reality upon us, and perhaps upon himself, for his portrayal of a world that fails to honor that solution is far more powerful than his thematic affirmation that it works.

Just as Shakespeare both believes in and doubts the perfectionistic solution, he both admires and despises the self-effacing one, especially when it is embraced by a man and a king. The code of martial and manly honor can be combined readily with that of loyalty, duty, and service, and this is the combination that makes a good king. It cannot be combined with Henry's Christian values, however; and this renders him impotent as a leader. "The smallest worm will turn, being trodden on," says Clifford (*3 Henry VI*, II, ii); but Henry is a worm that will not turn. It is difficult not to feel that Shakespeare shares some of Clifford's contempt, and he shows Henry's solution failing miserably in the plays that bear his name. But Henry is presented as an appealing human being, and his failures as a leader are at least partly the fault of the power-hungry nobles by whom he is surrounded and the weakness of his claim to the throne. His story can be read as either that of a deplorably weak leader who does terrible things to the state, or as that of a saintly man who cannot cope with an evil world and is martyred as a result. Are the plays an indictment of Henry or of the world in which he lives? They are both, of course, and each way of looking at them corresponds to one side of Shakespeare's personality.

Shakespeare is more ambivalent about the self-effacing solution than he is about any of the others. In *2 & 3 Henry VI*, Henry is presented as lacking in manly and martial qualities and as an easy prey for the Machiavels, but in *Richard III*, self-effacing values are strongly affirmed. The God of this play is not only the God of the perfectionistic solution who demands obedience to his law and hurls vengeance upon those who break it; He is also the God of the self-effacing solution who offers "redemption/ By Christ's dear blood shed for our grievous sins" (I, iv). The ailing King Edward is waiting for his "Redeemer to redeem [him] hence," and in order to prepare his soul he is doing "deeds of charity" and is trying to "make [his] friends at peace" (II, i). Clarence urges the men who have come to murder him to "Relent, and save your souls."

> *Murd.* Relent? 'tis cowardly and womanish.
> *Clar.* Not to relent is beastly, savage, devilish. (I, iv)

The murderer has conflated the codes of manly honor and personal ambition, so that it seems cowardly not to be a villain. From the perspective of the two codes, Christian values seem "womanish." Clarence's reply to the murderer is a powerful statement of the Christian perspective.

After the murder, the second murderer is overwhelmed by guilt and repentance and refuses to take his part of the fee. As we have seen, this is a common pattern in the play: a guilty deed activates remorseful feelings. On the eve of Bosworth, Richard is visited in his dreams by those against whom he has sinned, and he awakes pleading for Jesu's mercy. He is afflicted by his conscience, hates himself for his evil deeds, and pities himself because no one loves him (V, iii). He represses all of these feelings and marches bravely on to hell, but the play as a whole shows the inescapability of perfectionistic and self-effacing dictates. They can be denied, despised, and overridden, but they return again and again to haunt those who violate them.

Richmond triumphs because he lives up to both sets of values. He is "virtuous" *and* "holy" (V, iii). Before the battle, he stresses the right-eousness of his cause; afterward he minimizes the fact that it was he who killed Richard, he repeatedly gives credit to God for his victory, and he asks for divine blessing upon his reign. In the final scene, he is a combination of victorious soldier, righteous restorer of order, and humble servant of God.

Although it reveals neither the whole of his personality nor the degree of its complexity, the first tetralogy gives us a good introduction to Shakespeare's defenses and inner conflicts. Shakespeare endorses the code of martial and manly honor, is fascinated and repelled by Machiavellian behavior, believes in and doubts the perfectionistic bargain, and at once glorifies and despises self-effacing traits. The *Henry VI* plays seem to be written from the perspective of a disillusioned believer in the perfectionistic and self-effacing solutions. The world ought to honor these solutions, but it does not. Shakespeare seems unable to tolerate this; and in *Richard III* he makes the solutions work, if not from moment to moment, at least in the overall pattern of history. In order to accomplish this, he introduces unrealistic elements that were not present in the earlier plays. He repeats this oscillation between realism and fantasy many times, not only within individual plays but also as he shifts from genre to genre. In the histories and tragedies he often presents a world that does not honor any of the bargains, whereas in the comedies and romances wish-fulfillment dominates and the perfectionistic and self-effacing solutions triumph. In order to understand Shakespeare's defenses and conflicts more fully, I shall trace his treatment of the various codes and defenses through the rest of the corpus, reserving the main discussion of the self-effacing solution for Chapter 7.

MARTIAL AND MANLY HONOR

From *1 Henry VI* to *Cymbeline,* Shakespeare glorifies martial behavior in almost all the plays that deal with war, especially when it is linked to perfectionistic values. In *King John,* Philip the Bastard is among the most belligerent of Shakespeare's characters, but his aggressiveness is justified because it is directed against the French. In his famous speech on "commodity," he says that he will worship "gain," like everyone else (II, i); but he does not actually do so, and thus he retains his heroic stature. In *1 Henry IV,* Hotspur is excessive in his pursuit of military honor, which in his case is combined with "ill-weav'd ambition" (V, iv); but the satire is upon his obsessiveness rather than upon the martial code itself. Falstaff questions the code, of course; but his cowardice fits his role as buffoon, or Lord of Misrule, and his stabbing of Percy's corpse is disgraceful. Hal's redemption comes about largely through his performance in battle, and he is such a magnificent figure as king because of his conquest of France. In *Julius Caesar, Macbeth, Antony and Cleopatra, Coriolanus,* and *Cymbeline,* Shakespeare continues to celebrate martial valor, most of all when it is in a righteous cause, but, as in the case of Macbeth, even when it is not. Warriors like King Hamlet, Fortinbras, and Othello are treated positively because of heroic actions offstage or in the past.

The one play about war in which the martial code is questioned is *Troilus and Cressida,* where neither love nor war turns out to be very glamorous and no one lives up to his or her ideals. Martial honor is undermined by selfish individualism on the Greek side and is elevated above moral rectitude by the Trojans. Hector recognizes that the "moral laws/ Of nature and of nations" call for the return of Helen, but he votes to continue the war in order to maintain Troy's pride. Troilus elaborates:

> Why, there you touch'd the life of our design:
> . . . .
> She is a theme of honour and renown,
> A spur to valiant and magnanimous deeds,
> Whose present courage may beat down our foes,
> And fame in the time to come canonize us. (II, ii)

This is the most eloquent statement of the martial code in Shakespeare, but it is employed to justify a wrong course of action. The pursuit of martial honor prohibits a just settlement of the war because there is no glory to be won in peace. Two kinds of honor are in conflict here, and Shakespeare clearly indicates which should predominate. Hector is a perfectionist who knows what is right, but who allows the "promis'd glory/ . . . of this action" to seduce him into violating his own sense of justice. As a result, he is destroyed by Achilles, who violates the martial code by attacking Hector while he is unarmed. Neither Achilles' triumph nor Hector's death is glorious.

The code of manly honor is a major cause of the tragedy in *Romeo and Juliet.* It fuels the feud by sanctioning an endless cycle of violence and retaliation. When Tybalt recognizes Romeo at the ball, he wishes to attack him immediately: "Now, by the stock and honour of my kin,/ To strike him dead I hold it not a sin" (I, v). Once Romeo falls in love with Juliet, he wants to abandon the feud, but he is not permitted to do so. When he refuses to fight Tybalt, Mercutio accuses him of "calm dishonourable, vile submission" (III, i); and when he steps between the combatants, Tybalt thrusts beneath his arm and kills Mercutio. Romeo now turns upon his own lack of manliness: "O sweet Juliet,/ Thy beauty hath made me effeminate/ And in my temper soft'ned valour's steel!" (III, i). Full of "fire-ey'd fury," he retaliates for Mercutio's death by killing Tybalt. In this play, Shakespeare presents the code of manly honor as a primitive force that must be subordinated to the laws of the state. This is accomplished by the end, but only through the sacrifice of Romeo and Juliet. Although Shakespeare often seems like a typically combative male of his culture, there are times when he sees the code of martial and manly honor as a threat to such higher values as love, social order, and the "moral laws/ Of nature and of nations."

THE THREAT OF THE MACHIAVELS

As he does in the first tetralogy, Shakespeare always sees the code of personal ambition as a threat to the other codes. An ambitious man himself, Shakespeare may have identified to some extent with those characters who feel mistreated by society or by fate and who try to push their way ruthlessly to the top. He seems to have identified also with characters who feel wronged in their personal relationships and who react vindictively, often to their sorrow. As I have indicated, I believe that Shakespeare was obsessed with these kinds of characters and situations because he needed both to express his aggression and to show himself the danger of acting it out. He is afraid of aggressive tendencies not only in himself, but also in others. Such tendencies had been liberated and justified by the secularization of thought, and Shakespeare saw them as inimical to the social and political orders. A world governed by appetite is profoundly threatening to both his perfectionistic and his self-effacing belief systems, values, and bargains with fate.

Titus Andronicus is the first character in Shakespeare who is thrown into a state of psychological crisis because of the breakdown of his bargain. When the Emperor dies, Titus is chosen to succeed because of his bravery, nobility, and service to the state. He insists, however, that the

Emperor's eldest son is the rightful successor, and Saturninus promises never to forget his "unspeakable deserts" (I, i). Saturninus, Tamora, and Aaron the Moor all conspire against Titus, however. Two of his sons are killed, as is his son-in-law, Bassanius, his daughter is raped and mutilated, his last son is banished, and he loses a hand. As these wrongs are inflicted upon him by the Machiavels, Titus nearly goes mad with grief and rage. His bargain, like that of Coriolanus, is with Rome; but when he sees Lavinia with her hands lopped off, he wants to chop off his hands, too: "For hands to do Rome service, is but vain" (III, i). Instead of rewarding him for his loyalty and sacrifice, "ungrateful Rome" (IV, iii) has become "a wilderness of tigers": "Tigers must prey, and Rome affords no prey/ But me and mine" (III, i). The goddess of justice has left the earth (IV, iii), which is now little more than a jungle.

The wrongs done to Titus unleash vindictive impulses about which Shakespeare seems to have ambivalent feelings. He so structures the play that what is done to the Andronici seems horrible, but what they do in retaliation seems right. This allows him to relish acts of great cruelty, such as the murder of Tamora's sons. Titus tells the boys that he will cut their throats while Lavinia " 'tween her stumps doth hold/ The basin that receives your guilty blood" (V, ii). Then he will grind their bones to dust, combine it with their blood to make a paste, rear a coffin of the paste, "And bid that strumpet, your unhallowed dam,/ . . . swallow her own increase" (V, ii). Titus's behavior is made to seem justified; but, at the same time, revenge is, as Tamora says, "sent from th' infernal kingdom" (V, ii); and by pursuing it as he does, Titus violates his own moral standards. He must die, therefore, in the slaughter at the end, and his son must unfold his wrongs in order to clear his name (V, iii).

This play, for all its crudity, sets forth a problem with which Shakespeare continued to wrestle throughout his career: what is a good man to do when he is wronged, when he has lived up to his shoulds but his virtue is not rewarded. To accept the wrongs is unbearable, but to fight against them by "o'erreach[ing the villains] in their own devices" (V, ii) is to become bestial oneself.

In all of the plays that feature perfectionistic protagonists, Shakespeare shows them being threatened by Machiavellian characters who are either tormentors or tempters, and by aggressive tendencies in themselves that take the form either of ambition or of a desire for revenge. In *Titus Andronicus,* he portrays the destruction of Titus's bargain and the psychological transformation that results. There is a similar pattern in *Othello* where Iago destroys Othello's belief in Desdemona, who was to be the

reward for his virtue, and turns him into a bloodthirsty revenger. A varia-
tion on the pattern occurs in *Coriolanus,* where Rome's ingratitude leads
Coriolanus to turn against his native city and thus to violate the code of
loyalty, duty, and service by which he has guided his life. Like Othello, he
is torn by inner conflicts when vindictive trends emerge, and he reverts to
perfectionism at the end. In *Julius Caesar* and *Macbeth,* the threat to the
perfectionistic character is more from within than from without, though a
Machiavel is present in each play who stirs up the repressed aggressive
tendencies of the protagonist. Brutus is seduced by Cassius into conspir-
ing against Caesar, whose greatness both men envy; but he manages to
convince himself that he is remaining true to his perfectionistic conception
of honor, even as he violates it. He is never consciously aware of his
conflicts, though his self-hate manifests itself in a variety of ways. Macbeth's inner conflicts are much closer to the surface, both before and after
his crime. He would not have murdered Duncan had not his own ambition
been powerfully reinforced by Lady Macbeth, and he is immediately
overwhelmed by guilt and self-hate.

As we saw in the first tetralogy, the arrogant-vindictive characters are
a threat not only to perfectionists, like Duke Humphrey, but also to compliant types, like King Henry and Lady Anne. One of Shakespeare's most
positively presented self-effacing characters is Antonio in *The Merchant
of Venice,* whose bargain is that if he sacrifices all for love, his devotion
will be reciprocated (see Paris, 1989b). Since this is a comedy, his bargain
is ultimately honored by Bassanio, but his life is endangered, for a time at
least, by Shylock's vindictiveness. Shylock is so hostile because Antonio
thwarts his schemes and represents an opposite set of values by which he
stands condemned. Antonio's constant railing against Shylock's business
practices threatens to rouse Shylock's self-effacing side and to expose him
to self-hate. Shylock's elaborate justification of taking interest indicates
his inner conflicts. He plots against Antonio because he needs to prove
that his way is right by showing how Antonio's "low simplicity" (I, iii)
leads to his destruction. In seeking to cut out Antonio's heart, Shylock is
trying to cut out the last of his own self-effacing tendencies.

Shylock wants not only to remove Antonio as an economic and
psychological threat, but also to take revenge. He has been badly treated
by Antonio, who has called him names, has spat upon his beard, and has
kicked him like a dog. Even though he is now coming to Shylock for
money, Antonio says, "I am as like to call thee so again,/ To spet on thee
again, to spurn thee too" (I, iii). Antonio is threatened by Shylock as
much as Shylock is threatened by him. Each man repudiates his own

repressed tendencies as they manifest themselves in the other. Antonio's horror of usury is so great because of his need to be self-sacrificing and generous. If he behaved like Shylock, he would hate himself intensely. He reinforces the repression of his forbidden impulses by attacking them in Shylock. He releases his aggression in an innocent way, since it is in the service of self-effacing values and is directed toward a Jew. Because Shylock is not a member of Antonio's moral community, he can serve as a scapegoat upon whom Antonio discharges the anger that he represses in his dealings with fellow Christians or turns upon himself. Shylock wants revenge for the humiliations that have been inflicted upon him. The famous speech in which he reminds his listeners that Jews have the same faculties and feelings as Christians is very much to the point (III, i), for he has been denied human status by that kindest of gentlemen, Antonio.

As we can see from this brief analysis, Shakespeare's treatment of the relationship between arrogant-vindictive and self-effacing characters is far from schematic. His self-effacing characters often have a vindictive side that they seek to express in innocent or justified ways, and his vindictive characters often have reason to be hostile. Shylock's speech is so powerful because it leads us to enter into his perspective and to understand his desire for revenge. There are things in the play that justify the aggressive behavior of both Shylock and Antonio.

Shylock loses our sympathy when he insists on his bond, despite Bassanio's offers of money and Portia's plea for mercy. He justifies his behavior by a Hebraic appeal to the law. He does not need mercy because he has done no wrong, and "the decrees of Venice" will have no force if his bond is not upheld (IV, i). The conflict now is not only between revenge and mercy, but also between justice and mercy; and here, as in *Measure for Measure,* self-effacing values are favored. Mercy must season justice because "in the course of justice, none of us/ Should see salvation" (IV, i). Through Portia's legal quibble, Shakespeare avoids having to violate perfectionistic standards in order to free Antonio. Shylock is found to be deficient in both justice and mercy and can be punished severely as a result.

The Merchant of Venice dramatizes the threat of the arrogant-vindictive person by which Shakespeare seems to have been haunted and glorifies the self-effacing Antonio, who has much in common with the poet of the sonnets. The play is about greedy, vindictive characters and unselfish, forgiving ones, and about which set of characters is going to prevail. Bassanio wins Portia because he chooses the lead casket, which stands for sacrifice, while his competitors choose silver and gold. It looks as though Antonio will be destroyed as a result of his generosity, but Shylock is undone by his vindictiveness instead. The play dramatizes the triumph of the self-effacing solution and the defeat of the arrogant-vindictive one. In a last minute reversal, Antonio is rescued and experiences enormous triumphs—moral, psychological, and economic. This is a wish-fulfillment fantasy in which things turn out as they should.

The solutions are related to each other as they were, I suspect, in Shakespeare's personality. The arrogant-vindictive solution is disowned and punished, and the self-effacing and perfectionistic solutions are favored, with the former being superior to the latter. There is a lot of aggression, however, in the characters and in the author. Shylock's vindictiveness is condemned, but it is also made understandable as a reaction to having been wronged. Antonio's aggression comes out in his behavior toward Shylock, where it can be expressed without violating his self-effacing taboos. The play as a whole reenacts Antonio's behavior. Because Shylock has refused to be merciful, Antonio and the others can treat him with great cruelty at the end. Their vindictiveness is concealed by the fact that Shylock seems to have deserved his fate, that it is less severe than the law allows, and that it is being meted out in the name of mercy. "If a Jew wrong a Christian," asks Shylock, "what is his humility? Revenge" (III, i). Despite Portia's glorification of mercy, the play bears out Shylock's observation. Shakespeare's rhetoric conceals this from us because, like his characters, he is at once celebrating self-effacing values and releasing aggression in disguised or justified ways.

There are numerous other plays, of course, in which self-effacing values or characters are threatened by arrogant-vindictive characters who are the main source of mischief. It is the success of Claudius and the failure of his father's bargain that precipitate Hamlet's psychological crisis. Iago, like Shylock, needs to destroy those of free and open nature in order to justify his own value system. In *King Lear,* the four Machiavels attack the very foundations of social order, and there seems to be no way to cope with the evil they generate. Edgar and Albany survive; but, like other self-effacing characters in Shakespeare, they give little promise of effective leadership.

In the major tragedies, Shakespeare seems to have seen through all of the defensive strategies. There is a moment in *Macbeth* in which the inadequacy of the self-effacing solution to deal with the threat of the Machiavels is articulated with great explicitness. Lady Macduff's first response to the messenger's warning of impending danger is to say, "I have done no harm." She invokes the self-effacing bargain in which innocence is magically protected. She immediately realizes, however, that she is being unrealistic:

> But I remember now
> I am in this earthly world, where to do harm
> Is often laudable, to do good sometime
> Accounted dangerous folly. Why then, alas,
> Do I put up that womanly defense
> To say I have done no harm? (IV, ii)

In the comedies and romances, this womanly defense works well. In such plays as *Much Ado, As You Like It, Pericles, Cymbeline, The Winter's Tale,* and *The Tempest,* the threatening characters are ultimately destroyed, converted, or circumvented, whereas the self-effacing characters are vindicated, rewarded, or magically protected.

THE FATE OF PERFECTIONISTS

As we have seen, Shakespeare favors the value system and character traits of the perfectionistic solution and would like to believe in its world-view and its bargain with fate. Some of his most positively presented characters are perfectionists. Beginning with Bedford and Humphrey of Gloucester, they include Richmond, Philip the Bastard, Gaunt, Henry V, Kent, Cordelia, Banquo, and Malcolm. Other characters have inner conflicts or excesses that mar their perfectionism. Titus turns vindictive, as does Coriolanus; Othello is seduced by a Machiavel, as are Brutus and Macbeth; Hector violates the law of nature and of nations in order to pursue martial glory; Angelo and Isabella aspire to a superhuman purity; Duke Vincentio makes laws he cannot enforce; and Paulina is excessively punitive.

Shakespeare presents as most admirable those perfectionists who also have, but are neither paralyzed nor seduced by, self-effacing and martial traits. The most fully developed of such characters is Henry V, whom I discuss elsewhere (Paris 1991). Malcolm is another such character, as is Alcibiades in *Timon of Athens.* When Malcolm is trying to determine whether Macduff is to be trusted, he poses as a Machiavel, telling him that he has none of

> The king-becoming graces,
> As justice, verity, temp'rance, stableness,

> Bounty, perseverance, mercy, lowliness,
> Devotion, patience, courage, fortitude . . . (IV, iii)

This list encompasses the codes of martial and manly honor, loyalty, duty, and service, and Christian values. When Macduff proves his integrity by refusing to serve such a man, Malcolm unspeaks his "own detraction":

> I am yet
> Unknown to woman, never was forsworn,
> Scarcely have coveted what was mine own,
> At no time broke my faith, would not betray
> The devil to his fellow, and delight
> No less in truth than life. (IV, iii)

As I observed in my discussion of *Macbeth,* Malcolm seems superior to the other characters who are left in charge at the end of the tragedies. Cassio, Edgar, and Albany are weak; Antony (in *Julius Caesar*) is a schemer; Octavius (in *Antony and Cleopatra*) represents power and efficiency rather than any moral principle; and Fortinbras is merely a soldier. Malcolm has high moral standards, displays martial and manly qualities, and knows how to cope with evil, as his self-effacing father could not.

Alcibiades, in *Timon of Athens,* is less fully developed than Malcolm; but he, too, is favorably presented because of his combination of martial, perfectionistic, and self-effacing qualities. He is banished from Athens when he pleads for a friend who has been sentenced to death: "For pity is the virtue of the law,/ And none but tyrants use it cruelly" (III, v). He is angry that the Senate will not defer to him because of his military service and outraged when he is banished because of his anger. Like Titus and Coriolanus, he is infuriated by the ingratitude of his countrymen, and he is determined to lay waste his native city. He quickly responds, however, to the appeals of the Athenians that he take revenge only upon the guilty and not upon them all: "We were not all unkind, nor all deserve/ The common stroke of war" (V, iv). Shakespeare puts Alcibiades in Coriolanus's situation and has him respond in a strong but just way.

The perfectionistic value system corresponds to the code of loyalty, duty, and service that Shakespeare found in his culture. That code is based on the worldview set forth by Ulysses in *Troilus and Cressida.* Order in all realms, human and natural, depends upon "degree, priority, and place" (I, iii), and disorder in any realm produces a corresponding disruption in the others. "Take but degree away," says Ulysses, "And hark what discord follows!"

Force should be right; or rather, right and wrong
(Between whose endless jar justice resides)
Should lose their names, and so should justice too.
Then everything includes itself in power,
Power into will, will into appetite;
And appetite, an universal wolf,
So doubly seconded with will and power,
Must make preforce an universal prey,
And last eat up himself. (I, iii)

This is a vision of a world governed by the Machiavellian philosophy, which is, for Shakespeare, the chief threat to the perfectionistic bargain. The perfectionistic person knows exactly where he stands in the order of things and fulfills the duties belonging to his place. In a just universe, he is rewarded for his rectitude; but in a world ruled by force, he cannot control fate through the height of his standards.

Narcissism can also be a threat to degree. Ulysses' speech is occasioned by Achilles, who, "Having his ear full of his airy fame,/ Grows dainty of his worth and in his tent/ Lies mocking our designs" (I, iii). Achilles' sense of his own importance leads to an insubordination that is infecting the entire Greek army. It should be noted that Ulysses tries to solve the problem in a cynical way, by puncturing Achilles' pride, rather than by appealing to his sense of duty. If Ulysses' stratagem had worked, it would not have restored degree. Other plays in which narcissism is the villain are *Richard II* and *King Lear*. In both plays, discord is unleashed by a king who fails to recognize that he is part of a larger order in which he has not only rights, but also duties. Richard and Lear each has a perfectionistic adviser—Gaunt and Kent; but each ignores his adviser and brings destruction to himself and to his country. If Richard had not taken Hereford's rights away, the whole cycle of civil war might never have begun. Henry IV is afraid that when Hal becomes King, he will "from curb'd license [pluck]/ The muzzle of restraint," and that England will "be a wilderness again,/ Peopled with wolves, [its] old inhabitants" (*2 Henry IV*, IV, v). Hal shows that this will not happen when he submits himself to *his* perfectionistic adviser, the Lord Chief Justice.

Shakespeare's rhetoric favors perfectionistic characters and the universe of many of his plays *is* that of the perfectionistic solution. Again and again he shows us the terrible consequences of violating the code of loyalty, duty, and service, and he tends to end the plays in which that code has been violated with a restoration of order, often by a perfectionistic leader. The discord of the first tetralogy is resolved by Richmond, that of the second tetralogy by Henry V, and that of *Macbeth* by Malcolm. The problem is that the endings do not always sufficiently counterbalance the portrayal of absurd suffering that has preceded them. While the evil are always punished, the good are often also destroyed. If there is a just order in the universe, it manifests itself quite imperfectly in "this earthly world."

Sometimes the perfectionistic bargain works and sometimes it does not. It works for Richmond, but not for Humphrey of Gloucester; for Hal, but not for John of Gaunt; for Malcolm, but not for Banquo. It does not work, of course, for Titus, Coriolanus, Kent, or Cordelia. In the two tetralogies, Shakespeare shows it working in the form of trial by combat, at Bosworth and at Agincourt. His treatment of these battles is a reflection, I think, of his will to believe. In *Richard III* and *Henry V,* he shifts from the realism of the preceding plays to a mode in which supernatural intervention is emphasized. It may be argued that he is following the Tudor historians, and no doubt he is, but I think he is also seizing upon two fleeting moments in which history and "justice" coincided in order to affirm the perfectionistic world order. The wish-fulfillment quality of these plays reflects the magic nature of the bargain that is being celebrated. That bargain fares least well in *King Lear,* where the death of Cordelia and the despair of Kent leave us feeling that "All's cheerless, dark, and deadly" (V, iii).

In the 1590s, Shakespeare seems to be wavering between a belief in the perfectionistic bargain and a fear that life is governed by appetite, which "eat[s] up himself," but which consumes many innocent victims along the way. In the early 1600s, he seems to have succumbed to his disillusioned view of reality and to have stopped trying to cheer himself up. There is great bitterness that his expectations have been disappointed not only in *Lear,* but also in *Troilus and Cressida* and *Timon of Athens.* In *Troilus,* he sets forth the perfectionistic world view and value system primarily for satirical purposes, to develop the contrast between things as they are and things as they should be. Ulysses' behavior has little to do with his speech (he is not really an idealist, but a crafty manipulator); and the most attractive character in the play, Hector, sacrifices justice to the pursuit of martial glory. The play as a whole shows the ideals of Western civilization in a state of collapse. I shall discuss Shakespeare's other very bitter play, *Timon,* when I examine the transition from the tragedies to the romances, in which the perfectionistic world order is reaffirmed. Not only are the evil punished, but the innocent are, for the most part, preserved, sometimes by divine intervention.

INNER CONFLICTS IN *MEASURE FOR MEASURE*

So far our analysis of Shakespeare has shown that he rejects the Machiavellian code and embraces the codes of martial and manly honor, loyalty, duty, and service, and Christian values. In the structure of his personality, martial and manly attitudes are subordinated, for the most part, to the dictates of perfectionism, which are subordinated, in turn, to self-effacing values. This is not a static but a dynamic structure, and one that generates continual inner conflict. Since the favored solutions are not always in harmony with each other, satisfying the dictates of one may involve violating those of another; and this sets up a cross fire of conflicting shoulds that produces oscillation from solution to solution and makes it impossible to maintain any set of values wholeheartedly.

Shakespeare's plays seem very often to be generated by his efforts to resolve his conflicts, or at least to satisfy his contradictory needs in a way that temporarily evades or defuses self-hate. His most powerful inner conflict is between vindictive and self-effacing tendencies, and *The Tempest* is his most imaginative effort to resolve this conflict. Another important conflict is between his two most favored solutions, perfectionism and self-effacement. This conflict is evident in plays such as *Measure for Measure,* which deal with the issue of justice versus mercy. An analysis of this play will suggest the dynamics of the conflict, the way in which Shakespeare uses his art to achieve a sense of resolution, and the dominance in his personality of self-effacing trends.

Measure for Measure is a play of which I cannot make sense thematically. It begins by stressing the corruption in Vienna and the need for a stricter enforcement of the law, but it ends by celebrating mercy and forgiveness and perpetuating the conditions that have led to license in the first place. The demands of justice and of mercy are not reconciled, for everyone is pardoned, including the unregenerate murderer, Barnardine. Although the play is thematically puzzling, we can make sense of it, I believe, if we see it as the manifestation of a system of psychological conflicts in which contradictory attitudes are generated by different trends within the personality. Such conflicts occur in Duke Vincentio and account for his inconsistent behavior, and they are built into the structure of the play as a whole and are an expression of the warring impulses within the author. Although *Measure for Measure* does not have a coherent thematic structure, it does have a psychological structure in terms of which its contradictions become intelligible.

One of the Duke's motives for "leaving" Vienna is to have Angelo enforce the laws that he has "let sleep" for fourteen years (I, iii). He has been a "fond father" who has threatened his children but not punished them so that "the rod" has become "more mock'd than fear'd." As a result of his indulgence, "liberty plucks justice by the nose;/ The baby beats the nurse, and quite athwart/ Goes all decorum" (I, iii). Others share, and reinforce, this perception of the Duke's. Angelo says that if we do not enforce the law it will become an impotent "scarecrow" that "birds of prey" will make "their perch, and not their terror" (II, ii). Lucio recognizes that the object of Angelo's harshness is "to give fear to use and liberty,/ Which have for long run by the hideous law,/ As mice by lions" (I, iv). Even Escalus, who is opposed to Angelo's severity toward Claudio, acknowledges that "Mercy is not itself that oft looks so./ Pardon is still the nurse of second woe" (II, i).

It seems clear, then, that a major concern of the Duke, and a major theme of the play, is the corruption that results when the person in authority is too permissive. The primary thrust of the play, however, is to present a case against the strict enforcement of the law; and when the Duke reassumes his authority at the end, he gives no indication that he will behave in such a way as to curb the license in Vienna. The play cannot be said to favor license, but it seems to draw back from the firm judgment and exercise of authority that are necessary to control it. The case against strictness is developed along three lines: (1) the laws are too harsh; (2) no one is so pure that he is fit to be the judge of another; and (3) we should show mercy to our fellows, as God has shown mercy to us.

There is much in the play to suggest that the laws governing sexual behavior, and especially the one that condemns Claudio, demand an impossible perfection of human beings and should not be enforced. They are the irrational laws, so common in comedy, the bondage of which must be removed if a good society is to emerge at the end. These laws run counter to the course of nature. They cannot be enforced without drastic measures (gelding and spaying all the youth, chopping off a great many heads) that would be far more destructive than the evil they are attempting to cure. The punishments, moreover, do not fit the crimes and are too severe. Claudio is betrothed to Juliet and intends to marry her. As the Provost observes, "He hath but as offended in a dream!/ All sects, all ages smack of this vice—and he/ To die for 't!" (II, ii). There are similar statements from Lucio, but this one from the Provost carries great weight, since he is consistently presented in a favorable light.

Since the laws are too harsh, those in authority seem left with a choice between irrational severity and a leniency that leads to license. It should be noted, however, that the Duke appears to endorse the harsh laws he has not enforced. He tells Friar Thomas that Vienna's "strict statutes and most biting laws" are "the needful bits and curbs to headstrong steeds" (I, iii). When he transfers his authority to Angelo, he tells him, "your scope is as mine own,/ So to enforce *or qualify* the laws/ As to your soul seems good" (I, i, italics added). The Duke is not in the position of a magistrate who is obliged to enforce the law, whether he agrees with it or not, since he could have changed it if he had wished to do so. Angelo also has this option.

The condemnation of Claudio is presented as unfair not only because the law is too strict, the punishment too harsh, and Claudio too nice a fellow, but also because Angelo, his judge, is guilty of the same crime. The Duke insists that if Angelo's "own life answer the straitness of his proceeding" (III, ii), "he's just" (IV, ii); but he is "tyrannous" if it does not (IV, ii): "Shame to him whose cruel striking/ Kills for faults of his own liking!" (III, ii). Escalus and Isabella both urge Angelo to be lenient toward Claudio if he has done, or wanted to do, the same thing, if his heart confesses "a natural guiltiness such as is his" (II, ii). Angelo thinks he is free of Claudio's fault when he condemns him, but he learns that blood is blood and that he has the same desires as everyone else. He then feels that he has no right to condemn Claudio: "O, let her brother live! Thieves for their robbery have authority/ When judges steal themselves" (II, iii). He does not act upon this conclusion, of course, but he feels guilty about the inconsistency of his behavior.

The "strict statutes and most biting laws" of Vienna demand that men be morally perfect and condemn them to death if they are not. Those in authority have a right to enforce the law as long as they live up to its dictates; but since all men have "a natural guiltiness," no one has that right. G. Wilson Knight argues that the Duke has been lenient "because meditation and self-analysis, together with profound study of human nature, have shown him that all passions and sins of other men have reflected images in his own soul" (1970, 32). He knows already what Angelo must learn. The problem with this is that it leads to the moral anarchy from which Vienna is suffering at the outset and for which the play provides no remedy. The Duke says that lechery "is too general a vice, and severity must cure it" (III, ii); but severity is condemned by the play, and the Duke is incapable of it.

The argument for mercy resembles the argument against judging, and it leads to similar consequences. Under the terms of the divine law, "all the souls that were were forfeit once"; but God in his mercy "found out the remedy" (II, ii). "How would you be," Isabella asks Angelo, "If he which is the top of judgment" should "judge you as you are?": "O, think on that!/ And mercy then will breathe within your lips/ Like man new made" (II, ii). Mercy is preached by Isabella and practiced by the Duke, who upon his return pardons everyone except Lucio. Angelo feels that he deserves death and is ready to accept it, but the Duke gives him his blessing after subjecting him to a brief period of psychological torment. Angelo may not deserve death, but his crimes are grievous, and his punishment seems disproportionately light.

It might be argued that the Duke is a Christ figure who stands between man and the Old Testament law that condemns him to death for the sinfulness inherent in his nature. This may have been Shakespeare's intention, but even within this framework it is difficult to understand the pardoning of Barnardine, who, unlike the others, shows no signs of spiritual growth or repentance. Near the end of the play, moreover, the Duke seems as disturbed about the moral anarchy in Vienna as he was at the beginning. Speaking as the Friar, he says that he has seen "corruption boil and bubble/ Till it o'errun the stew; laws for all faults,/ But faults so countenanc'd that the strong statutes/ Stand like the forfeits in a barber's shop,/ As much in mock as mark" (V, i). Soon after this, he pardons all faults, except that of Lucio, who has offended him personally; and he looses upon society the incorrigible Barnardine. Neither the Duke nor the play, it seems to me, makes any effort to reconcile the case for mercy with the need for law and order.

The thematic confusion of *Measure for Measure* is the result, I believe, of the inner conflicts of the Duke, who acts as a moral norm, and of the implied author, whose psyche is expressed by the play as a whole. The Duke's basic conflict is between his perfectionistic and his self-effacing trends. The "strict statutes and most biting laws" of Vienna are an expression of his perfectionistic standards. His condemnation of vice is, in part, an attempt to reinforce his own repressions, which must be strictly maintained if he is to avoid self-hate. He does not relish "the loud applause and ave's vehement" of the multitude, nor does he "think the man of safe discretion/ That does affect it" (I, i); but he does want respect from others, especially for his wisdom and his moral character. The one person he cannot forgive is Lucio, who denies his moral perfection. The unfairness of Lucio's attack calls his secret "deal" into question; one of his darkest moments occurs when he realizes that "back-wounding calumny/ The whitest virtue strikes" (III, ii). Immediately following the scene with Lucio, he seeks recognition of his virtues from Escalus as a way of confirming his idealized image and reassuring himself that his perfectionistic solution works.

Along with his perfectionistic trends, the Duke has a number of self-effacing traits. He needs love and approval, which he pursues by being helpful, nonthreatening, and generous. He tends to take the blame on himself when things go wrong and has great difficulty in being openly critical of others. He believes in the strict laws of Vienna, but his self-effacing tendencies prevent him from enforcing them. He has succeeded in living up to his standards so far, but he is insecure about his virtue and is afraid of judging others. His refusal to judge is, in part, a defense against the self-hate he would feel if he should go astray, and it is in part the product of his desire to retain the affection of his people. Like the fond father in his analogy, he does not punish because he wants to be loved. He blames himself for his leniency, however, and holds himself responsible for the depravity of Vienna.

Inner conflict often produces detachment, as the individual tries to immobilize his contradictory trends by moving away from himself and others. The Duke has many traits that are characteristic of the detached person. He is shy, withdrawn, an observer of himself and others (III, ii). He avoids the spotlight, reminds Friar Thomas that he has "ever lov'd the life removed," and boasts of his imperviousness to "the dribbling dart of love" (I, iii). He seems so far to have avoided close relationships, especially with women. Because of a fear of forbidden or conflicting feelings, he engages in vicarious living. Escalus describes him as "rather rejoicing to see another merry than merry at anything which profess'd to make him rejoice" (III, ii). He is caught in a cross fire of perfectionistic and self-effacing shoulds that leaves him paralyzed as a ruler, unable either to "qualify" the laws or to enforce them.

As the play opens, the Duke has hit upon a plan that will allow him to satisfy all of his conflicting needs. He will turn over his authority to Angelo, a perfectionist who does not have his inner conflicts and insecurities, and Angelo will enforce the harsh laws he has let sleep. This will satisfy his need to judge others by his perfectionistic standards and will relieve his feelings of guilt for encouraging vice: "For we bid this be done/ When evil deeds have their permissive pass/ And not the punishment" (I, iii). It would be "tyranny" in him to punish the people for what he "bid them do"; but Angelo carries no such burden. Angelo will act out the Duke's perfectionistic impulses without making him feel hypocritical and without causing him to lose the love of the people. Indeed, Angelo's harshness will increase his popularity and make the people long for his return. Since the Duke is not actually leaving, he will be able to protect his people from the extreme consequences of Angelo's severity, thus satisfying his need to be merciful and forgiving. The Duke accomplishes all this in a way that is compatible with his need for detachment. His strategy is, literally, to move away, to remain in the background as a secret observer.

The final reason the Duke gives Friar Thomas for his plan is that it will provide a test for Angelo:

> Lord Angelo is precise,
> Stands at a guard with envy, scarce confesses
> That his blood flows or that his appetite
> Is more to bread than stone; hence we shall see,
> If power change purpose, what our seemers be. (I, iii)

The Duke wants Angelo to enforce the laws without harming his own relationship to the people; but, even more than this, he wants Angelo to fail morally. Because of his inner conflicts and his anxieties about his own vulnerability, the Duke has not been able to enforce his perfectionistic standards. As a result, he is full of guilt and feels that he has failed as a ruler. If Angelo succeeds in enforcing the laws, it will increase the Duke's sense of failure by showing that his perfectionistic goals were actually attainable. If Angelo succumbs to temptation, however, thus losing his right to judge others, Vincentio's self-hate will be assuaged; for then it will be evident that no one could have done any better.

The action of the play is like a wish-fulfillment fantasy of the Duke's. Angelo fails and Vincentio emerges as a Christ-like intercessor between sinful man and the harshness of the law. He pulls down and punishes Angelo, by whose self-righteousness he has felt threatened, but he does so in such a way that he seems extremely merciful. The failure of Angelo puts an end to the effort at strictness and justifies the Duke's earlier conduct of office. His marriage with Isabella is part of the wish-fulfillment pattern. Apparently the Duke is a sexually vital man who takes great pride in his purity and who has been struggling to remain continent. Hence his obsession with sexual license. Marriage will permit him to satisfy his needs and to retain his virtue. Isabella is a predominantly perfectionistic person who meets his high standards and who will reinforce his sense of rectitude. She has a compliant side, however, that will enable her to sympathize with his softness toward others. They are well matched because they have similar inner conflicts.

The only thing left unresolved for the Duke is that corruption is still boiling and bubbling in Vienna, and he has found no remedy for it. The claims of justice and mercy have not been reconciled. He felt that it was his "fault to give the people scope" (I, iii), but his behavior at the end is even more permissive than it was at the beginning. The laws are still too strict, but there is no indication that he will modify them. His inner conflicts have not been resolved, but they are less intense now because Angelo's failure has justified his self-effacing trends and made him more comfortable with his compulsive leniency.

What the play accomplishes for the Duke it seems also to accomplish for the author. The central conflict in the play as a whole is between perfectionistic and self-effacing attitudes. The conflict is not resolved, but it is diminished by a critique of perfectionism and a glorification of self-effacing values. Perfectionistic standards are shown to be too high for human nature; it is impossible to enforce them without an absurd amount of "heading and hanging" (II, i). As a successful perfectionist, Angelo is an unappealingly self-righteous and punitive figure. His fall reinforces the notion that even saints are subject to temptation, that no one is an angel. Who, then, has the right to demand perfection of his fellows? The author, like the Duke, offers us nothing between overstrictness and an abandonment of moral authority. Isabella, likewise, goes from one extreme to the other. She is least attractive when she is most perfectionistic, when she decides that her "chastity" counts "More than [her] brother" (II, iv) and when she turns on Claudio so viciously after he appeals to her to save him. Isabella can do nothing that would violate her idealized image; her self-hate would be unbearable. But, like the Duke, she also has a compliant side; and, with a little prodding, she makes eloquent pleas for the forgiveness of others. Her speech on mercy provides the rationale for the Duke's behavior in the final act, a rationale in terms of which it seems impossible for anyone to inflict the penalties of the law upon another. The Duke's indulgent behavior was identified at the beginning of the play as the reason why "quite athwart/ Goes all decorum" (I, iii), but at the end it is glorified as God-like.

Like the Duke, the author seems to be trying to work through his inner conflicts; and, like the Duke, he succeeds not in resolving but in muting them. The failures of perfectionism in the play reinforce and justify the self-effacing solution. The governing fantasy of the play is one in which self-effacing attitudes and values are vindicated and failure to live up to perfectionistic standards is excused. At the same time, Isabella and the Duke are admired for their moral purity, the laws are not modified, and the consequences of being overly permissive are clearly indicated. The play is not thematically integrated because of a lack of integration in the author. It is a remarkably vivid expression, however, of his inner conflicts.

CHAPTER 7

"What Fools These Mortals Be"

Self-Effacement in the Sonnets, the Comedies, *Troilus and Cressida,* and *Antony and Cleopatra*

Shakespeare's treatment of the self-effacing solution is complicated. Self-effacing traits are among the "king-becoming graces," which include "Bounty . . . mercy, lowliness, devotion," and "patience" (*Macbeth,* IV, iii); but, as we saw in the case of Henry VI, a predominantly self-effacing leader is unable to cope with a world full of aggression. Since not only kings, but all men live in such a world, self-effacing tendencies are regarded by Shakespeare and his culture as dangerous for a man, and they must be either subordinated to other tendencies or repressed. Self-effacing women are often as vulnerable as the men in the realistic plays, but self-effacing behavior is glorified in them and is, indeed, equated with "womanliness." The women who are treated most negatively are those who are deficient in self-effacing traits, and a number of the comedies castigate or tame aggressive women. Self-effacing men are treated differently in the comedies than they are in the histories and tragedies. Since these are domestic plays that are more concerned with love than with power, the males do not have to be so aggressive. There is mockery of self-effacing behavior toward the opposite sex, whether the lover be male or female, but many of the self-effacing males are presented in a positive way, especially in their relations with other men. The most fully developed self-effacing males in Shakespeare are the poet of the sonnets, Antonio in *The Merchant of Venice,* Hamlet, Duke Vincentio, Antony, Timon, and Prospero. The sonnets reveal how extremely self-effacing Shakespeare could be, which accounts for his sympathetic treatment of self-effacing males, and also how he hated this side of himself, which accounts for the mockery.

In this chapter, I shall examine Shakespeare's treatment of self-effacing behavior in the large group of works that deal with the problems of morbid dependency, betrayal, and the contrariness of love. Virginia Woolf felt that we know so little of Shakespeare because all desire "to proclaim an injury, to pay off a score, to make the world the witness of some hardship or grievance was fired out of him and consumed" (1957, 58–59). It seems to me that Woolf has the situation exactly backwards, that Shakespeare's "grudges and spites and antipathies" are not "hidden from us," but are evident in his obsessive reworking of the situation depicted in the sonnets. In addition to many of the comedies, *Troilus and Cressida* and *Antony and Cleopatra* reflect this obsession.

THE SONNETS

The poet of the sonnets displays many self-effacing traits in his relations with both the friend and the dark lady. He glorifies the friend and deprecates himself (sonnets 26, 38, 39, 62), but he participates in the friend's glory by identifying with and living vicariously through him: "I in thy substance am sufficed/ And by a part of all thy glory live" (Number 37). His possession of the friend's love is more important to him than "public honors and proud titles" (Number 25), than wealth, hawks, horses, and high birth (Number 91), or, indeed, than anything else. It compensates for his misfortunes, disgraces, and low birth, eases his self-contempt, and enables him to feel like a king (Numbers 25, 29, 30, 37, 91). The poet is morbidly dependent upon the friend. The friend is his only delight (Number 75), he cannot enjoy anything unless he shares it with him (Number 97), and only his opinion matters (Number 112). In sonnet 92, he says, in effect, that he will die if the friend stops loving him. The poet's desperate need of the friend's love is combined with a profound sense of his own unworthiness: "For how do I hold thee but by thy granting,/ And for that riches where is my deserving?" (Number 87; see Numbers 49, 71, 72). This combination intensifies his anxiety.

The greatest threat to the poet's relationship with the friend is his anger at the friend's mistreatment of him, with the dark lady and also in other situations. Like Desdemona with Othello, the poet employs a variety of self-effacing strategies to protect the friend's glory, upon which his own glory depends, and to preserve the relationship. He does not blame when he is wronged, or he blames without blaming, in indirect ways, or he blames so gently that it is hardly a reproach (Numbers 33, 40, 41). He denies his anger and hurt (Number 42), or he is quick to forgive and eager to make up (Number 34). In order to manage his resentment, he sees himself as a slave who has no right to judge or question anything his master does, even though it puts him through hell (Numbers 57, 58). In sonnets 57 and 58 he may be exaggerating his submission in order to make the friend feel guilty, but the submission is nonetheless genuine, and it gives him the masochistic satisfaction of possessing the friend through the friend's possession of him. He handles his resentments also by excusing the friend (Numbers 33, 35), especially in his behavior toward the dark lady (Numbers 40, 41, 42), by blaming himself (Numbers 118, 119), and by arguing on the friend's behalf: "Thy adverse party is thy advocate—/ And 'gainst myself a lawful plea commence" (Number 35; also Numbers 88, 89).

I do not have space to analyze the sonnets in detail, but we can see how self-effacing the poet can be in his relation to the friend in sonnet 88, where he is anticipating mistreatment and is preparing a way to handle it:

> When thou shalt be disposed to set me light
> And place my merit in the eye of scorn,
> Upon thy side against myself I'll fight
> And prove thee virtuous, though thou art forsworn.
> With mine own weakness being best acquainted,
> Upon thy part I can set down a story
> Of faults concealed wherein I am attainted,
> That thou in losing me shall win much glory.
> And I by this will be a gainer too,
> For, bending all my loving thoughts on thee,
> The injuries that to myself I do,
> Doing thee vantage, double-vantage me.
>> Such is my love, to thee I so belong,
>> That for thy right myself will bear all wrong.

When the friend "set[s him] light" or scorns his "merit," the poet will not defend himself or accuse the friend of being forsworn; rather he will fight on the friend's side against himself by revealing his own hidden faults. This will bring the friend "much glory" by justifying his rejection of the poet. Since the poet feeds his own pride through the friend, however, the friend's glory will also be his and he will thus be "double-vantage[d]" by the "injuries" he does to himself. Although the poet says he will fight against himself when the friend "place[s] his merit in the eye of scorn," the sonnet is, of course, a vindication of his merit in self-effacing terms, since he is so humble, loving, and self-sacrificial. His acceptance of responsibility for the friend's unjust criticisms proves the grandeur of his love: "Such is my love, to thee I so belong,/ That for thy right myself will bear all wrong." We have here again, as in sonnets 57 and 58, the strategy of possessing the friend through submission to him, so that the poet's acquiescence in the friend's rejection negates the friend's power to reject him.

The poet is also self-effacing in his relationship with the dark lady. He is a "slave" (Number 133), a vassal wretch" (Number 141), with a "doting heart" (Number 131), who is "mortgaged to [her] will" (Number 134). He partakes with her against himself (Number 149) and even hopes she will succeed with his rival so that she will be in a better humor with him (Number 143). She wrongs him, as does the friend; but he cannot tear himself away from her, so intense is his morbid dependency. He loves her not with his senses or his wits, but with his "foolish heart" (Number 141): "Who taught thee how to make me love thee more,/ The more I hear and see just cause of hate?" (Number 150; also Numbers 131, 137, 148).

Although the poet is equally bewitched by his "two loves" (Number 144), he has very different attitudes toward them. The friend is his "better angel"; the poet's identification with him feeds his pride and makes him feel like his idealized self.[1] The dark lady is his "worser spirit"; his enslavement by her damages his pride and makes him feel like his despised self. He is enraged with both the friend and the dark lady for their betrayal of him, but he has a powerful interest in protecting his image of the friend, and so he expresses his rage toward him in much more indirect ways and places the blame primarily upon the dark lady. In sonnet 144, he is afraid that the dark lady will "corrupt [his] saint to be a devil" and that he will therefore lose the source of his glory. There is no evidence, of course, that the friend was at all saintlike before the dark lady arrived upon the scene. In sonnet 148, the poet exclaims, "what eyes hath Love put in my head,/ Which have no correspondence with true sight!" He is speaking of his perception of the dark lady, but his perception of the friend is equally distorted.

The poet has different attitudes not only toward the friend and the dark lady, but also toward his self-effacing behavior in relation to each. Whereas he exalts such behavior in relation to the friend, he condemns it in relation to the dark lady. He hates himself for being so enslaved, so doting, so abject. He has a strong sense of his own helplessness and irrationality. In sonnet 147, he sees his love "as a fever" which longs for that which "nurseth the disease." He has tried to cure himself with "reason," but to no avail, and now he is "Past cure . . ./ And frantic-mad with evermore unrest." He sees himself as a madman because his "thoughts" are so "At random from the truth": "For I have sworn thee fair, and thought thee bright,/ Who art as black as hell, as dark as night." Not only has he misperceived her, but even when he perceives her correctly, there is nothing he can do about it, and he loathes himself for the compulsiveness and self-destructiveness of his behavior. He feels at once spellbound and contaminated by the dark lady, and he takes a certain satisfaction in her mistreatment of him (Number 141), since this fulfills his need to punish himself for being in love with a whore. Given his character structure, the poet would not have been spellbound by either the friend or the dark lady if they had not mistreated him, but he glorifies his submission to the friend while despising himself for accepting the dark lady's abuse.

Despite the conventional elements in them, the sonnets have seemed to many to be Shakespeare's most autobiographical work. We can never know exactly how autobiographical they are, but critics have noted the recurrence in the corpus of dark ladies and triangular relationships, and this recurrence supports the idea that the sonnets reflect Shakespeare's personal experience, or at least the kinds of preoccupations that experience induced. Without losing sight of the speculative nature of the enterprise, I shall adopt the hypothesis that the sonnets are autobiographical and that many of the plays, the comedies in particular, were efforts on Shakespeare's part to reimagine the situation depicted in the sonnets and to comfort himself. This hypothesis seems plausible to me not because of historical evidence, but because it both illuminates and is corroborated by the plays.

TWO GENTLEMEN OF VERONA

We can account for much that happens in the comedies by citing their sources, but there were psychological reasons why these stories appealed to Shakespeare in the first place. *The Taming of the Shrew,* for instance, is a fantasy of male power over women. Instead of submitting to a domineering woman, Petruchio makes such a woman submit to him, to the point of embracing the self-effacing code of womanly conduct more thoroughly than her ostensibly meek and mild sister. Petruchio is not unmanned by love, as is the poet in the sonnets. He is the self-effacing Shakespeare's fantasy of how he would like to be.

In *Two Gentlemen of Verona,* there is a love triangle similar to that of the sonnets in that Valentine's friend, Proteus, falls in love with his betrothed. The situation of the sonnets is reimagined, for here the woman is faithful and the friend is clearly at fault. In this play, Shakespeare undoes his betrayal by the dark lady and, through the indirection of drama, accuses the friend much more directly than he could allow himself to do in the sonnets. The hero of the play, like the poet of the sonnets, is nobly forgiving. When he intercepts Proteus as he is about to ravish Silvia, he seems to be disillusioned forever; but Proteus repents and Valentine forgives him immediately:

> Who by repentance is not satisfied
> Is nor of heaven nor earth; for these are pleas'd;
> By penitence th' Eternal's wrath's appeas'd.
> And, that my love may appear plain and free,
> All that was mine in Silvia I give thee. (V, iv)

Critics have been amazed by these lines and have sought an explanation of Valentine's behavior, especially his yielding of Silvia. One explanation, and a good one, I think, is to see it in terms of the Renaissance code of male friendship. Whereas the code of martial and manly honor prohibited the display of self-effacing tendencies, the code of male friendship idealized such tendencies and permitted them to be expressed in certain situations. Shakespeare would have been attracted to this code because it justified his own compulsive behavior. In addition, Valentine is behaving in accordance with the code of Christian values, which also celebrates self-effacing behavior. His generosity toward and forgiveness of one who has wronged him makes perfectly good sense in psychological terms, though it would seem less startling in a more fully developed character. It is similar to the poet's behavior toward the friend, Orlando's behavior toward Oliver, Duke Vincentio's behavior toward Angelo, Posthumus's behavior toward Iachimo, and Prospero's behavior toward his enemies. It is in keeping with the speeches on mercy that recur in the corpus. Valentine's self-effacing bargain (or gamble) works in that Proteus declines his offer.

Like the poet, Valentine is self-effacing in relation to both his friend and his lady. The difference is that, unlike the poet's, his lady is faithful, reciprocates his love, and is above him socially. She is, therefore, worthy of his devotion. The poetry inspired by his love of her reminds us of the poet's sonnets to the friend:

> Banish'd from her
> Is self from self—a deadly banishment!
> What light is light, if Silvia be not seen?
> What joy is joy, if Silvia be not by?
> Unless it be to think that she is by
> And feed upon the shadow of perfection.
> Except I be by Silvia in the night,
> There is no music in the nightingale.
> Unless I look on Silvia in the day,
> There is no day for me to look upon. (III, i)

The courtly love tradition, which is strongly felt in this play, provides another cultural code that idealizes self-effacing behavior on the part of the male.

THE MERCHANT OF VENICE

The most striking portrait of male friendship outside the sonnets is that between Antonio and Bassanio in *The Merchant of Venice*. As has often been noted, Bassanio is similar to the friend of the sonnets in his higher social status, his narcissism, and his shallowness; and Antonio is similar to the poet in his self-sacrificial devotion. Whether Antonio has a sexual attachment to Bassanio or not, he is clearly the self-effacing partner in the relationship. He has a morbid dependency upon his friend—"he only loves the world for him" (I, viii). He is melancholy because Bassanio is involved with a woman, but he cannot admit, or perhaps even feel, the true cause of his condition because this would violate his taboos against selfishness and make him feel unworthy of love. Instead, he arranges a loan for Bassanio, offering his flesh for a bond, in order to help him pursue his rival, even though Bassanio is indebted to him already and admits to improvidence. He will do his "uttermost" to help Bassanio succeed (I, i) and will never let him know how much he is suffering. It is no wonder that Bassanio feels Antonio to be "the kindest man" who "draws breath in Italy" (III, ii).

Antonio's ill-fortune seems like a wish-fulfillment. With the intrusion of Portia between himself and Bassanio, life seems empty and he is ready to die; but he would like to go out as a martyr, and so he welcomes the opportunity to suffer for his friend and to demonstrate his love. He wants to possess Bassanio in the only way possible: by winning his eternal gratitude for this last and most glorious of his sacrifices. His self-effacing bargain works better than he dares to hope; for when Bassanio sees how much Antonio loves him, he is ready to sacrifice "life itself, [his] wife, and all the world" to "deliver" his friend (IV, i). Antonio has won the contest with Portia for first place in Bassanio's heart. His victory is confirmed in the affair of the ring, when his wish is valued more than Portia's commandment. He provokes the tension between Portia and Bassanio and then resolves it by offering his "soul" as security for Bassanio's faithfulness (V, i), thus putting his friend once again into his debt.

At the beginning of the play, Antonio is in a state of psychological crisis. He is threatened with the loss of the person without whom life has no meaning, and he is compelled by his shoulds to help his friend succeed with his rival. His self-effacing behavior pays off, however, for instead of losing Bassanio as he had feared, he gains assurance that his devotion is reciprocated, and he is taken into the Bassanio-Portia relationship. From the point of view of the author, this is another reimagining of the situation of the sonnets. It is a fantasy in which sacrifice is given its proper reward and the self-effacing male is the most honored member of the triangle. The price of all this for Antonio is sexual fulfillment (for a fuller discussion, see Paris 1989b).

UNIVERSALIZING HIS PLIGHT

Shakespeare tends to glorify self-effacing behavior on the part of men, then, when it is manifested within a male friendship (see also Antonio and Sebastian in *Twelfth Night*). Self-effacing behavior toward women is sometimes idealized, as with Valentine and Silvia, but more often it is treated ambivalently or is made the matter of comedy. In the sonnets, the poet condemns himself for his irrational attraction to and enslavement by the dark lady. In the comedies that deal with love, Shakespeare is trying to universalize the situation described in the sonnets and thus to reduce its painfulness. Again and again, he shows heterosexual love (on the part of both men and women) to be blind, foolish, and compulsive. If all mortals are fools, his is the common lot and he need not despise himself so much. By treating behavior similar to his own in a comic manner, moreover, he denies its seriousness and distances himself from it. He reduces his discomfort by employing the strategy of detachment.

TWO GENTLEMEN AGAIN

Two Gentlemen begins with the love-sick Proteus doting upon Julia. Valentine tries to bring his friend to his senses, but to no avail:

> Even so by love the young and tender wit
> Is turn'd to folly, blasting in the bud,
> Losing his verdure, even in the prime,
> And all the fair effects of future hopes.
> But wherefore waste I time to counsel thee
> That art a votary to fond desire? (I, i)

Valentine is punished "for contemning Love" by falling in love with Silvia, upon whom *he* dotes with all the symptoms that had before afflicted Proteus (II, iv). No one escapes the "high imperious thoughts" and discomforts of love. The situation is complicated when Proteus falls in love with Silvia at first sight and compulsively violates his vows both to Valentine and to Julia. He tries to assuage his self-hate by telling himself that it is "Love [that] bids [him] forswear" (II, vi), and Shakespeare seems at least partially to excuse him, much as the poet excuses the friend in the sonnets. People just cannot help themselves in these matters. Proteus is so bewitched by Silvia because she does not reciprocate his affection: "Yet, spaniel-like, the more she spurns my love,/ The more it grows, and fawneth on her still" (IV, ii). Many critics have noted Shakespeare's negative attitude toward fawning dogs. I believe that it is an externalization of his contempt for the self-effacing side of himself.

Just as Proteus dotes on Silvia, so Julia dotes on Proteus, even though he has betrayed her. As she says to him, under the cover of her disguise:

> She dreams on him that has forgot her love;
> You dote on her that cares not for your love.
> 'Tis pity love should be so contrary;
> And thinking on it makes me cry "Alas!" (IV, iv)

This cry could come from the poet of the sonnets. The contrariness of love is one of the chief blocking forces in Shakespearean comedy. It can be overcome, it seems, only by the arbitrary resolutions of that genre.

LOVE'S LABOUR'S LOST

In *Love's Labour's Lost,* men are once again shown to be helplessly subject to love's overpowering force. The men of King Ferdinand's court swear "Not to see ladies, study [and] fast" for a period of three years; but Berowne, Shakespeare's spokesman in this play, predicts that "Necessity will make [them] all forsworn" (I, i), for will-power is helpless against our natural impulses. The first to be forsworn is the clownish Armado, who, like the poet of the sonnets, falls in love with a socially inferior wench of dubious reputation. He excuses himself by calling love "a devil" and citing other examples of its power: "Yet was Samson so tempted, and he had an excellent strength. Yet was Salomon so seduced, and he had a very good wit. Cupid's buttshaft is too hard for Hercules' club, and therefore too much odds for a Spaniard's rapier . . . . His disgrace is to be called boy, but his glory is to subdue men" (I, ii).

The other men of the court are soon subdued, including Berowne, who, like Valentine, sees himself as being punished for his "neglect" of Cupid's "almighty dreadful little might" (III, i). Now he, too, must "love, write, sigh, pray, sue, and groan," and wear Cupid's "colours like a tumbler's hoop" (III, i). Each of the courtiers feels guilty and foolish because of his lovesick behavior, and each hopes that the others are in the same condition: "For none offend where all alike do dote" (IV, iii). They obtain relief, much as Shakespeare, I am arguing, did himself, by discovering that they are all fools together. "You three fools," says Berowne, "lacked me fool to make up the mess" (IV, iii). Since they "cannot cross the cause why [they] were born," they have been "As true . . . as flesh and blood can be" (IV, iii). Once again Shakespeare presents the doting male as being unable to control his behavior.

The men seem like fools not only because they are forsworn and engage in love-sick behavior, but also because they are treated as such by the ladies, who are less in love than they are and regard them with a certain detachment. To the ladies, their "letters, full of love" are merely "pleasant jest, and courtesy" (V, ii). This lack of reciprocity gives the ladies a power over their lovers that they use with great delight. Rosaline, in particular, enjoys tormenting Berowne:

> That same Berowne I'll torture ere I go.
> O that I knew he were but in by th' week!
> How I would make him fawn, and beg, and seek,
> And wait the season, and observe the times,
> And spend his prodigal wits in bootless rhymes,

> And shape his service wholly to my hests,
> And make him proud to make me proud that jests!
> So pertaunt-like would I o'ersway his state
> That he should be my fool, and I his fate. (V, ii)

Since Berowne is a wit, like Shakespeare, and Rosaline is a dark lady (though not, in this case, an unworthy one), Shakespeare seems again to be reimagining the situation of the sonnets and to be trying to understand his plight by entering into the woman's perspective.

The dialogue that follows the lines quoted above seems to be a commentary by Shakespeare on himself:

> *Princess.*   None are so surely caught, when they are catch'd,
>   As wit turn'd fool. Folly, in wisdom hatch'd,
>   Hath wisdom's warrant, and the help of school,
>   And wit's own grace to grace a learned fool.
> *Rosaline.*   The blood of youth burns not with such excess
>   As gravity's revolt to wantonness.
> *Maria.*   Folly in fools bears not so strong a note
>   As fool'ry in the wise when wit doth dote;
>   Since all the power thereof it doth apply
>   To prove, by wit, worth in simplicity. (V, ii)

Shakespeare sees himself very clearly here, more clearly, perhaps, than in the sonnets; but one of the things that he sees and illustrates in his portrait of Berowne is the inability of insight to save us from folly.

The ending of the play is strikingly antiromantic. When the Princess must leave because of the death of her father, Ferdinand asks the ladies "Now at the latest minute of the hour" to "grant [them their] loves" (V, ii). "A time methinks too short," the Princess replies, "To make a world-without-end bargain in." It is the relative lack of passion on the women's part that permits them to be so wise. There is more than wisdom at work here, however. Now that they are sure of the men's affections, the women follow Rosaline's program of making them "wait the season and observe the times" and "shape [their] service wholly to [their] hests." Ferdinand must spend a year in "some forlorn and naked hermitage,/ Remote from all the pleasures of the world"; and Berowne must spend twelve months visiting "the speechless sick" and trying to make them laugh (V, ii). This is supposed to cure him of his "gibing spirit," but Rosaline is much more gibing than he, and her criticism hardly seems fair. She seems motivated less by a concern for his moral reformation than by a desire to "o'ersway his state."

A MIDSUMMER-NIGHT'S DREAM

One of Shakespeare's darkest portrayals of love occurs in one of his lightest plays, *A Midsummer-Night's Dream*. Puck's comment, "What fools these mortals be," applies to most of the characters in the play, including the fairies, and most of the relationships are quite disturbed. The contrariness of love is very much in evidence here. Helena dotes on Demetrius, who scorns her and dotes on Hermia, who is in love with Lysander. Lysander reciprocates Hermia's affection, but the course of their love does not run smooth because of her father's objections and Lysander's sudden transfer of his affections to Helena.

This is caused by Puck's error in administering the magic drops, but the effect of the magic drops corresponds to the fickleness and irrationality of ordinary human behavior. Theseus compares the lover to "the lunatic" (V, i); Bottom observes that "reason and love keep little company together now-a-days" (III, i); and, according to Puck, "the fate o'errules, that, one man holding troth,/ A million fail, confounding oath on oath" (III, ii). The lover, like the lunatic, has hallucinations: "One sees more devils than vast hell can hold:/ That is the mad man. The lover, all as frantic,/ Sees Helen's beauty in a brow of Egypt" (V, i). This is a reference, perhaps, to Shakespeare's delusion about a dark lady. He simultaneously mocks and excuses himself by having Titania fall in love with the ass-headed Bottom, thus eliciting Bottom's remark about the divorce of love and reason. "The more the pity," Bottom continues, "that some honest neighbours will not make them friends" (III, i). Those who hold troth in the play tend, in the heat of their passion, to be self-destructive. Helena will "make a heaven of hell/ To die upon the hand [she loves] so well" (II, i); Hermia is ready to die when she wakes to find Lysander gone (II, ii); and Pyramis and Thisbe, like Romeo and Juliet, kill themselves rather than live on without their lovers. The constant lovers are morbidly dependent upon their partners.

The magic in this play is used not only to create situations that are comparable to those of everyday life, as Shakespeare sees it, but also to rectify these situations. The dark view of love can be treated lightly because it occurs within a comic world where we can regard all the complications with a detached amusement, a Puckish delight. Puck enjoys the consequences of his error, "As this their jangling I esteem a sport" (III, ii). He looks at the human scene from a very great distance. Oberon, the playwright figure in the play, is more sympathetic and makes sure that the mischief is undone. Indeed, he goes farther than that and uses his magical powers to bring about an ideal resolution. Helena gets Demetrius, Hermia gets Lysander back, and all of the couples, as a result of his blessing, shall "Ever true in loving be" (V, i).

Through the figure of Puck, Shakespeare dramatizes the process by which he gains the distance that permits him to laugh at his folly; and through the figure of Oberon, he dramatizes the process by which he creates a version of life as he wants it to be. Oberon's magic is equivalent to the poet's imagination, "That, if it would but apprehend some joy,/ It comprehends some bringer of that joy" (V, i). Through its unrealistic components, the play expresses Shakespeare's wish for faithful, reciprocal, rational love. This leads us back to the dark view, for the play seems to be saying that such love can come about only through magic, that happiness in love is a miracle. The couples who are united at the end are being exempted from the vicissitudes of fate and vagaries of normal human behavior.

In *A Midsummer-Night's Dream,* then, Shakespeare comforts himself by laughing at folly like his own as part of the human condition and by using the magic of his imagination to make friends of love and reason. He reimagines the situation of the sonnets in other ways as well. The play contains two strong males who master powerful women. Theseus woos Hippolyta "with [his] sword/ And [wins her] love doing [her] injuries," while Oberon forces Titania to capitulate by humiliating her with his magic. Her defiance creates discord in nature (II, i), but after her submission "all things shall be peace" (III, ii). The situation of the sonnets is reversed. It is the woman, here, who is in love "with a monster" (III, ii) and the men who gain mastery by inflicting pain.

In the Helena-Demetrius-Hermia triangle, Helena and Demetrius dote upon those who do not love them, as the poet does in the sonnets; but it is the woman who most vividly displays the kind of self-effacing behavior of which Shakespeare is ashamed. Helena "dotes in idolatry,/ Upon this spotted and inconstant man" (I, i) and tells him that the more he beats her, the more she will "fawn" on him:

> Use me but as your spaniel—spurn me, strike me,
> Neglect me, lose me; only give me leave
> (Unworthy as I am) to follow you.
> What worser place can I beg in your love
> (And yet a place of high respect with me)
> Than to be used as you use your dog? (II, i)

Her abjectness arouses Demetrius's "hatred" and contempt, which makes her love him more.

This is all very realistic psychologically if we understand the dynamics of the self-effacing personality. Demetrius's rejection places him above her and at once crushes her pride and permits her to restore it by transferring her pride to him. If he uses or abuses her, then he is acknowledging his possession of her, which allows her to merge with him and thus to participate in his superiority. If he reciprocated her affection, he would seem less valuable to her, given her insecurity about her own worth. Her insecurity produces marvelous comedy in the scene in which both Demetrius and Lysander profess to love her and she thinks that she is being mocked by them (III, ii).

Demetrius is also a self-effacing person; he loves Hermia for the same reason that Helena loves him. He scorns Helena partly because he is externalizing his self-hate and partly because she is so abject that it would damage rather than feed his pride to accept her devotion. Shakespeare has a wonderful intuitive understanding of these dynamics.

Like the poet in the dark lady sonnets, Helena is aware of her folly but can do nothing about it:

> And as he errs doting on Hermia's eyes,
> So I, admiring of his qualities.
> Things base and vile, holding no quantity,
> Love can transpose to form and dignity.
> Love looks not with the eyes, but with the mind;
> And therefore is wing'd Cupid painted blind.
> Nor hath Love's mind of any judgment taste;
> Wings, and no eyes, figure unheedy haste.
> And therefore is Love said to be a child,
> Because in choice he is so oft beguil'd. (I, i)

Like Shakespeare, Helena disowns responsibility for her behavior by blaming it on "Love," as though that were a force independent of her personality. Indeed, since her feelings toward Demetrius are compulsive, they feel like something imposed upon her. As Puck says, "Cupid is a knavish lad/ Thus to make poor females mad" (III, ii). Helena is so mad that she decides to tell Demetrius of Hermia's flight in order to gain his "thanks" and the sight of him "thither and back again" (I, i).

Shakespeare both mocks and excuses Helena, along with everyone else, but there is no glorification of self-effacing behavior in this play. The contrariness of love is presented in considerable psychological detail, but Shakespeare is unable to imagine a realistic resolution of the problem, here or anywhere else. In *A Midsummer-Night's Dream,* he uses Oberon's magic (that is, his license as a playwright) to make it disappear.

MUCH ADO ABOUT NOTHING

Like *A Midsummer-Night's Dream, Much Ado About Nothing* contains a dark view of love within its comic structure. There are recurring
references to the arbitrariness of love, the foolishness of lovers, and the
pain of disillusionment. When Benedick and Beatrice are tricked into
loving, Hero observes: "then loving goes by haps;/ Some Cupid kills with
arrows, some with traps" (III, i). Claudio has always spoken of "how
much another man is a fool when he dedicates his behaviors to love" (II,
iii), but he quickly begins mooning over Hero; and even Benedick, who
has sworn to be a bachelor, becomes melancholy, shaves his beard, wash-
es his face, wears perfume, and writes poetry to Beatrice (III, ii). Here, as
elsewhere in the comedies, the moral is that there is no fighting Mother
Nature. As Benedick says, "the world must be peopled" (II, iii). There is
a great fear, however, of marriage. When he hears that there has been a
betrothal, Don John asks, "What is he for a fool that betroths himself to
unquietness?" (I, iii). Benedick and Beatrice have vowed to avoid, as
Beatrice puts it, "wooing, wedding, and repenting" (II, iii). Both men
and women are afraid of being betrayed. Balthasar sings, "Men were
deceivers ever,/ . . . To one thing constant never" (II, iii); and the horn
imagery that runs through the play reflects the men's anxiety about being
cuckolded. Perhaps it is this anxiety that leads Claudio to believe the worst
about Hero.

There is a potential triangle in the play similar to that of the sonnets.
When Don Pedro woos Hero on behalf of Claudio, Don John, to make
mischief, tells Claudio that Pedro is "enamour'd on Hero" himself (II, i).
Although he is not presented as especially prone to distrust, Claudio
believes this immediately:

> 'Tis certain so. The Prince woos for himself.
> Friendship is constant in all other things
> Save in the office and affairs of love:
> . . . .
> Let every eye negotiate for itself
> And trust no agent; for beauty is a witch
> Against whose charms faith melteth into blood.
> This is an accident of hourly proof. (II, i)

Claudio's fears are confirmed by Benedick, who tells him, "the Prince
hath got your Hero" (II, I). Benedick observes to Don Pedro that
Claudio's is "the flat transgression of a schoolboy who, being overjoyed

with finding a bird's nest, shows it his companion, and he steals it" (II, i). Don Pedro has been acting in good faith, however, and he replies: "Wilt thou make a trust a transgression? The transgression is in the stealer" (II, i). In this reworking of the relationship between lover, friend, and mistress, it is not the lover who is foolish for trusting his friend, but the friend who would be at fault if he betrayed his trust. The ideal of friendship is redeemed through Don Pedro.

Indeed, Shakespeare seems in this play to be both expressing and trying to work through his anxiety and cynicism about love and friendship. Claudio is quick to feel betrayed, but both Don Pedro and Hero turn out to be true, and it is Claudio who is at fault for mistrusting them. The fact that some have been false does not mean that no one is faithful. Perhaps the most anxious lovers in Shakespeare are Benedick and Beatrice, another wit and dark lady. In order to avoid being cuckolded, Benedick resolves to remain unmarried; and Beatrice, who is insecure about her attractiveness, drives men away with her "shrewd . . . tongue" (II, i) so that they cannot spurn or disappoint her. Beatrice is especially wary of Benedick because he has jilted her in the past, and she punishes him cruelly with her witty assaults. Benedick is attracted to her, but he is injured and frightened by her attacks. He fears being unmanned, as Hercules was by Omphale, and says that he "would not marry her though she were endowed with all that Adam had left him before he transgress'd" (II, i).

Benedick and Beatrice are brought together by a trick that is not so much an accident, a "hap," as a form of therapy. When friends assure them that they are loved by the other, they can become less defensive and allow their love needs to rise to the surface. With the emergence of their self-effacing sides, they are particularly susceptible to accusations of pride and have a need to demonstrate that they have mended their faults. Beatrice is a dark lady whose cruelty is shown to be a product of her vulnerability and who is not ultimately unkind. She is a shrew who is tamed by being assured that she is loved rather than by being mastered, like Kate. She does not become submissive, but retains a strong personality. Both she and Benedick are wary lovers. They have allowed themselves to entertain love after a period of cynicism, and they are still afraid of a whole-hearted commitment. Benedick tells Beatrice that he "love[s her] against [his] will" (V, ii), and Beatrice says that she yields "upon great persuasion, and partly to save [his] live, for [she] was told [he] was in a consumption" (V, iv). Benedick defends himself against being mocked for his inconsistency by generalizing it— "for man is a giddy thing" (V, iv); and he protects himself against the possible pain of marriage by seeing cuckoldry as the common lot: "Prince, thou art sad. Get thee a wife, get thee a wife! There is no staff more reverent than one tipp'd with horn" (V, iv). The play is saying, in effect, that we may be deceived if we marry, but we'll be sad if we do not.

The play also seems to be holding out the possibility of faithfulness and to be rejecting excessive distrust. It is the first of a group of plays in which a woman turns out to be true after being suspected of unfaithfulness. The others are *Othello, Cymbeline,* and *The Winter's Tale.* In all of these plays, Shakespeare seems to be at once dramatizing and trying to purge himself of his fear of betrayal.

AS YOU LIKE IT

In *As You Like It,* there is once again a chorus of cynical comments on love, friendship, and human nature. According to Rosalind, "love is merely a madness" (III, ii), and Touchstone says that "all nature in love [is] mortal in folly" (II, iv). The lover is made to seem foolish indeed in Jaques' "seven ages" speech: "And then the lover,/ Sighing like a furnace, with a woeful ballad/ Made to his mistress' eyebrow" (II, vii). The ardor of love soon passes ("Men are April when they woo, December when they wed"—IV, i) and inconstancy follows. At the end, Touchstone presses in "amongst the country copulatives, to swear and to forswear, according as marriage binds and blood breaks" (V, iv). As in *Much Ado,* there is a preoccupation with horns and a resigned acceptance of marriage as a lesser evil than bachelorhood: "Is the single man therefore blessed? No; as a wall'd town is more worthier than a village, so is the forehead of a married man more honorable than the bare brow of a bachelor" (III, iii). Nature drives us to marry in order to perpetuate the species: "'Tis Hymen peoples every town" (V, iv). In Amiens's song, friendship is treated as satirically as love: the winter weather does "not bite so nigh/ As benefits forgot./ . . . As friend rememb'red not" (V, iv). Little of the human scene escapes negative comment. Celia says that Fortune makes women either fair or honest (I, ii), and Duke Senior prefers "the icy fang/ . . . of the winter's wind" to the "flattery" and "peril [of] the envious court" (II, i). Orlando and Rosalind are hated by Oliver and Duke Frederick because of their virtues. "O, what a world is this," exclaims Adam, "when what is comely/ Envenoms him that bears it!" (II, iii).

The tone of much of the play is set by Jaques's detached, disillusioned perspective, which "pierceth through/ The body of the country,

city, court" (II, i). As in the "seven ages" speech, everything is demythified, including romantic love and life in the Forest of Arden. The
playwright defends himself against feeling like a fool by seeing through
everyone's folly, including his own. He has Touchstone quote the old saw,
"The fool doth think he is wise, but the wise man knows himself to be a
fool" (V, i). Knowing oneself to be a fool is the mark of superior wisdom.

Even the process of demythification is demythified. When Jaques
wishes that he had the fool's license to speak his mind so that he could
"Cleanse the foul body of th' infected world," Duke Senior undercuts his
right to chide others by pointing to his own sins:

> Most mischievous foul sin, in chiding sin.
> For thou thyself hast been a libertine,
> As sensual as the brutish sting itself;
> And all th' embossed sores and headed evils
> That thou with license of free foot hast caught,
> Wouldst thou disgorge into the general world. (II, vii)

These lines seem to apply to Shakespeare as well as to Jaques. The sonnets
express not only anger toward those who have wronged him, but also guilt
for his sensuality (Number 129) and for his betrayal of his wife (Number
152). There is evidence elsewhere that he felt too much in need of forgiveness to be comfortable judging others. Like the playwright, Jaques
observes the human scene and pierces through its absurdities and vices.

In Duke Senior's lines, Shakespeare shows his awareness that neither
he nor Jaques is an objective observer, that both tend to project their own
behavior onto others in order to allay their feelings of guilt. By showing
inconstancy as the rule of human behavior, Shakespeare reduces the sting
not only of what others have done to him, but also of what he has done
himself. He, too, has sworn and forsworn, "according as marriage binds
and blood breaks."

I do not mean to suggest that Jaques's is the predominant perspective.
One of the most striking things about *As You Like It* is what might be
called its antithetical vision. In its treatment of almost every theme, the
play oscillates among a variety of conflicting perspectives (II, vii is a good
example). Cynicism is balanced by idealism, and idealism is balanced by a
comic awareness of absurdity or a detached deromanticization. The play is
at once optimistic and pessimistic, festive and melancholy. The action
both supports and contradicts the choral commentary: there is much betrayal, but also much faithfulness; much contrariness and folly in love, but
also the most attractive pair of lovers in Shakespeare. There are fratricidal

brothers (Duke Frederick and Oliver), but also a loyal servant and master (Adam and Orlando), true friends (Celia and Rosalind), and a wise and benevolent ruler (Duke Senior). Even as he continues to make dark comments on human nature, Shakespeare allows his wish to believe in love and goodness to rise to the surface.

The play's antithetical vision is a manifestation of Shakespeare's inner conflicts. The play's three predominant moods—idealism, cynicism, and detachment—correspond to the defensive strategies of moving toward, against, and away from people. The expression of one of these moods tends to activate the others. For instance, when he expresses idealistic attitudes, Shakespeare needs to counterbalance them with cynicism and comic or melancholy detachment to protect himself against being disappointed or feeling like a fool.

The play's antithetical vision is evident in its treatment of self-effacing behavior in heterosexual relationships. Such behavior is both mocked and idealized, with idealization dominating at the end. Once again, Shakespeare seems to be trying to come to terms with his own self-effacing tendencies. Phebe is another dark lady ("inky brows," "black silk hair," and "bugle eyeballs"—III, v), and Silvius is her doting lover. Silvius begs Phebe not to scorn him, but his abjectness only increases her contempt. When Rosalind witnesses the interchange between them, she intervenes with an attack on both parties:

> You foolish shepherd, wherefore do you follow her,
> Like foggy south, puffing with wind and rain?
> You are a thousand times a properer man
> Than she a woman. 'Tis such fools as you
> That makes the world full of ill-favour'd children.
> 'Tis not her glass, but you, that flatters her,
> And out of you she sees herself more proper
> Than any of her lineaments can show her. (III, v)

This is a brilliant analysis of the way in which Silvius's devotion feeds Phebe's pride and leads to her contempt for him, even though he is a "properer" person. The more he suffers the weaker he seems and the less his chance of winning her. Rosalind's mockery of Silvius is Shakespeare's mockery of himself, for he has behaved in exactly the same way in relation to his own dark lady. In a later scene, Celia pities Silvius, but Rosalind refuses to do so: "No, he deserves no pity. Wilt thou love such a woman? What, to make thee an instrument, and play false strains upon thee? Not to be endur'd! Well, go your way to her (for I see love hath made thee a tame snake)" (IV, iii). This is similar to the contempt for himself that the poet expresses in the sonnets.

Rosalind's attack on Silvius contains an attack on Phebe as well that she continues more directly:

> But, mistress, know yourself. Down on your knees,
> And thank heaven, fasting, for a good man's love;
> For I must tell you friendly in your ear,
> Sell when you can! You are not for all markets.
> Cry the man mercy, love him, take his offer. (III, v)

This assault on her pride makes Phebe fall in love with Rosalind (who is disguised as Ganymede), much as Demetrius's rejection turns Helena into his spaniel: "Sweet youth, I pray you chide a year together./ I had rather hear you chide than this man woo" (III, v). By feeding her pride, Silvius made Phebe feel too good for him. By crushing her pride, Rosalind brings out her self-effacing side and arouses her feelings of dependency. We become attached to the person who has injured our pride because only through that person's love or approval can our pride be restored. Phebe is now as morbidly dependent upon Ganymede as Silvius is upon her. She can pity Silvius because she is in the same state as he, and she is willing to "endure" his presence because it affords her an opportunity to talk of love. Silvius is such a "tame snake" that he is glad to have her company on these terms:

> So holy and so perfect is my love,
> And I in such a poverty of grace,
> That I shall think it a most plenteous crop
> To glean the broken ears after the man
> That the main harvest reaps. Loose now and then
> A scatt'red smile, and that I'll live upon. (III, v)

Silvius glorifies his self-effacing behavior, but in view of Rosalind's contempt for his abjectness we are not meant, I think, to regard his love as "holy" and "perfect." Phebe's behavior is just as extreme as Silvius's. She pursues Ganymede with declarations of passion and says that she will "study how to die" if he does not reciprocate (IV, iii).

Rosalind is the most fascinating character in this play. She seems in many ways to be a surrogate for Shakespeare; she is a spokesman, an actor, and a playwright within the play. Through her attacks on Silvius and Phebe, Shakespeare mocks himself and the dark lady and shows himself how he should have managed the relationship. Through her relationship with Orlando, Shakespeare is trying to imagine a heterosexual love that transcends contrariness, fickleness, and folly despite the fact that the relationship has much in common with the irrational ones that are typical of the comedies. Rosalind and Orlando fall in love at first sight, without real knowledge of each other, they cannot control their affections, and they display many of the signs of lovesickness. Orlando, whom Jaques calls "Signior Love" (III, ii), "abuses . . . young plants with carving 'Rosalind' on their barks; hangs odes upon hawthorns, and elegies on brambles; all, forsooth, deifying the name of Rosalind" (III, ii). His verses are mocked by Touchstone and by Rosalind herself, who says that some have "in them more feet than the verses would bear" (III, ii). Like Phebe, Orlando says that he will "die" if his passion is not reciprocated. Rosalind is as "love-shaked" (III, ii) as Orlando. She identifies with Silvius's passion— "Alas, poor shepherd! Searching thy wound,/ I have by hard adventure found my own"—and she agrees with Touchstone's remark that "We that are true lovers run into strange capers" (II, iv). Indeed, it is Rosalind who speaks of love as "madness" and "lunacy" (III, ii). She tells Celia that she "cannot be out of the sight of Orlando" (IV, i), and she swoons when she sees the "napkin/ Dy'd in his blood" (IV, iii). Her affection, she says, "cannot be sounded": it "hath an unknown bottom, like the Bay of Portugal" (IV, i).

The ingredients are here for a satirical treatment, and, indeed, there is some gentle mockery; but the relationship is an authorial fantasy in which love at first sight does not turn out to be foolish. Unlike Silvius and Phebe or Touchstone and Audrey (or the poet and the dark lady), Orlando and Rosalind are equal in worth and attractiveness, especially after Oliver turns over the estate to Orlando. Their love is reciprocal, and we are encouraged to believe that they will be true to each other. There is much joking about horns, even by Rosalind; but, as Orlando says, "Virtue is no horn-maker, and my Rosalind is virtuous" (IV, i). The whole flavor of their relationship is profoundly affected by Rosalind's disguise, by her play-acting. Orlando does not make a fool of himself to Rosalind because he does not know it is Rosalind to whom he is confessing his passion, and Rosalind's disguise prevents her from letting Orlando see the depth of her devotion. Her confessions are made to Celia. She can enjoy the knowledge of Orlando's love without having to deal with its excesses. Indeed, when he says that he will die if Rosalind does not have him, Rosalind, as Ganymede, mocks him: "Men have died from time to time, and worms have eaten them, but not for love" (IV, i).

It seems that Rosalind is able to be in and out of the game, to love passionately, but to keep passionate love in perspective. As Rosalind, she falls in love with Orlando when he displays his mastery in the wrestling match; and, in the heat of her passion, she is in danger of running "into strange capers." She cannot very well do this, however, as Ganymede. As Ganymede, that is, as playwright and actor, she gains a distance from her emotions that permits her to recognize her danger and to guard against it by mocking her self-effacing tendencies as they manifest themselves in others. As Rosalind, she identifies with Silvius's passion; but as Ganymede, she ridicules it. As Ganymede, she is clear-sighted, unillusioned, even a bit cynical; as Rosalind, she is desperately in love. The split in Rosalind corresponds, I propose, to a split in Shakespeare. In his role as a playwright, he gained distance from his emotions and insight into himself. Whether he was able to utilize this insight in an effectual way, we shall never know. Ganymede's lessons seem to have been lost on Silvius.

Although there is much mockery of self-effacing behavior and much cynicism about human nature and the human condition early in *As You Like It,* the end of the play honors self-effacing values. Orlando saves his brother instead of taking revenge, and his nobility results in Oliver's conversion and makes him a suitable mate for Celia. While he is on his way to kill his brother, Duke Frederick is converted by "an old religious man" (V, iv) and retires from the world, bequeathing his crown to Duke Senior. The wrongs with which the play began are easily set right by the forces of goodness, which have a magical potency. A self-effacing view of love is embraced when the wooers assent to Silvius's account of "what 'tis to love":

> It is to be all made of sighs and tears;
> . . . .
> It is to be all made of faith and service;
> . . . .
> It is to be all made of fantasy,
> All made of passion, and all made of wishes,
> All adoration, duty, and observance,
> All humbleness, all patience, and impatience,
> All purity, all trial, all observance . . . (V, ii)

Silvius's self-effacing bargain finally works when, after Ganymede turns out to be a woman, Phebe says, "Thy faith my fancy to thee doth combine" (V, iv). The play's earlier psychological realism is simply ignored in a wish-fulfillment ending. Rosalind, in her role as playwright and/or magician, arranges all the matches and brings Hymen on the scene. Like Oberon in *A Midsummer-Night's Dream,* Hymen assures the happiness of the couples, with the possible exception of Touchstone and Audrey. There is Touchstone's remark about "the country copulatives," but, on the whole, marriage is presented in a favorable light—"O blessed bond of board and bed!" (V, iv). Even Jaques seems mellow. He departs, wishing all well, and taking with him the satirical perspective.

TWELFTH NIGHT

Irving Ribner feels that Shakespeare's treatment of love in *Twelfth Night* may have been in part suggested by Barnaby Rich's prefatory remarks to "Apolonius and Silla," which is the play's primary source:

> If a question might be asked, what is the ground indeed of reasonable love, whereby the knot is knit of true and perfect friendship, I think those that be wise would answer—desert: that is where the party beloved doth requite us with the like; for otherwise, if the bare show of beauty, or the comeliness of personage might be sufficient to confirm us in our love, those that be accustomed to go to fairs and markets might sometimes fall in love with twenty in a day. Desert must then be (of force) the ground of reasonable love, for to love them that hate us, to follow them that fly from us, to fawn on them that frown on us, to curry favour with them that disdain us, to be glad to please them that care not how they offend us—who will not confess this to be an erroneous love, neither grounded upon wit nor reason. (Kittredge and Ribner 1966, xv)

This is an interesting passage, but we do not need it to explain *Twelfth Night,* for the kinds of "erroneous love" that Rich describes pervade the sonnets and the comedies that precede this play.

Twelfth Night repeats many of the patterns we have been examining. Here, too, there are numerous instances of love at first sight. Orsino falls in love with Olivia at "the bare show of beauty," as does Olivia with the disguised Viola (I, v) and Sebastian with Olivia (IV, iii). Shakespeare seems to excuse such love by having Olivia attribute it to fate: "Ourselves we do not owe./ What is decreed must be—and be this so!" (I, v). The contrariness of love is very much in evidence in this play, as Viola observes: "My master loves her dearly;/ And I (poor monster) fond as much on him;/ And she (mistaken) seems to dote on me" (II, iii). Orsino and Olivia "follow them that fly from" them and "fawn on them that frown" upon them. Olivia feels humiliated by her own behavior but cannot control it:

> I have said too much unto a heart of stone
> And laid mine honour too unchary out.

> There's something in me that reproves my fault;
> But such a headstrong potent fault it is
> That it but mocks reproof. (III, iv)

Viola points out that Orsino is in the same state: "With the same havior that your passion bears/ Goes on my master's griefs." In this play, too, Shakespeare is rationalizing his own self-effacing behavior by portraying love as an uncontrollable, compelling force.

Ribner sees Barnaby Rich as attacking "the absurdities of [the] fashionable Petrarchism" of the day and feels that Shakespeare's "lovers also expose the affectations of the Petrarchan love conventions" (p. xvi). He makes an exception of Viola, who represents the Platonic "'love of the understanding,' the love proper to angels, an intuitive union of soul in which the lover surrenders all awareness of self and becomes a part of the beloved object. It is a love of complete self-sacrifice, as Viola illustrates when she is ready to die for the whim of Orsino. By Viola's standard of true devotion, all of the other varieties of love in the play are measured and found wanting" (pp. xvi–xvii).

It seems to me that Rich is attacking the absurdities of self-effacing behavior, which are culturally encoded in and sanctioned by the Petrarchan conventions, and that Viola's love is just as "erroneous" as the love of Orsino for Olivia or of Olivia for Cesario. Viola is slavishly devoted to an undeserving, immature man who is foolishly in love with another. She is probably just as much "charm'd" by his "outside" as Olivia is by hers (II, ii). As she indicates in act 2, scene 2, they are all doting lovers, and there is not much to choose between them. She is just as lovesick as Orsino and Olivia, but, like Rosalind, she is prevented from behaving foolishly by her disguise. She does not even have a confidant, though she does confess her state indirectly when the Clown says that he will ask Jove, "in his next commodity of hair," to send her "a beard": "By my troth, I'll tell thee, I am almost sick for one, though I would not have it grow on my chin" (III, i). The intensity of her passion, as well as its self-sacrificial nature, is expressed in the eloquence with which she woos Olivia on Orsino's behalf. When Orsino wants to kill her (as Cesario) in order to spite Olivia, she is not appalled by this revelation of his character but is thrilled at the thought of his taking possession of her in this ultimate way: "And I, most jocund, apt, and willingly,/ To do you rest a thousand deaths would die" (V, i).

Critics see Viola's self-sacrifice as noble rather than as pathological in part because Shakespeare's rhetoric presents it that way. Through Viola, and through Antonio, he glorifies self-effacing behavior in this play.

The Antonio of *Twelfth Night* is much like the Antonio of *The Merchant of Venice*. He "adore[s]" Sebastian, who is socially above him, and he risks his life in order to serve him (II, i). He gives Sebastian his purse in case his "eye shall light upon some toy/ [He has] desire to purchase" (III, iii), and he intervenes on his behalf when he thinks he is in danger. It is Viola whom he rescues, of course. When he is arrested as a result of his concern and faces the penalty of death, he is grieved more for Sebastian than for himself, since his "necessity" makes him ask for his purse. He becomes terribly upset when Cesario denies knowing him, for this calls his bargain into question and forces him to assert his claims, which is something he is not supposed to do:

> Is't possible that my deserts to you
> Can lack persuasion? Do not tempt my misery,
> Lest that it make me so unsound a man
> As to upbraid you with those kindnesses
> That I have done. (III, iv)

Antonio is in the position here of the poet in the sonnets when he feels betrayed by the ingratitude of his friend. Through him, Shakespeare seems to be getting in touch with his anger and allowing himself to express it more directly (see V, i). The difference, of course, is that Sebastian, like Bassanio, reciprocates his friend's affection, as is evident upon their reunion: "Antonio! O my dear Antonio!/ How have the hours rack'd and tortur'd me/ Since I have lost thee!" (V, i). This is how the poet would like the friend to feel about him. Antonio's bargain works.

Shakespeare may be reimagining his relationship to the friend in another way in his portrayal of Viola's love for Orsino. The kind of merger with the other that the self-effacing person craves often takes the form of sexual union, especially union in which one plays a submissive role and feels possessed by a masterful partner. The love problems in *Twelfth Night* are caused, in part at least, by Viola's disguise: "As I am man,/ My state is desperate for my master's love./ As I am woman . . ./ What thriftless sighs shall poor Olivia breathe!" (II, iii). These problems are resolved when sexual differentiation is established by the appearance of Sebastian, who can take Viola's place with Olivia, and by Viola's revelation of her identity as a woman. In *Twelfth Night,* Shakespeare seems to be splitting his identity between Viola and Antonio, with Orsino and Sebastian both being versions of the friend. In the Viola story, he seems to be wishing that his masculine identity were only a disguise and that he could transcend his inability to merge with the friend by becoming

a woman. The Antonio-Sebastian story depicts an eroticized male relationship ("My desire,/ More sharp than filed steel, did spur me forth"—
III, ii); but Antonio cannot achieve ultimate union with his friend, except,
perhaps, through self-sacrifice, because they are of the same sex. Like the
poet, therefore, and like the merchant of Venice, he must share his friend
with a woman.

ALL'S WELL THAT ENDS WELL

There are three other plays in which Shakespeare seems to be reimagining the experience depicted in the sonnets: *All's Well That Ends
Well, Troilus and Cressida,* and *Antony and Cleopatra. All's Well* is the
story of a relatively lowborn but meritorious young woman whose value is
recognized by everyone except the highborn but shallow young man with
whom she is in love. Helena displays a mixture of self-effacing and
aggressive qualities that corresponds to a similar mixture in the poet, and
Bertram's narcissism is similar to that of the friend. Helena feels worthy of
Bertram because of her merit but unworthy because of her birth. She feels
that her love is hopelessly "ambitious" ("The hind that would be mated
by the lion/ Must die for love"—I, i), but also that it is bound to succeed:
"Who ever strove/ To show her merit that did miss her love?" (I, i). She
forces Bertram into marriage by asserting her claims, but then becomes
completely submissive ("In everything I wait upon his will"—II, iv),
while continuing to pursue him relentlessly. She is blind to Bertram's
faults and loves him despite, or perhaps because of, the fact that he treats
her so badly. She is attracted to him because of his superiority and must
continue to idealize him, as the poet does the friend, in order to protect the
value of her prize. Through the Countess, the King, and Lefew, however,
Shakespeare attacks Bertram and glorifies Helena, thus expressing his
anger toward the friend and asserting his claims for himself. Parolles is
used to excuse some of Bertram's behavior so that a reconciliation can
take place at the end without excessively reducing Bertram's stature.

The ending of the play is unsatisfactory if we regard *All's Well* as a
story of romantic or sexual love, but it is not. Helena's is an "ambitious
love," about which the self-effacing side of her feels guilty (III, iv). She
gets what she wants from Bertram, which is recognition of her worthiness
to enter his family. Winning Bertram is so important not only because it
elevates her socially, but also because it confirms her value system, in
which true honor comes from deeds rather than birth, and her version of

reality, in which our virtues enable us to master our fate—"Our remedies oft in ourselves do lie,/ Which we ascribe to heaven" (I, i). Like Shakespeare, Helena is a gifted person who is insecure because of her birth and who needs to have her claims confirmed by recognition from those of higher social status. Through her medical skill and her ingenious compliance with Bertram's seemingly impossible conditions, she wins the man who can give her the position she deserves. Her perfectionistic and self-effacing bargains have worked: merit and submission have been rewarded. The play is the story of the triumph of genius over the inequities of the social order.

TROILUS AND CRESSIDA

Troilus and Cressida is one of the most direct expressions of Shakespeare's anxiety, disillusionment, and anger. The cynical commentary that is present in the comedies is present here also. Lovers are always fools, "for to be wise and love/ Exceeds man's might" (III, ii). "This love," says Helen, "will undo us all. O Cupid, Cupid, Cupid!" (III, i). There is much fear of inconstancy and an anxious sense that "love is food for fortune's tooth" (IV, v). Nowhere is love more consistently equated to lust, and not only by Thersites, who sees "nothing but lechery" and "incontinent varlets" everywhere (V, i). According to Paris, Troilus "eats nothing but doves . . . and that breeds hot blood, and hot blood begets hot thoughts, and hot thoughts begets hot deeds, and hot deeds is love." "Is this the generation of love?" responds Pandarus, "hot blood, hot thoughts, hot deeds? Why they are vipers! Is love a generation of vipers?" (III, i). In the comedies, the commentary expresses a disillusioned view of love that is often illustrated through the folly or fickleness of the lovers; but by the end, things are set right and the lovers are frequently exempted, through some form of magic, from the pitfalls of the human condition. The action partly confirms and partly transcends the dark view of love in the commentary. In *Troilus,* the commentary is completely confirmed by the action. The idealism of the protagonist is thoroughly shattered and his fears prove to have been very well founded.

Troilus and Cressida are both anxiety-ridden lovers who are very much afraid of disappointment. Cressida falls in love with Troilus at first sight (III, ii) but holds out because she fears that he will lose interest if she capitulates. When she confesses the "unbridled" nature of her passion, she feels like a fool for having said too much (III, ii). In response to her fear that there are "more dregs than water" in the "fountain" of their love, Troilus assures her that "In all Cupid's pageant there is presented no monster" (III, ii), but he himself is afraid that fulfillment will overwhelm him or that he will not be able to fully appreciate the experience. Each of the lovers distrusts the constancy of the other. Their anxiety continues the morning after. Cressida is upset because Troilus will not "tarry" and is afraid that he is "aweary" of her. When they learn that she must join her father in the Grecian camp, there is again much concern about each other's "truth" and much protestation of fidelity. Now it is Troilus who is the most nervous lover.

At one point Cressida becomes irritated with Troilus's constant pleas that she "be true," and Troilus explains that he is insecure about his own "merit": "I cannot sing,/ Nor heel the high lavolt, nor sweeten talk,/ Nor play at subtile games—fair virtues all/ To which the Grecians are most prompt and pregnant . . ." (IV, iv). Much as Shakespeare must have felt at a disadvantage in competition with the friend, Troilus feels inferior to the "Grecian youths," who are "full of quality." Although he is a Trojan prince, he speaks of the Greeks as though they were of a higher social class, which may be an indication of Shakespeare's identification with him. Cressida's inconstancy may be traceable to Troilus's insecurity. She is a shallow young woman who has fallen in love with Troilus for superficial reasons. His glamor as a warrior has been magnified by Pandarus; but instead of being a masterful lover who is confident of his own attractiveness, he turns out to be a man known for "mere simplicity" (IV, iv) who is uncertain of his worth. He makes the Greeks seem far more glamorous than he is; indeed, he does for them what Pandarus has done for him. His fidelity is touching, but being "plain and true" (IV, iv) is not very exciting, and it loses much of its value because of his self-deprecation. Troilus is a self-effacing lover who loses out to the masterful Diomedes, much as King Hamlet loses out to Claudius, or the poet, I would surmise, to the friend. When Cressida tries to withhold from Diomedes the sleeve that Troilus had given her as a token of love, Diomedes immediately begins to leave: "No, no, good night. I'll be your fool no more" (V, ii). "Thy better," says the listening Troilus, "must." Cressida gives in, of course. In this play, the good guy finishes last.

Shakespeare has an ambivalent attitude toward Troilus that corresponds, I suspect, to an ambivalence toward himself. He creates in the praise of Ulysses an idealized image (of himself as well as of Troilus?) that combines the virtues of the various codes or solutions he favors:

> a true knight;
> Not yet mature, yet matchless; firm of word;
> Speaking in deeds and deedless in his tongue;
> Not soon provok'd, nor being provok'd soon calm'd;
> His heart and hand both open and both free,
> For what he has he gives, what thinks he shows,
> Yet gives not till judgment guide his bounty,
> Nor dignifies an impair thought with breath;
> Manly as Hector, but more dangerous;
> For Hector in his blaze of wrath subscribes
> To tender objects, but he in heat of action
> Is more vindictive than jealous love. (IV, v)

Troilus is modest, generous, and transparent, though not excessively so; and, at the same time, he is very "manly" and "dangerous." He is "a true knight" who is "firm of word" and pure of speech. This image of Troilus is subverted by Diomedes and Cressida, who make him look foolish: "That dissembling abominable varlet, Diomed, has got that same scurvy doting foolish young knave's sleeve of Troy there in his helm. I would fain see them meet, that the same young Troyan ass that loves the whore there, might send that Greekish whoremasterly villain with the sleeve back to the dissembling luxurious drab of a sleeveless errand" (V, iv). Through Thersites, Shakespeare may be calling the friend a "dissembling abominable varlet" and "whoremasterly villain" and the dark lady a "dissembling luxurious drab"; but he is also striking out at himself for being a "doting foolish" "ass that loves [a] whore." If Ulysses presents Shakespeare's idealized image of himself, Thersites may be presenting his despised image, what he feels himself to be as a result of having been betrayed.

Cressida's betrayal produces a psychological crisis in Troilus that is similar to the crises of the tragic heroes when their bargains fail. Troilus's bargain is that his truth will be rewarded by her fidelity. His idealization of women, his sense of reality, his whole orientation toward life are threatened by Cressida's betrayal. It is important to note, however, that like the poet in the sonnets, he does not stop loving the lady: "Never did young man fancy/ With so eternal and so fix'd a soul" (V, ii). His attitude toward Cressida is similar in some ways to the poet's attitude toward the friend: "O Cressid! O false Cressid! false, false, false!/ Let all untruths stand by thy stained name/ And they'll seem glorious" (V, ii). In order to preserve his love, he glorifies her fault.

Troilus deals with his crisis in part, then, by continuing to be true, by living up to his exalted conception of himself as a lover, which he can do no matter how Cressida behaves. This is similar to the poet's response to his mistreatment by the friend. The anger that is directed toward the dark lady in the sonnets is here directed against Diomedes, whom Troilus holds responsible for Cressida's fall, just as the poet holds the dark lady responsible for her affair with the friend. Diomedes has characteristics of both the friend and the dark lady, and Shakespeare discharges onto him the anger that he feels toward both. This anger can be expressed directly through Troilus's martial activity, which is one reason why this play does not become a tragedy. The meetings between Troilus and Diomedes are inconclusive, but Troilus does "Mad and fantastic execution" (V, vi) against the Greeks, fighting with the energy of rage and the boldness of despair. The Trojan war provides a heroic outlet for his turbulent emotions and a means by which he can restore his pride.

Through Troilus, Shakespeare is imagining how a self-effacing person who has been wronged can express his murderous rage without losing his innocence. Troilus does this by directing all of his rage toward Diomedes, and toward the Greeks in general, whom he has a license to kill because they are at war. After the death of Hector, he tries to comfort the Trojans with "Hope of revenge" (V, x). Revenge is an acceptable way of dealing with "inward woe" here because of the military form that it takes.

ANTONY AND CLEOPATRA

The last play in which Shakespeare seems to be reimagining the experience of the sonnets is *Antony and Cleopatra*. Antony, like the poet, is a doting lover who is bewitched by a dark lady of dubious reputation and who is given both to compulsive sensuality and to self-disgust. He is "the triple pillar of the world transform'd/ Into a strumpet's fool" (I, i), the "noble ruin" of Cleopatra's "magic" (III, x). He feels that he must "break" his "Egyptian fetters" or "lose [himself] in dotage" (I, ii), but he cannot do so, and he seems to have "lost [his] way for ever" (III, xi) when, at the battle of Actium, he "flies after" Cleopatra "like a doting mallard" (III, x).

In the first three acts of the play, Antony's compulsive behavior is consistently condemned as shameful and self-destructive, but in the last two acts he is surrounded with a favorable rhetoric that obscures his faults and turns him into a glamorous figure. Much of this is accomplished in act 4, where Shakespeare emphasizes his generosity and allows him to refurbish his image as a warrior. Whereas before he had been a man who would "make no wars without doors" (II, i), he now rises "betime" to business that he loves and declares war to be a "royal occupation" (IV, iv). Antony is in danger of losing everything when his fleet yields and he is convinced that Cleopatra has betrayed him; but once he is reassured by the false news of her death, he begins to glorify himself, her, and their relationship. Since his "torch is out," he is ready to die, but he envisions a kind of glory in death which far exceeds that of a Roman emperor. He and Cleopatra will be the most famous lovers in history, outdoing in Elysium even Dido and Aeneas. Antony receives tributes from others as well as himself, and most of all from Cleopatra. For her he is the "crown o' th' earth," without whom "this dull world . . . is/ No better than a sty" (IV, xv).

Cleopatra's point of view dominates the last act of the play and becomes one of the chief vehicles of Shakespeare's rhetoric. In its presentation of Cleopatra, the play follows a vindication pattern. From the outset, there are two views of Cleopatra—the Roman view of her as a strumpet and Antony's view of her as a majestic woman who is worthy of his devotion. Whereas the Romans see a "ne'er-lust-wearied Antony" under the spell of "salt Cleopatra" (II, ii), Antony sees himself and Cleopatra as "peerless" lovers in whose relationship lies "The nobleness of life" (I, i). As the play unfolds, Antony's view of Cleopatra comes more and more to prevail. Her vindication is completed in acts 4 and 5, in which she demonstrates her loyalty to Antony and proves herself, through the manner of her death, to be most royal. Like Antony, she sees suicide as the means to achieve a reunion: "Go fetch/ My best attires. I am again for Cydnus/ To meet Mark Antony" (V, ii). She remains so beautiful in death that even the prosaic Caesar imagines her as ready to "catch another Antony/ In her strong toil of grace."

The most powerful tribute to Antony and Cleopatra is put into the mouth of Caesar, the man who had been their greatest detractor. Even though Antony was married to Octavia, Caesar recognizes that he and Cleopatra belong together in death:

> She shall be buried by Antony.
> No grave upon the earth shall clip in it
> A pair so famous. High events as these
> Strike those that made them; and their story is
> No less in pity than his glory which
> Brought them to be lamented. (V, ii)

Cleopatra had been regarded through most of the play as a strumpet and

Antony as a fool, but this speech confirms Antony's view of himself and of Cleopatra. Caesar sees his own glory as a derivative of theirs.

Shakespeare seems to have a need both to criticize and to justify the self-effacing side of himself through Antony. The first three acts of the play are governed by his contempt for his own foolish behavior, whereas the last two acts rewrite the story of the sonnets and make the self-effacing bargain work. Cleopatra is a combination of the "two loves" of the sonnets. The Roman view of her corresponds to the poet's "worser spirit," or the dark lady. If this view is correct, then Antony is a fool indeed for doting upon her. Most of the time, Antony's view of Cleopatra corresponds to the poet's "better angel," that is, to his idealized view of the friend. If this view is correct, then she is worthy of his devotion; and his love for her, instead of being foolish, is a means of fulfilling his search for glory. The vindication of Cleopatra vindicates Antony and obscures the self-destructiveness of his morbid dependency. The story of Antony and Cleopatra provides Shakespeare with a way of glorifying an extreme form of self-effacing behavior in a heterosexual relationship (for a fuller discussion of this play, see Paris 1991).

CHAPTER 8

Shakespeare's Leap of Faith
From the Tragedies to the Romances

Shakespeare's attitude toward self-effacing behavior is complex and ambivalent. The code of martial and manly honor calls for the repression of "womanly" feelings; and, in a world full of personal ambition, to be direct and honest is not safe. His preoccupation with the theme of appearance versus reality derives, in large part, from his awareness that Machiavels try to manipulate self-effacing people by pretending to subscribe to their values. He is afraid also of his tendency to enter into compulsive love relationships, and he makes such relationships the subject of about a third of his plays, most of which were discussed in Chapter 7. Sometimes he satirizes such relationships, sometimes he glorifies them, and sometimes he does both. In *Romeo and Juliet,* for example, it is difficult to determine whether the protagonists are meant to be perceived as foolish, doting lovers or as grand, romantic figures. Through much of the play the rhetoric supports both perspectives, though, as in *Antony and Cleopatra,* the emphasis upon the external forces that contribute to the deaths of the lovers obscures the destructiveness of their mutual morbid dependency and makes the play seem, by the end, to be a tragedy of fate.

Despite his ambivalence, Shakespeare is predominantly self-effacing. He glorifies the values of the self-effacing solution and wants to believe in its bargain with fate. Even when he shows the bargain failing, as he does with Henry VI, Hamlet, Troilus, Desdemona, and Timon, he presents the protagonists in a favorable light. The inability of such characters to cope with the world in which they live is at once a tragic flaw and a mark of their moral superiority. In *Hamlet,* Shakespeare shows what happens to a man who, out of his desire to preserve his innocence and nobility, cannot cope with the harsh realities of life; but he also celebrates that innocence and nobility and arraigns a world in which such a man is destroyed. The ending of the play shows the tragic consequences of Hamlet's paralysis, but it also allows him to preserve his idealized image by providing overwhelming justification for his murder of Claudius and by leaving a final impression of him in the words of Horatio and Fortinbras.

TIMON OF ATHENS

The period of the tragedies begins with *Julius Caesar* and *Hamlet* and it concludes with *Timon of Athens,* which seems to be a pivotal play in Shakespeare's development, though the dating of the play is still in dispute. The focus here is not upon sexual love but upon friendship, which Timon seeks to buy through his excessive generosity. As the play opens, his strategy seems to be working, though there are intimations that his behavior is foolish, that he is surrounded by flatterers, and that his popularity would not survive a decline in his fortunes. He is shattered when he goes bankrupt and is deserted by those whom he has benefitted. Outraged by the ingratitude of man, he becomes bitterly misanthropic, trusts no one, and longs for the destruction of his native city. Many critics feel that "no attempt . . . is made to give his sudden change from philanthropy to misanthropy a psychological basis" (Charney 1965, xxiii), but Timon's transformation is intelligible, I believe, if we see it as a result of the collapse of his self-effacing bargain and of his attempt to develop new strategies of defense.

Timon's compulsive generosity is itself a defense against feelings of insecurity. We do not know why he feels insecure, but it is evident that he desperately needs friends and is afraid that no one will love him for himself. He seeks to win love by lavish gifts, favors, and entertainments, and he discourages reciprocation so as to keep everyone in his debt. He has developed an idealized image of himself as a noble friend, patron, and benefactor who behaves as he does out of lofty ideals. This image is confirmed by the praise he receives from others, both from the flatterers by whom he is surrounded and from those who genuinely believe in his moral nobility. Of course, Timon does desire a return for his generosity: he wants affection and esteem and a feeling of assurance that his friends will come to his aid if he needs them.

It is no wonder, then, that Timon thinks he "could deal kingdoms to
[his] friends,/ And ne'er be weary" (I, ii). His generosity brings him
enormous rewards—the love and esteem of others, a sense of his own
moral grandeur, and protection against the uncertainties of fate. It is no
wonder, also, that he defends his version of reality against the contrasting
views of Apemantus. Apemantus and Timon have embraced very different
defensive strategies. Whereas Timon protects himself against his insecurities by moving toward people, Apemantus's defense is to move away,
to gain a sense of invulnerability by not needing or trusting anyone.
Whereas Timon believes in the love and loyalty of his friends, Apemantus
has a cynical view of men and of human relations: "Who lives that's not
depraved or depraves?" (I, ii). He gains his sense of worth not from
feeling loved, as does Timon, but from seeing through everything and
everybody. It is important for him, therefore, to call Timon's attention to
his folly, but Timon cannot possibly take him seriously, for to do so would
undermine his entire solution.

Timon cannot be completely confident of the loyalty of his friends,
however, until he has need of them, and it is evident that he wants
something to happen that will put their love to the test: "O no doubt my
good friends, but the gods themselves have provided that I shall have
much help from you: how had you been my friends else?" (I, ii). Perhaps
this is one reason why Timon is so careless with his money. He may want
to go bankrupt so as to gain the assurance that other people really care
about him. When Timon is finally made to confront his financial situation,
he is by no means distraught. He seems to feel little self-blame ("Un-
wisely, not ignobly, have I given"—II, ii) and to be confident that his
friends will come to his rescue. This is the moment for which he has been
waiting, when his doubts about his worth will be laid to rest and his
values, his actions, and his view of human nature will all be vindicated.
He has lived up to his shoulds, and his claims are going to be honored.

When Timon's bargain breaks down, he becomes extremely aggressive. He hates not only those who have wronged him, but "all humanity." He would like to restore his pride through revenge, but he lacks the
power to do this; and so, like Lear, he curses his fellows instead. As he
leaves Athens, he calls for the undoing of "Degrees, observances,
customs, and laws" and invokes the reign of "confusion" (IV, i). His
sense of order has been shattered, and he wants to retaliate by having
everyone else go through the same experience. His fantasies of revenge
take even more horrible forms when he finances Alcibiades' war against
Athens:

> Let not thy sword skip one.
> Pity not honour'd age for his white beard:
> He is an usurer. Strike me the counterfeit matron:
> It is her habit only that is honest,
> Herself's a bawd. Let not the virgin's cheek
> Make soft thy trenchant sword: for those milk paps,
> That through the window-bars bore at men's eyes,
> Are not within the leaf of pity writ,
> But set them down horrible traitors. Spare not the babe
> Whose dimpled smiles from fools exhaust their mercy:
> Think it a bastard, whom the oracle
> Hath doubtfully pronounced thy throat shall cut,
> And mince it sans remorse. Swear against objects.
> Put armor on thine ears and on thine eyes,
> Whose proof nor yells of mothers, maids, nor babes,
> Nor sight of priests in holy vestments bleeding,
> Shall pierce a jot. (IV, iii)

Because the people in whom he has believed have turned out to be insincere, Timon sees all human beings as vile.

This attitude is, in part, an externalization of self-hate and, in part, a way of excusing himself for his folly. He has been totally indiscriminate in his generosity, and to discriminate now in his rage would mean having to blame himself for poor judgment. In order to protect his pride, he must attribute the disappointing behavior of others to their evil nature rather than to his unrealistic expectations or unlovability. No matter what he does, however, he cannot escape his self-hate: "His semblable, yea himself, Timon disdains" (IV, iii). He feels that he has been annihilated (indeed, his idealized image has been destroyed), and he wishes to annihilate the whole human race in return. The collapse of his self-effacing bargain converts Timon to the arrogant-vindictive view of human nature and the human condition.

The disenchanted Timon moves not only against his fellow humans but also away from them, and he does this in such an extreme way as to make the detached Apemantus seem well-balanced by comparison. Even when he is moved by the loyalty of Flavius and is persuaded that he is the "singly honest man," he will not allow his former servant to "stay and comfort" him (IV, iii). The only way he can "stop affliction" (V, i) and find peace is through the ultimate withdrawal of death. His death is psychologically willed and appears to be the result of his sense of the horror and emptiness of life: "My long sickness/ Of health and living now begins to mend,/ And nothing brings me all things" (V, i). Through the words he leaves behind, he continues to express his hatred of his fellows.

I have been talking so far about Timon's personality and the changes that it undergoes. Shakespeare's personality is revealed in this play by his rhetorical treatment of Timon, which reflects the ambivalence he so frequently manifests toward the self-effacing solution. The primary source for the play is a satire by Lucian that is directed against the evils of wealth. In one of the speeches by Hermes, Timon is characterized in a way that seems quite consistent with Shakespeare's attitude toward him:

> You *could* say it was his goodness and philanthropy and the way he took pity on everyone in need that ruined him. But the truth of the matter is, it was his senselessness, stupidity, and lack of judgment in choosing friends. The man never realized he was indulging a pack of crows and wolves. The poor devil imagined that all those vultures, who were tearing out his liver, were his bosom friends, who enjoyed eating his food because they liked him so much.
> (quoted in Charney 1965, 162)

Before he is betrayed, Timon is genuinely admired by some characters ("The noblest mind he carries/ That ever governed man"—I, i); but his folly and the impurity of his motives are made quite clear. His excessive trust and unrealistic expectations are mocked by Apemantus, and one of the Senators comments tellingly upon his imprudence and absurd generosity: "Still in motion/ Of raging waste? It cannot hold, it will not./ If I want gold, steal but a beggar's dog/ And give it Timon—why the dog coins gold" (II, i). Even Flavius, who greatly admires his master, sees that his course is "unwise" (II, ii). The satire is directed at flatterers and false friends and the ingratitude of man, but it is also directed at Timon, whose self-effacing behavior brings many of his troubles on himself.

Timon never understands his true motives or his own contribution to his downfall, but, through a variety of rhetorical devices, Shakespeare makes these things clear to the audience. Once Timon's friends fail him, however, the rhetoric shifts, and his earlier behavior is glorified. He becomes an innocent victim, and those who have disappointed him seem all the more monstrous because of his nobility. The loyal Flavius articulates the play's new perspective:

> Poor honest lord, brought low by his own heart,
> Undone by goodness. Strange, unusual blood,
> When man's worst sin is, he does too much good.
> Who then dares to be half so kind again?
> For bounty that makes gods, do still mar men. (IV, ii)

This is a lament for the failure of the self-effacing solution. Timon's virtues are godly, but we live in a world in which to be honest, good, and bountiful is dangerous. Timon is no longer a fool who has brought his troubles on himself, but an "unmatched mind" who has been destroyed by others. The play begins with a clear understanding of Timon's compulsive behavior; but once Timon's bargain breaks down, Shakespeare loses his distance and identifies with his character, as he does with Lear in a similar situation. This is another play in which thematic inconsistencies are explicable in terms of the author's psychological conflicts. He begins by seeing self-effacing behavior as foolish and ends by seeing it as grand.

Timon does not become a hero as the play proceeds, however. There is a great deal of sympathy for his misanthropy and rage, but they are so excessive that they, in turn, become objects of satire. Even the sympathetic Alcibiades observes that "his wits/ Are drowned and lost in his calamities" (IV, iii). There is evidence in the play that Timon's indiscriminate condemnation of mankind is unjustified. Flavius is loyal and generous, both to Timon and to his fellow servants; Timon's own servants and those of his debtors are scornful of his false friends and sympathetic toward him; and even strangers react with compassion for Timon and indignation "at the monstrousness of man/ When he looks out in an ungrateful shape" (III, ii). The "when" is important here; man is not always monstrous. Even when Alcibiades says, "I am thy friend and pity thee, dear Timon" (IV, iii), Timon persists in seeing himself as a man "who all the human sons do hate" (IV, iii). This is partly passive externalization in which he experiences his self-hate by feeling hated by others and partly a defense against being hurt. If he feels hated by everyone, he will not hope to be loved and thereby expose himself to further disappointment.

Timon feels that Apemantus's version of reality has proved to be right, and he adopts his strategy of resignation and distrust, only in a more extreme form. Some critics see Apemantus as Shakespeare's spokesman in the play, and he does express the detached side of Shakespeare's personality; but he, too, is presented, I think, as having adopted an inflexible and life-denying solution. When he says grace, he prays that he "may never prove so fond" as to trust anyone (I, ii). He is just as indiscriminate in his distrust as the disillusioned Timon. He reacts to other people not in terms of evidence he has about them, but in terms of his compulsive strategy of defense. When Timon asks him why he calls his friends "knaves" when he "know'st them not," Apemantus replies, "Are they not Athenians?" (I, i). This is similar to Timon's later condemnation of all his townsfolk.

Indeed, Apemantus, no less than Timon, condemns the whole human race and wishes for its destruction. If he had the world in his power, he would "Give it to the beasts, to be rid of the men" (IV, iii).

The norm in this play is not Apemantus but Alcibiades, who is a foil to both Timon and Apemantus. Like Timon, Alcibiades is wronged but he neither withdraws nor seeks an indiscriminate revenge. He takes Timon's gold to support his war against Athens, but not "all [his] counsel" (IV, iii). Though he punishes those who have wronged Timon and himself, he does not "kill . . . all together" (V, iv). He sees that not all men are alike and he pursues his revenge in a rational manner. He is a man of action who seeks to remedy wrongs instead of retreating, like Apemantus, behind a shield of cynicism. Apemantus takes fewer risks, but he pays for his safety by leading a sterile existence.

Shakespeare seems to be warning himself in this play against the danger of being too self-effacing and the danger of becoming too cynical as a result of disillusionment. I have examined at length his satirical treatment of self-effacing behavior, as well as his glorification of it, but I have only touched upon his apparent recognition of and reaction against his Timon-like tendency to distrust everyone. This is present most strikingly in the four plays that deal with unjustly accused women—*Much Ado, Othello, Cymbeline,* and *The Winter's Tale*—in which the male is too prone to distrust. It is also present in *Hamlet,* where Gertrude's act "Calls virtue hypocrite, takes off the rose/ From the fair forehead of an innocent love/ And sets a blister there" (III, iv). In *Troilus and Cressida,* Cressida's fall has a similar effect upon Troilus's conception of women, but there is nothing to counterbalance his disillusioned point of view. In *Macbeth,* as we have seen, Malcolm refuses to distrust everyone because the evil often appear to be good: "Angels are bright still, though the brightest fell./ Though all things foul would wear the brows of grace,/ Yet grace must still look so" (IV, iii). Malcolm is a good man who is not a dupe, as good men often are in Shakespeare, but who is able to test reality. In his exploration of the problem of trust, Shakespeare seems at times to be seeking self-cure. The unjustifiably or excessively distrustful males like Claudio, Hamlet, Othello, Timon, Posthumus, and Leontes show what happens when we allow our minds to be poisoned by suspicion, while characters like Malcolm and Alcibiades provide models for dealing realistically with the world as it is, rather than as it ought to be.

It is striking, however, that in many of the plays in which Shakespeare seems to be seeking self-cure there are some of the most violent denunciations of women and/or of human nature. Shakespeare seems to be simultaneously expressing his distrust and criticizing himself for its irrationality. He is able to give vent to feelings of tremendous hostility because he is articulating them through characters who are presented as disturbed or deranged and whose rantings are repudiated by the rhetoric. In the plays in which women are first condemned and then exonerated, he is taking the responsibility for his misogynistic feelings on himself (the male) and is telling himself that it is not their fault but his that he thinks so ill of them. The combination of irrational men and angelic women suggests a reaction formation in which Shakespeare, unable to cope with his real feelings toward women, denies them (or expresses them in a disowned way) and turns his anger and condemnation on himself. This is, of course, a self-effacing way of dealing with rage (which is taboo) and with the feeling of having been wronged.

Timon of Athens is a pivotal play in that after Timon Shakespeare seems to become progressively more self-effacing. Through the experience of its protagonist, Timon portrays some extreme consequences of the collapse of the self-effacing solution—namely, a vision of universal chaos and evil and a desire to die. Like the major tragedies, it dramatizes what we would now call a confrontation with the absurd. In the psychological terms that I have been using, a sense of the absurd arises when life does not honor our bargain, when the world order that is posited by our solution is disconfirmed by reality. As we have seen, different solutions posit different world orders, and different kinds of experiences can, therefore, confront the individual with the absurd. What happens to Timon shatters his view of reality, but it only confirms that of Apemantus. Shakespeare's conflict between faith and cynicism comes to a head in Timon, where he shows that idealists like Timon and himself cannot embrace the dark view of human nature and the world order and continue to live. He shows the dark view to be diseased, moreover, and counterbalances it with the positive figures of Flavius and Alcibiades. In the works that follow Timon, he seeks to escape the dark view altogether by using the unrealistic conventions of romance to affirm the perfectionistic and self-effacing bargains and to punish or convert the evil. In the period of the tragedies, he finds that none of the solutions work; in the romances, he solves this problem not by finding a workable solution, but by making a leap of faith.

PERICLES

Pericles is a story of hardship and suffering at the hands of evil people and stormy seas. There is far more good than evil, however, in the world of the play. Pericles, Simonides, Cerimon, and Lysimachus are wise and just princes, Helicanus is a loyal minister, and Thaisa and Marina are models of feminine virtue. Through providential interventions, Antiochus and Dionyza receive their just punishments and the virtuous characters are protected and rewarded. When Marina is about to be killed by Dionyza's servant, she pleads her innocence:

> I never did her hurt in all my life.
> I never spake bad word nor did ill turn
> To any living creature. Believe me, la,
> I never kill'd a mouse, nor hurt a fly.
> I trod upon a worm against my will,
> But I wept for it. (IV, i)

The bargain that Lady Macduff recognized as unrealistic works for Marina. Instead of being killed, she is captured by pirates who sell her into a brothel with her virginity intact. There, under the protection of Diana, she preaches divinity and converts her would-be violators: "I'll do anything now that is virtuous, but I am out of the road of rutting forever" (IV, v). In this play, virtue *has* the power that is attributed to it in the self-effacing solution. The gods intervene in various ways on behalf of those who have the right attitude. The seemingly dead Thaisa is restored by Cerimon, whose quasi-magical art is the means by which "the gods have shown their power" (V, iii); Marina is saved and Pericles is led to her by happy accidents; and Diana appears to Pericles in a dream in order to effect his reunion with Thaisa. For good people, even the blows of fortune turn out to be blessings in disguise. Although they undergo much suffering, "wishes" ultimately "fall out as they're will'd" (V, ii) and the "present kindness" of the gods more than makes up for "past miseries" (V, iii). We must assume that everything has a meaning and accept life as it is.

CYMBELINE

In *Cymbeline,* too, there is a strong supernatural presence. The loyal Pisanio prays for "heavenly blessings" on Imogen (III, iii), as had a Lord earlier (II, i); and when he finds himself "Perplex'd in all," he puts himself in the hands of the gods: "Fortune brings in some boats that are not steer'd" (IV, iii). "All was lost" for the British "But that the heavens fought" on their side (V, iii). Cymbeline responds to the revelation of his mistaken trust in the Queen by saying, "Heaven mend all!" (V, v), and it does. As in *Pericles,* those who are evil are punished or converted and those who are good are protected and rewarded.

Cymbeline affirms a bargain with fate that had been called into question in the tragedies. In Posthumus's dream (where, strangely, he knows of Imogen's innocence), his father complains to Jupiter of the injustice done to his son: "No more, thou Thunder-master, show/ Thy spite on mortal flies" (V, iv). "Since, Jupiter, our son is good," pleads his mother, "Take off his miseries." "Help, Jupiter!" exclaim his brothers, "or we appeal/ And from thy justice fly." Jupiter is offended by their impatience and threatens to become impatient in turn, but he is not spiteful or capricious, and he recognizes their claims:

> Be not with mortal accident opprest.
> No care of yours it is; you know 'tis ours.
> Whom best I love I cross; to make my gift,
> The more delay'd, delighted. Be content.
> Your low-laid son our godhead will uplift;
> His comforts thrive, his trials well are spent.
> . . . .
> He shall be lord of Lady Imogen,
> And happier much by his affliction made. (V, iv)

This passage explains the ways of the gods in the romances, which are designed to justify them to man. In *Cymbeline,* as in *Pericles,* earlier unwarranted sufferings are made up for by the joyousness of the resolution: "Laud we the gods" (V, v).

Cymbeline is one of the plays in which a virtuous woman is maligned and then later vindicated. The source of the mischief is Iachimo, an Iago-like character who convinces Posthumus that Imogen has been unfaithful. Iachimo has a cynical view of women to which he converts Posthumus by his lie, but Posthumus's original idealistic view of his wife is restored by the end, and it is Iachimo who must acknowledge himself to have been wrong. What makes this play different from *Much Ado* or *Othello* or *A Winter's Tale* is that after his murderous rage and perhaps the bitterest denunciation of women in Shakespeare, Posthumus repents having had Imogen killed (as he thinks) *before* he discovers her innocence.

After responding to Imogen's supposed infidelity in a typically vindictive way, Posthumus becomes quite self-effacing. He feels that he was more sinful than Imogen even before he had her murdered and wishes that the gods had taken "vengeance on [his] faults" so that he would not have lived to commit his greater sin (V, i). He accuses himself and excuses Imogen, who has "wry[ed] but a little"; and he also excuses the gods, whom he had seemed at times to arraign. They have snatched Imogen "hence for little faults" in order to have her "fall no more," while they have left him here to sin so that he will be led to repentance. Whatever the gods do is right, and our place is "to obey." The claims his mother makes for Posthumus's goodness do not ring true (since he had tried to have Imogen murdered) unless we see him as having been purified by his repentance. His charitable attitude toward Imogen sets the tone for the end of the play, where he forgives the repentant Iachimo and inspires Cymbeline to proclaim a pardon for all (V, v).

THE WINTER'S TALE

The Winter's Tale differs from the other plays in which innocent women are falsely accused in that Leontes has no grounds whatever for his suspicions. Since he is entirely self-deluded, there seems to be no way to convince him of Hermione's innocence, as she herself well understands: "it shall scarce boot me/ To say 'Not guilty.' Mine integrity,/ Being counted falsehood, shall, as I express it,/ Be so receiv'd" (III, ii). Hermione's plight is the same as that of Desdemona, who only damns herself further in Othello's eyes by denying his charges. Like the other pious characters in the romances, Hermione submits herself to the will of the gods and assumes that her present trials are for her "better grace" (II, i). She is confident that there is a just order in the universe and that "innocence shall make/ False accusation blush and tyranny/ Tremble at patience" (III, ii). Her bargain works, her claims are honored, when the oracle proclaims her chastity and the still sceptical Leontes is forced to believe the oracle by the death of his son. The descent of the gods cures Leontes of his paranoia and solves the appearance/reality problem by bringing absolute truth into the world.

The unfounded nature of Leontes' jealousy marks a further step on Shakespeare's part in the direction of a self-effacing assumption of responsibility for his mistrust of women. Claudio, Othello, and Posthumus are deceived by others (too easily, it is true), but Leontes has only himself to blame. And blame himself he does, through a long ordeal of guilt and penitence. He has a rage toward women that he vents upon Hermione, but when that rage is proved to be unwarranted, he turns it against himself and spends sixteen years in self-flagellation. Posthumus's brief period of self-castigation is trivial by comparison. Leontes' sense of guilt is exacerbated, of course, by Paulina, whose reproofs he accepts because of his need for self-punishment. He submits to her control because he distrusts himself profoundly and hopes that he will avoid additional guilt by doing whatever she tells him. He is a psychologically crippled man who has lost his sense of authority and who seeks safety and forgiveness through compliance with the dictates of his perfectionistic mentor. The rhetoric of the play does not present him that way, of course. His suffering (some of which is unwarranted, since Hermione is not really dead) is ultimately for his better grace; and his penitence, guilt, and self-hate purify him and prepare him for the "exultation" of the ending.

Leontes earns the happy ending through his self-effacing behavior. Paulina helps to bring it about through her compliance with the oracle, which states that "the king shall live without an heir, if that which is lost is not found" (III, iii). She does her part by preventing the conception of a new heir, and the heavens do theirs by "directing" (V, iii) Florizel and Perdita to each other and bringing about the necessary recognitions. The power of the gods is confirmed by the fact that "The oracle is fulfill'd" (V, ii); and the play ends, like the other romances, with an outburst of wonder and joy. If bargains with fate are to work, there must be a just and powerful force with which to bargain. The romances are so appealing because they affirm that such a force exists.

HENRY VIII

Shakespeare continues to affirm the self-effacing solution in *The Tempest,* which I shall discuss in Chapter 9, and in *Henry VIII,* which combines features of the history play and the romance. Indeed, *Henry VIII* is his most sustained celebration of self-effacing values. The play contains many idealized characters (Henry, Buckingham, Katherine, Anne, Cranmer, and even Wolsey after his fall); evils are presented as a man- ifestation of the divine will, to which all the characters submit; and those who are wronged forgive their enemies instead of craving revenge. They are avenged, however, by a divine justice that punishes the guilty. Al- though the innocent sometimes suffer, as in the case of Buckingham, they are sometimes shielded from evil, as Cranmer is by Henry, who is the deus ex machina in this play. The theme of the play is that high place leads to sorrow, that it is better to be a "humble liver" than "to be perk'd up in a glist'ring grief" (II, iii). Its first three episodes deal with the fall of the mighty—Buckingham, Katherine, and Wolsey. The play ends on a positive note with the rise of Anne Bullen, who is presented as humble and virtuous, with the rescue of Cranmer, and with the birth of Elizabeth, for whom great things are predicted (V, v).

The characters who fall all behave in extremely self-effacing ways. Buckingham is completely innocent, but he submits to "the will of heaven" (I, i) when he is arrested, as does the equally innocent Abergavenny. Although he speaks "in choler" when he is condemned to death, he soon shows "a most noble patience" (II, i). Like many characters in the histories and tragedies, he is done in by Machiavellian practice; but unlike most of his fellow victims, he does not call for revenge. He "heartily forgive[s]" those who have plotted against him and wishes that they could be "more Christians" (II, i). He feels that "Heaven has an end in all," blesses the king, and accepts his fate. Not only does he forgive Wolsey, but his son-in-law Surrey forgives him also when Wolsey is about to fall (III, ii). The codes of marital and manly honor and of personal ambition are rejected in this play in the name of Christian values.

No one better exemplifies those values than Queen Katherine, who has, according to Henry himself, a "saintlike" "meekness" (II, iv), and who is the perfectly compliant wife:

> Heaven witness
> I have been to you a true and humble wife,
> At all times to your will conformable,
> Ever in fear to kindle your dislike.
> . . . .
> When was the hour
> I ever contradicted your desire
> Or made it not mine too? (II, iv)

Katherine asks for "right and justice" (II, iv), but her "virtue finds no friends" (III, i), and she is indignant:

> Have I with all my full affections
> Still met the King? lov'd him next heav'n? obey'd him?
> Been (out of fondness) superstitious to him?
> Almost forgot my prayers to content him?
> And am I thus rewarded? 'Tis not well, lords. (III, i)

Katherine's bargain has broken down, but instead of undergoing a psychological crisis, she turns to the religious virtue of "patience," which permits her to maintain her idealized image as the perfectly submissive woman and to accept her fate without losing faith in the ultimate meaning of life. She is rewarded by a vision of "spirits of peace" who promise her "eternal happiness" and bring her "garlands" that she feels "not worthy yet to wear" (IV, ii). In the self-effacing value system, her feeling of unworthiness is proof of her spiritual grandeur. She exits from the play as a noble figure who asks to be remembered in "all humility" to Henry and who promises to "bless" him "in death" (IV, ii).

Wolsey is a villain who deserves his fate, but his fall turns out to be a fortunate one since it brings about the most thoroughgoing conversion of a Machiavel in all of Shakespeare. According to Katherine's woman, Griffith, "His overthrow heap'd happiness upon him;/ For then, and not till then, he felt himself/ And found the blessedness of being little" (IV, ii). When Wolsey's predominant solution fails, his subordinate trends rise to the surface, and he turns against the arrogant-vindictive values that have led to his destruction. He repudiates his "high-blown pride" and the "Vain pomp and glory of this world" (III, ii) and sees the earthly honor he had so diligently pursued as "a burden/ Too heavy for a man that hopes for heaven!" (III, ii). He urges Cromwell to "fling away ambition":

> By that sin fell the angels. How can man then
> (The image of his Maker) hope to win by it?
> Love thyself last. Cherish those hearts that hate thee;
> Corruption wins not more than honesty.
> Still in thy right hand carry gentle peace
> To silence envious tongues. Be just, and fear not.
> Let all the ends thou aim'st at be thy country's,
> Thy God's, and truth's. Then if thou fall'st, O Cromwell,
> Thou fall'st a blessed martyr. (III, ii)

Wolsey feels that the King has "cur'd" him by giving him self-knowledge and peace: "I know myself now, and I feel within me/ A peace above all earthly dignities,/ A still and quiet conscience" (III, ii). He seems to have been torn between conscience and ambition; now that ambition is fruitless, his inner conflicts have ceased.

The story of Cranmer illustrates the precepts that Wolsey lays down to Cromwell. Cranmer is an honest, just, and peaceful man who preaches "Love and meekness" (V, iii) and whose ends are God's, his country's, and the truth's. He is surrounded by Machiavels who, led by Gardiner, seek his undoing. He lacks the skills to outmaneuver his enemies and must rely on God and King Henry to "Protect [his] innocence" (V, i). Henry reminds him that "truth and honesty" do not always win out here on earth and points to the example of Christ, but he gives Cranmer his ring so that he can summon him to judge his case if his enemies are about to triumph. Like the oracle in *The Winter's Tale,* Henry knows the absolute truth, and he uses his absolute power to rescue Cranmer from "the gripes of cruel men" (V, iii). Cranmer then forgives Gardiner, and Henry makes a comment that points out how very self-effacing Cranmer is: "The common

voice I see is verified/ Of thee, which says thus: 'Do my Lord of Canter-
bury/ A shrewd turn, and he's your friend for ever' " (V, iv). This is
praise, I think, of his Christianity, rather than criticism of his excessively
forgiving nature.

The self-effacing solution works for Cranmer because in King Henry
he has a just and powerful ruler who shares his values and honors his
bargain. But even if there had been no deux ex machina to save him from
worldly injustice—as there is not for Katherine and Buckingham—his
solution still would have worked, for, according to Wolsey's precepts, he
would have fallen "a blessed martyr." Shakespeare shows in this play that
the self-effacing solution cannot fail if only we are self-effacing enough.
The historical process is often absurd, but it can be transcended through
patience and faith in a supernatural order, the existence of which is affirmed in all of the romances. The ambivalence with which Shakespeare
has treated self-effacing behavior throughout his corpus has disappeared
by *Henry VIII,* which is a play in which Henry VI could have been an
unequivocal hero. Perhaps Shakespeare resolved some of his own inner
conflicts by giving up his guilty ambition and returning to his family in
Stratford, where he found, like Wolsey, "the blessedness of being little."

CHAPTER 9

The Tempest
Shakespeare's Ideal Solution

As we read the criticism, we find many versions of Shakespeare. One reason for this is the differences in temperament and perspective among critics; but another, I think, is the multiplicity of trends, conflicts, and ambivalences in Shakespeare himself. Each of us tends to focus upon the aspect of Shakespeare to which we have a particularly strong response and to ignore or downplay the others. I have tried to account for many facets of Shakespeare's personality from my own psychoanalytic perspective, though I remain confined, of course, within the limitations of my sensibilities and my approach.

As the preceding chapters have shown, in my Shakespeare there are conflicts between arrogant-vindictive and self-effacing, perfectionistic and self-effacing, and perfectionistic and arrogant-vindictive tendencies, as well as impulses toward detachment. Although there is an oscillation among all these tendencies, I think that some are stronger than others and that it is possible to establish their order of strength. Shakespeare favors the aggressive code of martial and manly honor, but feels that it should be subordinated to the perfectionistic code of loyalty, duty, and service. He is ambivalent toward self-effacing behavior, especially in leaders and lovers, but self-effacing values come more and more to dominate his works. In the conflict between the perfectionistic value of justice and the self-effacing value of mercy, mercy always wins out. This indicates the primacy of self-effacing tendencies in Shakespeare, which are reinforced, I think, by a sense of guilt that makes it difficult for him to pass moral judgment.

Among Shakespeare's conflicts, the most powerful are those between his perfectionistic and self-effacing tendencies on the one hand and his impulses toward vindictiveness and violence on the other. As we have seen in the preceding pages, Shakespeare attempts to resolve these conflicts in a variety of ways. Both McCurdy and I feel that *The Tempest* is Shakespeare's "ideal solution" (1953, 162), but we differ in defining the problem he is trying to solve. McCurdy sees Shakespeare as a predominantly aggressive person who is afraid of his softer emotions and whose problem is how to "admit the loving-kindness of Christian charity" without feeling spineless (1953, 162). I see Shakespeare as a predominantly self-effacing person who is more afraid of his aggressive side than he is of his submissive or charitable tendencies and whose problem is how to give expression to his sadistic and vindictive impulses without violating his stronger need to be loving, noble, and innocent. The solution is to create situations that permit disguised or justified aggression and innocent revenge. *The Tempest* embodies his ideal solution because Prospero's magical powers permit him to satisfy his needs for revenge without sacrificing his moral nobility.

From *1 Henry VI* to *The Tempest,* a frequent concern of Shakespeare's plays is how to cope with wrongs, how to remain good in an evil world. In the histories and the tragedies, the tendency of the main characters is to respond to wrongs by taking revenge, but this contaminates the revenger and results in his own destruction. The arrogant-vindictive solution, with its emphasis upon retaliation, does not work. But neither does the self-effacing solution work in these plays, because many innocent, well-intentioned, but weak characters perish. As I see it, Hamlet's problem is how to take revenge and remain innocent. The problem is insoluble and nearly drives him mad. In a number of the comedies and romances, Shakespeare explores a different response to being wronged—namely, mercy and forgiveness. Because of the conventions of these genres, with their providential universe and miraculous conversions, wronged characters do not have to take revenge; either fate does it for them or they forgive their enemies, who are then permanently transformed. In these plays, the self-effacing solution, with its accompanying bargain, works very well, but only because the plays are unrealistic.

What I infer about Shakespeare from his plays is that he has strong vindictive impulses, but even stronger taboos against those impulses and a fear of the guilt and punishment to which he would be exposed if he acted them out. He does act them out imaginatively in the histories and tragedies and is purged of them through the destruction of his surrogate aggressors. He also has a fear of his self-effacing side, however; and through characters like Henry VI, Hamlet, Desdemona, and Timon, he shows that people who are too good and trusting cannot cope with the harsh realities of life. In the histories and tragedies, he portrays the inadequacy of both solutions. In some of the comedies and in the romances, he fantasizes the triumph of good people and avoids guilt either by glorifying forgiveness or leaving revenge to the gods. In *The Tempest,* through Prospero's magic, he imagines a solution to Hamlet's problem; for Prospero is at once vindictive and noble, vengeful and innocent. He raises a tempest and inflicts various psychological torments; but he does not really "hurt" anybody; and when he has had his revenge, he renounces his magic and forgives everyone.

THE FUNCTION OF PROSPERO'S MAGIC

The Tempest is one of only two Shakespearean plays whose plot, as far as we know, is entirely the author's invention. More than any other play, it is Shakespeare's fantasy. What, we must ask, is it a fantasy of? What psychological needs are being met? What wishes are being fulfilled? One way of approaching these questions is to look at the unrealistic elements in the play, particularly Prospero's magic. The function of magic is to do the impossible, to grant wishes that are denied to us in reality. What is his magic doing for Prospero? And for Shakespeare? What impossible dream does it allow to come true?

These questions can be approached from a variety of psychological perspectives. In Freudian theory, for instance, magic is associated with a belief in the omnipotence of thought, and it is employed in an effort to restore the delusions of grandeur that accompanied infantile megalomania. By giving him magical powers, Shakespeare grants Prospero the mastery of time, space, and matter that we once thought we enjoyed and that we still desire. In *Totem and Taboo,* Freud argued that man's conception of the universe has passed through three stages, the animistic, the religious, and the scientific:

> we have no difficulty in following the fortunes of the "omnipotence of thought" through all these phases. In the animistic stage man ascribes omnipotence to himself; in the religious he has ceded it to the gods, but without seriously giving it up, for he reserves to himself the right to control the gods by influencing them in some way or other in the interest of his wishes. In the scientific attitude toward life there is no longer any room for man's omnipotence; he has acknowledged his smallness and has submitted to death as to all other natural necessities in a spirit of resignation. (n.d., 115)

Most of Shakespeare's comedies and romances are written from a religious perspective; wishes are fulfilled through the cooperation or even the direct intervention of providential forces. Perhaps Northrop Frye, for whom domination by the pleasure principle is the glory of literature, calls *The Tempest* "the bedrock of drama" (1969, 67) because it is written from an animistic perspective. Prospero is indebted to "providence divine" for guiding him to the island and for placing his enemies within his reach, but to a large extent the powers given to the gods and to providence in the other romances are conferred here upon a human being. No doubt, the appeal of *The Tempest* lies, in part, in the directness and immediacy of its wish-fulfillment, in its regression to one of the earliest stages of primary-process thinking. One question we must ask, of course, is why Prospero gives up his magic. Is it a sign of movement to a religious or a scientific perspective?

This approach sheds a good deal of light upon the play, especially upon the ending, but it does not relate Prospero's magic to his personality and show us how it helps him to satisfy his specific psychological needs. Before he is overthrown, Prospero is a predominantly detached person. The detached person craves serenity, dislikes responsibility, and is averse to the struggle for power. His "two outstanding neurotic claims are that life should be . . . effortless and that he should not be bothered" (Horney 1950, 264). Prospero turns his responsibilities as duke over to his brother, rejects the pursuit of "worldly ends," and retires into his library, which is "dukedom large enough!" (II, ii). He immerses himself in a world of books, seeking glory not through the exercise of his office, which involves him in troublesome relations with other people, but through the pursuit of knowledge. As a result of his studies, he becomes "the prime duke, being so reputed/ In dignity, and for the liberal arts/ Without a parallel" (II, ii). He is not without ambition and a hunger for power, but he satisfies these needs in a detached way.

Prospero's study of magic is highly congruent with his personality. The detached person has an aversion to effort and places the greatest value upon freedom from constraint. Magic is a means of achieving one's ends without effort and of transcending the limitations of the human condition. It is a way of enforcing the claim that mind is the supreme reality, that the material world is subject to its dictates. Indeed, it symbolizes that claim. Through his withdrawal into the study of magic, Prospero is pursuing a dream of glory that is far more grandiose than any available to him as Duke of Milan. It is no wonder that he "prize[s]" his "volumes . . . above [his] dukedom." He becomes "transported/ And rapt in secret studies" and grows a "stranger" to his state (I, ii).

Reality intrudes upon Prospero in the form of Antonio's plot, which leads to his expulsion from the dukedom. Although many critics have blamed Prospero for his neglect of his duties, Prospero does not seem to blame himself or to see himself as being responsible in any way for his fate. He interprets his withdrawal as a commendable unworldliness and presents his behavior toward his brother in a way that is flattering to himself:

> and my trust,
> Like a good parent, did beget of him
> A falsehood in its contrary as great
> As my trust was, which had indeed no limit,
> A confidence sans bound. (I, ii)

There are strong self-effacing tendencies in Prospero that lead him to think too well of his fellows and to bestow upon them a trust they do not deserve. Overtrustingness has disastrous consequences in the history plays and in the tragedies, but it has no permanent ill-effects in the comedies and romances. Prospero glorifies his excessive confidence in his brother and places the blame for what happens entirely upon Antonio's "evil nature." He seems to have no sense of how his own foolish behavior has contributed to his fate.

Antonio's betrayal marks the failure of Prospero's self-effacing bargain; his goodness to his brother, which he had expected to be repaid with gratitude and devotion, is used by Antonio to usurp the dukedom. This trauma is similar to those that precipitate psychological crises in the protagonists of the tragedies, crises from which none of them recover. Prospero's case is different because of his magic. Like the protagonists of the tragedies, Prospero is furious with those by whom he has been injured and craves a revenge that will assuage his anger and repair his idealized image. Unlike the characters in the realistic plays, however, he has a means of restoring his pride without being destructive to himself and others. He spends the next twelve years dreaming of his revenge and perfecting his magic in preparation for his vindictive triumph. *The Tempest* is the story of his day of reckoning.

Prospero has numerous objectives on this day, all of which he achieves through his magic. He wants to punish his enemies, to make a good match for his daughter, to get back what he has lost, to prove through his display of power that he was right to have immersed himself in his studies, and to demonstrate that he is the great man that he has felt himself to be, far superior to those who have humiliated him. The most important function of his magic, however, is that it enables him to resolve his psychological conflicts. Once he has been wronged, Prospero is caught between contradictory impulses. He is full of rage that he has a powerful need to express, but he feels that revenge is ignoble and that he will be as bad as his enemies if he allows himself to descend to their level. What Prospero needs is what Hamlet could not find and what Shakespeare is trying to imagine: a way of taking revenge and remaining innocent. This is a problem that only his magic can solve. *The Tempest* is above all a fantasy of innocent revenge. The revenge is Prospero's, but the fantasy is Shakespeare's, whose conflicting needs are similar to those of his protagonist.

The storm with which the play opens is an expression of Prospero's rage. It instills terror in his enemies and satisfies his need to make them suffer for what they have done to him. If the vindictive side of Prospero is embodied in the storm, his compassionate side is embodied in Miranda, who is full of pity for the suffering of the "poor souls" who seem to have "perish'd" (I, ii). Since Miranda is the product of Prospero's tutelage, she represents his ideal values, at least for a woman; and it is important to recognize that she is extremely self-effacing. When Prospero begins to tell the story of their past, her "heart bleeds/ To think o' th' teen that I have turn'd you to"; and when he describes their expulsion, she exclaims, "Alack, what trouble/ Was I then to you!" (I, ii). She wants to carry Ferdinand's logs for him, feels unworthy of his love, and swears to be his servant if he will not marry her (III, i). Like her father before his fall, she has an idealistic view of human nature. The "brave vessel" that has sunk "had no doubt some noble creature in her" (I, ii), and when she first sees the assembled company, she exclaims, "How beauteous mankind is! O brave new world/ That has such people in't!" (V, i). Prospero is no longer so idealistic, but he has retained many of his self-effacing values and has instilled them in Miranda. He approves of her response to "the wrack, which touch'd/ The very virtue of compassion in thee" (I, ii) and assures her that "There's no harm done." Through his "art" he has "So safely ordered" the storm that there is "not so much perdition as an hair/ Betid to any creature in the vessel/ Which thou heard'st cry." Miranda says that if she had "been any god of power" she would never have permitted the wreck to happen, and neither does Prospero. Through his magic, the wreck happens and does not happen. His magic permits him to satisfy his vindictive needs without violating the side of himself that is expressed by Miranda.[1] To further alleviate his discomfort with his sadistic behavior and Miranda's implied reproaches, Prospero claims that he has "done nothing but in care" of her and justifies his actions by telling the story of Antonio's perfidy.

Prospero's delight in the discomfiture of his enemies is revealed most vividly in his response to Ariel's account of his frightening behavior during the tempest. He asks Ariel if he has "Perform'd to point the tempest" he had commanded; and when Ariel replies that he has, Prospero's sadistic pleasure is evident: "My brave spirit!/ Who was so firm, so constant, that this coil/ Would not infect his reason?" His enthusiastic response inspires Ariel to elaborate:

> Not a soul
> But felt a fever of the mad and play'd
> Some tricks of desperation. All but mariners
> Plung'd in the foaming brine and quit the vessel,
> Then all afire with me. The King's son Ferdinand,
> With hair up-staring (then like reeds, not hair),
> Was the first man that leapt; cried "Hell is empty,
> And all the devils are here!" (I, ii)

Once again Prospero expresses his approval: "Why, that's my spirit!" Since Ariel has carried out his orders "To every article," we must assume that the madness and desperation Ariel describes are precisely what Prospero intended. He is pleased not only by the terror of his enemies, but also by that of Ferdinand, his future son-in-law. He is rather indiscriminate in his punishments, as he is later in his forgiveness.

Prospero can enjoy the terror of his victims because he has not injured them physically: "But are they, Ariel, safe?" Not only are they safe, but their garments are "fresher than before" (I, ii). In the history plays and the tragedies, revengers incur guilt and bring destruction upon themselves by doing physical violence to their enemies. Prospero is a cunning and sadistic revenger who employs his magic to inflict psychological violence upon his enemies while he shields them from physical injury and thereby preserves his innocence. In his mind, as long as no one is physically injured, "There's no harm done" (I, ii). Having everyone fear imminent destruction, including the good Gonzalo, having them run mad with terror at Ariel's apparitions, having Ferdinand and Alonso believe each other dead, such things, for Prospero, do not constitute harm.

PROSPERO'S CRUELTY TO ARIEL AND CALIBAN

Prospero's cruelty toward his enemies may not appear to say much about his character because it seems justified by their outrageous treatment of him. He is prone to react with aggression, however, whenever he

can find a justification, however slight, for doing so.[2] He says he will put
Ferdinand in chains and force him to drink sea water and to eat mussels,
withered roots, and acorn husks, and he makes him remove thousands of
logs, "lest too light winning" of Miranda "Make the prize light" (I, ii).
This seems a weak excuse for his sadistic behavior. His pleasure with
Ariel for his management of the tempest is followed by a scene in which
he threatens to "rend an oak/ And peg [him] in his knotty entrails till/
[He] has howl'd away twelve winters" (I, ii). He even threatens Miranda
when she beseeches him to have pity upon Ferdinand: "Silence! One word
more/ Shall make me chide thee, if not hate thee" (I, ii).

Prospero is usually benevolent until he feels that his kindness has
been betrayed or unappreciated, and then he becomes vindictive. He feels
betrayed by Antonio, of course, and unappreciated by Ariel when that
spirit presses for liberty. He justifies his enslavement of Ariel by reminding him that it was his "art" that freed him from Sycorax's spell, and he
threatens him with torments similar to those Sycorax had inflicted if he
continues to complain. Prospero's threats seem to me an overreaction. He
will peg Ariel in the entrails of an oak merely for murmuring. Prospero
makes enormous claims on the basis of his kindness, and if others do not
honor these claims he becomes enraged. If he is ready to punish Ariel and
to hate Miranda for very slight offenses, think of the vindictiveness that he
must be feeling toward Antonio. Ariel is self-effacing and knows how to
make peace with Prospero. He thanks him for having freed him and
promises to "be correspondent to command/ And do [his] spriting gently"
(I, ii). This allows Prospero to become benevolent once again, and he
promises to discharge Ariel in two days. Ariel then says what Prospero
wants to hear: "That's my noble master!" This is the way Prospero insists
upon being perceived. Indeed, his anger with Ariel when he murmurs
derives partly from the fact that Ariel has threatened his idealized image
by making him seem unkind.

Ariel plays Prospero's game, but Caliban does not. Prospero is initially very kind to Caliban; he strokes him, gives him treats, educates him,
and lodges him in his cell. And Caliban initially reciprocates; he loves
Prospero and shows him "all the qualities o' the' isle" (I, ii). Prospero
turns against Caliban, however, when he seeks to violate Miranda's honor,
and from this point on he treats Caliban with great brutality. Here, too,
Prospero overreacts. He is so enraged, I propose, because Caliban has
repeated Antonio's crime, accepting Prospero's favors and repaying them
with treachery. Prospero discharges onto him all the anger that he feels
toward the enemies back home who, before the day of reckoning, are

beyond his power. Even after he enslaves Caliban, Prospero expects him to behave submissively. He complains to Miranda that Caliban "never/ Yields us kind answer," but then he summons Caliban in a way that reveals the unreasonableness of his expectation: "What, ho! slave! Caliban/ Thou earth, thou! Speak!" (II, ii). When Caliban responds to being treated like dirt by being bitterly resentful, Prospero takes this as a sign of his irreclaimable nature.

There is a major contradiction in Prospero's attitude toward Caliban. He feels that Caliban is subhuman, but he holds him morally responsible for his acts and he punishes him severely. If Caliban is subhuman, then he is not morally responsible and should simply be kept away from Miranda, a precaution Prospero could easily effect. If he is a moral agent, then he needs to be shown the error of his ways; but Prospero's punishments are merely designed to torture him and to break his spirit. The contradiction in Prospero's attitude results from conflicting psychological needs. He needs to hold Caliban responsible because doing so allows him to act out his sadistic impulses, but he also needs to regard Caliban as subhuman because this allows him to avoid feeling guilt. If Caliban is subhuman, he is not part of Prospero's moral community, and Prospero's behavior toward him is not subject to the shoulds and taboos that are operative in his relations with his fellow human beings. Caliban provides Prospero with a splendid opportunity for justified aggression, for being vindictive without losing his nobility.

Prospero's rationalization of his treatment of Caliban works so well that the majority of critics have accepted his point of view and have felt that Caliban deserves what he gets, though some have been sympathetic toward Caliban's suffering and uneasy about Prospero's behavior (Auden 1962, 129). Prospero is constantly punishing Caliban, not just for the attempted rape, but also for the much lesser crimes of surliness, resentment, and insubordination. When Caliban is slow in responding to Prospero's summons ("Slave! Caliban!/ Thou earth, thou!"), Prospero calls him again in an even nastier way: "Thou poisonous slave, got by the devil himself/ Upon thy wicked dam, come forth!" (I, ii). Caliban does not yield a "kind answer" but enters with curses: "As wicked dew as e'er my mother brush'd/ With raven's feather from unwholesome fen/ Drop on you both!" Prospero responds by promising horrible punishments:

> For this, be sure, to-night thou shalt have cramps,
> Side-stitches that shall pen thy breath up; urchins
> Shall, for that vast of night that they may work,
> All exercise on thee; thou shalt be pinch'd

As thick as honeycomb, each pinch more stinging
Than bees that made 'em. (I, ii)

This is a very unequal contest, since Caliban's curses are merely words, an expression of ill-will, while Prospero has the power to inflict the torments he describes. Despite his "crime" in attempting Miranda (a natural act for an uncivilized being), Caliban seems to have reason for his resentment. He feels that the island is his (he was his "own king" before Prospero arrived), he has been turned into a drudge, and he is subject to vicious abuse. Prospero looks for penitence, submissiveness, and gracious service from Caliban and punishes him severely for his spirit of defiance. He seems to be trying to torture him into being a willing slave, like Ariel, and he is embittered by his lack of success.

Prospero and Caliban are caught in a vicious circle from which there seems to be no escape. The more Caliban resists what he perceives as Prospero's tyranny, the more Prospero punishes him; and the more Prospero punishes him, the more Caliban resists. He curses Prospero even though he knows that his spirits hear him and that he may be subject to retaliation—"yet I needs must curse" (II, ii). The need for this emotional relief must be powerful indeed in view of what may be in store for him:

For every trifle are they set upon me;
Sometime like apes that mow and chatter at me,
And after bite me; then like hedgehogs which
Lie tumbling in my barefoot way and mount
Their pricks at my footfall; sometime am I
All wound with adders, who with cloven tongues
Do hiss me into madness. (II, ii)

It is remarkable that Caliban's spirit has not been broken as a result of such torments. And it is no wonder that Caliban seizes the opportunity he thinks is presented by Stephano and Trinculo to revolt against Prospero. "I am subject," he tells them, "to a tyrant,/ A sorcerer, that by his cunning hath/ Cheated me of the island" (III, ii). Is this far from the truth? He claims that Prospero's spirits "all do hate him/ As rootedly as I." It is impossible to say whether or not this is true, but it might be. Even Ariel must be threatened with terrible punishments and reminded once a month of what Prospero has done for him.

Prospero does not need to use his magic to resolve inner conflicts in his relationship with Caliban because regarding Caliban as subhuman allows him to act out his vindictive impulses without guilt or restraint. The combination of his sadistic imagination and his magic makes him an ingenious torturer. He could have used his magic more benignly if he had regarded Caliban as part of his moral community, but this would have generated conflicts and deprived him of his scapegoat. (See Berger 1970, 261, on Caliban as scapegoat.) He insists, therefore, that Caliban is uneducable: "A devil, a born devil, on whose nature/ Nurture can never stick! on whom my pains,/ Humanely taken, all, all lost, quite lost!" (IV, i). His judgment is reinforced by Miranda, who abhors Caliban, in part, because his vindictiveness violates her self-effacing values, and by Caliban's plot, which seems to demonstrate his innate depravity. Since there is no point in being humane to a born devil, Prospero is free to "plague" him "to roaring."[3]

Many critics agree that Caliban is a hopeless case, but some are impressed by his sensitivity in "The isle is full of noises" speech (III, ii) and by his declaration that he will "seek for grace" (V, i) (see also Berger 1970, 255). His plot can be seen as a reaction to Prospero's abuse rather than as a sign that he is an "abhorred slave/ Which any print of goodness wilt not take" (I, ii). Prospero must hold onto his image of Caliban as a devil in order to hold onto his idealized image of himself. If Caliban is redeemable, then Prospero has been a monster. The exchange of curses between Prospero and Caliban indicates that they have much in common. What Prospero hates and punishes in Caliban is the forbidden part of himself. His denial of moral status to Caliban is in part a rationale for his vindictive behavior and in part a way of denying the similarities that clearly exist between them. Prospero is doing to Caliban what Caliban would do to Prospero if he had the power.

THE NOBLE PROSPERO?

Prospero is much more careful in his treatment of his fellow humans, some of whom strike us as being considerably more depraved than Caliban. Indeed, Prospero calls Caliban a devil but feels that Antonio and Sebastian "are worse than devils" (III, iii). Nonetheless, he regards them as fellow human beings and his shoulds and taboos are fully operative in relation to them. Not only does he conceal his vindictiveness from himself (and from many of the critics) by employing his magic to punish them without doing any "harm," but he justifies his treatment of them by seeing it as conducive to their moral growth. His object is not revenge but regeneration and reconciliation. Ariel articulates Prospero's perspective in the banquet scene. He accuses the "three men of sin" of their crimes against "good Prospero," threatens them with "ling'ring perdition," and indicates that they can escape Prospero's wrath only by "heart's sorrow/ And a clear life ensuing" (III, iii). Even as Prospero is knitting them up in "fits" and exulting in the fact that "they are now in [his] pow'r," he is being presented in a very noble light. He manages to take revenge in such a way that he emerges as the benefactor of his victims.

After he has tormented them so much that "the good old Lord Gonzalo" is in tears at the sight and even Ariel has "a feeling/ Of their afflictions," Prospero relents, as he had intended to do all along:

> Though with their high wrongs I am struck to th' quick,
> Yet with my nobler reason 'gainst my fury
> Do I take part. The rarer action is
> In virtue than in vengeance. They being penitent,
> The sole drift of my purpose doth extend
> Not a frown further. (V, i)

Although Prospero is still furious with the evil three, his perfectionistic and self-effacing shoulds are stronger than his vindictive impulses. He releases them from his spell, in part, because his cruelty is making him uneasy and, in part, because his need for revenge has been assuaged by their suffering. He proclaims that "the rarer action is/ In virtue than in vengeance," but he says this only after he has gotten a goodly measure of vengeance. He makes it seem that his only purpose has been to bring the men of sin to penitence, but that is hardly the case. This is a play not only about renouncing revenge but also about getting it.

There has been much debate over whether Prospero's enemies are indeed repentant. Prospero's forgiveness is made contingent upon penitence and a clear life after, but only Alonso seems to merit his pardon. Alonso displays his remorse again and again, but Sebastian and Antonio show no sign of repentance or promise of reformation. They have plotted against Prospero in the past; they try to kill Alonso during the course of the play; and they seem at the play's end still to be dangerous fellows. Many critics have speculated upon the likelihood of their continued criminality upon the return to Italy. In 1797, F. G. Waldron wrote a sequel to *The Tempest* in which Antonio and Sebastian betray Prospero during the voyage home and force him to retrieve his magic.

Why, then, does Prospero forgive them? It may be that he thinks they have repented, but I do not think he does. While Antonio is still under his spell, Prospero says, "I forgive thee,/ Unnatural though thou art" (V, i); and when he has returned to full consciousness, Prospero forgives him again, in an even more contemptuous way:

> For you, most wicked sir, whom to call brother
> Would even infect my mouth, I do forgive
> Thy rankest fault—all of them . . . (V, i)

As Bonamy Dobrée (1952) suggested, there is a nasty quality about Prospero's forgiveness. More like revenge than a movement toward reconciliation, it is a vindictive forgiveness that satisfies his need to express his scorn and bitterness while appearing to be noble. Antonio's undeservingness contributes to Prospero's sense of moral grandeur; the worse Antonio is, the more charitable is Prospero to forgive him. This is Prospero's perspective and that of the play's rhetoric; but from a psychological point of view, Prospero's forgiveness seems compulsive, indiscriminate, and dangerous. It is inappropriate to the practical and moral realities of the situation but necessary if Prospero is to maintain his idealized image.

For most of the play, Prospero's idealized image contains a combination of arrogant-vindictive and self-effacing traits that are reconciled by means of his magic. He needs to see himself as a humane, benevolent, forgiving man, and also as a powerful, masterful, dangerous man who cannot be taken advantage of with impunity and who will strike back when he has been injured. The first four acts of the play show Prospero satisfying his needs for mastery and revenge, but in ways that do not violate his perfectionistic and self-effacing dictates. By the end of act 4, he has achieved his objectives. He has knit up Antonio, Sebastian, and Alonso in his spell and has thwarted the plot of Caliban, Stephano, and Trinculo, with a final display of innocent delight in the torture of the conspirators. Prospero sets his dogs (two of whom are aptly named Fury and Tyrant) upon them, and tells Ariel to charge his "goblins that they grind their joints/ With dry convulsions, shorten up their sinews/ With aged cramps, and more pinch-spotted make them/ Than pard or cat o' mountain" (IV, i). "At this hour," Prospero proclaims, "Lie at my mercy all mine enemies." From this point on, he becomes increasingly self-effacing. At the beginning of the next act, he gives up his vengeance and determines to renounce his magic. Once he gives up his magic, he has no choice but to repress his vindictive trends, for it was only through his magic that he was able to act them out innocently.

Prospero represses his vindictive side for a number of reasons. He has shown his power. Now, in order to satisfy his self-effacing shoulds, he must show his mercy. He cannot stop behaving vindictively until his anger has been partially assuaged, but he cannot continue once his enemies are in his power. That he is still angry is clear from the manner of his forgiveness, but the imperative to forgive is now more powerful than the need for revenge. Given his inner conflicts, Prospero is bound to feel uncomfortable about his aggressive behavior; and now that he has had his day of reckoning, his negative feelings about it become dominant. He regards revenge as ignoble and "abjures" his "rough magic" (V, i). His choice of words here is significant. He seems to feel ashamed of his magic (even as he celebrates its powers) and guilty for having employed it. Why else would he use the word "abjure," which means to disavow, recant, or repudiate? Whereas earlier he was able to enjoy his power, he now has a self-effacing response to it. He gives up his magic because he needs to place himself in an humble position and to show that he has not used his power for personal aggrandizement, but only to set things right, to bring about moral growth and reconciliation.

Although *Henry VIII* was yet to come, *The Tempest* is often read as Shakespeare's farewell to the theater, and Prospero is seen as his supreme embodiment of the artist figure. Though it is impossible to tell to what extent Prospero is Shakespeare's alter ego, there are some striking parallels. Prospero uses his magic and Shakespeare uses his art to attain mastery and to achieve disguised or innocent revenge. Shakespeare condemns or even kills off in his plays the kinds of people who have hurt him or of whom he is most afraid, but, like Prospero, he maintains a posture of benevolence and wisdom.[4] Again like Prospero, he seems after a certain point (*Timon*) to become more and more self-effacing; and he prematurely relinquishes his magic, perhaps because he, too, feels guilty about his exercise of power and needs to embrace "the blessedness of being little" (*Henry VIII*, IV, ii).

In the Epilogue, with his "charms . . . o'erthrown," Prospero adopts an extremely self-effacing posture. Since he can no longer "enchant," "he can "be reliev'd" only by prayer,

> Which pierces so that it assaults
> Mercy itself and frees all faults.
> As you from crimes would pardon'd be,
> Let your indulgence set me free.

Prospero sees himself here not as the avenger, but as the guilty party, perhaps because of his revenge; and he tries to make a self-effacing bargain in which he judges not so that he will not be judged. We can now understand more fully his motives for forgiving the men of sin. Beneath his self-righteousness, Prospero has hidden feelings of guilt and fears of retribution. By refusing to take a more severe form of revenge, to which he certainly seems entitled, he protects himself against punishment. By forgiving others, he ensures his own pardon. Giving up his magic serves a similar purpose. It counteracts his feelings of pride and places him in a dependent, submissive position. Although Prospero's remarks in the Epilogue are partly a conventional appeal to the audience, he remains in character and expresses sentiments that are in keeping with his psychological development.

When we understand Prospero's psychological development, he seems different from the figure celebrated by so many critics. Those who interpret *The Tempest* as a story of magnanimity, forgiveness, and reconciliation are responding correctly, I believe, to Shakespeare's thematic intentions, whereas those who take a more "hard-nosed" view of the play are responding to the psychological portrait of Prospero. There is in this play, as in some others, a disparity between rhetoric and mimesis that generates conflicting critical responses and reflects the inner divisions of the author (see Paris 1991).

In his presentation of Prospero, Shakespeare employs a powerful rhetoric both of justification and of glorification. He employs numerous devices that justify Prospero's behavior toward Antonio, Sebastian, Alonso, Caliban, Ariel, Ferdinand, Stephano, and Trinculo—toward all the characters, in effect, whom Prospero treats harshly. Early in the play, there is some rhetoric of glorification and some rhetoric of justification toward the end, but by and large the justification occurs when Prospero is being punitive and the glorification occurs after he gives up his vengeance. We learn early in the play of Prospero's betrayal by his brother, of the dangers to which he was exposed, of Ariel's impatience, of Caliban's treachery, of the need to test Ferdinand, and of the continued perfidy of Antonio and Sebastian. All these things justify Prospero's harshness, as does Miranda's condemnation of Caliban and Ariel's acceptance of Prospero's reproaches. As the play progresses, Prospero is increasingly surrounded by a rhetoric of glorification. He is praised by Ariel ("my noble master") and Ferdinand ("so rare a wond'red father"), and he receives a tribute even from Caliban, who is impressed by his fineness and determines to "seek for grace." (Though Prospero cannot afford to recognize it, Caliban reforms when Prospero stops torturing him and holds out the prospect of pardon.)

The rhetoric of the play justifies the vindictive Prospero and glorifies the self-effacing one. It confirms Prospero's idealized image of himself as a kindly, charitable man who punishes others much less than they deserve and only for their own good. Meanwhile, the action of the play shows us a Prospero who is bitter, sadistic, and hungry for revenge. The disparity between rhetoric and mimesis is a reflection of Prospero's inner conflicts and of Shakespeare's. The rhetoric rationalizes and disguises Prospero's vindictiveness and celebrates his moral nobility.[5] Its function is similar to that of Prospero's magic. The magic enables Prospero to have his revenge and to remain innocent in his own eyes and in the eyes of the other characters. The magic and the rhetoric together enable Shakespeare to deceive himself and the audience as to Prospero's true nature.

NO LONGER DIVIDED

The Tempest offers an ideal solution to the problem of how to cope with wrongs without losing one's innocence, but only through the first four acts. The solution collapses when Prospero renounces his magic, for his magic was the only means by which he could reconcile his conflicts and keep evil under control. At the end, he does not seem to have attained emotional balance or to have discovered a viable way of living in the real world.

Magic enables Prospero to attain only a temporary psychological equilibrium. It solves one set of problems, but it generates new inner conflicts, which he attempts to resolve by becoming extremely self-effacing. As we have seen, he abjures his magic because of a need to disown his pride and to assuage the feelings of guilt aroused by his exercise of power. Prospero has never been comfortable with power, which is one reason why he delegated his authority to Antonio, and he seems unduly eager to relinquish it here. The problem is that though he feels guilty with power, he feels helpless without it, as he indicates in the Epilogue. He has achieved all his objectives, but he seems weary rather than triumphant at the end. He will see the nuptials solemnized in Naples, "And thence retire me to my Milan, where/ Every third thought shall be my grave" (V, i). Since he has given up his secret studies and has no taste for governance, what is there, indeed, for Prospero? It is no wonder that he longs to withdraw into the quietude of death.

We see Prospero at the end in the grip of self-effacing and detached trends that do not promise to make him an effective ruler. Even so "sentimental" a critic as Northrop Frye observed that Prospero "appears to have been a remarkably incompetent Duke of Milan, and not to be promising much improvement after he returns" (1969, 63–64). There have been many misgivings about Prospero's forgiveness of Antonio and doubts about his ability to cope upon the return to Italy. As we have seen, the forgiveness is compulsive and indiscriminate. There is no evidence of repentance on Antonio's part and no reason to think that he will meekly submit to Prospero's rule. At the least, Antonio should be put into jail; but Prospero can neither do this nor, I suspect, keep him under control. Like the Duke in *Measure for Measure* and many other of Shakespeare's self-effacing characters, Prospero cannot exercise authority and deal effectively with the guilty. At the end of *The Tempest* Shakespeare seems back to where he started in the plays about Henry VI, with a nobly Christian ruler who cannot cope with the harsh realities of life.

Like Prospero at the end of *The Tempest,* Shakespeare at the end of his career seems to have resolved his inner conflicts by repressing his aggressive impulses and becoming extremely self-effacing. In *Henry VIII,* he begins at the point he had reached by the end of *The Tempest.* The desire for revenge, which had inspired such a marvelous fantasy in *The Tempest,* is no longer present. Character after character is wronged and responds in a remarkably charitable manner, asking forgiveness and blessing his or her enemies. There is no need to cope with evil; rather we must submit ourselves patiently to the divine will, which has a reason for everything. Priestly said that Shakespeare was "a deeply divided man" the "opposites" of whose nature gave "energy and life to his works" (1964, 82). In *Henry VIII,* the opposites are gone, and the result is a vapid moral fable in which we no longer feel the presence of a complex and fascinating personality. This play makes it clear that Shakespeare's inner conflicts had much to do with the richness and ambiguity of his art.

Notes

INTRODUCTION

1. For other recent criticism that supports my approach to character, see Kantak 1977, Chatman 1978, Levine 1981, Bredin 1982, Price 1983, Nuttall 1983, Docherty 1984, Hochman 1985, Newman 1985, Frattaroli 1987, and Alter 1989. There is beginning to develop in Shakespearean criticism a reaction against the reaction against Bradley.

2. One of the finest statements of this position is by Wyndham Lewis in *The Lion and the Fox*: "It is actually . . . impossible . . . for an artist to be 'impersonal'. . . . There are only different ways of being personal; and one of them is that admired method of insinuation whereby a particularly compendious pretended reality enables its creator to express himself as *though he were nature,* or a god. But it is never as nature, or as the god responsible for this world, that a great creative artist speaks . . . . Artistic creation is always a . . . *personal* creation" (n.d., 285–286).

3. For recent discussions of the relation of Shakespeare's early experience to his adult personality, see Barber and Wheeler 1986 and Holland, Homan, and Paris 1989.

CHAPTER 1. BARGAINS, DEFENSES, AND CULTURAL CODES

1. Because I quote so much from Horney, I shall follow her practice in using the masculine pronoun.

2. Horney speaks of "aggressive" and "compliant" solutions in *Our Inner Conflicts* (1945) and of "expansive" and "self-effacing" solutions in *Neurosis and Human Growth* (1950). She did not establish a clear distinction between these terms, and I use them more or less interchangeably, choosing whichever seems most appropriate to the

behavior under discussion. The division of expansive solutions into narcissistic, perfectionistic, and arrogant-vindictive occurs in *Neurosis and Human Growth*.

3. I am indebted to Bertram Wyatt-Brown for helping me to clarify the treatment
of honor in Shakespeare. Part I of his *Southern Honor* (1982) provides a useful
background to this discussion.

4. Except where otherwise indicated, I shall be using the Kittredge-Ribner edi-
tions of Shakespeare.

CHAPTER 2. *HAMLET*

1. There have been, of course, many fine psychological studies of *Hamlet*. See
Holland 1966 and Noland 1974 for surveys of criticism. For bibliographies, see Holland 1966 and Schwartz and Kahn 1980, which updates Holland. Among the more
relevant recent studies are Leverenz 1978, Kahn 1981, Kirsch 1981, and Erickson
1985.

2. I am using, with a few exceptions, the Hardin Craig text of *Hamlet*. I prefer
"solid" to "sullied" in act 1, scene 2, line 129; and I read act 3, scene 4, line 149 as
"curb the devil."

3. Psychological considerations aside, I do not believe that the play's structure
encourages us to see Hamlet's decision not to kill Claudius at this point as further
procrastination. The whole situation is so ordered as to produce powerful ironies that
would be lost if we did not take Hamlet's reasons at face value. The Mousetrap
achieves what Hamlet intended: it conclusively reveals Claudius's guilt and releases
Hamlet's bloodthirsty aggression. Because Hamlet has caught the conscience of the
king, however, Claudius is now praying. This at once gives Hamlet the opportunity to
take him unguarded and prevents him from using it, since he is afraid that Claudius's
soul will go to heaven if he dies in a state of purgation. We discover as soon as Hamlet
leaves that Claudius's effort at prayer has failed: "My words fly up, my thoughts
remain below;/ Words without thoughts never to heaven go" (III, iii). This would have
been a good time to kill him, after all. It is difficult to reconcile the contention that we
are meant to see Hamlet as delaying with this striving for ironic effects.

4. The flow of the action makes it appear that Hamlet went directly from the
prayer scene to his mother's chamber. If he did, he must have known that the person
behind the arras could not have been the king, and we need, then, a psychological
explanation of why he acts as though it might have been. Other evidence suggests that
it could have been the king and that Hamlet did, in fact, take Polonius for his better.
When Claudius hears of the murder, he says, "It had been so with us, had we been
there" (IV, i). At the end of the closet scene, Hamlet displays his knowledge of
Claudius's plan to send him to England in the company of Rosencrantz and
Guildenstern: "There's letters seal'd: and my two schoolfellows,/ Whom I will trust as
adders fang'd,/ They bear the mandate" (III, iv). Although Claudius first thought of
sending Hamlet to England after overhearing his tirade to Ophelia, he does not give

Rosencrantz and Guildenstern their commission until after the play, in a scene that culminates with his attempt to pray (III, ii). This indicates that there is an interval between the prayer scene and Hamlet's arrival at the Queen's chamber during which he learns of Claudius's plan. There would have been time, then, for the King to have gone to the Queen's closet and to have concealed himself there. In the absence of clear stage directions, there is no way of arguing this point conclusively. Each interpreter (and director) must make his own choice. It is quite consonant with my interpretation of Hamlet's character for him to have been able to kill the king at this point in the play, and I shall take the position that it was physically possible for Claudius to have been behind the arras.

CHAPTER 3. *OTHELLO*

1. Iago has been discussed from a Horneyan perspective by Rosenberg 1961 and by Rabkin and Brown 1973. For representative Freudian readings, see Wangh 1950, Smith 1959, Orgel 1968, and Hyman 1970. Other interesting psychological studies include Staebler 1975 and West 1978.

2. This is Bradley's position. It has been echoed by many others and has been most eloquently defended in recent years by Rosenberg 1961, 185–205.

3. The leading exponents of the negative view have been Bodkin 1934, Leavis 1964, Heilman 1956, and Kirschbaum 1962. Rosenberg, Heilman, and Kirschbaum have bibliographic footnotes that trace the history of the dispute; and Berman 1973 summarizes the negative views. For a review of psychoanalytic studies, almost all of which see Othello's character as responsible, in some way, for his fate, see Holland 1966. The most interesting of the recent psychoanalytic studies are Shapiro 1964, Reid 1968, and Faber 1974.

4. There have been few detailed psychological studies of Desdemona, however. Two of particular interest are Reid (1970b) and Dickes (1970).

5. In the Kittredge-Ribner text, "rites" has been changed to "rights." I have restored the original word, which makes more sense than the emendation.

CHAPTER 4. *KING LEAR*

1. I am using Karen Horney's concept of narcissism, which sees it as a reactive rather than as a primary phenomenon. For other psychological perspectives on *King Lear,* see Holland 1966, Kanzer 1965, Kaplan 1967, Burke 1969, Cavell 1969, Lesser 1970, Reid 1970a, Dundes 1976, Sinfield 1976, Holland 1978, McLaughlin 1978, McFarland 1981, Muslin 1981, Porter 1984, and Coursen 1986.

2. I am indebted to Michael Warren for making me more vividly aware of the disparities between the Quarto and Folio texts of *King Lear* and of how they might

affect my reading of the play. Although I have used the conflated Kittredge-Ribner text instead of the Folio alone, as Warren recommends, I do not think that my reading of the ending is incompatible with the one that Warren derives from the Folio: "In summary, Q and F embody two different artistic visions. In Q, Edgar remains an immature young man and ends the play devastated by his experience, while Albany stands as the modest, diffident, but strong and morally upright man. In F Edgar grows into a potential ruler, a well-intentioned, resolute man in a harsh world, while Albany, a weaker man, abdicates his responsibilities. In neither text is the prospect for the country a matter of great optimism, but the vision seems bleaker and darker in F, where the young Edgar, inexperienced in rule, faces the future with little support" (Warren 1978, 105).

3. The ellipsis is the author's. I had arrived at essentially the same position before I encountered Rosenberg's interpretation, though I was not aware of the folk tale parallels. I refer the reader to his fascinating chapter entitled "The *Lear* Myth."

4. This analysis of the play as a fantasy conceived from the wronged child's point of view may make it seem more integrated than it is. We must remember that from the end of act 1 to the end of act 4, the wronged father's point of view predominates.

CHAPTER 5. *MACBETH*

1. Important contributions to our understanding of Macbeth's individuality have also been made by Stewart 1949, McElroy 1973, Heilman 1977, Lesser 1977, and Egan 1978. There are other character studies, of course; but these along with Rosenberg's have seemed to me especially perceptive.

2. Perhaps the central myth in Horney is that of "the devil's pact," which she sees as a symbol of the relationship between self-hate and the search for glory: "Man in reaching out for the Infinite and Absolute also starts destroying himself. When he makes a pact with the devil, who promises him glory, he has to go to hell—to the hell within himself" (1950, 154).

3. See Paris (1978b). A major printing error in this essay was corrected in the following issue.

CHAPTER 7. "WHAT FOOLS THESE MORTALS BE": Self-Effacement in the Sonnets, the Comedies, *Troilus and Cressida*, and *Antony and Cleopatra*

1. In an essay that is complementary to my brief discussion of the sonnets, Catherine R. Lewis used Horney's theory to analyze the sonnets that express the poet's "contentment in his relationship with the friend" (1985, 177). As she observed, these sonnets "directly reveal the requirements of his defense system and allow us to

understand exactly why the friend's failures to meet the Poet's expectations are so devastating" (177).

CHAPTER 9. *THE TEMPEST*: SHAKESPEARE'S IDEAL SOLUTION

1. Kahn observed that Prospero achieves "a brilliant compromise between revenge and charity, which allows him to have his cake and eat it too." The trials to which he subjects Antonio, Sebastian, and Alonso "would add up to a tidy revenge were they not sheer illusion . . . and were they not perpetrated for the sake of arousing 'heart-sorrow and a clear life ensuing.' They are and are not revenge" (1981, 223).

2. I am one of the relatively small number of critics who subscribe to what Harry Berger, Jr. calls "the hard-nosed" as opposed to the "sentimental" view of Prospero (1970, 279). See also Leech (1961), Abenheimer (1946), Auden (1962, 128–34), and Dobrée (1952).

3. In his response to my interpretation of *The Tempest* at the 1985 Florida Conference on Shakespeare's Personality, J. Dennis Huston pointed out that Prospero may have yet another motive for classifying Caliban as subhuman: "he does not have to recognize that he, like Antonio, has used raw power to usurp a kingdom belonging to another: if Caliban is really subhuman, he can hardly have valid claims to the island."

4. As A. D. Nuttall observed in his response to this chapter, "You can kill people in plays without hurting anyone."

5. David Sundelson observed that "much in the play that might pass for dissent only adds to Prospero's stature—the brief quarrel with Ariel, for example." He speaks of the "sanctioned narcissism of Prospero" (1980, 38, 39).

Works Cited

Abenheimer, K. M. 1946. "Shakespeare's *Tempest*: A Psychological Analysis." *Psychoanalytic Review* 33:339–415.

Adelman, Janet, ed. 1978. *Twentieth Century Interpretations of* King Lear. Englewood Cliffs, NJ: Prentice-Hall.

Alter, Robert. 1989. *The Pleasures of Reading in an Ideological Age*. New York: Simon & Schuster.

Auden, W. H. 1962. *The Dyer's Hand*. New York: Random House.

Auden, W. H., ed. 1964. *Shakespeare's Sonnets*. New York: New American Library.

Barber, C. L., and Richard Wheeler. 1986. *The Whole Journey: Shakespeare's Power of Development*. Berkeley and Los Angeles: University of California Press.

Berger, Harry, Jr. 1970. "The Miraculous Harp: A Reading of Shakespeare's *Tempest*." *Shakespeare Studies* 5:254–83.

Berman, Ronald. 1973. *A Reader's Guide to Shakespeare's Plays,* rev. ed. Glenview, Ill.: Scott, Foresman.

Bodkin, Maud. 1934. *Archetypal Patterns in Poetry*. London: Oxford University Press.

Bradley, A. C. [1909]. 1963. "Shakespeare the Man." In *Oxford Lectures on Poetry*. London: Macmillan & Co.

Bradley, A. C. [1904]. 1964. *Shakespearean Tragedy*. London: Macmillan & Co.

Brandes, George. 1899. *William Shakespeare: A Critical Study*. New York: Macmillan.

Bredin, Hugh. 1982. "The Displacement of Character in Narrative Theory." *The British Journal of Aesthetics* 22:291–300.

Burke, Kenneth. 1969. "*King Lear*: Its Form and Psychosis." *Shenandoah* 21:3–18.

Cavell, Stanley. 1969. "The Avoidance of Love: A Reading of *King Lear*." In *Must We Mean What We Say?* New York: Charles Scribner's Sons.

Charney, Maurice, ed. 1965. *The Life of Timon of Athens*. New York: New American Library.

Chatman, Seymour. 1978. *Story and Discourse*. Ithaca: Cornell University Press.

Coursen, H. R. 1986. *The Compensatory Psyche: A Jungian Approach to Shakespeare*. Lanham, NY: University Press of America.

Dickes, Robert. 1970. "Desdemona: An Innocent Victim?" *American Imago* 27:279–97.

Dobrée, Bonamy. 1952. "The Tempest." *New Series of Essays and Studies* 5:13–25.

Docherty, Thomas. 1984. *Reading (Absent) Character: Towards a Theory of Characterization in Fiction.* Oxford: Oxford University Press.

Dowden, Edward. 1910. "Is Shakespeare Self-Revealed." In *Essays Modern and Elizabethan.* London: J. M. Dent & Sons.

Dundes, Alan. 1976. "'To Love My Father All': A Psychoanalytic Study of the Folktale Source of *King Lear.*" *Southern Folklore Quarterly* 40:353–66.

Egan, Robert. 1978. "His Hour Upon the Stage: Role-Playing in *Macbeth.*" *The Centennial Review* 22:327–45.

Eliot, T. S. 1950. *Selected Essays.* new ed. New York: Harcourt, Brace.

Erickson, Peter. 1985. *Patriarchal Structures in Shakespeare's Drama.* Berkeley and Los Angeles: University of California Press.

Faber, M. D. 1974. "*Othello*: Symbolic Action, Ritual, and Myth." *American Imago* 31:159–205.

Feiring, Candice. 1983. "Behavior Styles in Infancy and Adulthood: The Work of Karen Horney and Attachment Theorists Collaterally Considered." *Journal of the American Academy of Child Psychiatry* 22:1–7.

Forster, E. M. [1927] 1949. *Aspects of the Novel.* London: Edward Arnold.

Fraser, Russell, ed. 1963. *King Lear.* Signet Classics. New York: New American Library.

Frattaroli, Elio J. 1987. "On the Validity of Treating Shakespeare's Characters as if They Were Real People." *Psychoanalysis and Contemporary Thought* 10:407–37.

Freud, Sigmund. 1958. "Some Character-Types Met with in Psycho-Analytic Work." In *On Creativity and the Unconscious.* Edited by Benjamin Nelson. New York: Harper & Row.

Freud, Sigmund. [n.d.]. *Totem and Taboo.* New York: Vintage Books.

Frye, Northrop. 1969. Introduction to *The Tempest.* In *Twentieth Century Interpretations of the Tempest.* Edited by Hallet Smith. Englewood Cliffs, NJ: Prentice-Hall.

Gottschalk, Paul. 1972. *The Meanings of Hamlet.* Albuquerque: University of New Mexico Press.

Harrison, G. B., and R. F. McDonnel. 1962. *King Lear: Text, Sources, Criticism.* New York: Harcourt, Brace & World.

Heilman, Robert. 1956. *The Magic in the Web.* Lexington: University of Kentucky Press.

Heilman, Robert. 1977. "The Criminal as Tragic Hero: Dramatic Methods." In *Aspects of Macbeth.* Edited by Kenneth Muir and Philip Edwards. Cambridge: Cambridge University Press.

Hochman, Baruch. 1985. *Character in Literature.* Ithaca: Cornell University Press.

Holland, Norman N. 1966. *Psychoanalysis and Shakespeare.* New York: McGraw-Hill.

Holland, Norman N. 1978. "How Can Dr. Johnson's Remarks on Cordelia's Death Add to My Own Response?" In *Psychoanalysis and the Question of the Text.* Edited by Geoffrey Hartman. Baltimore: Johns Hopkins University Press.

Holland, Norman N., Sidney Homan, and Bernard J. Paris, eds. 1989. *Shakespeare's Personality.* Berkeley and Los Angeles: University of California Press.

Horney, Karen. 1937. *The Neurotic Personality of Our Time.* New York: Norton.

Horney, Karen. 1939. *New Ways in Psychoanalysis.* New York: Norton.

Horney, Karen. 1942. *Self-Analysis.* New York: Norton.

Horney, Karen. 1945. *Our Inner Conflicts.* New York: Norton.

Horney, Karen. 1950. *Neurosis and Human Growth: The Struggle Toward Self-Realization.* New York: Norton.

Horney, Karen. 1967. *Feminine Psychology.* Edited by Harold Kelman. New York: Norton.

Hunter, G. K. 1977. "*Macbeth* in the Twentieth Century." In *Aspects of* Macbeth. Edited by Kenneth Muir and Philip Edwards. Cambridge: Cambridge University Press.

Hyman, Stanley Edgar. 1970. *Iago: Some Approaches to the Illusion of His Motivation.* New York: Atheneum.

Jones, Ernest. [1949]. 1954. *Hamlet and Oedipus.* New York: Anchor Books.

Kahn, Coppélia. 1981. *Man's Estate: Masculine Identity in Shakespeare.* Berkeley and Los Angeles: University of California Press.

Kantak, V. Y. 1977. "An Approach to Shakespearean Tragedy: The 'Actor' Image in *Macbeth.*" In *Aspects of* Macbeth. Edited by Kenneth Muir and Philip Edwards. Cambridge: Cambridge University Press.

Kanzer, Mark. 1965. "Imagery in *King Lear.*" *American Imago* 22:3–13.

Kaplan, Bert. 1967. "On Reason in Madness in *King Lear.*" *Challenges of Humanistic Psychology.* Edited by James Bugental. New York: McGraw-Hill.

Kirsch, Arthur. 1981. "Hamlet's Grief." *ELH* 48:17–36.

Kirschbaum, Leo. 1962. *Character and Characterization in Shakespeare.* Detroit: Wayne State University Press.

Kittredge, George Lyman and Irving Ribner, eds. 1967. *The Tragedy of Hamlet, Prince of Denmark.* 2d ed. Waltham, Mass.: Blaisdell.

Kittredge, George Lyman and Irving Ribner, eds. 1966. *Twelfth Night.* New York: John Wiley.

Knight, G. Wilson. [1949]. 1970. "*Measure for Measure* and the Gospels." In *Twentieth Century Interpretations of* Measure for Measure. Edited by George Geckle. Englewood Cliffs, NJ: Prentice-Hall.

Knights, L. C. 1965. *Further Explorations.* Stanford: Stanford University Press.

Kott, Jan. [1966]. 1974. *Shakespeare Our Contemporary.* Translated by Boleslaw Taborski. New York: Norton.

Leech, Clifford. 1961. *Shakespeare's Tragedies.* London: Chatto & Windus.

Leavis, F. R. [1952]. 1964. *The Common Pursuit.* New York: New York University Press.

Lesser, Simon O. 1970. "Act One, Scene One, of *Lear.*" *College English* 32:155–71.

Lesser, Simon O. 1977. "*Macbeth*: Drama and Dream." In *The Whispered Meanings, Selected Essays of Simon O. Lesser.* Edited by Robert Sprich and Richard W. Noland. Amherst: University of Massachusetts Press.

Leverenz, David. 1978. "The Woman in Hamlet: An Interpersonal View." *Signs* 4:291–308.

Levine, George. 1981. *The Realistic Imagination.* Chicago: University of Chicago Press.

Lewis, Catherine. 1985. "Poet, Friend, and Poetry: The Idealized Image of Love in Shakespeare's Sonnets." *American Journal of Psychoanalysis* 45:176–190.

Lewis, Wyndham. [n.d.]. *The Lion and the Fox.* New York: Barnes & Noble.

McCurdy, Harold Grier. 1953. *The Personality of Shakespeare.* New Haven: Yale University Press.

McElroy, Bernard. 1973. *Shakespeare's Mature Tragedies.* Princeton: Princeton University Press.

McFarland, Thomas. 1981. "The Image of the Family in *King Lear.*" In *On* King Lear. Edited by Lawrence Danson. Princeton: Princeton University Press.

McLaughlin, John J. 1978. "The Dynamics of Power in *King Lear*: An Adlerian Interpretation." *Shakespeare Quarterly* 29:37–43.

Mack, Maynard. 1972. *King Lear in Our Time.* Berkeley and Los Angeles: University of California Press.

Maugham, W. Somerset. 1919. *The Moon and Sixpence.* New York: Grosset & Dunlap.

Maslow, Abraham. 1968. *Toward a Psychology of Being.* 2d ed. New York: Van Nostrand.

Maslow, Abraham. 1970. *Motivation and Personality.* 2d ed. New York: Harper & Row.

Muslin, Hyman L. 1981. "King Lear: Images of Self in Old Age." *Journal of Mental Imagery* 5:143–55.

Newman, Karen. 1985. *Shakespeare's Rhetoric of Comic Character*. New York: Methuen.

Noland, Richard. 1974. "Psychoanalysis and *Hamlet*." *Hartford Studies in Literature* 6:268–81.

Nuttall, A. D. 1983. *A New Mimesis: Shakespeare and the Representation of Reality*. London: Methuen.

Orgel, Shelly. 1968. "Iago." *American Imago* 25:274–93.

Paris, Bernard J. 1974. *A Psychological Approach to Fiction: Studies in Thackeray, Stendhal, George Eliot, Dostoevsky, and Conrad*. Bloomington: Indiana University Press.

Paris, Bernard J. 1977. "Hamlet and His Problems: A Horneyan Analysis." *Centennial Review* 21:36–66.

Paris, Bernard J. 1978a. *Character and Conflict in Jane Austen's Novels: A Psychological Approach*. Detroit: Wayne State University Press.

Paris, Bernard J. 1978b. "The Two Selves of Rodion Raskolnikov." *Gradiva* 1:316–28.

Paris, Bernard J. 1978c. "Horney's Theory and the Study of Literature." *American Journal of Psychoanalysis* 38:343–53.

Paris, Bernard J. 1980. "Bargains with Fate: A Psychological Approach to Shakespeare's Major Tragedies." *Aligarh Journal of English Studies* 5:144–61.

Paris, Bernard J. 1981. "The Inner Conflicts of *Measure for Measure*." *Centennial Review* 25:266–76.

Paris, Bernard J. 1982. "Bargains with Fate: The Case of Macbeth." *American Journal of Psychoanalysis* 42:7–20.

Paris, Bernard J. 1983. "Richard III: Shakespeare's First Great Mimetic Character." *Aligarh Journal of English Studies* 8:40–67.

Paris, Bernard J. 1984a. "Iago's Motives: A Horneyan Analysis." *Revue Belge de Philologie et d'Histoire* 62:504–20.

Paris, Bernard J. 1984b. "'His Scorn I Approve': The Self-Effacing Desdemona." *American Journal of Psychoanalysis* 44:413–24.

Paris, Bernard J. ed. 1986. *Third Force Psychology and the Study of Literature*. Rutherford, NJ: Fairleigh Dickinson University Press.

Paris, Bernard J. 1987. "Brutus, Cassius, and Caesar: An Interdestructive Triangle." In *Psychoanalytic Approaches to Literature and Film*. Edited by Maurice Charney and Joseph Reppen. Rutherford, NJ: Fairleigh Dickinson University Press.

Paris, Bernard J. 1989a. "Interdisciplinary Applications of Horney." *American Journal of Psychoanalysis* 49:181–88.

Paris, Bernard J. 1989b. "The Not So Noble Antonio: A Horneyan Analysis of Shakespeare's *Merchant of Venice*." *American Journal of Psychoanalysis* 49:189–200.

Paris, Bernard J. 1989c. "*The Tempest*: Shakespeare's Ideal Solution." In *Shakespeare's Personality*. Edited by Norman Holland, Sidney Homan, and Bernard Paris. Berkeley and Los Angeles: University of California Press.

Paris, Bernard J. 1991. *Character as a Subversive Force in Shakespeare: The History and the Roman Plays*. Rutherford, NJ: Fairleigh Dickinson University Press.

Porter, Laurel. 1984. "*King Lear* and the Crisis of Retirement." In *Aging in Literature*. Edited by Laurel Porter and Laurence Porter. Troy, MI: International Book Publishers.

Price, Martin. 1983. *Forms of Life: Character and Moral Imagination in the Novel*. New Haven: Yale University Press.

Priestley, J. B. 1964. "The Character of Shakespeare." *Show* 3:82.

Quinn, Susan. 1987. *A Mind of Her Own: The Life of Karen Horney*. New York: Summit Books.

Rabkin, Leslie Y., and Jeffrey Brown. 1973. "Some Monster in His Thought: Sadism and Tragedy in *Othello*." *Literature and Psychology* 23:59–67.

Reid, Stephen. 1968. "Othello's Jealousy." *American Imago* 25:274–93.

Reid, Stephen. 1970a. "In Defense of Goneril and Regan." *American Imago* 27:226–44.

Reid, Stephen. 1970b. "Desdemona's Guilt." *American Imago* 27:245–62.

Rosenberg, Marvin. 1961. *The Masks of Othello.* Berkeley and Los Angeles: University of California Press.

Rosenberg, Marvin. 1972. *The Masks of King Lear.* Berkeley and Los Angeles: University of California Press.

Rosenberg, Marvin. 1978. *The Masks of Macbeth.* Berkeley and Los Angeles: University of California Press.

Rossiter, A. P. 1961. *Angel with Horns and Other Shakespeare Lectures.* Edited by Graham Storey. New York: Theatre Arts Books.

Rubins, Jack L. 1978. *Karen Horney: Gentle Rebel of Psychoanalysis.* New York: Dial Press.

Schoenbaum, Samuel. 1970. *Shakespeare's Lives.* New York: Oxford University Press.

Scholes, Robert, and Robert Kellogg. 1966. *The Nature of Narrative.* New York: Oxford University Press.

Schwartz, Murray, and Coppélia Kahn, eds. 1980. *Representing Shakespeare.* Baltimore: Johns Hopkins University Press.

Shapiro, Stephen. 1964. "Othello's Desdemona." *Literature and Psychology* 14:56–61.

Sinfield, Alan. 1976. "Lear and Laing." *Essays in Criticism* 26:1–16.

Smith, Gordon Ross. 1959. "Iago the Paranoic." *American Imago* 16:155–67.

Staebler, Warren. 1975. "The Sexual Nihilism of Iago." *Sewanee Review* 83:284–304.

Stewart, J. I. M. 1949. *Character and Motive in Shakespeare.* New York: Barnes & Noble.

Stoll, E. E. 1933. *Art and Artifice in Shakespeare.* Cambridge: Cambridge University Press.

Stoll, E. E. 1940. *Shakespeare and Other Masters.* Cambridge: Harvard University Press.

Sundelson, David. 1980. "So Rare a Wonder'd Father: Prospero's *Tempest.*" In *Representing Shakespeare: New Psychoanalytic Essays.* Edited by Murray M. Schwartz and Coppélia Kahn. Baltimore: Johns Hopkins University Press.

Wangh, Martin. 1950. "*Othello*: The Tragedy of Iago." *Psychoanalytic Quarterly* 19:202–12.

Warren, Michael J. 1978. "Quarto and Folio *King Lear* and the Interpretation of Albany and Edgar." In *Shakespeare, Pattern of Excelling Nature.* Edited by David Bevington and Jay L. Halio. Newark: University of Delaware Press.

Watson, Curtis Brown. 1960. *Shakespeare and the Renaissance Concept of Honor.* Princeton: Princeton University Press.

West, Fred. 1978. "Iago the Psychopath." *Shakespeare Association Bulletin* 43:27–35.

Westkott, Marcia. 1986. *The Feminist Legacy of Karen Horney.* New Haven: Yale University Press.

Wheeler, Richard. 1981. *Shakespeare's Development and the Problem Comedies.* Berkeley and Los Angeles: University of California Press.

Woolf, Virginia. [1929]. 1957. *A Room of One's Own.* New York: Harcourt, Brace & World.

Wyatt-Brown, Bertram. 1982. *Southern Honor.* New York: Oxford University Press.

Index